FOREWORD

The authors of this volume set themselves a seemingly impossible task: to provide a comprehensive yet meaningful discussion of the WTO regulatory framework within a few pages. The result is remarkable. They managed to address all the critical issues regarding the multilateral trade integration process, and shed light on a series of questions that have been occupying centre-field in modern literature. They thus produced a book which is a great introduction to the WTO, and, at the same time, a point of reference for the WTO practitioner.

There are many good things I could have written about this volume. I will restrict myself to two comments who could serve as presentation to what follows: *first*, the structure of the book. The authors follow a path which makes the understanding of their material very accessible. Starting with the history and the various (economic and international relations) rationales for the GATT, the authors first establish what the negotiators of this international contract aimed at. This chapter, along with the chapter on the objectives of the GATT that immediately follows, serve as the compass that will orientate the discussions on the substance of the multilateral agreements that follow. And I can only side with their choice in this respect: absent an understanding of the objectives of the GATT, the student and interpreter risks moving into the area of a-contextual interpretations with all risks that such an endeavour inherently carries with it. With the compass now firmly in place, they move to discuss first the substance of the WTO legal regime, and then its institutional background. The reader will thus be in the position to appreciate and evaluate each and every agreement in light of its natural context: the objectives sought by the framers.

Second, and this is probably the authors' most important achievement while writing this book, the discussion of the regulatory framework is not long, but not cursory either. In fact, they manage to put within few pages the most important questions that students of the WTO, like myself, ask when dealing with these documents. At the same time, they include references to a large number of primary and secondary literature, so as to satisfy the interests of the reader eager to move to a more detailed discussion of any given question. Indeed, the number of references, as well as their organization and classification, is one of the highlights of this volume.

The authors did more than honour the task they assigned to themselves. This book is, in my view, a great addition to the existing literature, a necessary companion to students and practitioners of the WTO alike. It is highly recommendable not only to those interested in an overview of the world trading system, but to all those interested in specific questions regarding the WTO and its modern day evolution.

Petros C. Mavroidis
Edwin B. Parker professor of law at Columbia Law School, New York,
Professor of Law at the University of Neuchâtel, &
Research Fellow at CEPR

INTRODUCTION

The World Trade Organization (WTO) has become a centrepiece of global economic governance in a fragmented international legal and institutional system. Building upon the General Agreement on Tariffs and Trade (GATT), an international agreement from 1947 which over many years had evolved towards a *de facto* international organization, it was set up as a full-fledged international organization in 1995. Today, the WTO oversees an extensive body of international trade rules in a rather successful manner. Nevertheless, it has also become a widely contested organization. The trade rules administered by the WTO indeed affect various national and international regulations. Rules and principles on environmental protection, public health, technical standards, cultural diversity and financial stability, professional qualifications all potentially become subject to the trade scrutiny of the WTO. Thus, national regulatory autonomy as well as the use of standards developed by international organizations may become seriously restricted. Whether it likes it or not, the WTO is put at the centre of global economic governance and no internationally oriented legal practitioner, government official, academic or student can afford to neglect this swiftly developing body of law.

This book introduces the institutional and substantive legal aspects of the WTO. It thereby addresses both the vertical interactions of WTO law with domestic legal systems and horizontal interactions between WTO rules and other areas of international regulation. In the opening chapter, the theory and history of international trade law is explained. The second chapter spells out the objectives of the organization and introduces the basic principles on which the law of the WTO is based and which reappear, sometimes in different guises, in the various WTO Agreements. The third chapter gives an overview of the different WTO Agreements with a basic explanation of their content and function. Throughout the discussion of the substantive aspects of the law of the WTO, it will be explained how the rules relate to other bodies of (domestic and international) law. Finally, in the fourth chapter, the institutional aspects of the WTO will be addressed. Special attention will be paid to the way the WTO, as an international organization, relates to other global and regional international organizations and groupings. Furthermore, the decision-making process of the WTO, which has given rise to concerns on efficiency and legitimacy, will be discussed. The fourth chapter finishes with the 'cherry on the cake' of WTO law: the dispute settlement system.

Introduction

It is in this system that the frictions between WTO rules, on the one hand, and domestic and international rules, on the other hand, are concretely addressed.

Our aim in writing this book is to present the institutional and substantive legal aspects of the WTO in an accessible way for non-specialist law students, practising lawyers, diplomats, magistrates, officials and policymakers. It is hoped that an understanding of these legal rules may help the reader better grasp the impact of the law of the WTO on the daily work and life of everyone.

Last but not least, we would like to thank Dominic Coppens for his many valuable comments as well as Alistair Maclean for his language review and editing.

Leuven, 1 October 2007

Prof. Dr. Jan Wouters
Bart De Meester

TABLE OF CONTENTS

Foreword by P.C. Mavroidis v

Introduction vii

List of Tables and Figures xiii

Abbreviations xv

CHAPTER I. FROM GATT TO WTO 1

§ 1. The Theory of International Trade 1
§ 2. The Road to GATT 6
§ 3. WTO 12
§ 4. The WTO Agreement and Its Annexes 14

CHAPTER II. OBJECTIVES AND BASIC PRINCIPLES OF THE WTO ... 19

§ 1. Objectives and Functions of the WTO 19
§ 2. Basic Principles 22
    A. Market Access 22
    B. Non-Discrimination 23
        1. Most Favoured Nation 24
        2. National Treatment 27
    C. Exceptions 29

CHAPTER III. OVERVIEW OF THE WTO AGREEMENTS 33

§ 1. Multilateral Agreements on Trade in Goods 34
    A. GATT 35
        1. Tariffs 37
        2. Most Favoured Nation 44
        3. National Treatment 46
        4. Quantitative Restrictions 55

		5.	General Exceptions 56

           5.   General Exceptions 56
           6.   Free Trade Areas and Customs Unions 60
           7.   Special and Differential Treatment of Developing Countries .. 64
    B.   Agreement on Sanitary and Phytosanitary Measures 69
    C.   Agreement on Technical Barriers to Trade 73
    D.   Agreement on Safeguards..................................... 76
    E.   Agreement on Subsidies and Countervailing Measures 79
    F.   Agreement on Antidumping 86
    G.   Agreement on Agriculture 89
    H.   Agreement on Textiles and Clothing 94
    I.   Agreement on Trade-Related Investment Measures............... 96
    J.   Agreement on Customs Valuation.............................. 98
    K.   Agreement on Preshipment Inspection 100
    L.   Agreement on Import Licensing Procedures................... 102
    M.   Agreement on Rules of Origin 102

§ 2. GATS 104
           1.   Services 104
           2.   General Obligations and Disciplines 107
           3.   Specific Commitments 113
           4.   Exceptions... 117

§ 3. TRIPS 120
§ 4. Dispute Settlement Understanding 123
§ 5. Trade Policy Review Mechanism................................... 123
§ 6. Plurilateral Trade Agreements 123
    A.   Agreement on Trade in Civil Aircraft.......................... 123
    B.   Agreement on Government Procurement 125
    C.   International Dairy Agreement 126
    D.   International Bovine Meat Agreement 126

CHAPTER IV. INSTITUTIONAL FRAMEWORK. 127

§ 1. The WTO as an International Organization 127
    A.   International Legal Personality 127
    B.   Relationship with Other Intergovernmental Organizations....... 128
           1.   Observer Status 129
           2.   Cooperation Agreements................................. 129
    C.   Relationship with Non-Governmental Organizations............ 152
    D.   Membership 153
           1.   Procedure 153
           2.   Groupings and Alliances in the WTO 160
           3.   Separate Customs Territories as Member of the WTO 168
           4.   Developing Countries in the WTO 176

		E.	Budget.	178
§ 2.	Decision-Making Bodies.			179
	A.	Decision-Making and Voting Procedures		180
		1.	Ministerial Decisions	184
		2.	Interpretations	184
		3.	Amendments	184
		4.	Waivers	186
		5.	Negotiating New Agreements	187
	B.	Ministerial Conference		187
	C.	General Council		189
		1.	Acting on Behalf of the Ministerial Conference	190
		2.	Dispute Settlement Body	217
		3.	Trade Policy Review Body	218
	D.	WTO Secretariat		220
		1.	Secretariat	220
		2.	Director-General	220
	E.	Legitimacy, Democracy and Efficiency in the WTO		221
§ 3.	Dispute Settlement Mechanism			226
	A.	Accessibility of the WTO Dispute Settlement System and *Locus Standi*		228
	B.	Legal Basis for Initiating a WTO Dispute Settlement Case		229
	C.	Consultations		233
		1.	Procedure	233
		2.	Third Parties	234
	D.	Panel		234
		1.	Request for a Panel	234
		2.	Establishment and Composition of Panels	235
		3.	Procedure before the Panel	237
		4.	Third Parties	241
		5.	Standard of Review and Treaty Interpretation	241
	E.	Standing Appellate Body		246
		1.	Composition of the Appellate Body	246
		2.	Appeal Process	247
		3.	Third Parties	249
	F.	Implementation and Enforcement		249
	G.	Transparency of the Dispute Settlement Process –*Amicus Curiae* Briefs		251
	H.	Position of Developing Countries in the Dispute Settlement System		254

SELECT BIBLIOGRAPHY 259

INDEX. 297

LIST OF TABLES AND FIGURES

Table 1. NGO Attendance at Ministerial Conferences 153
Table 2. Table of Members of the WTO 158
Figure 1. Groups and Alliances in the WTO for Agriculture Negotiations.. 166
Figure 2. Organization Chart of the WTO 192
Figure 3. Schematic Overview of Dispute Settlement Procedure 232

ABBREVIATIONS

ACFTA	ASEAN-China Free Trade Area
ACWL	Advisory Centre on WTO Law
AFTA	ASEAN Free Trade Area
APQLI	Augmented Physical Quality of Life Index
ASEAN	Association of Southeast Asian Nations
CEPA	Mainland China and Hong Kong Closer Economic Partnership Arrangement
CU	Customs Union
DDA	Doha Development Agenda
DSB	Dispute Settlement Body
DSU	Dispute Settlement Understanding
EC	European Community
ECOSOC	United Nations Economic and Social Council
EEC	European Economic Community
Enabling Clause	Decision on Differential and More Favourable Treatment
ERG	Expert Review Group
EVI	Economic Vulnerability Index
FAO	Food and Agriculture Organization
FOGS negotiations	Negotiations on the Functioning of the GATT System
FTA	Free Trade Area
GATS	General Agreement on Trade in Services
GATT	General Agreement on Trade in Goods
GSP	Generalized System of Preferences
G20	Group of 20
G20+	Group of 20+
G90	Group of 90
G33	Group of 33
Harmonized System	Harmonized Commodity Description and Coding System
ICITO	Interim Commission for the International Trade Organization
ILC	International Law Commission
I.L.M.	International Legal Materials
ILO	International Labour Organization
IMF	International Monetary Fund
IOS	International Organization for Standardization
ITO	International Trade Organization

Abbreviations

ITU	International Telecommunications Union
LDCs	Least-Developed Countries
MATG	Multilateral Agreements on Trade in Goods
MFN	Most Favoured Nation
NAFTA	North-American Free Trade Area
NGO	Non-Governmental Organization
OIE	Office International des Epizooties
Quad	Quadrilaterals
RTA	Regional Trade Agreement
SCM	Subsidies and Countervailing Measures
SPS	Sanitary and Phytosanitary Measures
TBT	Technical Barriers to Trade
TPRM	Trade Policy Review Mechanism
TRIMS	Trade-Related Investment Measures
TRIPS	Trade-Related aspects of Intellectual Property Rights
UN	United Nations
UNCTAD	United Nations Conference on Trade and Development
UNDP	United Nations Development Programme
UNTS	United Nations Treaty System
VCLT	Vienna Convention on the Law of Treaties
WCO	World Customs Organization
WHO	World Health Organization
WIPO	World Intellectual Property Organization
WTO	World Trade Organization

CHAPTER I
FROM GATT TO WTO

§ 1. THE THEORY OF INTERNATIONAL TRADE

1. International legal rules with regard to economic relations between States are a relatively recent phenomenon. However, trading with foreigners has for a long time been part of each government's policy concerns.[1] These policies have swung between openness for trade and restriction of trade. This is due to the gradual development of the economic theory of free trade and the different political reactions to this theory. Although many criticisms of free trade point at undeniable problems linked to the theory, many others are simply caused by a lack of understanding of it. Nevertheless, from the 18th century on, there has been a constant call for trade liberalization. This culminated in 1995 in the establishment of the World Trade Organization (WTO) to monitor an extensive range of trade agreements. Today, advocates of free trade are more vociferous than ever before. Nonetheless, also the critics are raising their voices. To understand this friction, and the institutional and substantive law of the WTO, it is essential to provide a brief introduction to the economic theory of free trade as it has evolved over time.

2. In the 17th and 18th centuries, mercantilism[2] pleaded for restrictions on imports from other countries. It was believed that in order to become a wealthy country, one had to collect as much precious materials as possible. Therefore, a country should try to export as much as possible and limit imports. If a country had a surplus of imports, it would lose its precious materials (*specie*) to other countries. Moreover, the export of raw materials should be limited. Domestic production should process raw materials and export manufactured goods.

---

[1] For an overview, see M.J. TREBILCOCK and R. HOWSE, *The Regulation of International Trade*, (London, Routledge 2005), pp. 1–20 and D. IRWIN, *Against the Tide: An Intellectual History of Free Trade*, (Princeton, Princeton University Press 1996), viii + 265 p.
[2] The minister of finance of France under Louis XIV, Colbert (1619–1683), was a proponent of mercantilism. But also in Britain, these thoughts took root, although the English mercantilism was less directive than that of the French. See E.D. HANSEN, *European Economic History: from Mercantilism to Maastricht and beyond*, (Copenhagen, Copenhagen Business School Press 2001), pp. 59–65.

Therefore, countries had to subsidize the manufacturing industry and tax exports of raw materials as well as imports of manufactured goods.

3. In the late 18th and early 19th century, Adam SMITH and David RICARDO challenged the idea that trade exchange between countries was bad. According to Adam SMITH, wealth had to be measured by the standard of living of a country's inhabitants and not by the stock of gold the national bank holds. Already in 1776, he described in his book *An Inquiry into the Nature and Causes of Wealth of Nations*[3] how a government's attempts to protect its own producers by limiting imports not only hurt the country that normally exports the goods, but also the country that introduces the import barriers. Indeed, if one country could make a product cheaper than another country, the latter country would be better off buying the good from the former. Some countries have an advantage in producing a certain good because of favourable geographic conditions, a warmer climate, and the presence of certain resources. Every country should therefore specialize in making those products at which it is best and all countries should start trading their products with each other. In that case, goods would be produced at the lowest price possible and consumers would have access to a quasi-unlimited array of products to choose from. According to Smith, unilateral trade liberalization would be advantageous irrespective of the trade policies pursued by other countries. This theory is called the theory of *absolute advantage*.

4. It was David RICARDO who reformulated this insight in 1817 into the theory of *comparative advantage*.[4] Surely, Adam SMITH's theory did not explain what should be done if a country had no absolute advantage at all in producing anything. RICARDO explained that even in case a certain country is better at producing all possible products, when compared to another country, the former country still has an interest in specializing in producing the goods at which it is best while the latter country should produce those products at which it is *comparatively* best. Indeed, the first country should devote *all* its resources to the production of the good that it can produce best. The second country should then use its resources to manufacture the goods at which it is best, even if the first (which is now also focusing on what it is best at) could do this better. In doing so, the welfare of both countries will increase since all resources are used for the most efficient production. If the first country still produces some products at which it is not the best, there will be a *misallocation* of resources. These resources could have been used for

---

[3] A. SMITH, R.H. CAMPBELL and A.S. SKINNER (eds.), *An Inquiry into the Nature and Causes of the Wealth of Nations*, (Oxford, Clarendon Press 1967), pp. 450–472.

[4] D. RICARDO, *On the Principles of Political Economy and Taxation*, reprinted in P. SRAFFO and M.H. DOFF (eds.), *The Works and Correspondence of David Ricardo*, I, (Cambridge, Cambridge University Press 1962), pp. 128–149.

producing the products in which the country was better, and hence, could have created more wealth. A well-known example can clarify this. Suppose a lawyer has a secretary to do his typing. A lawyer is better at providing legal advice than his secretary. However, to a certain extent, the lawyer is also more efficient at doing his typing because he knows exactly how he wants to have the layout of his letters and papers. Nonetheless, the lawyer should focus on providing legal advice; an hour of work spent typing a letter could better be spent on advising clients, since the lawyer gets a high hourly rate from his clients. Yet, the lawyer's typing work also has to be done. The lawyer thus has to devote some of its resources to paying a secretary.

5. In sum, all countries, even the poorest, have assets that they can employ to produce goods and services for their domestic markets or to compete overseas. These countries can benefit when these goods are traded. In other words, the theory of comparative advantage says that countries are better off when first taking advantage of their assets in order to concentrate on what they can produce best, and then by trading these products for products those other countries produce (comparatively) best.[5] This insight has been confirmed by statistical data. Since the conclusion of the General Agreement on Tariffs and Trade (GATT; see *infra* paras. 47-92) world trade has grown exponentially. Indeed, in the first 25 years after World War II, world trade grew on average 8% per year.[6]

6. The theory of comparative advantage, formulated almost two centuries ago, still forms the basis for the theory of international free trade.[7] However, this supposes that all products can be freely traded all over the world. Producers in countries should not face barriers when exporting to other countries. This would make their products more expensive, thus diminishing the comparative advantage. Consumers would therefore pay too much and have too little choice. Yet,

---

[5] WORLD TRADE ORGANIZATION, *Understanding the WTO*, (Geneva, World Trade Organization 2007), p. 13.
[6] *Ibid.*
[7] However, the basic theory has been adapted and specified over time. An important contribution was made by the Heckscher-Ohlin theorem (1920). The theory of comparative advantage did not give due account to the fact that, when more than one factor of production was taken into account, combining land and labour at ever increasing costs would not necessarily entail similar costs. Moreover, practical evidence showed that States did never specialize in one product solely, but rather produced to a large extent one product, combined with some other products. The Heckscher-Ohlin theory stated that countries have comparative advantages in the production of commodities that are intensive in the use of factors of production with which their endowments are relatively abundant. It should also be noted that 'comparative advantage' is a dynamic notion because it is not solely defined by exogenous factors such as climate or geographic characteristics. Governments could influence the comparative advantage of the country by *inter alia* investing in education. See R. LIPSEY, P. STEINER, D. PURVIS and P. COURANT, *Economics*, (9th ed., New York, Harper & Row Publishers 1990), p. 837.

protectionism is still omnipresent and takes several forms. First, States may limit the amount or value of allowed imports of a certain good. These *quantitative restrictions* thus reduce the possibilities for foreign producers or service providers to sell their product (good or service) in the country. Second, States may impose *tariffs*. These are duties levied when a good is imported. It is obvious that the higher a tariff, the more expensive the goods will be once put for sale in the import country. Because of the 'intangible' nature of services, no duties are levied on them. These two modes of protecting the own industry are rather obvious. Nonetheless, other forms of protectionism exist which are less overt. States may impose non-tariff barriers. This category is very broad and includes a large variety of State measures.[8] States may impose certain standards and requirements (e.g. a prohibition on containing hormones) on products. If these products do not comply with these standards, they cannot be sold in the territory. Likewise, States may require that imported goods undergo expensive and time-consuming testing and controls before they can be sold. This increases the costs for the product significantly. With regard to services, conditions relating to qualification and licensing of foreign service providers and the assessment of these conditions may limit service supply by foreign providers in a country. Industrial nations like, for instance, the United States and the Member States of the European Union also subsidize their farmers, protecting them against competition of cheaper agricultural products from developing countries. States may also modify their exchange rates in order to make their own economy more competitive. Once the products are imported, they can still be discriminated against by the imposition of high internal taxes and restrictive regulations. Finally, other domestic policies, such as rules on intellectual property, competition law or protective labour law[9], can be used to shield the own industry against foreign competition. Such measures may discriminate between imported and domestic goods and services. Yet, even rules that are not discriminatory may create barriers to trade because they impose double burdens on foreign producers and service providers that have to comply with the diverse regulations of the countries in which they want to operate.

7. Surely, global ambitions and national objectives are not the same. Liberalizing trade requires short-term sacrifices (adjustment costs), although the benefits are

---

[8] In principle, they include quantitative restrictions, since quantitative restrictions limit imports, without the use of tariffs. Nonetheless, in the WTO agreements, they are dealt with separately.

[9] It was, for instance, claimed that the Belgian Labelling Law for Socially Responsible Production (creating a label which companies can affix to their products only if the products meet, among others, certain criteria and standards of certain specified ILO Conventions) was used to protect producers in developed countries against products originating in developing countries. Producers in developing countries often do not have the means (or willingness) to comply with all ILO Conventions. Indeed, having such low standards may constitute a comparative advantage for certain countries.

only experienced in the long term.[10] Opening the market of a State will subject its domestic producers to foreign competition. Consequently, less efficient producers might go out of business. However, it might turn out that a whole industry is less efficient than like industries in other countries, leading to massive lay-offs and social disruption.[11] According to SMITH's and RICARDO's theories, this is a mere reallocation of resources, diverting them from less efficient production, and relocating them in those industries where the country has a comparative advantage. Yet, this is a long process. Taking account of the fact that 'all politics is local'[12], many politicians who are concerned to be re-elected choose not to upset the electorate rather than introducing measures that would hurt domestic producers and would only produce benefits in the long term. On the other hand, politicians experience pressure by international economic actors, not least the own exporting industry, to engage in global free trade. Political leaders thus continually have to grapple with this dilemma between protectionism and free trade.[13]

8. Trade agreements may help surpass short-term policymaking and to commit States to abolishing barriers to free trade. Even though economic theory suggests that unilateral liberalization is beneficial for a State, States are not willing to open up their markets if other countries do not do the same.[14] Otherwise, producers in the State that unilaterally opens its market will suffer from the cheap imports, while at the same time not having increased access to foreign markets. Countries may therefore withhold any trade concessions until its major trading partners lower their trade barriers first. This situation is a clear application of the *prisoner's' dilemma*. This economic concept describes how actors achieve a situation which is much worse than when they had cooperated because they only pursue their own interests. Cooperation would increase the well-being of all actors.[15] However,

---

[10] Moreover, redistributive effects follow from trade liberalization, which may create social problems. Owners of a country's abundant factors (part of the comparative advantage) gain from trade, although owners of the country's scarce factors lose in relative terms.

[11] When the United States considered in 1992 establishing, together with Canada and Mexico, the North American Free Trade Association (NAFTA), the then presidential candidate Ross Perot warned of a 'giant sucking sound' that would be heard when 5 million jobs would be 'sucked away' from the US to Mexico.

[12] T. O'NEILL and G. HYMEL, *All Politics is Local, and other Rules of the Game*, (New York, Times Books 1994), xvi + 190 p.

[13] See J.H. JACKSON, *The Jurisprudence of GATT and the WTO*, (Cambridge, Cambridge University Press 2000), p. 4.

[14] With the exception of large and powerful countries that in theory could adopt an 'optimal tariff'. By restricting the trade at a certain optimal level, the State would be able to modify the terms of trade in its own favour. Yet, such may not happen soon, since other States may react by also raising tariff barriers. See A. NARLIKAR, *The World Trade Organization. A Very Short Introduction*, (Oxford, Oxford University Press 2005), p. 4.

[15] R. COOTER and T. ULEN, *Law and Economics*, Reading, (Mass., Addison-Wesley 2000), p. 34.

the prisoner's dilemma is a one-shot game, in which the actors do not take into account future interactions. In reality, actors take into account what might happen in future, when making decisions. Therefore, countries have realized that, in the long run, cooperation to liberalize world trade is better. Nonetheless, cooperation is very fragile and requires an external authority to enforce cooperative agreements. The law of world trade, supervised by the WTO, can provide such authority.

9. What is more, States often want to adopt policies that are aimed at protecting consumers, safeguarding public health, defending a clean environment, maintaining the cultural identity or promoting underdeveloped regions, etc. These non-trade policy goals, no matter how laudable, may constitute formidable barriers for foreign traders and thus may conflict with the goal of free trade. It cannot be left to the market to achieve these aims either. Market forces have no particular conscience or willingness to pursue fairness and quality of life. When the market fails – and it often does – law has its role to play. Also Adam SMITH recognized the role of government in providing essential goods such as a legal system, infrastructures and defence, the provision of which could not be handled efficiently through market mechanisms.[16] In addition, he – and many authors with him – realized that a "rule-based or rule-oriented system of human institutions is essential to a beneficial operation of markets".[17] In sum, as has been rightly observed, the "need for greater international trade, and the advent of globalization, call for a supra-national regime ensuring co-operation, order and harmonization".[18] The following chapters indicate how the legal rules of world trade try to strike a delicate balance between guaranteeing the functioning of a free market and promoting other values that are defined within domestic legal systems.

§ 2. THE ROAD TO GATT

10. The theories of SMITH and RICARDO were only very slowly taken up in countries' trade policies. Even though free trade was realized within countries (no more tolls were levied at the gates of a city), trade protectionism for a long

---

[16] See J.W. CAIRNS, 'Adam Smith and the Role of the Courts in Securing Justice and Liberty' in R.P. MALLOY and J. EVENSKY (eds.), *Adam Smith and the Philosophy of Law and Economics*, (Dordrecht, Kluwer 1994), p. 31. On the need for regulating market failures, see E.-U. PETERSMANN, 'The Transformation of the World Trading System through the 1994 Agreement Establishing the World Trade Organization', *European Journal of International Law* (1995), pp. 13-18.

[17] J.H. JACKSON, *supra* note 13, p. 7. See *e.g.* R. COASE, *The Firm, the Market and the Law*, (Chicago, University of Chicago Press 1988), Chapter 5 and T. COWEN, *The Theory of Market Failure*, (New Brunswick, Transaction Publishers 1992), p. 20.

[18] A.H. QURESHI, *International Economic Law*, (London, Sweet & Maxwell 1999), p. 230.

time seemed more attractive than an opening up to foreign goods. After the Napoleonic wars (1799-1815), during which the French emperor tried to boycott Britain, suddenly cheap continental grain was imported into the United Kingdom. English landowners complained and wanted protection against the import of this grain. However, the civil middle class did not like this: the cheap grain after all allowed them to produce cheap bread. Nonetheless, the landowners managed to convince the British government and in 1815 the 'Corn Laws' were introduced. Import of grain below a certain price level was prohibited. The theories of SMITH and RICARDO eventually helped to convince the government of the disadvantages of protectionism[19] and in 1846, the Corn Laws were repealed. Other European countries followed this example and decided to open up their markets through bilateral agreements. 'Friendship, Commerce and Navigation' treaties were concluded between Britain and France[20] and between France and the *Deutsche Zollverein*, the German Customs Union.[21] These treaties already included the principle of Most Favoured Nation (*infra* paras. 30-35). They were without any doubt concluded for strategic reasons[22], but also today, international trade policy is used as a tool for States' foreign policies. Most of the States adopted a policy of *laissez faire* with regard to the international economy: with the exception of customs rules and import limits, there were hardly any controls and limits on commercial and financial transactions with foreigners. The international trade system was primarily based on liberal national legislation (*inter alia* involving a gold standard and convertibility of national currencies) and on bilateral trade and investment treaties.

11. This preference for free trade did not last long. When Europe suffered a severe recession in 1870, protectionist policies became common again. The Chancellor of the German Empire, Otto von Bismarck, believed that it was necessary to respond to these economic difficulties and raised tariffs substantially. This also helped to protect the young, emerging German industries.[23] France too withdrew from free trade, together with a number of other European countries,

---

[19] In combination with the urgent need to find a solution for the Irish famine at that time.
[20] The 'Cobden-Chevalier Treaty' of 1860. See D. LAZER, 'The Free Trade Epidemic of the 1860s and Other Outbreaks of Economic Discrimination', *Kennedy School of Government Politics Research Group Working Paper*, 1998, available on http://www.ksg.harvard.edu/prg/lazer/contagin.pdf.
[21] Entered into force on 1 January 1834.
[22] It has for instance been stated that Germany's treaties with France were motivated by the German policy to isolate Austria, which was seen as a threat to the hegemony of Prussia in the German-speaking world. Moreover, it was believed that these treaties would foster French neutrality with respect to the disputes Germany had at that time with Denmark. See M.J. TREBILCOCK and R. HOWSE, *supra* note 1, p. 21.
[23] He was influenced by Friedrich List, who had returned from the United States. In the US, the use of high tariffs to protect 'infant industries' was believed to be essential.

with the exception of the United Kingdom, which kept a great interest in free trade. Britain's industry had a clear advantage over those of other countries. Nevertheless, at the turn of the century, it began to adopt trade-restrictive measures too. The major break with free trade in Britain came in 1915 when the government imposed tariffs of 33.3 per cent on motor cars and parts, musical instruments, clocks, wrist watches, and movie films. Subsequent legislation extended the list of items subject to protectionist tariffs.[24]

12. In the meantime, the United States had gained independence from Britain. Before 1776, the British adopted mercantilist policies towards the colonies. The colonies were required to conduct external trade by means of British ships. Certain goods had to be shipped to Britain first before they could be sent to their final destination. After independence, many Americans advocated protectionist policies. Between 1789 and 1832, US Congress adopted several protectionist tariffs. Thereafter, tariffs were scaled back. At the end of the 19th century and the beginning of the twentieth, the US again gradually increased tariffs.

13. The period between the two world wars, in the aftermath of the Wall Street Crash in 1929, was characterized by monetary instability. The gold standard, re-established after the First World War, was based on unrealistic currency relations, especially of the British pound. The disconnection of the pound from gold in 1931 led to a series of competing devaluations between several countries and a spiral of protectionism. Modifying a country's currency rate is of course a way to improve its terms of trade. States introduced tariff walls in order to protect their economy, which in turn led to analogous reactions by other countries. The practice of 'beggar thy neighbour' was common. One such example was the infamous Smoot-Hawley Tariff act, adopted by the US Congress in 1930. This act raised import duties on average 38 to 52 per cent. As a result of such measures, and the reactions to them by other countries, the volume of world trade decreased by no less than 60% in the period from 1929 to 1932. The collapse of the world economy and the ensuing Great Depression in the 1930s lead to political instability and was one of the foundations for the emergence of fascism in Europe, which in turn resulted in the outbreak of the Second World War.

14. Although the war was still raging, plans were being made for a new international economic constitution.[25] At the Bretton Woods conference (July

---

[24] C. KINDLEBERGER, 'Commercial Policy between the Wars', *in* P. MATHIAS and S. POLLARD (eds.), *Cambridge Economic History of Europe*, vol. 8 (New York, Cambridge University Press 1989), pp. 162–163.

[25] The Allies started thinking about the future post-war world economy and the rebuilding of Europe as soon as it became reasonably clear that the war would end shortly.

1944) it was decided to establish the International Monetary Fund (IMF) and the International Bank for Reconstruction and Development (the 'World Bank') in order to *inter alia* promote international monetary cooperation, facilitate the expansion and balanced growth of international trade and promote exchange stability.[26] A third institution was to be added to these two 'Bretton Woods Institutions', namely the International Trade Organization (ITO). Like the IMF and the World Bank, this ITO was meant to be a specialized agency of the United Nations.[27] Meanwhile, without waiting for the completion and entering into force of the agreement on the ITO, 23 of the 50 participating States began negotiations in 1946 to bind or reduce tariffs. In 1947, this led to a 'package' of trade rules and tariff concessions in the form of the General Agreement on Tariffs and Trade (GATT).[28] The GATT became provisionally applicable in January 1948.[29] Although the ITO Charter was adopted in Havana in March 1948, it never entered into force. Even though the US had taken the initiative to introduce a resolution in the United Nations in order to start negotiations in an International Conference for Trade and Employment, it proved to be impossible to get approval by the US Congress.[30] When the US President finally decided in 1950 not to submit the Havana Charter to Congress, the ITO died.[31]

---

[26] See art. I (i)–(iii) Articles of Agreement of the International Monetary Fund, signed at Bretton Woods on 22 July 1944, available on http://www.imf.org/external/pubs/ft/aa/; Art. I (iii) Articles of Agreement of the International Bank for Reconstruction and Development, signed at Bretton Woods on 22 July 1944, available on http://web.worldbank.org/WBSITE/EXTERNAL/EXTABOUTUS/0,,contentMDK:20049557~menuPK:58863~pagePK:43912~piPK:44037~theSitePK:29708,00.html.

[27] T. FLORY, *L'organisation mondiale de commerce. Droit institutionnel et substantiel*, (Brussels, Bruylant 1999), p. 3.

[28] GATT 1947 now forms a part of 'GATT 1994', which is added as Annex 1A to the WTO Agreement.

[29] On the basis of a Protocol on the Provisional Application of the GATT of 30 October 1947, 55 *UNTS* 1947, 308.

[30] The main reason being the fear of the US that the ITO would be too large a check on its sovereignty. On the various reasons, see *inter alia* J. H. JACKSON, *World Trade Law and the Law of GATT: A Legal Analysis of the General Agreement on Tariffs and Trade*, (Charlottesville, Michigan 1969), Chapter 2.4.; K. VAN DE CASTEELE, 'Internationale handel', *in* X., *Handels- en Economisch recht. Commentaar met overzicht van rechtspraak en rechtsleer*, (Antwerp, Kluwer 1995), p. 263.

[31] See generally W. DIEBOLD, *The end of ITO. Essays in International Finance no. 16*, (Princeton, Princeton University Press 1952), 37 p. Also later attempts in the 1950s in order to establish a – much less ambitious – Organization for Trade Cooperation (OTC), failed to achieve this approval. See *inter alia* J. JACKSON, *The World Trading System. Law and Policy of International Economic Relations*, (Cambridge, MIT Press 1997), pp. 39–42; A.F. LOWENFELD, *International Economic Law*, (Oxford, Oxford University Press 2003), pp. 23–26; P. DEMARET, 'Les métamorphoses du GATT: De la Charte de la Havane à l'Organisation Mondiale du Commerce', *Journal des Tribunaux – Droit Européen* (1994), pp. 121–130; J.-C. GRAZ, *Aux sources de l'OMC: la Charte de la Havane 1941–1950 / Precursor of the WTO: the stillborn Havana charter, 1941–1950*, (Geneva, Droz 1999), 367 p.

Chapter I

15. The GATT remained 'provisionally'[32] applicable and evolved over the years into a *de facto* international organization with a secretariat in Geneva. These secretariat functions were in fact performed by the secretariat of the Interim Commission for the International Trade Organization (ICITO). The ICITO was established during the Havana Conference in order to prepare for the expected coming into existence of the ITO. The ICITO only met once, at Havana, and its powers were delegated to an Executive Committee. As the ITO never came into existence, the ICITO's only function was to perform secretariat functions for GATT.[33] Importantly, the ICITO was part of the UN family. This stands in contrast with the WTO, which was later established outside the UN family. This 'splendid isolation' of the WTO is now increasingly challenged (see *infra* para. 173).

16. Until 1994, the GATT was the only multilateral instrument to regulate global commerce. Despite its difficult beginnings, the GATT became a success story: eight negotiation rounds in the framework of the GATT led to major reductions in tariffs and other trade barriers.[34] Each round resulted in a tariff protocol, containing reductions on tariffs for goods, and several new legal texts to be added to the GATT. It concerned decisions, memoranda of understanding and sometimes 'side codes'. The latter led to a '*GATT à la carte*', making it for the public, media, government officials and lawyers extremely difficult to grasp.[35]

17. The various trade negotiation rounds gradually increased their scope. The first six negotiation rounds (Geneva (April-October 1947); Annecy (1949); Torquay (1950–1951); Geneva (1955–1956); Geneva (Dillon Round) (1961–1962)

---

[32] Such a provisional entering into force was necessary to avoid a real 'stand-still' of the economy. If the tariff concessions became public before they were concluded, traders would no longer want to export but would rather wait until the lower tariffs entered into force. World trade could thus have been seriously disrupted. Therefore, the GATT had to become effective immediately. On the other hand, this provisional application was one of the 'constitutional' problems of the GATT, taking into account the uncertain internal legal status of a treaty that was never submitted to national parliaments. The 'Protocol of Provisional Application' exempted the Contracting Parties from applying Part II of the GATT (which includes the principle of National Treatment) if this would be inconsistent with *existing* national legislation. Existing national legislation was thus 'grandfathered'. This stands in contrast with the WTO Agreement, which clearly indicates in art. XVI.4 that WTO Members must ensure conformity with their laws, regulations and administrative procedures with their obligations under the WTO.

[33] See W. Davey, 'Institutional Framework', *in* P. Macrory, A. Appleton and M. Plummer (eds.), *The World Trade Organization: Legal, Economic and Political Analyses*, (New York, Springer 2005), Volume I, p. 54.

[34] See, for a description of the different trade rounds: A. Hoda, *Tariff Negotiations and Renegotiations under the GATT and the WTO. Procedures and Practices*, (Cambridge, Cambridge University Press 2001), pp. 25–52. Specifically for the Tokyo Round (1973–79), see *inter alia* J. Steenbergen, 'De Tokyo Ronde', *Sociaal-Economisch Wetgeving* (1980), pp. 752–773.

[35] J.H. Jackson, *supra* note 13, p. 401.

and Kennedy Round (1963–1967)[36] solely focused on the reduction of tariffs on manufactured goods. The 1947 Geneva Round was the round that led to the adoption of the GATT. The Annecy Tariff Conference provided for negotiations between the then existing Contracting Parties and eleven governments that had requested to accede to the GATT. Torquay was the first round where additional concessions were negotiated.[37] During this round it emerged that countries that had already comparatively low tariff rates when compared with other countries had nothing to offer. However, the trade negotiations were based on reciprocity: no government was required to grant unilateral concessions or to grant concessions without receiving adequate concessions in return. This issue seriously inhibited the negotiations at Torquay. The 1955–1956 Geneva Round was initially meant to be a round of negotiations between two or more parties, *i.e.* on a non-multilateral basis. However, in the end all major trading nations participated and exchanged concessions, making the round in fact a multilateral one. The Dillon Round led to the introduction of new concessions and to the renegotiation of certain concessions because the European Economic Community (EEC) had seen the light of day and its customs union was in the process of being established. During the Kennedy Round, an attempt was made to broaden the negotiations to a general agreement on agriculture. Nonetheless, this proved unsuccessful and the round only resulted in new tariff concessions. It should be noted that the Ministerial Resolution which launched the Kennedy Round stated that "the developed countries cannot expect to receive reciprocity from the less-developed countries". Moreover, whereas in the previous rounds the negotiations took place on a product-by-product basis, it was also agreed to negotiate reductions across the board. This meant that an average percentage of tariff reductions had to be agreed, which countries would have to meet within a certain period of time. Once an average percentage had been agreed, countries would negotiate on deviations for individual products or groups of products.[38]

18. Starting from the Tokyo Round, the domain in the scope of the negotiations became much larger. By then, tariffs on industrial products had been reduced substantially and did not constitute the major impediment to trade. Therefore, negotiations now included both tariff and non-tariff barriers for manufactured goods and the creation of several plurilateral agreements. The latter 'codes' were

---

[36] The latter two rounds were named after the persons who provided the inspiration for the negotiations. Douglas DILLON was US Under Secretary of State and J.F. KENNEDY was President of the US.
[37] It is remarkable that the first three rounds were conducted according to the rules and procedures included in the ITO Charter, with a view of including the agreements into the framework of the ITO.
[38] According to LOWENFELD, "the Kennedy Round became a hybrid of product-by-product and linear negotiations." See A.F. LOWENFELD, *supra* note 31, p. 52.

open to all parties and were only binding on the signatories. On the one hand, this mode of working allowed new international rules to be developed within the given time frame. On the other hand, they undermined the claim that the GATT was a universal organization.[39]

19. However, the GATT proved increasingly less adapted to the new circumstances of world trade in the 1980s. The legal uncertainty of the provisional application, the lack of a true institutional framework, the rigidity of the amendment procedure (which gave rise to the drafting of all sorts of 'codes') and defective competences regarding rule-making and dispute settlement led to calls for a review.[40] Moreover, although one had managed to reduce tariffs through the GATT to a relatively low level, subsequent recessions in the 1970s and early 1980s led governments to introduce all kinds of (non-tariff) trade barriers. Increasingly, the need grew for legal certainty and predictability in the international trade framework, along with the realization that a multilateral trade system based on rules of law – and not on economic power – ('rules-based system') was in everyone's interest.

§ 3. WTO

20. The Uruguay Round (1986–1994) achieved a far-reaching change.[41] It was the longest negotiation round so far. It was agreed that there would be negotiations on the functioning of the GATT system. These so-called 'FOGS negotiations' (negotiations on the Functioning of the GATT System) were aimed at (i) improving regular monitoring of trade policies of Contracting Parties; (ii) improving the overall effectiveness and decision-making of GATT as an institution and (iii) improving coherence in global economic policymaking. Thus, the Ministerial

---

[39] Moreover, the introduction of these codes lead to a modified, conditional Most Favoured Nation rule (*infra* paras. 35 and 62). Whereas normally under GATT, the possible benefits in the code would have to be granted to all other WTO Members, it was agreed that the benefits in question would only be granted to those countries that had signed the code. This system was intended to avoid 'free riding'. See A.F. LOWENFELD, *supra* note 31, p. 56.

[40] See J. JACKSON, 'Strengthening the International Legal Framework of the GATT-MTN System: Reform Proposals for the New GATT Round 1991', in E.U. PETERSMANN and M. HILF (eds.), *The New GATT Round of Multilateral Trade Negotiations: Legal and Economic Problems*, (Deventer, Kluwer 1991), p. 17.

[41] For an overview, see *inter alia* J.H.J. BOURGEOIS, F. BERROD and E. GIPPINI FOURNIER (eds.), *The Uruguay Round Results. A European Lawyers' Perspective*, (Brussels, European Interuniversity Press 1995), 541 p.; J.H. JACKSON and A.O. SYKES (eds.), *Implementing the Uruguay Round*, (Oxford, Clarendon Press 1997), xxix + 481 p.; J. STEENBERGEN, 'De Uruguay Ronde', *Sociaal-Economische Wetgeving* (1994), pp. 632–660 and P. VAN DEN BOSSCHE, 'Het oude GATT is dood, leve de WTO. Het langverhoopte einde van een succesvol begin', *Nederlands Juristenblad* (1994), pp. 901–905.

Conference of Punta del Este[42], which launched the Uruguay Round, did not include an explicit call for the establishment of a new international organization.[43] Negotiations proceeded relatively well and it was agreed in the Trade Negotiations Committee that the concluding Uruguay Round Ministerial Conference would be held at Brussels in December 1990. However, the Brussels Conference failed, the main reason being the disagreement between the US and the EEC on the reduction of the subsidies the latter provided to its farmers.[44] Yet, as explained above, the need for a proper international organization was undeniable. It was the GATT Director-General, Arthur DUNKEL, who kept the Uruguay Round alive and provided in December 1991 a summary of the negotiations so far. The so-called 'Dunkel Draft'[45] also included a draft statute for a Multilateral Trade Organization. In November 1992, the US and the EEC largely settled all their disputes on agriculture.[46] The subsequent GATT Director-General, Peter SUTHERLAND, pushed the negotiations further. During 1993 the negotiations proceeded significantly on market access and services. Finally, the Marrakesh Agreement of 15 April 1994 established the World Trade Organization, an international organization with legal personality, whose work was to lead to "raising standards of living, ensuring full employment and a large and steadily growing volume of real income [...] while allowing for the optimal use of the world's resources in accordance with the objective of sustainable development, seeking both to protect and preserve the environment and to enhance the means for doing so in a manner consistent with [its Members'] respective needs and concerns at different levels of economic development".[47]

---

[42] Ministerial Declaration on the Uruguay Round, GATT MIN.DEC, done at Punta del Este on 20 September 1986, GATT B.I.S.D. (33rd Supp.).

[43] Nonetheless, the Ministerial Declaration of Punta del Este did establish negotiating groups on dispute settlement and on the functioning of the GATT. See J.H. JACKSON, *supra* note 13, p. 400.

[44] It has been argued that this was not only a dispute between the US and the EEC. Japan, Australia, Canada and a number of developing countries (who played, unlike in the previous rounds, a substantially greater role; see P. GALLAGHER, *Guide to the WTO and Developing Countries*, (The Hague, Kluwer 2000), p. 5) stated that they would not accept the package if they did not get increased access to industrial countries for their agricultural goods. See A.F. LOWENFELD, *supra* note 31, pp. 63–65.

[45] *Draft Final Act Embodying the Results of the Uruguay Round of Multilateral Trade Negotiations*, GATT Doc. MTN.TNC/W/FA, dated 20 December 1991.

[46] The agreement became known as the 'Blair House Accord', named after the Presidential guest house in Washington where the agreement was reached. The EEC finally achieved the right to cut back agricultural subsidies more slowly than expected. In exchange, the US and other producers achieved the right for increased access to the European market. It is clear that the contentious agriculture issue and the weak deal that was finally agreed, already sowed the seeds for later tensions between the developing and developed countries.

[47] First recital preamble WTO Agreement.

§ 4. THE WTO AGREEMENT AND ITS ANNEXES

21. It suffices to look at the Marrakesh Agreement to realize what a broad range of subjects come under WTO law. The WTO Agreement itself only comprises 16 articles and is no more than the skeleton of the WTO system.[48] The flesh and bones is made up of the six annexes to the Agreement.
- Annex 1A contains 13 *multilateral agreements on Trade in Goods* (MATG), including the GATT 1947 in a slightly changed form as GATT 1994.[49] A number of these agreements are new; others pick up on – with some amendments – agreements that had been concluded within the framework of the older GATT rounds, with the important difference that while the GATT Contracting Parties could decide autonomously which agreement they wanted to become a party to[50], this is impossible in the WTO: the whole package of 'multilateral agreements' (see *infra* on the 'plurilateral agreements') must be accepted.[51] Next to the GATT, there are agreements concerning Agriculture; Sanitary and Phytosanitary measures (the so-called 'SPS Agreement'); Textiles and Clothing (terminated on 1 January 2005); Technical Barriers to Trade (the so-called 'TBT Agreement'); Trade-Related Investment Measures (TRIMS); Antidumping[52]; Customs Valuation[53]; Pre-shipment Inspection; Rules of Origin; Import Licensing Procedures; Subsidies and Countervailing Measures; and Safeguards.
- Annex 1B contains the *General Agreement on Trade in Services* (GATS).[54] GATS is a framework agreement that is strongly inspired by the GATT principles, but in most instances requires further negotiations for the implementation of these principles.

---

[48] See L. Cuyvers and B. Kerremans, *Internationale economische organisaties*, (Leuven, Garant, 1997), p. 140.
[49] A large number of memoranda have been added to GATT 1994, which interpret several provisions of the GATT.
[50] An example is the GATT-antidumping code which – as a replacement for an earlier antidumping code that dated from the Kennedy Round (1962–1967) – was adopted in the framework of the Tokyo Round and to which not all GATT Contracting Parties were party. On the contrary, the Antidumping Agreement of the WTO binds all WTO Members.
[51] According to art. II, 2, WTO Agreement, all multilateral trade agreements are binding for all Members.
[52] Formally called 'Agreement on Implementation of Article VI of the General Agreement on Tariffs and Trade 1994'.
[53] Formally called 'Agreement on Implementation of Article VII of the General Agreement on Tariffs and Trade 1994'.
[54] 33 I.L.M. 44 (1994). The GATS has 8 annexes, which deal *inter alia* with the Movement of Natural Persons, Supplying Services, Air Transport Services, Financial Services, Maritime Transport Services and Telecommunications. Four protocols are added to this Agreement: The Second and Fifth Protocol on lists on Financial Services (24 July 1995 and 3 December 1997); the Third Protocol on Movement of Natural Persons (24 July 1995); the Fourth Protocol on Basic Telecommunications (30 April 1996). (No First Protocol exists.)

- Annex 1C contains the *Agreement on the Trade-Related Aspects of Intellectual Property Rights, Including Trade in Counterfeit Goods* (TRIPS).
- In order to ensure the effectiveness of WTO law, Annex 2 contains the essential *Memorandum of Understanding on Rules and Procedures Governing the Settlement of Disputes* (DSU[55]).
- Annex 3 contains the *Agreement on the Trade Policy Review Mechanism* (TPRM).
- Finally, Annex 4 contains two so-called *plurilateral trade agreements,* i.e. agreements that (in contrast to the previously mentioned multilateral agreements) do not by definition apply to all WTO Members: these are the *Agreement on Trade in Civil Aircraft* and on *Government Procurement*.[56] Although these agreements are concluded between a limited number of WTO Members, they are nevertheless an integral part of the WTO system: e.g. the mechanisms concerning dispute settlement[57] and trade review are applicable.

22. The Marrakesh Agreement does not consist of these texts alone. The most voluminous part is the 22,500 pages of schedules that spell out the commitments individual Members have undertaken with regard to well-defined categories of goods and services.[58] The commitments range from the reduction and binding of customs tariffs to the reduction of these tariffs to zero. The number of 'bound' tariffs – i.e. tariffs that are fixed in the WTO framework and can be raised again only with difficulty[59] – has increased remarkably[60], which particularly for agricultural products meant considerable progress.[61] All these schedules form an

---

[55] Dispute Settlement Understanding.
[56] The two other plurilateral agreements that had been concluded in 1994, namely on dairy and bovine meat, were terminated in 1997.
[57] Note that the applicability of the dispute settlement system to the plurilateral agreements is subject to the adoption of a decision by the parties to such agreement setting out the terms for the application of the DSU to the individual agreement. This decision may specify any special or additional rules or procedures. See Appendix 1 to the DSU. The Committee on Government Procurement made such decision, but not the Committee on Trade in Civil Aircraft.
[58] To GATS there is also a list added which indicates for each Member the agreed exceptions to the principle of Most Favoured Nation.
[59] Raising of these tariffs is possible, but the Member concerned has to negotiate with Members that are most affected, which can result in compensation to trade partners for the loss of trade.
[60] The developed countries have increased their number of bound tariffs from 78% up to 99% of the product lines; for developing countries, it concerns an increase of 21% to 73%. Bound tariffs lead to a larger legal certainty for traders and investors.
[61] Almost all import barriers, which do not take the form of tariffs, such as quotas, have been transformed into tariffs. This 'tarification' makes agricultural markets considerably more predictable thanks to the bound character of the tariffs. On the other hand, the Agreement on Agriculture allows a system of 'tariff quotas', whereby lower tariffs are applicable if one stays below the quota, but (often considerably) higher tariffs if one exceeds the quota. It has been

integral part of the Marrakesh Agreement. On the basis of the principle of Most Favoured Nation, every WTO Member must apply its commitments, in principle[62] equally to imports from all WTO Members, even of those Members that have not agreed to specific commitments themselves.[63]

23. Next to the Agreements that are included in the framework of the Marrakesh Agreement, in the past eight years the WTO *acquis* has been extended with a number of further engagements and a swiftly increasing number of decisions within the framework of the dispute settlement mechanism. Since the most important principles are included in the previously mentioned Agreements, negotiations have focused on achieving specific commitments by Members in the area of market access. Within the framework of GATS, in 1997 a Protocol on Basic Telecommunications[64] and a Protocol on Financial Services were concluded, among others.[65] Within the framework of GATT, an Agreement on Trade in Information Technology Products was reached in 1996.[66]

24. The WTO provides a permanent forum for multilateral negotiations. Officials meet constantly on a wide variety of topics. In 2000 new negotiations on agriculture and services began on the basis of a 'built-in agenda' in the WTO Agreements.[67] More generally, following the failure of the 1999 Ministerial Conference in Seattle, in November 2001, the WTO started a new multilateral trade round on the Ministerial Conference in Doha, called the Doha Development Agenda (DDA).[68] Negotiations suffered a major setback with the failure of the

---

agreed that developed countries will decrease their tariffs (in the case of tariff quotas, the higher tariffs which apply outside the quota) with 36% on average over 6 years. See M. G. DESTA, *The Law of International Trade in Agricultural Products: From GATT 1947 to the WTO Agreement on Agriculture*, (The Hague, Kluwer Law International 2002), xvii + 468 p.

[62] Unless of course a specific exception to MFN applies, such as the temporary exceptions to MFN in the framework of GATS.

[63] This leads indeed to the 'free rider' problem: See R. FRID, 'Multilateral liberalization of trade in services under the GATS', *Sociaal-Economische Wetgeving* (1998), p. 414.

[64] Fourth Protocol to the General Agreement on Trade in Services, done at Geneva on 15 April 1997, http://www.wto.org/english/docs_e/legal_e/4prote_sl20_e.pdf.

[65] Fifth Protocol to the General Agreement on Trade in Services, done at Geneva on 27 February 1998, http://www.wto.org/english/docs_e/legal_e/5prote_sl45_e.pdf.

[66] Agreement on Trade in Information Technology Products, done at Singapore on 13 December 1996, http://www.wto.org/english/docs_e/legal_e/itadec_e.pdf.

[67] See art. 20 on the Agreement on Agriculture; art. XIX GATS. See also the built-in agenda in art. 27.3.b TRIPS (patentability).

[68] See the Ministerial Declaration of Doha, done on 14 November 2001, WT/MIN(01)/DEC/1, available on http://www.wto.org/english/thewto_e/minist_e/min01_e/mindecl_e.htm. See *inter alia* M. MOORE, *Doha and Beyond. The Future of the Multilateral Trading System*, (Cambridge, Cambridge University Press 2004), xx + 184 p.; S.P. SUBEDI, 'The road from Doha: the issues for the Development Round of the WTO and the future of international trade', 52 *International and Comparative Law Quarterly* (2003), pp. 425–446 and PH. VINCENT, 'Les

Ministerial Conference in Cancún in September 2003, and only began again in early 2004.[69] The objective was to achieve an agreement on 1 January 2005. Nonetheless, this deadline was not met. After the failure of Cancún, WTO Members agreed the so-called 'July Decision'[70] (named after the compromise achieved in July 2004) on 1 August 2004. In this Decision, the developed countries committed themselves to reducing domestic support and export subsidies. In return, an agreement could be reached with the developing countries to further open up their markets and make new steps in liberalizing the services sector. However, the July Decision provided only for a framework. More concrete commitments needed to be reached at the sixth WTO Conference in Hong Kong in December 2005. Although the Ministerial Declaration adopted at the end of this conference indeed contains a large number of references to development, the general feeling is that the developing countries did not achieve what they wished. The fear of a new failure, like the one in Cancún, probably motivated some Members to agree to the final Declaration, even if they were not entirely happy with it. There was indeed a danger that a failure in Hong Kong would have ended any prospect of completing the Doha Round in a reasonable time frame. Yet, as these lines are written, it becomes increasingly doubtful whether the Doha Round really constitutes a *development Round*, as was initially promised.

---

résultats de la quatrième Conférence ministérielle de l'OMC : vers un cycle du développement ?', *Revue belge de droit international* (2003), pp. 111–130.

[69] See for the EC perspective on that failure, European Commission, *Communication from the Commission to the Council, to the European Parliament, and to the Economic and Social Committee*, 26 November 2003, COM(2003) 734, available on http://www.eu-oplysningen.dk/upload/application/pdf/c1219a61/com2003_0734en01.pdf.

[70] Decision Adopted by the General Council of the WTO on 1 August 2004, WT/L/579.

CHAPTER II
OBJECTIVES AND BASIC PRINCIPLES OF THE WTO

§ 1. OBJECTIVES AND FUNCTIONS OF THE WTO

25. The ultimate objectives of the WTO are to raise standards of living, ensuring full employment and a large and steadily growing volume of real income and effective demand, and the expansion of the trade in and production of goods and services.[1] The pursuit of free trade[2], through reciprocal and mutually advantageous arrangements directed at the reduction of trade barriers and the elimination of discrimination[3], is a means to achieve this end. The Preamble of the WTO Agreement therefore makes clear that free trade is not an end in itself. Moreover, it qualifies the pursuit of free trade. First, WTO Members can only do this "in accordance with the objective of sustainable development, seeking both to protect and preserve the environment and […] in a manner consistent with their respective needs and concerns at different levels of development". Thus, the WTO Agreement recognizes explicitly the importance and legitimacy of policies aimed at environmental protection. Further obligations in the Agreements always have to be read in the light of this consideration.[4] Second, it is also specified in the Preamble that there is a need to ensure that developing countries, especially the least developed ones, "secure a share in the growth in international trade commensurate with the needs of their economic development".[5] Arguably, the

---

[1] Agreement Establishing the World Trade Organization, done at Marrakesh on 15 April 1994, *UNTS* no. 31874, para. 1 of the Preamble. For a comparison with the Havana Charter (ITO), see R. VERNON, 'The World Trade Organization: a New Stage in International Trade and Development', *Harvard International Law Journal* (1995), pp. 332-336.

[2] According to the principle of comparative advantage, free trade will lead to an optimal allocation of resources. The Preamble itself states that international trade relations should allow "… for the optimal use of the world's resources…". In this regard, QURESHI concludes that "the rationale of the theory of comparative advantage may be stated to be embedded in the preamble of the agreement establishing the WTO". A.H. QURESHI, *International Economic Law*, (London, Sweet & Maxwell 1999), p. 238.

[3] Two basic principles of the WTO, see *infra* §2.

[4] See Appellate Body report: United States – Import Prohibition of Certain Shrimp and Shrimp Products, WT/DS58/AB/R, 12 October 1998, paras. 129 and 153.

[5] Agreement Establishing the World Trade Organization, *supra* note 1, para. 2 of the Preamble. See also para. 2 of the Ministerial Declaration of Doha, done on 14 November 2001, WT/

Preamble points to the possibility of differential treatment of developing countries, since they "may have different needs according to their levels of development and particular circumstances".[6] These objectives are not only relevant for the interpretation of the Marrakesh Agreement, but are also relevant to the interpretation of each and every Uruguay Round Agreement, since it is an integral part of the Marrakesh Agreement.[7]

26. According to Article III of the WTO Agreement, the WTO has five major functions. The WTO's first and broadest task is to administer and implement the multi- and plurilateral agreements that together form the WTO Agreements. Second, the WTO provides the forum for multilateral negotiations between Members.[8] Various Uruguay Round Agreements have a 'built-in agenda' for further trade negotiations. What is more, the Ministerial Conference may decide to introduce new subjects into the WTO. It is also possible that negotiations take place which are not specifically authorized by the Ministerial Conference. For instance, during the Singapore Ministerial Conference, a number of WTO Members and accession candidates concluded an Agreement on Trade in Information Technology Products.[9] This Agreement, not part of the WTO Agreements, resulted in changes in tariff bindings. The WTO finally also provides a forum for bilateral negotiations between Members. The third task of the WTO consists of finding solutions when trade disputes arise between WTO Members on the various agreements. The WTO is one of the few intergovernmental organizations with effective enforcement of its rules.[10] As a fourth task, the WTO periodically reviews the national trade policy of WTO Members. The Trade Policy Review Mechanism (TPRM) accordingly is designed to contribute "to the smoother functioning of the multilateral trading system, by achieving greater transparency in and understanding of the trade policies and practices of Members".[11] The four countries (or groups of countries) with the greatest impact on international trade[12] are subject to review every two years, the next 16 countries

---

MIN(01)/DEC/1, available on http://www.wto.org/english/thewto_e/minist_e/min01_e/mindecl_e.htm.

[6] Appellate Body report: European Communities – Conditions for the Granting of Tariff Preferences for Developing Countries, WT/DS246/AB/R, (7 April 2004), para. 161. On the principle of 'special and differential treatment', see *infra* paras. 84–92.

[7] J. CROOME, *Guide to the Uruguay Round Agreements*, (The Hague, Kluwer 1999), p. 3 and A.H. QURESHI, *supra* note 2, p. 237.

[8] It is sometimes said that the WTO is no more than an enormous 'negotiation table'. See WORLD TRADE ORGANIZATION, *Understanding the WTO*, (Geneva, World Trade Organization 2007), p. 9.

[9] Ministerial Declaration on Trade in Information Technology Products, WTO/MIN(96)/16, 13 December 1996.

[10] On WTO dispute settlement, see *infra* Chapter 4, §3.

[11] Trade Policy Review Mechanism, A.i.

[12] Currently the EU, the US, Japan and Canada.

in importance every four years, and the remainder every six years.[13] The mechanism should allow the WTO to anticipate trade problems. The TPRM does not examine the legal compatibility of a country's trade measures with the WTO agreements.[14] The purpose is merely to examine the impact of these policies on the trading system, which increases transparency and understanding of other country's trade policies.[15] Nevertheless, the fact that the reviews are made public[16] has a certain (positive or negative) impact on the reputation of the country.[17] Finally, the WTO also cooperates with other international institutions that deal with the formulation of global economic policy. To be sure, the WTO is but one of many international organizations dealing with international trade, even though it can be seen as one of the main pillars of the international economic order. The WTO has concluded a cooperation agreement with the IMF and the World Bank and coordinates its actions with these institutions.[18] In contrast with these two institutions, the WTO is not a specialized agency of the United Nations (see also *infra* para. 161), although some critics have called for an adjustment in that direction.[19] In addition, Article V of the WTO Agreement indicates that the "General Council shall make appropriate arrangements for effective cooperation with other intergovernmental organizations that have responsibilities related to those of the WTO". The International Organization for Standardization (IOS), the World Customs Organization (WCO), the World Intellectual Property Organization (WIPO), the Codex Alimentarius Commission, the United Nations Conference for Trade and Development (UNCTAD) and the International Office

---

[13] For least-developed countries longer periods can be fixed: Trade Policy Review Mechanism, C.ii.
[14] This is the task of the WTO dispute settlement mechanism.
[15] J. CROOME, *supra* note 7, pp. 31–35.
[16] They are published on the website of the WTO. See http://www.wto.org/english/tratop_e/tpr_e/tpr_e.htm.
[17] B. HOEKMAN and M. KOSTECKI, *The Political Economy of the World Trading System*, (Oxford, Oxford University Press 2001), p. 63 and A.F. LOWENFELD, *International Economic Law*, (Oxford, Oxford University Press 2003), p. 71.
[18] See art. III, (5) WTO Agreement and the *Declaration on the Contribution of the World Trade Organization to Achieving Greater Coherence in Global Economic Policymaking*, para. 5, in annex to the WTO Agreement. On 9 December 1996 the WTO signed a cooperation agreement with the IMF, on April 28 with the World Bank.
[19] See the recommendations of the Parliamentary Working Group 'Globalization' of the Belgian Chamber of Representatives, para. 2.1.5 (Documents of the Belgian Parliament, 2002-2003, no. 50, Doc. 2330/003, based on the report by external experts, Doc. 2230/001–002), as adopted by the Chamber of Representatives of the Belgian Parliament by Motion of 13 March 2003 (Doc. 2230/004). Nevertheless the WTO is represented in the 'United Nations System Chief Executives Board for Coordination', but this body does not work adequately: see J. WOUTERS in cooperation with C. RYNGAERT, *Vers un renforcement de l'encadrement juridique et institutionnel de la globalisation*, Belgian Chamber of Representatives, 2002-2003, no. 50, Doc. 2330/001, (93), pp. 108–110. See also *infra* para. 173.

of Epizootics all have connections with the WTO.[20] The WTO is also increasingly interacting with non-governmental organizations.[21]

§ 2. BASIC PRINCIPLES

27. The substantive law of the WTO is extremely extensive and technical. The basic principles are *in se* not difficult, but 'the devil is in the detail'. It must be verified for each and every agreement which role the basic principles fulfil within the framework of that agreement and the extent to which they apply. Sometimes, a principle only becomes operational or exemptions only apply when there are specific commitments by WTO Members. Despite the fact that the basic principles appear in the whole of the WTO law, caution should be exercised: in the case of conflict of norms, the specific agreement prevails.[22] Two basic principles can be identified: market access and non-discrimination. Both principles have several exceptions, which will be explained briefly here and will be further elaborated upon for the various agreements.

A. MARKET ACCESS

28. The principle of market access is *in se* not an operational norm, but rather follows from various WTO rules that are each based on agreed concessions "on a reciprocal and mutually advantageous basis".[23] Economic operators of different WTO Members must, in principle, be granted unlimited access to another Member's market. Although customs duties do undoubtedly make access more difficult, under WTO law they are not prohibited.[24] WTO Members have nevertheless to comply with the agreed commitments. As explained earlier, ordinary customs duties were the object of different trade negotiation rounds within the framework of GATT and as a consequence, import duties on industrial products have steadily decreased from 40% in the 1940s to between 3% and 5% today. Other duties or charges on or in connection with importation, other than

---

[20] On the relations with some of these organizations, see *infra* paras. 165–201.
[21] See *infra* paras. 202–203.
[22] See, relating to conflicts between the GATT and provisions of other agreements on trade in goods, the 'General interpretative note to Annex 1A' in the chapeau of Annex 1A to the WTO Agreement. However, this does not mean that the specific agreements replace GATT 1994. They have to be read together and in case of a conflict between the provisions, the provisions of the specific agreements will prevail. See Appellate Body report: Brazil – Measures Affecting Desiccated Coconut, (WT/DS22/AB/R), 21 February 1997, para. 13.
[23] See *inter alia* third preliminary consideration and art. XXVIII*bis* GATT; third preliminary consideration GATS.
[24] Art. II.1 GATT.

ordinary customs duties, are possible in so far as they are included in a schedule of commitments for each Member.[25] Restrictions on the volume of imported goods or services, so-called quantitative restrictions[26] are, in principle, prohibited.[27] Finally, to a certain extent also the use of regulations imposing technical standards, sanitary measures, qualification or licensing requirements is restricted.[28] In order to further ensure market access, governmental regulations must be predictable and transparent.[29]

Market access is different in case of GATS (*infra* para. 144). Market access for services and service providers of one Member to the market of other Members is not granted automatically but depends on the specific commitments by sector or subsector that Members are willing to undertake.

B. NON-DISCRIMINATION

29. Having access to the market of other Members is not enough: this access also has to take place on a non-discriminatory basis. The principle of non-discrimination is without doubt the *leitmotiv* of the entire corpus of WTO law[30] and takes two forms in the WTO provisions on goods, services and intellectual property. On the one hand, a Member cannot discriminate among all his trading partners. This is the principle of Most Favoured Nation (MFN). On the other hand, in principle, once the imported products, services, persons etc have crossed the border, the imported products must receive national treatment.[31]

---

[25] Art. II.1 (b), second sentence GATT. During the GATT 1947 period, there was no obligation for WTO Members to record these 'other duties and charges' in their schedules of concessions. However, to increase transparency, the GATT Understanding on the Interpretation of Article II:1 (b) made this obligatory. See Understanding on the Interpretation of Article II:1 (b) of the General Agreement on Tariffs and Trade 1994, para. 1. See A. HODA, *Tariff Negotiations and Renegotiations under the GATT and the WTO. Procedures and Practices*, (Cambridge, Cambridge University Press 2001), p. 19.

[26] E.g. quotas or import licences.

[27] Art. XI GATT and art. XVI GATS.

[28] See specifically the TBT Agreement and the SPS Agreement as well as art. VI GATS.

[29] Art. 10 TBT, art. 7 SPS, art. III GATS and art. 63 TRIPS.

[30] It should be noted here that requirements in some WTO agreements go beyond non-discrimination. The Agreement on Trade Related Intellectual Property Rights (TRIPS) and the Agreement on Technical Barriers to Trade (TBT) lay down minimum standards and requirements that limit the freedom of governments to take measures, even if they constitute no discrimination. See *infra* para. 93.

[31] Applied in art. III GATT, art. XVII GATS and art. 3 TRIPS. See for an extensive discussion *inter alia* G. VERHOOSEL, *National Treatment and WTO Dispute Settlement: Adjudicating the Boundaries of Regulatory Autonomy*, (Oxford, Hart 2002), xi + 124 p.

It should first be noted that the principle of non-discrimination requires that similar situations are treated in the same way. Obviously, this does not apply to dissimilar situations. Therefore, it will be important to define the degree of 'likeness' of products or services. This primary assessment that has to be made when one considers whether States are discriminating in their trade relations gives rise to considerable doctrinal and jurisprudential discussion.[32]

1. Most Favoured Nation

30. The Most Favoured Nation rule (MFN) requires that a good, service or service provider originating in one WTO Member is not treated less favourably than a 'like' good, service or service provider that originates in any other Member.[33] The principle is phrased more generally – i.e. not necessarily applied on trade relations – in the International Law Commission's Draft Articles on Most-Favoured-Nation Clauses.[34] MFN treatment is described as "treatment accorded by the granting State to the beneficiary State, or to persons or things in a determined relationship with that State, not less favourable than treatment extended by the granting State to a third State or to persons or things in the same relationship with that third State".[35] In other words, if a Member grants another Member an advantage, this advantage has to be granted to all others.[36] In the end, there cannot be any 'most favoured' Member among WTO Members, since they all have to be equally favoured.

31. Already in the 19th century, the principle of MFN was rather popular in the liberal Europe of that time. The United Kingdom often included the principle in its trade agreements. This contrasted with the United States, which adopted only after World War I a multilateral rather than a bilateral approach. Admittedly, the US had achieved an economic advantage over other countries during the war years and the multilateral approach laid down in MFN provided strong opportunities for market expansion. In addition, MFN fitted perfectly in one of the 14 points of US President Woodrow Wilson, namely, the "establishment of an equality of trade conditions among all the nations". Also the Covenant of the

---

[32] On the difficult issue of defining 'likeness', see also *infra* paras. 66–67.
[33] B. HOEKMAN and M. KOSTECKI, *supra* note 17, p. 29.
[34] International Law Commission, *Draft Articles on Most-Favoured-Nation Clauses*, 1978, http://www.un.org/law/ilc/texts/mfnfra.htm.
[35] *Ibid*, art. 5.
[36] Applied in art. I GATT, art. II GATS and art. 4 TRIPS. See *inter alia* M. BROESSKAMP, *Meistbegünstiging und Gegenseitigkeit im GATT*, Cologne, Heymann, 1990, 145 p.; W. SCHWARTZ and A. SYKES, 'Towards a Positive Theory of the Most Favored Nation Obligation and its Exceptions in the WTO/GATT system', *International Review of Law and Economics* (1996), pp. 27–51 and UNCTAD, *Most-favoured-nation treatment*, (New York, United Nations 1999), viii + 54 p.

Objectives and Basic Principles of the WTO

League of Nations had a provision calling for "equitable treatment for the commerce of all members".[37] The depression in the 1930s drastically reduced interest in MFN. It was only in 1947, with the drafting of GATT, when the principle again became the focus of attention.[38]

32. Even though, today, the principle of MFN figures in several instruments relating to international trade, it is not accepted as being part of customary international law. A rule has to comply with two conditions in order to be accepted as a norm of customary international law. First, it should be an expression of an *opinio juris* among States. Second, there should be sufficient State practice in accordance with the rule.[39] With regard to the principle of MFN, both conditions do not seem to be fulfilled yet. Even though it is acknowledged that certain agreements that contain the principle of MFN (e.g. GATT) may eventually become part of customary international law, it is not accepted that MFN has already reached this stage.[40] It should be noted that the ILC Draft Articles on Most-Favoured-Nation Clauses merely address such clauses contained in treaties.[41]

33. Nonetheless, the importance of MFN as a basic pillar of the WTO cannot be ignored. States recur to MFN in trade agreements for a number of reasons.[42] First, MFN helps lower transaction costs. Transaction costs are the cost of concluding trade agreements. Negotiating multilateral trade concessions with 151 Members is extremely difficult and time-consuming. Thanks to the principle of MFN, the results of a negotiation with one country are extended to all other WTO Members. Second, MFN is an essential instrument in making the process of comparative advantage in a free market work. If all producers have equal access to a certain

---

[37] Art. 22 (5), Covenant of the League of Nations, done at Versailles on 28 June 1919, available on www.yale.edu/lawweb/avalon/leagcov.htm; J.H. JACKSON, *The World Trading System*, (Indianapolis, Bobbs-Merrill 1969), pp. 250–251.

[38] For a complete historical overview, see *inter alia* E.A. LAING, 'Equal access/non-discrimination and legitimate discrimination in international economic law', *Wisconsin International Law Journal* (1996), pp. 255–264.

[39] See ICJ, Continental Shelf (Libyan Arab Jamahiriya/Malta), *I.C.J. Rep.* 1985, p. 29, para. 27; ICJ, Case concerning military and paramilitary activities in and against Nicaragua (Nicaragua/USA.) (Merits), *I.C.J. Rep.* 1986, p. 14, para. 183 and ICJ, Legality of the use by a State of nuclear weapons in armed conflict, Advisory opinion, *I.C.J. Rep.* 1996, p. 66, para. 70. P. DAILLIER and A. PELLET, *Droit International Public*, (Paris, L.G.D.J. 2002), p. 381.

[40] The reluctance of Western nations to grant the same benefits to Communist nations used to be one of the reasons for the rejection of MFN as a rule of customary international law. Today, MFN is being eroded by various exceptions. E.A. LAING, *supra* note 38, p. 251 and J.H. JACKSON, W.J. DAVEY and A.O. SYKES, *Legal Problems of International Economic Relations*, (Saint Paul, West Publishing 1995, 3rd ed.), pp. 438 and 444.

[41] Art. 4 International Law Commission, *Draft Articles on Most-Favoured-Nation Clauses*, 1978, http://www.un.org/law/ilc/texts/mfnfra.htm.

[42] See B. HOEKMAN and M. KOSTECKI, *supra* note 17, p. 30 and J.H. JACKSON, W.J. DAVEY and A.O. SYKES, *supra* note 40, p. 437.

The World Trade Organization

market, importers and consumers in this market will be able to choose to buy from the producer with the lowest price. It will be perfectly possible to compare prices because national import rules and duties affect them all in the same way. Thus, MFN helps to establish equality of competitive opportunities.[43] Third, and following from the previous reason, MFN makes it impossible for States with large economies to neglect or abuse States with small economies. No matter how small a State, it can benefit from the same concessions as any other Member. Large States cannot "exploit their market power by raising tariffs against them in periods when times are bad and domestic industries are clamouring for protection, or alternatively, give specific countries preferential treatment for foreign policy reasons".[44] In the end, this results in peace and stability of international relations. Fourth, MFN treatment makes international trade interactions transparent and predictable. This is obviously advantageous for traders, but also for the negotiating Members themselves. Merely making use of bilateral deals can lead to uncertainty about the envisaged benefits accruing from the deal. It may indeed be possible that a bilateral deal between countries A and B erodes benefits of country C, which resulted from a previous bilateral deal between countries A and C. Finally, because of the obligation to grant benefits on a multilateral basis, special interest groups will have less impact on the executive (negotiating) branch in order to obtain special trade preferences.[45]

34. Of course, the principle of MFN also has disadvantages. The main problem resulting from the application of MFN is that of Members free riding on the efforts of other Members to achieve certain advantages. Since negotiation on for instance trade concessions within the WTO is a process of give and take, Members will have to give some advantages to a trading partner in order to achieve benefits for the products in which that Member itself has a trade interest. Other Members will immediately benefit from these concessions, without having to make any concessions themselves. Countries which enjoy a benefit without submitting themselves to a discipline such as a restraint on using certain trade barriers, are such 'free riders'.[46] Therefore, participants in multilateral negotiations may choose to refrain from making concessions in the hope that they can take advantage of concessions by others without offering something in return. Clearly, in the end, no concessions at all will occur.[47]

---

[43] UNCTAD, *supra* note 36, p. 8.
[44] B. HOEKMAN and M. KOSTECKI, *supra* note 17, p. 30.
[45] J.H. JACKSON, W.J. DAVEY and A.O. SYKES, *supra* note 40, p. 437.
[46] J.H. JACKSON, *The Jurisprudence of GATT and the WTO*, (Cambridge, Cambridge University Press 2000), p. 416, note 8.
[47] M.J. TREBILCOCK and R. HOWSE, *The Regulation of International Trade*, (London, Routledge 2005), p. 52.

35. In order to avoid the 'free rider' problem, States might recur to a conditional MFN.[48] This implies that a country willing to benefit – on the basis of MFN – from a privilege given by another country to a third country, only achieves the advantage if this country grants the privilege itself. Such MFN treatment would thus only be granted on condition of strict and specific reciprocity.[49] In the WTO agreements, MFN applies unconditionally.[50]

2. National Treatment

36. Once imported goods have entered the domestic market, a Member cannot treat them less favourably than its own domestic goods. The same rule applies with regard to treatment of services and service providers, be it then subject to specific commitments made by the WTO Member. National treatment may also restrict the application of rules on intellectual property rights.[51] Thus, in general, national treatment requires that a nation treats within its own borders, goods, services, persons etc. originating from outside its borders in the same manner as it treats those which are of domestic origin.[52] Clearly, the principle complements MFN. Liberalization commitments, applied on a non-discriminatory basis, would be valueless if there were not some limitations on the types of internal taxation or regulation that a country could impose. The rule is clearly wide-ranging. Therefore, almost every domestic policy measure – be it in the form of taxation or regulation – will come within its scope. Consequently, many domestic policies clash with the principle of national treatment, leading to several disputes before the Dispute Settlement Body of the WTO.[53] However, national policies that treat national products, services, persons etc. more favourably than like imported products, services or persons, and thus are discriminating on basis of origin, may be doing so for perfectly valid reasons. Indeed a government may for instance want to protect public health, improve welfare in underdeveloped regions, preserve the cultural identity, or protect the environment. To this end, the WTO agreements provide for a number of exceptions, which will be discussed later.[54] Moreover,

---

[48] J.H. JACKSON, W.J. DAVEY and A.O. SYKES, *supra* note 40, p. 439.
[49] UNCTAD, *supra* note 36, p. 9.
[50] Except in case of the Tokyo 'Codes'. However, this is not a traditional conditional MFN since there is no requirement of reciprocity. Instead, it is required that one becomes a party to the code in order to be granted the benefits of the code. See J.H. JACKSON, W.J. DAVEY and A.O. SYKES, *supra* note 40, p. 439. Moreover, under the GATS, WTO Members were allowed to inscribe exemptions to the MFN principle. Such an exception may include a reciprocity requirement before the MFN principle applies. See *infra* para. 138.
[51] See G. VERHOOSEL, *supra* note 31.
[52] J.H. JACKSON, *supra* note 46, p. 57.
[53] J.H. JACKSON, 'National treatment obligations and non-tariff barriers', *Michigan Journal of International Law* (1989), p. 209.
[54] *Infra* paras. 38–43.

national regulations and taxation that at first sight are origin-neutral, might in fact be unfavourable to imported products when applied in practice. This 'disguised discrimination' can be a purposeful protective policy of a State, but may equally just be an unintended side effect of an acceptable policy goal. It is clear that this dilemma always involves a difficult and delicate balancing act between free trade and other objectives.[55]

37. The principle of national treatment of 'like' domestic and imported products more often than not gives the impression of imposing a constraint on State sovereignty. A GATT Panel recognized that "the treatment of imported and domestic products as like products under Article III may have significant implications for the scope of obligations under the General Agreement and for the regulatory autonomy of contracting parties with respect to their internal tax laws and regulations [...]. In the view of the Panel, therefore, it is imperative that the like product determination in the context of Article III be made in such a way that it does not necessarily infringe upon the regulatory autonomy and domestic policy options of contracting parties".[56] There is a serious fear that an indirect, 'creeping expansion' of competences from Members to the WTO will occur. Moreover, it is feared that WTO decision-making does not provide sufficient democratic guarantees.[57]

---

[55] This balancing has *inter alia* been done in Appellate Body Report: European Communities – Measures Affecting Asbestos and Asbestos-containing Products, WT/DS135/AB/R (12 March 2001); Appellate Body Report: European Communities – Measures Concerning Meat and Meat Products (Hormones), WT/DS26 and 48/AB/R (16 January 1998) and Appellate Body Report: United States – Import Prohibition of Certain Shrimp and Shrimp Products, WT/DS58/AB/R (12 October 1998). See *infra* para. 75.

[56] Panel Report: United States – Measures Affecting Alcoholic and Malt Beverages, DS23/R (19 June 1992), BISD 39S/206, para. 5.72.

[57] See on the legitimacy and democracy discussion concerning the WTO, *infra* paras. 311–320 and *inter alia* J. ATIK, 'Democratizing the WTO', *George Washington International Law Review* (2001), pp. 451–472; M. BRONCKERS, 'Betere regels voor een nieuw millennium. Een waarschuwing tegen ondemocratische ontwikkelingen in de WTO', *Sociaal-Economische Wetgeving* (1999), pp. 414–423; P. M. GERHART, 'The Two Constitutional Visions of the World Trade Organization', *University of Pennsylvania Journal of International Economic Law* (2003), pp. 1–75; R. HOWSE, 'How to Begin to Think About the 'Democratic Deficit' at the WTO', in S. GRILLER (ed.), *International Governance and Non-Economic Concerns: New Challenges for the International Legal Order*, (Wien, Springer 2003), pp. 79–101; R. HOWSE and K. NICOLAIDIS, 'Enhancing WTO Legitimacy: Constitutionalization or Global Subsidiarity?', *Governance* (2003), pp. 73-94 and L. WALLACH and M. SFORZA, *Whose Trade Organization? Corporate Globalization and the Erosion of Democracy: An Assessment of the World Trade Organization*, (Washington D.C., Public Citizen 1999), xii + 229 p.

C. EXCEPTIONS

38. As has been explained above, there is a need to exempt certain national measures from the principle of Most Favoured Nation and the principle of National Treatment. WTO law recognizes that governments should be able to restrict trade in specific circumstances.[58] Admittedly, the Contracting Parties of the GATT and later, Members of the WTO, would never have been willing to sign agreements including commitments for which there is no exit option at all. A number of the exceptions that will be mentioned are only effectively used in the agreements relating to trade in goods. This is due to the fact that in case of trade in services or the trade aspects of intellectual property rights, the basic principles do not always apply to their full extent. However, as negotiation in these areas of international trade proceeds, the basic principles will achieve their full effect. As a result, the exceptions will have an equally important role to play.

39. The first important exception to the principle of Most Favoured Nation is that of free trade agreements.[59] Members might want to establish such agreements in a process to reinforce the economic ties with other countries (often neighbouring countries or countries with intertwined interests). Countries in the same region often have common interests and important economic ties. These can be promoted by the granting of certain trade preferences to each other, without their being extended to other WTO Members. Obviously, this practice is contrary to the principle of MFN. Yet, the WTO agreements contain provisions allowing such agreements. Apparently, the drafters of the agreements believed that regional economic integration was a process to be encouraged.[60]

40. A second departure from the principle of non-discrimination (both MFN and National Treatment) is the possibility for Members to use certain 'safety valves' when pursuing their economic policies. When foreign competition is extremely vigorous and the import of foreign products or services unexpectedly peaks so as to severely hurt national competitors, Members have the possibility of adopting safeguard measures.[61] It is also possible that foreign competitors price their goods well below a normal market price in order to destroy national competitors. This type of 'unfair' trade practice is called dumping.[62] Foreign producers may also be subsidized by their own government. In these two cases of 'unfair' trade practices, Members have – in limited circumstances and under

---

[58] B. HOEKMAN and M. KOSTECKI, *supra* note 17, p. 36.
[59] Art. XXIV GATT, art. V GATS, art. 4 TRIPS.
[60] See for a more elaborated discussion, *infra* paras. 78–83 (GATT) and para. 148 (GATS).
[61] Art. XIX GATT and Agreement on Safeguards.
[62] See *infra* paras. 108–111.

specific conditions – the right to impose antidumping duties or countervailing duties on the 'dumped' or subsidized imports. Safety valves are also provided for cases where a Member suffers balance of payments difficulties[63] or wants to protect its 'infant industries'.[64]

41. The Uruguay Round Agreements also provide Members with the option of obtaining a 'waiver' for their obligations under the Agreements. The 'waiver' will be granted if consensus is reached within the Ministerial Conference in a period of maximum 90 days. If consensus cannot be reached, this 'waiver' will only be granted after a majority of three quarters of WTO Members has agreed. Waivers are only granted for a limited period and are subject to annual review.[65]

42. Finally, the WTO agreements also have a limitative list of national non-trade policies that are accepted, even though they result in trade barriers (e.g. violate the MFN or National Treatment obligation).[66] Nonetheless, these provisions always include a section requiring that measures do not result in "arbitrary or unjustifiable discrimination" between countries, and are not a "disguised restriction on international trade".[67] These exceptions concern *inter alia*[68] the protection of public morals[69], the protection of human, animal or plant life or health[70], the control of importations or exportations of gold or silver[71], the control and prevention of imports of goods produced with prison labour[72], the conservation of exhaustible natural resources[73], the protection of cultural heritage.[74] As will be discussed below, the lists of exceptions in GATT and GATS differ to a certain extent (*infra* para. 147). Measures needed to secure compliance with laws or regulations that are not inconsistent with the provisions of the multilateral agreements are also allowed.[75] Finally, they also include interventions on national security grounds.[76] There have been discussions on whether WTO

---

[63] Art. XII and XVIII (b) GATT and art. XII GATS.
[64] Art. XVIII (a) and (c) GATT. The GATS does not contain provisions allowing for contingent or infant industry protection. In large part this reflects the difficulty of applying these concepts to trade in services. See B. HOEKMAN and M. KOSTECKI, *supra* note 17, p. 304.
[65] Art. IX.3 and 4 WTO Agreement.
[66] Art. XX GATT and art. XIV GATS.
[67] Art. XX, para. 1, GATT and art. XIV, para. 1, GATS.
[68] The exceptions will be discussed further in detail for each agreement, *infra* paras. 74 (GATT) and 147 (GATS).
[69] Art. XX (a) GATT and art. XIV (a) GATS.
[70] Art. XX (b) GATT and art. XIV (b) GATS.
[71] Art. XX (c) GATT.
[72] *Ibid.* art. XX (e).
[73] *Ibid.* art. XX (g).
[74] *Ibid.* art. XX (f).
[75] Art. XX (d) GATT and art. XIV (c) GATS.
[76] Art. XXI GATT, art. XIV*bis* GATS and art. 73 TRIPS.

Members should extend the exceptions to the basic principles to *inter alia* human rights measures, protective labour laws or development concerns. At present, there is no consensus to increase the number of exceptions.

43. The exceptions have to allow WTO Members to make sovereign policy choices without the creating of disproportionate barriers to international trade.[77] The question is whether the restriction of trade, driven by other objectives rather than free trade, is in a proportionate relationship to the value of the objective pursued.[78]

---

[77] This balancing has *inter alia* been done in Appellate Body Report: European Communities – Measures affecting asbestos and asbestos-containing products, WT/DS135/AB/R (12 March 2001); Appellate Body Report: European Communities – Measures Concerning Meat and Meat Products (Hormones), WT/DS26 and 48/AB/R (16 January 1998) and Appellate Body Report: United States – Import prohibition of certain shrimp and shrimp products, WT/DS58/AB/R (12 October 1998).

[78] The Appellate Body has stated on this matter: "It seems to us that a treaty interpreter assessing a measure claimed to be necessary to secure compliance of a WTO-consistent law or regulation may, in appropriate cases, take into account the relative importance of the common interests or values that the law or regulation to be enforced is intended to protect. The more vital or important those common interests or values are, the easier it would be to accept as 'necessary' a measure designed as an enforcement instrument." Appellate Body Report: Korea – Measures Affecting Imports of Fresh, Chilled and Frozen Beef, WT/DS161/AB/R and WT/DS169/AB/R (11 December 2000), para. 162.

CHAPTER III
OVERVIEW OF THE WTO AGREEMENTS

44. It has been explained above that the Marrakesh Agreement establishing the World Trade Organization merely provides a framework for the WTO system: the main rules governing international trade are included in the annexes to the Marrakesh Agreement. These annexes cover trade in goods, services and the trade-related aspects of intellectual property rights. The total of legal texts amounts to 60 agreements, decisions, annexes and understandings. This chapter discusses the substantive law of international trade; the institutional framework of the WTO is discussed in the next chapter. Therefore, the WTO Dispute Settlement Mechanism (annex 2) and the Trade Policy Review Mechanism (annex 3) are not explained here. We first address the Multilateral Agreements on Trade in Goods (MATG) (annex 1A), of which the GATT is the main component. The provisions of GATT are further clarified and modified in the other Multilateral Agreements on Trade in Goods. In the next section of this chapter, we attempt to clarify the rules governing trade in services, as laid down in the GATS (annex 1B). The third aspect of trade that is covered by the Uruguay Round Agreements, intellectual property, is discussed in the third section of this chapter. Finally, this chapter considers the two still existing plurilateral trade agreements: those on civil aircraft and government procurement. These agreements are included in annex 4 to the WTO Agreement. Membership to these two plurilateral agreements is voluntary. In contrast, every Member of the WTO has to accept upon accession the 'single undertaking' of all other agreements.

45. It should be noted that the two largest subject areas of the Uruguay Agreements, *i.e.* trade in goods (GATT) and trade in services (GATS), have a similar three-tiered structure.[1] Their first part contains the basic principles governing trade in that area, together with important exceptions. Thereafter follow specific agreements and annexes on particular issues (e.g. agriculture, and telecommunications). The extensive schedules of commitments form the third part of the Agreements. In contrast to GATT (where the commitments concern

---

[1] WORLD TRADE ORGANIZATION, *Understanding the WTO*, (Geneva, WTO Publications, 2007), to be consulted on www.wto.org, p. 23. The third subject area, trade-related aspects of intellectual property rights, has until now only the first of the three mentioned parts. As negotiations proceed, there might equally emerge specific agreements on particular aspects and schedules of commitments.

tariff reductions and bindings), the schedules in GATS indicate to what extent foreign service providers in specific sectors have access to a Member's market. They also contain exceptions to the application of MFN.

§ 1. MULTILATERAL AGREEMENTS ON TRADE IN GOODS

46. The majority of the trade agreements negotiated in the Uruguay Round concern trade in goods (Annex 1A of the Marrakesh Agreement). The objective of the multilateral system for trade in goods is to provide industries and business enterprises from different countries a secure, stable and predictable environment in which they can trade with one another under conditions of fair and equitable competition. This open and liberal trading system is expected to promote, through increased trade, greater investment, production and employment and thus facilitate the economic development of all countries.[2] The General Agreement on Tariffs and Trade (GATT) is the main agreement of the MATG (A). The GATT annexed to the WTO Agreement is a slightly modified version of GATT 1947. However, it became clear that some aspects of the GATT were insufficient and needed clarification. This has been done by the inclusion of several notes and memoranda of understanding to the GATT. For provisions where this was insufficient, the Uruguay Round negotiators drafted specific agreements with further elaboration and modification. First, it was realized that, even though tariffs had steadily been decreased, other non-tariff barriers still existed and had even been increased. To tackle this form of trade protection, but at the same time to give due account to the regulatory autonomy of Members, an Agreement on the Application of Sanitary and Phytosanitary Measures (B) and an Agreement on Technical Barriers to Trade (C) were concluded. Another GATT provision that proved unsatisfactory was Article XIX GATT ('Emergency Action on Imports of Particular Products', the so-called 'safeguards'). Since safeguards had to be taken on a non-discriminatory basis, this article was little used.[3] The Agreement on Safeguards introduced the option of adopting safeguard measures that affect only the imports from the exporting country (D). This helped to "improve and strengthen the international trading system".[4] A similar reasoning lies behind the drafting of the Agreement on Subsidies and Countervailing Measures (E). This agreement is a further elaboration of Article XVI GATT. The Agreement on

---

[2] See Preamble to the GATT and INTERNATIONAL TRADE CENTRE/COMMONWEALTH SECRETARIAT, *Business Guide to the World Trading System*, (London, Commonwealth Secretariat 1999), p. 55.
[3] States prefer to use Voluntary Export Restraints (VERs). See *infra* paras. 70 and 102–103.
[4] First paragraph of the Preamble of the Agreement on Safeguards.

Antidumping is another additional agreement, aimed at combating 'predatory pricing' (lower than normal prices in order to force another firm out of the market) by foreign firms and thus ensuring 'fair' competition (F). One of the most pressing needs at the time of the negotiating of the Uruguay Round Agreements was the need to reform trade in agricultural products. Still, as has been explained above, this was also one of the most contentious issues. The European Economic Community was hesitant to reform its Common Agriculture Policy, which included extensive subsidies to European farmers. These subsidies depressed world market prices for agricultural goods, which in turn kept many farmers in developing countries in poverty. An Agreement on Agriculture was finally reached (G). Many (mostly developing) Members of the WTO were unsatisfied with this arrangement, and trade in agricultural products is today still the main discussion point within the WTO. Another agreement with relevance to development, the Agreement on Textiles and Clothing (H), was designed to eliminate the quotas that had been established on imports of textiles, an essential condition for developing countries to accept the inclusion of GATS and TRIPS in the Uruguay Round Agreements. This Agreement expired on 31 December 2004, which means that textiles and clothing are now covered by the GATT regime. The Agreement on Agriculture and the Agreement on Textiles and Clothing are called 'sector-specific multilateral trade agreements'.[5] Negotiators also wanted to make a start on negotiating an agreement on Trade-Related Investment Measures (TRIMS) (I). Finally, agreements were concluded on certain border measures related to customs procedures, such as customs valuation (J), preshipment inspection (K) and import licensing procedures (L). Also related is the Agreement on Rules of Origin (M). It should again be noted that, in case of conflict between the provisions of the specific agreements and those of the GATT, the provisions of the specific agreement prevail.[6]

A. GATT

47. As is explained above, the GATT existed long before the WTO. When the latter was established in 1994, 'GATT 1947' was added in the annex to the WTO Agreement, slightly modified as 'GATT 1994'.[7] The GATT 1947 Contracting Parties decided on 8 December 1994 that the GATT 1947 should cease to have

---

[5] B. HOEKMAN and M. KOSTECKI, *The Political Economy of the World Trading System*, (Oxford, Oxford University Press 2001), p. 208.
[6] See *supra* para. 27.
[7] GATT 1994 contains a large number of memoranda that interpret the various provisions of the GATT. However, GATT 1947 and GATT 1994 are legally distinct agreements. Art. II.4 WTO Agreement. See T.J. DILLON, 'The World Trade Organization: A new legal order for world trade?', *Michigan Journal of International Law* (1995), p. 358.

effect. In fact, it is still necessary to read the text of GATT 1947 since GATT 1994 only refers to the 1947 provisions.[8] In addition, the GATT 1994 contains also[9] the provisions of protocols and certifications relating to tariff concessions; protocols of accession; decisions on waivers that were still in force on 1 January 1995[10] and other decisions of the Contracting Parties to GATT 1947.[11] Six different understandings are added to this.[12] Annexed to the GATT (and as a part of it[13]) is the 'Uruguay Round Protocol'. This is the legal instrument by which the 'schedules of concessions' – in which participants have made commitments to eliminate or reduce tariff rates and non-tariff measures applicable to trade in goods – as well as the schedules themselves, became an integral part of the GATT.[14] The term 'GATT' is now commonly used to refer to GATT 1947 together with all the legal instruments and decisions adopted by GATT Contracting Parties before 1 January 1995. Therefore, the following paragraphs will only use the term 'GATT' in this sense, unless it is appropriate to make a distinction.

48. In principle, GATT follows a system of 'negative integration'. Governments have the freedom to pursue their economic policies, as long as this is done in a way that is in line with the provisions of GATT. The GATT does not proscribe specific measures, but only requires that these measures be the least trade restrictive. Since it was impossible to remove all protectionist barriers from the start, a system in which market access is limited as little as possible was opted for.[15] It has been argued, though, that the WTO is now increasingly moving towards 'positive integration' because other Agreements also impose positive obligations upon Members.[16]

---

[8] Para. 1 (a) GATT 1994. See J. CROOME, *Guide to the Uruguay Round Agreements*, (The Hague, Kluwer 1999), p. 39. In fact, the text of GATT 1947 is that which was published in 1969, as Volume IV in the series Basic Instruments and Selected Documents. See Preface to the GATT 1947, para. 1. Indeed, Part IV ('Trade and Development') was added only in 1965, under pressure by developing countries and UNCTAD. See M. TREBILCOCK and R. HOWSE, *The Regulation of International Trade*, (London, Routledge 2005), p. 27.

[9] See para. 1 (b) GATT.

[10] See the list in: Waivers Granted Under Article XXV of GATT 1947, WT/L/3, 27 January 1995.

[11] A decision fits into this category if it is a "formal legal text which represented a legally binding determination in respect of the rights and/or obligations generally applicable to all Contracting Parties to GATT 1947". See Panel Report: United States – Tax Treatment of Foreign Sales Corporations, WT/DS108/R (8 October 1999), para. 7.63. This would include *inter alia* the Decision on Differential and More Favourable Treatment, Reciprocity and Fuller Participation of Developing Countries, 26S/203, 28 November 1979.

[12] Para. 1 (c) GATT.

[13] *Ibid.* para. 1 (d).

[14] Art. II.7 GATT.

[15] See B. HOEKMAN and M. KOSTECKI, *supra* note 5, 145.

[16] See D. DE BIÈVRE, 'Governance in International Trade: Judicialization and Positive Integration in the WTO', *Max Planck Institute Collective Goods Preprint No. 2004/7* (July 2004), available on http://ssrn.com/abstract=566501 and J. TRACHTMAN, 'The World Trading System, the

49. The Preamble of GATT is similar to the first and third paragraph of the WTO Agreement. Still, there are some important differences, due to the fact that this preamble has been written in 1947. The preamble of the WTO Agreement has references to sustainable development, the preservation of the environment and the differences between countries because of different levels of economic development. Nonetheless, the Preamble of the WTO Agreement is relevant for all other annexed agreements; thus the concerns that are mentioned are also applying for trade in goods. Obviously, the preamble to GATT only refers to trade in goods, whereas the preamble of the WTO Agreement refers to trade in goods and services.

50. In the following paragraphs, we (1) first discuss the role of tariffs and tariff negotiations. When the GATT was concluded in 1947, the focus was indeed mainly on removing tariff barriers. Next, we discuss the two main manifestations of the principle of non-discrimination: Most Favoured Nation (2) and National Treatment (3). Further, the provisions dealing with Quantitative Restrictions will be considered (4). After having addressed these core provisions in the GATT, we turn to exceptions to these provisions. We subsequently discuss the general exceptions (5), the exception with regard to free trade agreements (6) and the specific special and differential treatment for developing countries (7).

1. Tariffs

51. Trade in goods can be limited in several ways. The most common way is by the use of tariffs. Tariffs are duties that a State levies on foreign products that cross its border. Because of the tariff, the price of an imported product will increase, allowing the domestic producers of competing products to charge a higher price. Tariffs are not prohibited by the GATT. In this respect, it should be noted that the WTO is only a 'would be' or 'would become' free trade organization. The organization aims to abolish all trade barriers, but has not yet achieved this. However, the GATT requires that States can only use tariffs to protect their markets. Tariffs are preferred to other protective measures, such as quantitative restrictions, subsidies or discriminatory regulations. It is indeed clear that tariffs provide income to the State levying them.[17] Moreover, compared to quantitative restrictions, tariffs are considered less trade distortive because they do not fix the trade volume at a certain level. They allow any import volume, though a certain

---

International Legal System and Multilevel Choice', *European Law Journal* (2006), pp. 469–485, especially at pp. 478–484.

[17] According to economists, the 'monopoly profit' that is created through tariffs is transferred to the government. J.H. JACKSON, W.J. DAVEY and A.O. SYKES, *Legal problems of international economic relations*, (Saint Paul, West Publishing 1995, 3rd ed.), p. 377. See also M.J. TREBILCOCK and R. HOWSE, *supra* note 8, p. 178.

price must be paid for it. They also give fewer incentives for special-interest lobbying than quantitative restrictions or subsidies. In sum, tariffs are the most transparent and predictable way of protecting the own industry. What is more, taking into account the objective of GATT to eventually abolish also all protective measures, this form of protection is much easier to negotiate on as well. Indeed, the level of nominal protection under a tariff is easier to calculate and thus easier to negotiate on.

52.   Most tariffs are *ad valorem*, *i.e.* they are levied as a percentage of the price of the imported product. Tariffs can also be levied per specific unit of a product, e.g. a certain amount levied per litre of wine. Finally there can also be a combination of both. The GATT has no explicit preference for a certain type of tariff. Nevertheless, *ad valorem* tariffs are most transparent: since a percentage is levied on the price, the impact of the tariffs on the price is clearly visible. What is more, other bases for setting tariffs, such as the value of competing products of national origin or arbitrary or fictitious values, cannot be used.[18] On the other hand, *ad valorem* tariffs suppose a valuation of the goods that are imported. This difficult problem of customs valuation[19] does not occur for specific tariffs.

53.   Once WTO Members are protecting their production with nothing but tariffs, the aim is to reduce these tariffs gradually. Therefore, Members negotiate within the WTO framework to bind their tariffs and to reduce them. The reduction of tariffs was already the basic purpose of the GATT 1947 and this has remained so under GATT 1994. This process of cutting tariffs takes place through negotiation rounds. A tariff negotiations committee composed of representatives of all Members and often also of States that plan accession[20], negotiates through a bargaining process of give and take. In the first five negotiation rounds[21], participating States submitted 'request lists' to their major importing partners, indicating for which products they want a reduction. They also prepared an 'offer list' with possible reductions of the State's own tariffs, in exchange for the granting of requests. It is thus clear that the tariff negotiations were – and still are – strictly

---

[18]   Art. VII.2 GATT
[19]   See *infra* paras. 126–128.
[20]   When developing countries joined the GATT under GATT 1947, they were allowed to do so without tariff concessions. In contrast, since the establishment of the WTO, States can only join the organization after submitting tariff schedules. See B. HOEKMAN and M. KOSTECKI, *supra* note 5, p. 145.
[21]   The rules and procedures adopted for the first three rounds were guided by the provisions of the ITO Charter. The aim was to fit the results of the tariff negotiations in the framework of the International Trade Organization. This proved illusory when finally in 1950, the US president decided not to submit the ITO Charter any more for approval to Congress. The later two rounds (Geneva 1956 and Dillon Round 1960) were held on the basis of art. XXVIII *bis*.

based on reciprocity.[22] States are only willing to give up some protection if they receive some access in exchange. This principle of reciprocity is indeed politically valuable[23] and also makes economic sense.[24] However, it also constitutes a major problem in trade negotiations. It is almost impossible to measure the exact volume of trade concessions.[25] Hence, States can hardly be sure that they receive as much as they offer. According to JACKSON "reciprocity can be termed a 'useful myth'"[26] to make politicians and the constituency accept the tariff reductions as 'fair'. Yet, reciprocity impedes swift negotiations still in other ways. Countries that already had relatively low tariff rates (especially the EEC Member States[27]) complained in the Kennedy Round that they had nothing to offer in return for tariff reductions by States who still had high tariffs. Be this as it may, today tariff negotiations still have to be conducted on a mutually advantageous and reciprocal basis.[28]

54. Nonetheless, tariff negotiations changed in other ways. Although in the first five rounds, negotiations took place product by product, from the Kennedy Round, tariff reductions were agreed 'across the board'. Negotiating tariff reductions on each and every product had indeed become very complex. Moreover, in practice, negotiations were only conducted with the 'principal supplier' of a product, which is the one that will gain most by the tariff reduction. Consequently, it would be willing to give more in return than a smaller supplier. Nevertheless this clearly marginalized developing countries, who were rarely involved in the negotiations from the beginning. In the sixth negotiation round, it was eventually agreed that there would be 'linear tariff reductions'. Negotiators would fix a general cut in all tariffs, with the possibility for States to indicate products to be

---

[22] In the rules of each negotiation round, it was indicated, explicitly or implicitly, that tariff reductions should be done on a reciprocal basis. See A. HODA, *Tariff Negotiations and Renegotiations under the GATT and the WTO. Procedures and Practices*, (Cambridge, Cambridge University Press 2001), p. 52.
[23] It is easier for governments to convince their constituencies of measures reducing import barriers if other countries also provide better export opportunities for the domestic industry.
[24] SMITH and RICARDO stressed that, even when unilateral, liberalization was the best thing to do for a country. Nevertheless, if a country that reduces its trade barriers can convince its trading partners to do the same, this will generate both import and export benefits. M.J. TREBILCOCK and R. HOWSE, *supra* note 8, p. 3.
[25] Governments have the freedom to use their own formula for measuring tariff reductions. See GATT Working Party Report, Schedules and Customs Administration, 26 February 1955, GATT L/329, BISD 3S/205 at 219–220, para. 38 and GATT Working Party, 19 November 1959, GATT COM/3, BISD 8S/103 at 110, para. 10.
[26] J. JACKSON, W.J. DAVEY and A.O. SYKES, *supra* note 17, p. 377.
[27] The EEC had implemented a common external tariff (an essential condition for the formation of a customs union, see *infra* para. 79), which on average significantly reduced the customs tariffs of Member States.
[28] See Preamble of the GATT, para. 3.

exempted from the general cut.[29] This system not only solved the problem of product-by-product negotiations, but also enabled States that already had low tariffs on one type of product, to offer tariff reduction on other products, thus saving reciprocity. The exceptions were "subject to confrontation and justification". In fact, this led to further bilateral negotiations on the exempted products. The "Kennedy Round became a hybrid of product-by-product and linear negotiations"[30] and did not escape the concept of reciprocity. Remarkably, the principle of linear tariff reductions did not apply to Australia, New Zealand, Canada and South Africa. These countries relied heavily on agriculture and raw material imports, which were most often exempted from linear reductions. Therefore, they would not have anything to offer in across-the-board negotiations. Moreover, it was agreed that reciprocity would not apply to less-developed countries vis-à-vis developed countries, taking into account the special status of these countries under Part IV GATT.[31] The same negotiation process was basically applied in later rounds. Yet, in the Tokyo Round, a formula was developed to fix the amount of the linear tariff cut. There was a need to find a formula that solved the problem of disparities of tariffs. The effect of cutting an already low tariff by the same amount as the reductions of high tariffs is clearly different. The low tariff becomes exceedingly low and thus provides almost no protection any more, whereas, comparatively, a reduced high tariff still provides significant protection. In addition, the four previously mentioned countries that were entirely exempted from the system of linear reduction had to comply with the system under the Tokyo Round, be it with several exceptions. During the Uruguay Round, both linear formula reductions and item-per-item reductions were used.[32] In the Doha Round, it was decided in the 'July Decision' to use a formula approach in the agricultural negotiations, but to use a 'request-and-offer' approach (item per item) in the services negotiations.[33]

55. When a Member agrees on tariff concessions for a specific product, in fact it freezes its tariffs at a certain rate. Once agreed upon, these 'bound' tariffs cannot be raised. Non-compliance with the bound rates results in a prima facie

---

[29] The Resolution setting out the system noted that tariff negotiations should be based "upon a plan of substantial linear tariff reductions with a bare minimum of exceptions […]". GATT Ministerial Meeting 16–21 May 1963, Resolution on Arrangements for the Reduction or Elimination of Tariffs and Other Barriers to Trade, and Related Matters, para. A(4), BISD 12S/36, at 47, para. 4 (1964).
[30] A.F. LOWENFELD, *International Economic Law,* (Oxford, Oxford University Press 2003), p. 52.
[31] The Developing Countries should have the opportunity to make commitments as far as they consider themselves able to do so, depending on their level of development, financial and trade needs. The idea for 'graduated reciprocity' is also included in art. XXXVI.8 GATT and the Enabling Clause. See A. HODA, *supra* note 22, p. 58.
[32] Framework for Negotiations for the Uruguay Round, MTN.TNC/7(MIN), 9 December 1988, p. 4.
[33] See Decision Adopted by the General Council of the WTO on 1 August 2004, WT/L/579.

nullification and impairment of a benefit accruing from the GATT (essential to bring a complaint before the WTO Dispute Settlement Body).[34] It should be noted that the tariff rate that is actually applied by a State is not necessarily equal to the bound rate. If the applied rate is lower than the bound rate, the latter rate is called a 'ceiling rate'. It is also possible that the applied rate is higher than the bound rate because the bound rate only enters into force on a future date. This bound rate is then called a 'negotiated rate'.[35] It is finally also possible that States renegotiate their tariffs temporarily[36] or permanently.[37] The tariff rates are included in detailed lists for each country. These lists consist of four parts: the first indicates the tariff that is applied on MFN basis[38]; a second part details preferential tariffs that are 'grandfathered'[39] because they result from special historical trading arrangements[40]; a third part indicates reduction of non-tariff barriers and a final part on the reductions of subsidies in the agricultural sector.[41] The lists of concessions can contain specific provisions, drafted by the State, that qualify the engagements of the State.[42] Nevertheless, these provisions cannot infringe upon other GATT provisions.[43] It must be reiterated that any concession has to be extended to all other Members because of the principle of MFN.

56. A Member's lists of concessions indicate for each product the bound tariff rate. This implies that an imported product first of all has to be classified. Customs authorities have to decide under which tariff heading the product falls. The World

---

[34] See *infra* para. 327, art. XXIII GATT.
[35] See B. HOEKMAN and M. KOSTECKI, *supra* note 5, p. 149. It has been noted, however, that developing countries have bound their tariffs at levels that are much higher than the actually applied tariff, hence agreed tariff reductions did not result in substantial liberalization. On the other hand, even though developed countries may have seriously reduced their tariffs, they maintain high tariffs on a number of selected products ('tariff peaks'), which are often main export interests of developing countries. Moreover, they make use of 'tariff escalation'. This means that they charge higher tariffs on processed products than raw materials. This implies that developing countries are discouraged from processing the raw materials into processed products on which they would have a higher profit margin.
[36] See art. XIX (safeguards), art. XXIII.2 (in the framework of dispute settlement), XXV (temporary waivers) GATT.
[37] The procedure of renegotiation of tariffs is described in Article XXVIII.
[38] Art. II.1 (b) GATT.
[39] 'Grandfathered clauses' are provisions in agreements that are accepted under the GATT because of historical circumstances that existed before the GATT was established, even though these agreements might conflict with GATT provisions.
[40] Art. II.1 (c) GATT.
[41] See D. LUFF, *Le droit de l'Organisation mondiale de commerce: analyse critique*, (Brussels, Bruylant 2004), p. 66.
[42] Art. II.1 (b) first sentence and Art. II.1 (c) first sentence GATT.
[43] See GATT Panel Report: United States – Restrictions on the Importation of Sugar and Sugar-Containing Products, (22 June 1989), BISD 36S/331, para. 5.8 and Appellate Body Report: European Communities – Regime Applicable to the Importation, Sale and Distribution of Bananas, WT/DS113/AB/R (9 September 1998), para. 154.

Customs Organization[44] has developed a 'Harmonized Commodity Description and Coding System' (hereinafter 'Harmonized System').[45] This system classifies goods using a four-digit code (indicating a product group) and a two-digit code (indicating a specific product line). This classification of goods under a tariff heading is of course important because it will define the competitive opportunities of the product on the market. Therefore, it often causes serious disputes. Moreover, new products are frequently developed for which no tariff heading is provided. In that case it is the question which tariff will apply. The World Customs Organization has drafted several notes interpreting the Harmonized System, which constitute a source of interpretation[46] of Members' lists.[47]

57. Once a product is classified under a tariff heading, the product has to be valued in order for the tariff to be applied. This is because most tariffs are *ad valorem*. The higher a product is valued, the higher the fee that will be due. Thus, 'customs valuation' is as delicate as customs classification. Article VII of the General Agreement on Tariffs and Trade lays down the general principles for an international system of valuation. It stipulates that the value for customs purposes of imported merchandise should be based on the actual value of the imported merchandise on which duty is assessed, or of like merchandise, and should not be based on the value of merchandise of national origin or on arbitrary or fictitious values. This has been complemented with an Agreement on Implementation of Article VII of GATT 1994, in which six different methods of valuation are set out. (This Agreement is discussed *infra* Section III.1.J.)

---

[44] See www.wcoomd.org.

[45] International Convention on the Harmonized Commodity Description and Coding System, done at Brussels on 14 June 1983 and the Protocol of Amendment thereto of 24 June 1986, entered into force on 1 January 1998, O.J., 2003, L198/3–10. See D. LUFF, *supra* note 41, p. 66, note 148.

[46] The notes form the context of and subsequent practice relating to the schedule of concessions. These should be used as a source of interpretation, according to art. 31.2–3 Vienna Convention on the Law of Treaties, done at Vienna on 23 May 1969, *UNTS* no. 18232.

[47] Appellate Body Report: European Communities – Customs Classification of certain Computer Equipment, WT/DS62/AB/R, WT/DS67/AB/R, WT/DS68/AB/R, (5 June 1998), paras. 90–91. This case concerned the classification of Local Area Network (LAN) equipment under the tariff schedules of the EC. There was no tariff heading explicitly mentioning LAN equipment. The EC claimed LAN should be classified as telecommunications equipment, implying high tariffs. The US, on the other hand, believed LAN should be classified as Automatic Data Processing (ADP) machines, on which the EC levied lower tariffs. The higher tariffs, applied by the EC, would thus constitute a violation of art. II GATT. The Appellate Body noted that in order to classify the goods, one had to look at the Harmonized System and its Explanatory Notes. Thereafter, one could look at the 'legitimate expectations' of the Parties. However, contrary to what the Panel found, the Appellate Body stated that one should consider the legitimate expectations of *all* Parties involved and not solely those of the importing Member.

58. Despite the principle of MFN, the tariffs that producers from different countries face when exporting to a certain country are not always the same. There are indeed several exceptions to MFN, the most important being free trade areas and customs unions, which result in different tariffs according to the country where the imported products originate.[48] Therefore, it is of major importance to determine the origin of the imported goods. This can be particularly difficult when the goods in question consist of parts that are produced in several countries, thereafter assembled in another country and finally packaged in still another country. Depending on the overriding factor that defines the origin of the good, tariffs will be lower or higher. Yet, no uniform rules on origin of goods exist. The GATT has no specific provisions that address the determination of the origin of goods. There is of course Article IX on marks of origin, but this article only addresses the requirements of marking the origin and not the criteria to *determine* the origin of goods. Article IX requires Members to treat other Members as equal with regard to marking requirements. This is another application of the principle of MFN. The article is further designed to limit the hindrances to trade caused by marking requirements.[49] A similar requirement arises from Article VIII GATT, which calls for minimal complexity of import and export formalities. In order to address the need for uniform rules of origin, the Uruguay Round Agreement on Rules of Origin was drafted.[50] (This Agreement is discussed *infra* Section III.1.M.)

59. Besides ordinary customs duties, States often levy other fees and charges on imports.[51] It may for instance be the case that an importer has to pay fees to use the port. These 'para-tariffs' are "frequently subject to arbitrary implementation

---

[48] It is also important to know the origin of goods in order to apply antidumping measures or countervailing duties.

[49] As far as possible, the marks of origin should be permitted to be attached at the time of importation (art. IX.3 GATT). The marking cannot cause damage to products, reduce their value or unreasonably increase their cost (art. IX.4 GATT).

[50] Before, there already existed an International Convention on the Simplification and Harmonization of Customs Procedures, done at Kyoto on 18 May 1973, *UNTS* No. 13561, O.J., 1975, L100/2. This convention was negotiated under auspices of the World Customs Organization (see *supra* para. 56) and was revised in 1999 (see Protocol of amendment to the International Convention on the Simplification and Harmonization of Customs Procedures, done at Brussels on 26 June 1999, O.J., 2003, L86/23). The revised convention entered into force on 3 February 2006. The Convention provides general rules relating to origin and a shortlist of products that should be considered as originating in a country because they are wholly produced or obtained there. The major problem of the Convention is the lack of enforcement mechanism. See B. HOEKMAN and M. KOSTECKI, *supra* note 5, pp. 168–169. See on the revised Convention: Z.V. GURULI, 'What is the best forum for promoting trade facilitation?', *Penn State International Law Review* (2002), pp. 168–170.

[51] These fees are different from internal taxes, which are addressed by the provisions on 'national treatment' (more precisely art. III.2 GATT, see *infra* para. 66). First, the fees are due when the goods enter the importing country and constitute a condition of entry. Second, the fees only

and are nontransparent".[52] Therefore, Members have to include these fees in their schedules of tariff concessions indicating the nature of the fees and the level.[53] Article VIII GATT specifically addresses fees and formalities connected with importation and exportation. Importantly, the fees must be cost based and shall not "represent an indirect protection to domestic products or a taxation of imports and exports for fiscal purposes".[54] It is recognized that there is a need to minimize the incidence and complexity of formalities for importation.[55]

2. Most Favoured Nation

60. As explained above, the Most Favoured Nation principle requires a Member of the WTO to treat all other Members equally in trading relations. MFN applies to its full extent in case of trade in goods (contrary to what is the case for trade in services, see *infra* para. 138). The principle is included in Article I GATT and prohibits *de jure* as well as *de facto* discrimination.[56] The MFN principle figures, implicitly or explicitly, in a number of other GATT provisions as well: *inter alia* in Article XIII (permitted quantitative restrictions must be applied to *all* trading partners); Article XIX (safeguard measures in the case of an unforeseen surge of imports of a product that causes a serious injury to domestic producers must be applied to *all* trading partners) or Article XX (general exceptions cannot be applied in a manner that discriminates between countries where the same conditions prevail).

61. The MFN principle in Article I GATT is not only applicable to charges and measures at the border (customs duties and charges imposed on or in connection with importation, exportation or transfer of goods and the rules and formalities connected to this). It also applies to internal measures and taxes, matters which are also covered by the national treatment obligation in Article III GATT. The

---

apply to the imported goods and do not have analogous counterparts for domestic products. See D. LUFF, *supra* note 41, p. 70.

[52] B. HOEKMAN and M. KOSTECKI, *supra* note 5, p. 151.

[53] Art. II.1 (b)–(c), second sentence GATT and Understanding on the Interpretation of Article II:1 (b) of the General Agreement on Tariffs and Trade 1994, para. 1. These 'other duties and charges' cannot be imposed above the level of the date of the GATT 1947 (30 October 1947) or, for subsequent concessions, the date of the Protocol when the new schedules were incorporated in the GATT 1947. For the concessions made during the Uruguay Round, this date is 15 April 1994. For a discussion of these issues: see A. HODA, note 22, pp. 19–21. Note that art. II.2 indicates three specific duties or charges that, when levied, do not infringe upon the concessions made.

[54] Art. VIII.1 (a) GATT.

[55] *Ibid.* art. VIII.1 (c).

[56] Appellate Body Report: Canada – Certain Measures Affecting the Automotive Industry, WT/DS139/AB/R and WT/DS142/AB/R (31 May 2000), para. 78.

application of Article I GATT to them means that internal measures or taxes cannot be applied in a discriminatory way to different trading partners.[57]

62. MFN treatment must be accorded immediately and unconditionally by WTO Members. This implies, first, that WTO Members must immediately extend a benefit granted to one trading partner to other WTO Members. Second, it means that the WTO Member cannot attach conditions to this extension of a benefit. The majority of WTO (and GATT 1947) case-law interprets this as a prohibition on attaching any conditions to the granting of an advantage.[58] Yet, there is another view on the meaning of the term 'unconditionally' expressed in some cases. This second view is less absolute and considers whether *additional* conditions are being imposed when the benefit under MFN treatment is extended, possibly on top of the conditions already attached to the benefit when it was granted in the first place.[59] If so, the MFN treatment would not be 'unconditional'. Certain authors have argued that the second view takes more account of the context in which a benefit is granted.[60] According to this second view, the conditions attached to MFN treatment should thus be assessed when one takes into account the conditions that were attached to the benefit in the first place.

63. A Member is only required to treat products originating in different countries in the same way if these products are sufficiently 'like'.[61] Because of the

---

[57] See GATT Working Party Report: Belgium – Family Allowances, (7 November 1952), BISD, 1S/59, para. 4. (This case concerned the application of Belgian law on the levy of a charge on foreign goods purchased by public bodies when these goods originated in a country whose system of family allowances did not meet specific requirements. Thus, a differentiation was made among different countries.) This should be contrasted with the National Treatment obligation in art. III GATT, which requires that international measures and taxes cannot be applied in a discriminatory way when one compares the treatment of *domestic* and *imported* products.

[58] See GATT Panel Report: EEC – Imports of Beef from Canada, (10 March 1981), BISD, 28S/92; GATT Working Party Report, Accession of Hungary, (30 July 1973), BISD 20S/34; Panel Report: Indonesia – Certain Measures Affecting the Automobile Industry, WT/DS54/R (2 July 1998), para. 14.143 and Panel Report: European Communities – Conditions for Granting of Tariff Preferences to Developing Countries, WT/DS246/R (1 December 2003), paras. 7.59–7.60.

[59] See GATT Working Party Report: Belgium – Family Allowances, (7 November 1952), BISD, 1S/59, para. 3; GATT Panel Report: EEC – Program of Minimum Import Prices, Licences and Surety Deposits for Certain Processed Fruits and Vegetables (19 October 1978), BISD, 25S/68 and Panel Report: Canada – Certain Measures Affecting the Automotive Industry, WT/DS139 and 142/R, paras. 10.22 and 10.24. The latter case notes that the term unconditionally does not mean that all conditions are prohibited but rather that the MFN treatment cannot be conditional on reciprocity by the Member who would benefit from the MFN treatment.

[60] M. Matsushita, T. Schoenbaum and P. Mavroidis, *The World Trade Organization. Law, Practice and Policy*, (Oxford, Oxford University Press, 2006), pp. 212–216. See also B. Hoekman and P. Mavroidis, *The World Trade Organization. Law, Economics and Politics*, (London, Routledge 2007), p. 34.

[61] See GATT Panel Report: Spain – Tariff Treatment of Unroasted Coffee, (11 June 1981), BISD, 28S/102 and GATT Panel Report: Japan – Tariff on Imports of Spruce, Pine, Fir (SPF) Dimension Lumber, (19 July 1989), BISD, 36S/167.

relatively few disputes involving Article I GATT, the concept of 'likeness' is more extensively discussed under Article III GATT.[62] A Panel noted that finding that a product is 'like' under Article III also justifies the finding of 'likeness' for the purpose of Article I GATT.[63] The criteria for likeness are indicated in the section dealing with Article III GATT.

3. *National Treatment*

64. The second manifestation of the principle of non-discrimination, the principle of 'national treatment', is provided in Article III GATT. As soon as a product enters the market, internal regulations and internal taxes or other internal charges cannot be applied to imported products so as to afford protection to domestic production. Article III obliges WTO Members to provide equality of competitive conditions for imported products in relation to domestic products.[64]

65. Similarly, internal taxes or regulations that apply to both imported and like domestic products, but in case the imported products are collected or enforced at the border, are subject to Article III GATT.[65] The fact that a tax is collected at the time and point of importation does not preclude it from qualifying as an internal tax measure.[66]

66. Despite its complex formulation, Article III has a logical structure. It concerns, on the one hand, internal[67] charges[68] (Article III.2 GATT) and on the other hand, regulations (Article III.4 GATT). With regard to *internal taxes*, the *first sentence* of Article III.2 states that imported products cannot be subject to internal taxes in excess of those applied to 'like' domestic products.[69] The degree of 'likeness' is assessed by considering the end-use of the product on the market,

---

[62] Note that the meaning of 'like products' does not necessarily need to be interpreted in the same way in each of the WTO provisions. See J. JACKSON, W.J. DAVEY and A.O. SYKES, *supra* note 17, p. 448.
[63] Panel Report: Indonesia – Certain Measures Affecting the Automobile Industry, WT/DS54, 55, 59 and 64/R (2 July 1998), para. 14.141.
[64] See Appellate Body Report: Japan – Taxes on Alcoholic Beverages, WT/DS8, 10 and 11/AB/R, (4 October 1996), p. 16; Appellate Body Report: Korea – Taxes on Alcoholic Beverages, WT/DS75 and 85/AB/R, (18 January 1999), para. 120 (declining to take a static view of the term 'directly competitive or substitutable') and Appellate Body Report: Canada – Certain Measures Concerning Periodicals, WT/DS31/AB/R, (30 June 1997), p. 18.
[65] See the interpretative note to art. III (*Ad* Article III, Annex I to GATT). With respect to charges, see also Article II.2(a) GATT.
[66] Panel Report: Argentina – Measures Affecting the Export of Bovine Hides and the Import of Finished Leather, WT/DS155/R, (19 December 2000), para. 11.145.
[67] In contrast to duties, which are levied at the border: these are covered by art. I GATT.
[68] It concerns e.g. taxes on added value or sales taxes such as excise duties.
[69] Only taxes on products are covered and thus not direct taxes, which are imposed on income or producers.

consumers' tastes and habits, as well as the product's properties, nature and quality (the so-called 'Border Tax Adjustment' criteria).[70] A further criterion to determine 'likeness' is the tariff classification in the Harmonized System. If two products are included in the same classification, they may be considered 'like'.[71] The slightest difference between the levels of taxation on the 'like' products is enough to cause a violation of Article III.2.[72] There are thus two conditions to be established: first, the likeness of the products in question and second, a difference in level of taxation. This is different for the *second sentence* of Article III.2. The second sentence concerns products that are not so similar as to allow one to talk about 'like products', but which are, nevertheless, in a competitive relationship.[73] The competitive relationship is defined with reference to the market place and the cross-price elasticity of the products.[74] In order to identify a violation in that case, one needs, next to a dissimilar taxation, proof that the difference in taxation is applied so as to afford protection to domestic production. The second sentence of Article III.2 indeed makes reference to Article III.1, where this additional condition is mentioned.[75] Thus, there are three conditions to be established: first, a competitive relationship between the goods; second, a dissimilar taxation and, third, the measure must be applied so as to afford protection. The second condition requires a higher standard than the taxation 'in excess' of the first sentence. Although in the first sentence *any* difference in taxation would lead to a violation, in the second sentence, the difference has to be more than *de minimis*.[76] The exact meaning of the third condition has given rise to much discussion. WTO case-law has attempted to clarify that the third condition is not an issue of subjective intent.[77] However,

---

[70] See Working Party Report on Border Tax Adjustments, (2 December 1970) BISD, 18S/97, para. 18. See also W.M. CHOI, *'Like Products' in International Trade Law: Toward a Consistent GATT/WTO Jurisprudence,* (Oxford, Oxford University Press 2003), xxi + 265 p.

[71] See Panel Report: United States – Standards for Reformulated and Conventional Gasoline, WT/DS2/R, (29 January 1996), para. 6.8. Nevertheless, the Appellate Body cautioned in a later case that the tariff bindings by WTO Members can be very broad so that they do not necessarily indicate likeness. See Appellate Body Report: Japan – Taxes on Alcoholic Beverages, WT/DS8, 10 and 11/AB/R, (4 October 1996), p. 23.

[72] If the products are very similar and there applies on imported products a tax in excess of those applied to like domestic products, there is a presumption that this tax is levied so as to afford protection to domestic products. In that case the tax constitutes a violation of art. III (2), first sentence GATT. See Appellate Body Report: Japan – Taxes on alcoholic beverages, WT/DS8/AB/R (4 October 1996), p. 20.

[73] Para. 1, *Ad* Article III, Annex I GATT.

[74] See Appellate Body Report: Japan – Taxes on Alcoholic Beverages, WT/DS8, 10 and 11/AB/R, (4 October 1996), p. 25.

[75] Art. III (2) *juncto* art. III (1) GATT. See Panel Report: Chile – Taxes on Alcoholic Beverages, WT/DS87/R (15 June 1999), para. 7.92.

[76] Whether the difference in taxation is *de minimis* or not is a matter that is decided on a case-by-case basis. See Appellate Body Report: Japan – Taxes on Alcoholic Beverages, WT/DS8, 10 and 11/AB/R, (4 October 1996), p. 28.

[77] *Ibid.* p. 28.

the protective application can sometimes be discerned *objectively* from the design, architecture and revealing structure of the measure.[78] In practice, though, factual evidence of intent will most probably have an impact on the analysis of whether the measure is 'so as to afford protection' (see further on the role of 'intent', *infra* para. 67).[79] Neither would there be a requirement that the tax measure necessarily has a protective 'effect'.[80] The only purpose is to provide equality in competitive opportunities and this is not linked to any particular trade volumes.[81] In our view, if protective effect – actual or potential – results from the application of dissimilar taxation, in the sense that the conditions of competition are modified, the tax is 'so as to afford protection'.

Article III.4, which relates to the application of *regulation* on internal sale, offering for sale, purchase, transportation, distribution or use, covers the same products as Article III.2. The concept of 'like products' in Article III.4 is thus wider than 'like products' in the first sentence of Article III.2.[82] Under the GATT provisions on discrimination, WTO Members are not allowed to differentiate between goods on the basis of the differences in production process.[83] This so-called 'product-process distinction' means that, the production process cannot be considered as

---

[78] Appellate Body Report: Korea – Measures Affecting Imports of Fresh, Chilled and Frozen Beef, WT/DS161 and 169/AB/R, (11 December 2000), para. 150 and Appellate Body Report: Chile – Taxes on Alcoholic Beverages, WT/DS87 and 110/AB/R, (13 December 1999), para. 62. On the difficulty of making such 'objective' assessment, see H. HORN and P. MAVROIDIS, 'Still Hazy after All These Years: The Interpretation of National Treatment in the GATT/WTO Case-law on Discrimination', *European Journal of International Law* (2004), pp. 39–69, at p. 58.

[79] See A. PORGES and J. TRACHTMAN, 'Robert Hudec and Domestic Regulation: The Resurrection of Aim and Effects', *Journal of World Trade* (2003), pp. 783–799, at p. 791. In a later case, a Panel noted that "the declared intention of legislators and regulators of a Member adopting the measure should not be totally disregarded, particularly when the explicit objective of the measure is that of affording protection to domestic production." See Panel Report: Mexico – Taxes on Soft Drinks, WT/DS308/R, (7 October 2005), para. 8.91.

[80] See Appellate Body Report: Japan – Taxes on Alcoholic Beverages, WT/DS8, 10 and 11/AB/R, (4 October 1996), p. 15, repeating the statements of the Panel in Panel Report: United States – Taxes on Petroleum and Certain Imported Substances, (17 June 1987), BISD 34S/136, para. 5.1.9.

[81] *Ibid.*

[82] If this were not the case, a WTO Member that protects its domestic products through a tax measure that is inconsistent with Art. III.2 could try to convert the tax measure into a regulatory measure with the same effect to avoid this inconsistency. Obviously, this needs to be avoided. See Appellate Body Report: European Communities – Measures affecting Asbestos and Asbestos-Containing Products, WT/DS135/AB/R (12 March 2001), para. 99.

[83] The distinction dates from the pre-WTO GATT period. See GATT Panel Report: United States – Restrictions on Imports of Tuna, DS21/R (3 September 1991), B.I.S.D. 39S/155 (unadopted), para. 5.11 and GATT Panel Report: United States – Restrictions on Imports of Tuna, DS29/R (16 June 1994), paras. 5.8 and 5.9. The distinction has been criticized because of not having a basis in the text of the GATT. See S. CHARNOVITZ, 'The Law of Environmental 'PPMs' in the WTO: Debunking the Myth of Illegality', *Yale Journal of International Law* (2002), pp. 59–110 and R. HOWSE and D. REGAN, 'The Product/Process Distinction – An Illusory Basis for

part of the characteristics of a good, thus cannot be the basis of finding different goods 'unlike'. Nonetheless, the production process of a product may be an important element in the decision of consumers on whether the goods are like.[84] Still, the distinction is maintained, probably because it is felt that allowing States to differentiate between goods on the basis of the production process opens the doors to hidden protectionism.[85]

When the imported products enjoy a less favourable treatment than the 'like' domestic products, there is a violation of this provision. Since Article III.4 contains no reference to Article III.1, there is no separate requirement that the measure is 'so as to afford protection'.[86] The determination of the 'less favourable treatment' again implies an assessment of the effect of the measure: are the conditions of competition modified?[87] Therefore, the fact that 'like' products are treated differently is not sufficient to find that Article III.4 has been violated.[88] Thus, for a regulation to be inconsistent with Article III.4, two conditions need to be established: first, the fact that the goods in question are 'like' or at least in a competitive relationship and, second, a less favourable treatment. This general provision was perceived as a serious threat to the national sovereignty of Members. Certainly, nearly every regulation can have an effect on trade[89] and could therefore be assessed under Article III.4 and thus be tested by the Dispute Settlement Body, which has little guidance besides these general non-discrimination principles. Nevertheless, it was unclear how far this provision, based on the principle of non-discrimination, could be stretched. Indeed, regulations often do not draw

---

Disciplining 'Unilateralism' in Trade Policy', *European Journal of International Law* (2000), pp. 249–289.

[84] Note that HUDEC interpreted the product/process distinction doctrine in such way that, for goods, regulatory distinctions can only be based on the qualities of the products themselves. This would involve the product qualities themselves *or other characteristics that indirectly govern product qualities*. He cites as examples of the latter slaughterhouse cleanliness or possession of a licence certifying certain requisite skills. This may be similar to considering e.g. the qualifications and reputation of a service provider in determining whether two services are like. See R. HUDEC, 'GATT/WTO Constraints on National Regulation: Requiem for an "Aim and Effects" Test', *International Lawyer* (1998), pp. 619–649, at p. 624. The problem is then of course to determine what characteristics of the provider indirectly influence the qualities of the service and what characteristics do not. See on 'likeness' in the GATS, *infra* para. 138.

[85] See J. JACKSON, 'Comments on Shrimp/Turtle and the Product/Process Distinction', *European Journal of International Law* (2000), pp. 303–307.

[86] Appellate Body Report: European Communities – Regime for the Importation, Distribution and Sale of Bananas, WT/DS27/AB/R, (9 September 1997), para. 216.

[87] Appellate Body Report: Korea – Measures Affecting Imports of Fresh, Chilled and Frozen Beef, WT/DS161 and 169/AB/R, (11 December 2000), para. 144.

[88] Appellate Body Report: European Communities – Measures affecting Asbestos and Asbestos-Containing Products, WT/DS135/AB/R (12 March 2001), para. 100.

[89] See *inter alia* A. DEARDORFF and R. STERN, *Measurement of Nontariff Barriers*, (Ann Arbor, University of Michigan Press 1998), 137 p.

distinctions in law or in fact and thus would not be discriminatory. Yet, the mere fact of their existence may create an impediment to cross-border trade. It does not seem desirable, however, to bring these measures under the non-discrimination provision of Article III.4. Clarification was obviously needed: on the one hand, Article III.4 GATT should not be applied to all possible measures; on the other hand, technical regulations, sanitary measures, licensing and qualification requirements could form a barrier to trade that needed to be disciplined. States often want to protect their citizens against unsafe or unhealthy products and want to determine what level of risk they themselves are willing to tolerate.[90] On the other hand, these measures cannot form a disguised protection of their own products. The Agreement on Technical Barriers to Trade (TBT) and the Agreement on Sanitary and Phytosanitary measures (SPS) provide for basic rules to introduce such regulations in a manner consistent with the fundamental principles of GATT.[91] Even though they form an important further limitation on the regulatory autonomy of WTO Members, they provide more guidance to the Dispute Settlement Body on how to scrutinize regulatory measures, for instance by reference to international standards. Also the Agreement on Trade Related Investment Measures (TRIMS) is a specification of Article III.4, in case of investment measures.

67. It remains unclear, however, whether internal measures exist that will *a priori* be excluded from the scrutiny of Article III. Article III contains only two explicit exclusions: the article does not apply to laws, regulations and requirements on government procurement and neither does it prevent the payment of subsidies to domestic producers.[92] The GATT remains mainly based on the principle of non-discrimination, contrary to what is the case for the TBT and SPS Agreements. National measures will come under scrutiny of the GATT as soon as they lead to discriminatory treatment. Yet, the concept of discrimination has been broadened: not only formal (*de jure*) discrimination is addressed, but also *de facto*

---

[90] A good example of the question at hand is the notorious trade dispute between the US, Canada and the EC with regard to hormones. Certainly, the EC still has a regulation that restricts the sale of bovine meat that is treated with hormones. Therefore, hormone-treated meat originating in the US or Canada cannot be sold in the EC. This has been found to violate art. III GATT. See Appellate Body Report: European Communities – Measures Concerning Meat and Meat Products (Hormones), WT/DS26/AB/R and WT/DS48/AB/R (16 January 1998). See also *inter alia* M.M. SLOTBOOM, 'The hormones case: an increased risk of illegality of sanitary and phytosanitary measures', *Common Market Law Review* (1999), pp. 471–491 and M. WYNTER, 'The agreement on sanitary and phytosanitary measures in the light of the WTO decisions on EC measures concerning meat and meat products (hormones)', in P. MENGOZZI (ed.), *International Trade Law on the 50th Anniversary of the Multilateral Trading System*, (Milano, A. Giuffrè, 1999), pp. 471–526.
[91] See *infra* paras. 93–95 (SPS) and 96–100 (TBT).
[92] See art. III.8 GATT.

discrimination.[93] Measures are *de jure* discriminatory if they make a formal distinction between goods according to their origin; measures are *de facto* discriminatory if they make no formal distinction according to the origin (they are 'origin-neutral'), but *in fact* lead to different treatment of the goods. Since the trade scrutiny of the GATT extends to formally non-discriminatory measures that nonetheless have a discriminatory effect, almost any national measure may become open to challenge. In a wide interpretation, a national measure with which a foreign producer needs to comply if it wants to sell its goods in the territory of another WTO Member, may, because of the mere fact that these rules are different from the rules to which this foreign producer has to comply in its own State, lead to *de facto* discrimination if it modifies the conditions of competition. For a foreign producer, whose products already conform to the own national standards, it is more difficult to comply with the foreign standard than for the domestic producer. One thus needs to draw the boundary line between measures that are discriminatory (*de jure* or *de facto*) and thus fall within GATT scrutiny, on the one hand, and non-discriminatory measures, which do not fall within GATT scrutiny, but may fall within the scope of application of TBT and SPS, which provide more guidance than the general non-discrimination principle in the GATT.[94] A broad concept of discrimination will lead to intensive scrutiny under the GATT and thus serious limitation of the regulatory autonomy of Members.[95]

Since discrimination may lead to such a wide scrutiny of national regulation, it may be questioned where the limitations of this scrutiny can be found. Indeed, if a wide range of national measures were to come under GATT scrutiny, all these measures would need to be justified by WTO Members on the basis of the limited explicit exceptions that are included in the GATT (see *infra* para. 74). It has been suggested that an excessive impact of the principle of non-discrimination could be avoided if one considers the 'intent' of the measure when assessing its compatibility with the GATT provisions on non-discrimination. Even if a measure *discriminates*, so this reasoning goes, this would not necessarily mean that the measure is intended to *protect* the domestic industry.

The aim of a measure can be considered at three stages in the application of the GATT to a measure: *first*, whether the products are 'like' or 'directly competitive

---

[93] See H. HORN and P. MAVROIDIS, *supra* note 78, at p. 40.
[94] Depending on whether they qualify as a Technical Barrier to Trade or a Sanitary or Phytosanitary Measure. It should be noted, however, that discriminatory Technical Barriers or discriminatory Sanitary or Phytosanitary Measures are also caught by the TBT or SPS Agreement. See *infra* paras. 93–95 (SPS) and 96–100 (TBT).
[95] On the difficulty of drawing such a line and the inherent 'fluidity' of the concept of discrimination, see G. DE BÚRCA, 'Unpacking the Concept of Discrimination in the EC and International Trade Law', in C. BERNARD and J. SCOTT (eds.), *The Law of the Single European Market. Unpacking the Premises*, (Oxford, Hart 2002), pp. 181–195.

or substitutable', *second,* whether the products get a different treatment,[96] and *third,* whether the measure is justified. The first two stages concern two aspects of the applying of Article III GATT. The third stage concerns mainly the application of Article XX and Article XXI GATT. Considering the aim of the measure when applying Article III GATT has proven to be highly controversial. As has been indicated, WTO case-law has established that it is irrelevant whether the tax is levied or the measure is adopted with the *intent* of discriminating against imported goods. The applicability of Article III.2 is not conditional upon the policy purpose of a tax measure.[97] It is not an issue of intent.[98] The Appellate Body noted that "in examining the issue of 'so as to afford protection', it is not necessary for a Panel to sort through the many reasons legislators and regulators often have for what they do and weigh the relative significance of those reasons to establish legislative or regulatory intent. The *subjective* intentions inhabiting the minds of individual legislators or regulators do not bear upon the inquiry, if only because they are not accessible to treaty interpreters. It does not follow, however, that the statutory purposes or objectives – that is, the purpose or objectives of a Member's legislature and government as a whole – to the extent that they are given *objective* expression in the statute, are not pertinent".[99] There have been cases, however, where it seems that the Panel or Appellate Body have been willing to give greater weight in their analysis to the question of intent.

During the GATT 1947 era, a GATT Panel developed the so-called 'aim and effects' test, which implied that the aim and the effect of a measure would be considered when domestic and imported products are considered.[100] The aim of the measure would thus be considered in the *first phase* of the scrutinizing of national measures. This meant that certain measures, even though they make a distinction, are nevertheless not discriminatory because they apply to products

---

[96] On these first two points, see A. PORGES and J. TRACHTMAN, *supra* note 79, at pp. 789–790.
[97] Panel Report: Argentina – Measures Affecting the Export of Bovine Hides and the Import of Finished Leather, WT/DS155/R, (19 December 2000), para. 11.144.
[98] Appellate Body Report: Japan – Taxes on Alcoholic Beverages, WT/DS8, 10 and 11/AB/R, (4 October 1996), pp. 18–19. The Appellate Body rejected the so-called 'aim-and-effect test'. See S.B. WILLE, 'Recapturing a Lost Opportunity: Article III.2 GATT 1994. Japan Taxes on Alcoholic Beverages 1996', *European Journal of International Law* (1998), available on http://www.ejil.org/journal/Vol9/No1/sr1b.html.
[99] Appellate Body Report: Chile – Taxes on Alcoholic Beverages, WT/DS87 and 110/AB/R, (13 December 1999), para. 62.
[100] See GATT Panel Report: United States – Taxes on Petroleum and Certain Imported Substances, L/6175 (17 June 1987), BISD 34S/136, para. 5.1.9; GATT Panel Report: United States – Measures Affecting Alcoholic and Malt Beverages, DS23/R (19 June 1992), BISD 39S/206, para. 5.74 and GATT Panel Report: United States – Taxes on Automobiles, DS31/R (29 September 1994, unadopted), para. 5.9. On the 'aim and effects' test, see R. HUDEC, 'GATT/WTO Constraints on National Regulation. Requiem for an "Aim and Effects" Test', *International Lawyer* (1998), pp. 619–649.

that are different. Imagine, for example, two products that share the same properties, nature and quality, end-uses and consumer tastes and habits, but are differently labelled. One label is in the official language of the State where it is sold, the other label is not only in this language but also in another language that is used in the State, but is on the verge of extinction. If the traditional 'Border Tax Adjustment' criteria were used, the products would be similar. Yet, if the aim of the measure (*e.g.* preservation of culture) would be considered, the two products could be regarded as different.[101] Hence, there is no discrimination; thus no violation of Article III GATT would be at hand. As has been indicated, later Appellate Body decisions rejected the use of intent to determine whether the products are different[102], be it that the characteristics of the products may sometimes be closely linked to the regulatory aim.[103] As explained, the main reason stated by the Appellate Body for the rejection was that Panels could not sort through all the subjective reasons a national regulator may have. Thus, the intent cannot be considered in the *first phase* of scrutinizing the measure.

Nonetheless, WTO case-law may suggest that the intent of the measure is still relevant when one considers the treatment of the products (*second phase* in scrutinizing the measure). Thus, even if the products are considered similar, there may still be no violation of Article III because there is no protective intent. Article III.1 notes that internal taxation and regulation "should not be applied to imported or domestic products so as to afford protection to domestic production". This provision 'informs' the other provisions of Article III.[104] The phrase 'so as to afford protection' may point to the need to consider the 'intent' of the measure, which WTO case-law has confirmed is possible as far as the *objective* intent can

---

[101] Note that it is not permitted to consider two products unlike because their production *method* is different. This is the so-called 'product-process' doctrine. See R. HUDEC, *supra* note 84, p. 624.

[102] Appellate Body Report: Japan – Taxes on Alcoholic Beverages, WT/DS8, 10 and 11/AB/R, (4 October 1996), pp. 18–19.

[103] Indeed, in the Asbestos case, the Appellate Body noted that the health risk linked to asbestos fibres makes them different from other fibres. Of course, the Appellate Body linked this distinction to the competitive relationship of the products. (Consumers are aware of this difference and thus will treat asbestos and non-asbestos fibres as different, thus they are not in a competitive relationship). Nevertheless, it is clear that it is precisely because of the aim of avoiding health risks that they receive different regulatory treatment. See Appellate Body Report: European Communities – Measures Affecting Asbestos and Asbestos-Containing Products, WT/DS135/AB/R, (12 March 2001), paras. 114–117. HOEKMAN and MAVROIDIS have argued that the Appellate Body implicitly applied a 'reasonable consumer' test, which had as implication that it was not necessary to look for factual evidence of such consumer perceptions in the market. They also argue that it makes little sense, from an economic viewpoint, to only consider criteria on the demand side of the market. See B. HOEKMAN and P. MAVROIDIS, *The World Trade Organization. Law, Economics, and Politics*, (London, Routledge 2007), pp. 41–42.

[104] Appellate Body Report: Japan – Taxes on Alcoholic Beverages, WT/DS8, 10 and 11/AB/R, (4 October 1996), pp. 16–17.

be established.[105] Nevertheless, only in Article III.2, second sentence is an explicit reference made to the phrase 'so as to afford protection' in Article III.1. For Article III.2, first sentence, any difference in taxation of like products is automatically so as to afford protection. With regard to Article III.4, the Appellate Body has found that it is not necessary to determine separately whether a measure is 'so as to afford protection', to define whether there is a violation of Article III.4.[106] However, in practice, this would mean that *any* regulatory measure that treats imported products less favourably than 'like' (in the wider interpretation of Article III.4) (see *supra* para. 66) domestic products would violate Article III and need justification under the explicit exceptions of the GATT. If the aim of a measure could be considered in determining whether Article III.4 is violated in the first place, measures that treat 'like' products different, may still not violate this provision. The Appellate Body has indeed stated that the term 'less favourable treatment' expresses the general principle, in Article III:1, that internal regulations "should not be applied ... so as to afford protection to domestic production".[107] Still, the Appellate Body did not examine further the implications of its statement. Hence it is not clear whether this means that merely a protective effect needs to be proven or whether also the intention to protect will be considered.

If the intent of a measure cannot be examined during the application of Article III, it will only be relevant in the *third phase* of applying GATT scrutiny to national measures. Once a violation of Article III is found, the measure will need to be justified under explicit GATT exceptions, especially Article XX and Article XXI. The intent of the measure thus has to fit with one of the explicitly stated aims in Article XX or Article XXI. The limited list of aims in these provisions may lead to a situation where some measures (e.g. to protect culture) cannot be justified (on the application of the exceptions, see *infra* para. 74).

---

[105] But see our remark, *supra* para. 66, that in practice factual evidence of subjective intent will most probably have an impact on the analysis of whether the measure is 'so as to afford protection'. See for instance: Appellate Body Report: Canada – Certain Measures Concerning Periodicals, WT/DS31/AB/R, (30 June 1997), p. 30, where the Appellate Body referred to the declared intentions in the preparatory works for Canadian legislation. See also, more recently, Panel Report: Mexico – Taxes on Soft Drinks, WT/DS308/R, (7 October 2005), para. 8.91, where the Panel stated that declared intention of legislators and regulators of Member adopting the measure should not be totally disregarded.

[106] Appellate Body Report: European Communities – Regime for the Importation, Distribution and Sale of Bananas, WT/DS27/AB/R, (9 September 1997), para. 216.

[107] Appellate Body Report: European Communities – Measures Affecting Asbestos and Asbestos-Containing Products, WT/DS135/AB/R, (12 March 2001), para. 100.

4. Quantitative Restrictions

68. Article XI GATT provides for the general elimination of quantitative restrictions and is 'one of the cornerstones of the GATT system'.[108] As explained, the only restrictions WTO Members are allowed to impose on trade must take the form of duties, taxes or other charges, which should be gradually brought to zero. A Member cannot impose quotas, import or export licences or other measures having equivalent effect upon goods that originate in another Member or on the export of a product that is destined for the territory of another Member. 'Measures having equivalent effect' are *border* measures that do not take the form of a quota, but nevertheless have such an effect. It is necessary to establish whether the measures constitute a prohibition or restriction on importation and thus affect the opportunities of importation itself.[109] Nevertheless, internal measures that apply both to imported and like domestic products, but are enforced in the case of the imported product at the time or point of importation, are not subject to Article XI, but to Article III GATT.[110] To distinguish between the scope of Article III and Article XI GATT, it is therefore essential to determine whether the measure in question also applies to the domestic like product (in which case Article III will be applicable) or not (in which case Article XI applies).[111] For Article III to be applicable, it is not necessary that the measure that is applied to the domestic product is *identical* to the one applied to the like imported product.[112]

69. Measures having the effect of quotas do not necessarily have to be legally binding or mandatory. Two essential criteria need to be satisfied in order to be such 'other measure'. First, there must be reasonable grounds to believe that sufficient incentives or disincentives exist for non-mandatory measures to take effect. Second, the operation of the measures should be essentially dependent on government action or intervention.[113]

---

[108] Panel Report: Turkey – Restrictions on Imports of Textile and Clothing Products, WT/DS34/AB/R, (22 October 1999), para. 9.63.

[109] One can think of a customs duty that is so high that no importer will ever be willing to pay it, thus a zero quota would be the result. Even less extreme situations than this one may give rise to such 'measures having equivalent effect'. It is however always "necessary to identify [an alleged inconsistent measure] as a condition that has a limiting effect on importation itself". See Panel Report: Dominican Republic – Measures Affecting the Importation and Internal Sale of Cigarettes, WT/DS302/R, (26 November 2004), paras. 7.252 and 7.261.

[110] See *Ad* art. III, Annex I GATT.

[111] Panel Report: European Communities – Measures Affecting Asbestos and Asbestos-Containing Products, WT/DS135/R, paras. 8.91–8.92.

[112] *Ibid.* paras. 8.94–8.95.

[113] GATT Panel Report: Japan – Trade in Semi-Conductors, (4 May 1988), BISD 35S/116, para. 109. Remarkably, in the Panel Report on *Argentina – Hides and Leather*, the Panel seemed to have clarified this provision and thereby restricted the scope of art. XI GATT. The Panel noted that a complainant must provide convincing evidence of a causal link between the government

70. Quantitative *export* restrictions are equally prohibited. It may occur that an exporting country voluntarily restricts its export to another country in the framework of an agreement with the importing country that wants to protect its own industry against the imports. Such 'voluntary export restraints' are contrary to Article XI GATT.

71. The prohibition of quantitative restrictions has a number of exceptions. It concerns export prohibitions or restrictions that are temporarily applied to prevent or relieve critical shortages of foodstuffs or other products essential to the exporting Member; import and export prohibitions that are necessary to the application of standards or regulations for the classification, grading or marketing of commodities in international trade; and import restrictions on agricultural or fisheries products necessary to the enforcement of certain governmental measures in these fields.[114]

5. *General Exceptions*

72. Article XX GATT contains a number of general exceptions to the above-mentioned fundamental principles. It concerns a difficult balancing act between free trade and other values, which often leads to conflicts between WTO Members. "Paragraphs (a) to (j) of Article XX GATT contain measures that are recognized as *exceptions to substantive obligations* established in the GATT 1994 because the domestic policies embodied in such measures have been recognized as important and legitimate in character."[115] Indeed, it was clear that the principles of GATT seriously curtail the regulatory autonomy of the Contracting Parties and that certain exceptions were needed to recognize the *right* of a Member to adopt certain policies, while at the same time taking into account the treaty rights of other Members.[116]

73. Article XX consists of two parts.[117] First, it has a list of measures that are not excluded by the GATT. Paragraphs (a) to (j) define the *contents* of the exceptions. Second, the chapeau (introductory paragraph) of Article XX limits the *way* these measures are *applied*.[118] The examination of a contested measure has to be

---

measure attacked and the reduced level of trade. See Panel Report: Argentina – Measures Affecting the Exports of Bovine Hides and the Import of Finished Leather, WT/DS155/R (19 December 2000), paras. 11.19–11.22.

[114] Art. XI.2 (a)–(c) GATT.
[115] Appellate Body Report: United States – Import Prohibition of Certain Shrimp and Shrimp Products, WT/DS58/AB/R, (12 October 1998), para. 121.
[116] *Ibid.* para. 156.
[117] Appellate Body Report: United States – Standards for Reformulated and Conventional Gasoline, WT/DS2/AB/R, (29 April 1996), p. 22.
[118] Appellate Body Report: United States – Import Prohibition of Certain Shrimp and Shrimp Products, WT/DS58/AB/R (12 October 1998), para. 120.

conducted in this particular order. It reflects 'the fundamental structure and logic of Article XX'.[119]

74. The closed list of exempted measures consists of measures (a) necessary to protect public morals; (b) necessary to protect human, animal or plant life or health[120]; (c) relating to the importations of gold or silver; (d) necessary to secure compliance with laws or regulations which are not inconsistent with the provisions; (e) relating to the products of prison labour; (f) imposed for the protection of national treasures of artistic, historic or archaeological value; (g) relating to the conservation of exhaustible natural resources[121] if such measures are made effective in conjunction with[122] restrictions on domestic production or consumption; (h) undertaken in pursuance of obligations under an intergovernmental commodity agreement; (i) involving restrictions on exports of domestic materials of which the essential quantities must be preserved for the domestic industry in periods when the domestic price is held below the world price as part of a governmental stabilization plan; (j) essential to the acquisition or distribution of products in general or local short supply.

75. In the paragraphs where the permitted measures must be *necessary* to pursue a certain goal, a balancing test must be performed to weigh the importance of the goal pursued and the restrictive impact of the measure. According to the Appellate Body "a treaty interpreter assessing a measure claimed to be necessary to secure compliance of a WTO-consistent law or regulation may, in appropriate cases, take into account the relative importance of the common interests or values that the law or regulation to be enforced is intended to protect. The more vital or important those common interests or values are, the easier it would be to accept as 'necessary' a measure designed as an enforcement instrument." It involves in every case "a process of weighing and balancing a series of factors which prominently include the contribution made by the compliance measure to the enforcement of the law

---

[119] *Ibid.* para. 119.
[120] The Appellate Body noted that "WTO Members have the right to determine the level of protection of health they consider appropriate in a given situation". The Panel and Appellate Body can only determine whether the measure is not 'necessary' to achieve that level of protection. See Appellate Body Report: European Communities – Measures Affecting Asbestos and Asbestos-Containing Products, WT/DS135/AB/R, (12 March 2001), para. 168.
[121] The Appellate Body has stated that 'exhaustible natural resources' contains both living and non-living sources. Also a measure to prevent the extinction of sea turtles can be justified under art. XX (g). See Appellate Body Report: United States – Import Prohibition of Certain Shrimp and Shrimp Products, WT/DS58/AB/R (12 October 1998), para. 131.
[122] The phrase 'made effective in conjunction with' is said to impose a requirement of 'even-handedness' in the imposition of restrictions on imported and domestic products. It does not require that imported and domestic products be treated equally, but merely that they be treated in an even-handed manner. See Appellate Body Report: United States – Standards for Reformulated and Conventional Gasoline, WT/DS2/AB/R, (29 April 1996), pp. 20–21.

or regulation at issue, the importance of the common interests or values protected by that law or regulation, and the accompanying impact of the law or regulation on imports or exports".[123] It should thus be assessed whether there is a 'reasonably available measure' that would serve the same end and that is less restrictive of trade.[124] This 'weighing and balancing' may result in the Panel or the Appellate Body interfering in the national policy choices of the WTO Member. Indeed, once the test implies that trade values are being balanced against other values, the adjudicator will be called upon to evaluate somehow the vitality of the objective that is pursued. Although in principle, WTO Members have the right to set their own level of protection,[125] an inquiry by the adjudicator into the vitality of the measure may seriously call this right into question. Of course, one could argue that the starting point should be the view the WTO Member has taken towards the vitality of the objective and that this point should not be questioned. Yet, the view taken by a Member as to the vitality and the appropriate level is not always obvious. Moreover, relying entirely on the view of the WTO Member may make the balancing test meaningless. For measures that involve health protection, the test may indeed be less intrusive. Nonetheless, for measures that pursue other objectives, for which the vitality may not so 'obvious', like e.g. cultural identity or consumer confusion, the test may be much more delicate.

In the paragraphs where the measures must *relate to* the policy goal, the measure must be *primarily aimed at* it.[126] There would here thus be no requirement that the measure be *necessary* to achieve the policy goal. Although it may seem that the burden of proof here is slightly lower than for measures which need to be 'necessary' to achieve the goal, the interpretation of the Appellate Body of this wording as a requirement that the measures "cannot be regarded as merely incidentally or inadvertently aimed at" the policy objective that is pursued makes this very close to a requirement of necessity.[127] The Appellate Body clarified that a "close and real" relationship would be required between the measure and the

---

[123] Appellate Body Report: Korea – Measures Affecting Imports of Fresh, Chilled and Frozen Beef, WT/DS161 and 169/AB/R, (11 December 2000), paras. 161–162 and 164.
[124] Appellate Body Report: European Communities – Measures Affecting Asbestos and Asbestos-Containing Products, WT/DS135/AB/R, (12 March 2001), para. 172.
[125] *Ibid.* para. 168. This statement stands indeed in striking contrast with the statements of the Appellate Body in Korea – Measures Affecting Imports of Fresh, Chilled and Frozen Beef, WT/DS161 and 169/AB/R, (11 December 2000), paras. 161–162 and 164.
[126] Appellate Body Report: United States – Standards for Reformulated and Conventional Gasoline, WT/DS2/AB/R, (29 April 1996), p. 16. The Appellate Body has stressed this interpretation to give a meaning to the different wording in the distinct paragraphs. Yet, at the same time, the Appellate Body expresses doubts on this interpretation. It notes "that the phrase 'primarily aimed at' is not in itself treaty language and was not designed as a simple litmus test for inclusion or exclusion from Article XX(g)." Nevertheless, since this point was not subject of appeal in the case, the Appellate Body continued applying this test.
[127] *Ibid.* p. 19.

policy objective. The measure cannot be "disproportionately wide in its scope and reach in relation to its policy objective".[128]

76. In its chapeau, Article XX GATT states that the allowed exceptions *may not be applied* in a manner which would constitute a means of arbitrary or unjustifiable discrimination between countries where the same conditions prevail, or a disguised restriction on international trade. The chapeau thus addresses the manner in which the measure is applied. It is the last 'safety valve' to ensure that a measure that restricts trade, but seems justified on the basis of one of the exceptions, still does not lead to an *abuse* of these exceptions under Article XX.[129] The way a measure under paragraphs (a)-(j) is applied is inconsistent with the chapeau if there is, first, a discrimination which is second, arbitrary or unjustifiable in character or a disguised restriction of international trade[130] and, third, occurs between countries where the same conditions prevail.[131] Some of these central concepts need further clarification. First of all, there needs to be *discrimination*. It cannot be intended by the drafters of the Agreements that the same discriminatory test as in, for instance, Article I or Article III is applied here. Therefore, it is secondly necessary that the discrimination is arbitrary or unjustifiable or leads to a disguised restriction of trade. The requirement that the measure does not amount to *arbitrary* discrimination rather affects the procedural aspects of the rule. This means that the measure must allow sufficient flexibility in application for the different situations of the affected countries to be taken into account.[132] The requirement that the exempted measure does not amount to *unjustifiable* discrimination, affects the substance of the rule. For instance, when

---

[128] Appellate Body Report: United States – Import Prohibition of Certain Shrimp and Shrimp Products, WT/DS58/AB/R (12 October 1998), para. 141.
[129] Appellate Body Report: United States – Standards for Reformulated and Conventional Gasoline, WT/DS2/AB/R, (29 April 1996), p. 22.
[130] The Appellate Body noted that "'[a]rbitrary discrimination', 'unjustifiable discrimination' and 'disguised restriction' on international trade may, accordingly, be read side by side; they impart meaning to one another". Appellate Body Report: United States – Standards for Reformulated and Conventional Gasoline, WT/DS2/AB/R, (29 April 1996), p. 25. A Panel noted that there will be a 'disguised restriction on international trade' if the "design, architecture and revealing structure" of the measure reveals that the measures pursues trade-restrictive and protectionist objectives. See Panel Report: European Communities – Measures Affecting Asbestos and Asbestos-Containing Products, WT/DS135/R, para. 8.236.
[131] Appellate Body Report: United States – Import Prohibition of Certain Shrimp and Shrimp Products, WT/DS58/AB/R (12 October 1998), para. 150.
[132] This implies that the measure a State imposes needs to provide for sufficient flexibility to ensure that measures by other States that are comparable in effectiveness need also to be found consistent with the first State's measures. Goods that comply with those measures that are comparable in effectiveness can thus not be denied access to the first State's market. It does not mean, however, that the State should anticipate the conditions in each and every individual Member. See Appellate Body Report: United States – Import Prohibition of Certain Shrimp and Shrimp Products, WT/DS58/AB/R (12 October 1998), para. 144.

adopting measures that restrict trade, but would fall under the exemptions of Article XX, the State has to ensure that WTO Members that may be affected are equally given the opportunity to minimize the effects of the measure on their trade. Multilateral solutions are preferred over unilateral solutions.[133] Finally, the trade-restrictive measure may not be a disguised restriction of trade. This would mean that the trade-restrictive measure is in fact taken "under the guise of a measure formally within the terms of an exception listed in Article XX".[134] Arguably, this may require again an inquiry into the 'intent' of the measure, be it that this intent is again objectively determined by looking at the "design, architecture and revealing structure" of the measure.[135] The fact that, as a third aspect of the chapeau of Article XX, the discrimination needs to be assessed between countries where the same conditions prevail means that comparisons need to be made not only between exporting countries but also between exporting countries and the importing country.[136]

77. Article XXI GATT, finally, also provides for exceptions that relate to national security. The provisions of the GATT cannot be interpreted (a) to require the disclosure by the WTO Members of information contrary to their essential security interests; (b) to prevent Members from taking measures that are necessary for its security interests; or (c) to prevent them from taking any action in pursuance of their obligations under the United Nations Charter.[137]

6. *Free Trade Areas and Customs Unions*

78. The question arises as to how customs unions (e.g. the EC) and free trade areas (e.g. NAFTA) are compatible with the principle of MFN. Those kinds of regional trade agreements (RTAs) grant advantages to a select group of countries that are not extended to other countries, thus violating MFN. Nonetheless, the WTO is, in principle, in favour of such agreements. Certainly, free trade agreements and customs unions can play an important role in the liberalization

---

[133] This may for instance imply that a State that is willing to take a measure under art. XX, needs to undertake attempts to secure a multilateral solution. The State should enter into negotiations with the trading partners before taking the measure unilaterally. *Ibid.* paras. 166 and 172.
[134] Appellate Body Report: United States – Standards for Reformulated and Conventional Gasoline, WT/DS2/AB/R, (29 April 1996), p. 25.
[135] Panel Report: European Communities – Measures Affecting Asbestos and Asbestos-Containing Products, WT/DS135/R, (18 September 2000), para. 8.236.
[136] Appellate Body Report: United States – Standards for Reformulated and Conventional Gasoline, WT/DS2/AB/R, (29 April 1996), p. 23.
[137] This is the only provision of the GATT where reference is made to the obligations as member of the United Nations. See A.F. Perez, 'WTO and UN Law: Institutional Comity in National Security', *The Yale Journal of International Law* (1998), pp. 301–381.

of world trade because they can lead to regional economic integration.[138] Enterprises within a free trade area or a customs union are being prepared for global free trade thanks to competition within a limited group of countries.[139] Moreover, these agreements can create a 'culture of multilateral negotiating' that can 'spill over' into other fields besides trade. On the other hand, there are also negative effects of the proliferation of economic integration agreements. The 'spaghetti bowl' of different agreements makes world trade less transparent than it could be under a general multilateral agreement. Also negative 'trade diversion' effects exist next to the positive 'trade creation' effects of such agreements.[140]

79. Article XXIV GATT makes a distinction between Free Trade Areas (FTA) and Customs Unions (CU). In a CU, the trade barriers between the members (*inter se*) will be abolished and a common customs tariff will apply with regard to goods originating in third countries. In an FTA, only the trade barriers *inter se* will be removed. The different members maintain their own trade barriers vis-à-vis third countries. The conditions Article XXIV sets out essentially come down to the principle that regional trade integration should impose no more trade diversion than is absolutely necessary. The main objective of the regional integration agreement must be to facilitate trade within the region and not to raise barriers to trade with outside economies.[141] The provision requires that: (a) the regional agreement covers substantially all trade between the constituent territories[142] (so-called internal trade requirement)[143]; and (b) the duties and other regulations of commerce in respect of trade with Contracting Parties not parties to the CU or FTA shall not be higher or more restrictive than those applicable in the constituent territories prior to the formation of such CU or FTA (so-called external trade requirement).[144] These two requirements can be seen as the main conditions for the establishment of a regional trade agreement.[145] In addition, countries establishing such agreement must make sure that (c) when

---

[138] See also Ministerial Declaration of Doha, done on 14 November 2001, WT/MIN(01)/DEC/1, available on http://www.wto.org/english/thewto_e/minist_e/min01_e/mindecl_e.htm, para. 4.
[139] Ministerial Declaration of Singapore, 13 December 1996, WT/MIN(96)/DEC, available on http://www.wto.org/english/thewto_e/minist_e/min96_e/wtodec_e.htm, para. 7.
[140] See N. LIMÃO, 'Preferential vs. Multilateral Trade Liberalization: Evidence and Open Questions', *World Trade Review* (2006), pp. 155–176.
[141] Art. XXIV.4 GATT.
[142] *Ibid.* art. XXIV.8 (a) and (b).
[143] For an extensive discussion: see J. MATHIS, *Regional Trade Agreements in the GATT/WTO: Art. XXIV and the Internal Trade Requirement*, (The Hague, T.M.C. Asser Press 2002), xxii + 328 p.
[144] Art. XXIV.5 (a) and (b) GATT. There is some difference in the wording of the provisions relating to CUs and FTAs. This is due to the fact that CUs suppose a common external customs policy. For a discussion, see M. MATSUSHITA, T.J. SCHOENBAUM and P.C. MAVROIDIS, *supra* note 60, p. 562–573.
[145] *Ibid.*

there is, because of the establishment of the CU[146], for a WTO Member a certain deviation from the tariffs that had been committed to by a party to the CU, these tariffs may need to be renegotiated in order to restore the previous balance[147]; and (d) an interim agreement leading to a formation of a CU or FTA shall be implemented within a reasonable period of time.[148]

80. Some of these conditions are rather vague and are subject to major discussions. It concerns first of all the principle that the CU or FTA must cover *'substantially all trade'*. The vagueness of this concept leads to the danger that States will exclude sensitive sectors from the regional trade liberalization and in fact use the CU or FTA to achieve some preferential arrangements while circumventing the principle of MFN. Some authors have suggested that the phrase *'substantially all trade'* should be replaced by *'all the trade'* or at least a certain clear percentage of all trade (80 or 90%).[149] The idea of requiring regional liberalization of all the trade has been criticized as "too ambitious and unrealistic", not only because it would lead to unfair treatment of existing and new regional integration efforts, but also because it does not take into account the depth of the integration. Also, applying a percentage criterion will not be without difficulties because it requires a difficult calculation of the trade flows.[150]

81. With the aim of establishing a CU or FTA, States may decide to adopt an interim agreement. Such agreements must include a plan or schedule for the CU or FTA.[151] They allow for a steady implementation of the agreement. Therefore, the obligation to comply with the above-mentioned conditions is delayed. Nevertheless, interim agreements to form a CU or FTA must be implemented within a *'reasonable length of time'*. This is again a vague formulation. The Understanding on the Interpretation of Article XXIV GATT has specified that such period should not be more than 10 years unless a full explanation is given for a longer period.[152]

---

[146] This requirement does not apply to the establishment of a Free Trade Area, since the participants in a FTA do not adopt a common external customs regime.
[147] Art. XXIV.6 GATT.
[148] *Ibid.* art. XXIV.5 (c).
[149] See J. BHAGWATI, 'Regionalism and Multilateralism: an overview', in J. DE MELO and A. PANAGARIYA (eds.), *New Dimensions in Regional Integration*, (Cambridge, Cambridge University Press, 1993), pp. 22–46 and J. HUBER, 'The Past, Present and Future ACP-EC Trade Regime and the WTO, *European Journal of International Law* (2000), pp. 427–438.
[150] S.-H. PARK, 'Regionalism, Open Regionalism and Article XXIV GATT: Conflicts and Harmony', in F. SNYDER (ed.), *Regional and Global Regulation of International Trade*, (Oxford, Hart 2002), pp. 278–279.
[151] Art. XXIV.5 (c) GATT.
[152] Understanding on the Interpretation of Article XXIV of the General Agreement on Tariffs and Trade 1994, available on http://www.wto.org/english/docs_e/legal_e/10-24.pdf, para. 3.

82. Both interim agreements leading to a CU or FTA and agreements establishing a CU or FTA have to be notified promptly to the Council for Trade in Goods.[153] Note that such trade agreements that also concern trade in services also have to be notified to the Council for Trade in Services[154] and that agreements entered into pursuant to the Enabling Clause (see *infra* paras. 88-92) have to be notified to the Committee on Trade and Development. The Goods Council will adopt the terms of reference for the *Committee on Regional Trade Agreements*, a Committee coming under the General Council. This Committee will examine the compatibility of the notified regional trade agreement/interim agreement with the provisions of the WTO Agreements.[155] All WTO Members are represented in this Committee. The Committee can make "reports and recommendations to contracting parties as they may deem appropriate".[156] Nonetheless, since most trade agreements are only notified after their establishment, there is a clear tolerance of WTO-incompatible trade agreements.[157] It seems that only when an *interim* agreement has been notified, the Committee has effective power to steer the implementation of this agreement in order to make it WTO compatible. In such case, the Committee can make recommendations which have to be followed by the parties to the agreement. If they do not, the interim agreement cannot be maintained or put into force.[158] Even if an agreement or interim agreement is notified in time, it does not often occur that a regional trade agreement is found incompatible. Decision-making in the Committee on Regional Trade Agreements is done by consensus. Thus, WTO Members that are involved in the notified agreement may refuse to decide that the agreement is incompatible.

83. Differences between Members on how to interpret the criteria for assessing the consistency of RTAs with WTO rules have created a lengthening backlog of uncompleted reports in the Committee. In fact, consensus on GATT consistency has been reached in only one case so far: the customs union between the Czech Republic and the Slovak Republic after the break-up of Czechoslovakia. This was an RTA assessed during the GATT 1947 period. Since 1995 (the establishment of the WTO) no RTA examination has yet been finalized. On 10 July 2006, an Agreement on Regional Trade Agreements was concluded within the WTO

---

[153] The Council for Trade in Goods works under the supervision of the General Council of the WTO. It monitors the functioning of the Multilateral Trade Agreements.
[154] Art. V.7 GATS. See also *infra* para. 148.
[155] Understanding on the Interpretation of Article XXIV of the General Agreement on Tariffs and Trade 1994, *supra* note 152, para. 3. M. MATSUSHITA, T.J. SCHOENBAUM and P.C. MAVROIDIS, *supra* note 60, pp. 559–562.
[156] *Ibid.*, p. 560.
[157] *Ibid.*
[158] Art. XXIV.7 (b) GATT.

Negotiation Group on Rules.[159] This agreement established a new transparency mechanism for Regional Trade Agreements. Notification of an RTA should take place as early as possible and no later than directly following the ratification of the Regional Trade Agreement. Agreements falling under Article XXIV GATT and Article V GATS will be reviewed by the Committee on Regional Trade Agreements. Agreements falling under the Enabling Clause[160] will be considered by the Committee on Trade and Development. The review should normally be concluded within one year after notification.

7. Special and Differential Treatment of Developing Countries

a. Specific substantive-law provisions relating to developing countries

84. Several provisions in the WTO agreements take into account the specific situation of developing countries in the WTO.[161] There are first of all measures that recognize that the interests of developing and least-developed countries are a general matter. In the Preamble of the Marrakesh Agreement, it is recognized that "there is a need for positive efforts designed to ensure that developing countries, and especially the least developed among them, secure a share in the growth in international trade commensurate with the needs of their economic development".[162] There is even a specific Ministerial Decision on Measures in Favour of Least-Developed Countries.[163] This Decision grants special treatment to least-developed countries with regard to all aspects of all WTO Agreements and requires regular review of their needs. It permits least-developed countries to apply only those commitments which are consistent with their development needs and individual capabilities, and it sets a framework for other countries to follow when formulating and implementing their national trade policies so that these are helpful to the least-developed countries.[164]

85. Second, there are measures in the WTO agreements that ease the rules or number of obligations to be met by developing countries. Some examples in the three main WTO agreements (GATT, GATS and TRIPS) can be given. Article XVIII GATT gives developing countries the right to restrict imports if this would

---

[159] Negotiation Group on Rules, Transparency Mechanism for Regional Trade Agreements (Draft Decision), JOB(06)/59/Rev.5, 29 June 2006.
[160] See *infra* paras. 88–92.
[161] On the definition of Developing Countries and Least-Developed Countries, see *infra* paras. 231–232.
[162] Agreement Establishing the World Trade Organization, done in Marrakesh on 15 April 1994, *UNTS* no. 31874, para 2 of the Preamble.
[163] Decision on Measures in Favour of Least-Developed Countries, LT/UR/D–1/3, 15 April 1994.
[164] See J. CROOME, *supra* note 8, p. 224.

promote the establishment or maintenance of a particular industry, or assist in cases of balance-of-payments difficulties.[165] Part IV of the GATT includes provisions on the concept of non-reciprocal preferential treatment for developing countries – when developed countries grant trade concessions to developing countries they should not expect the developing countries to make matching offers in return. However, developing countries claim that Part IV has been without practical value, as it does not contain any *obligations* for developed countries. Article IV GATS aims at increasing the participation of developing countries in world trade. It refers, among other things, to strengthening the domestic services competitiveness of developing countries through access to technology and improving their access to information networks. Article XII GATS allows developing countries and countries in transition to restrict trade in services for reasons of balance-of-payment difficulties. Article 66 TRIPS, finally, encourages technology transfer to developing countries.

86. Third, many provisions in the WTO agreements provide longer time frames for the implementation of obligations to be met. Several of these provisions are mentioned in the following discussion of the multilateral agreements on trade in goods.

87. Finally, WTO agreements include several provisions that set out measures for technical assistance for developing countries. The delivery of WTO technical assistance is designed to assist developing and least-developed countries and low-income countries in transition to adjust to WTO rules and disciplines, implement obligations and exercise the rights of membership, including drawing on the benefits of an open, rules-based multilateral trading system. The WTO also regularly organizes training courses for government officials from developing countries.

b.   Enabling Clause

88. A particularly important decision in the WTO framework is the Decision on Differential and More Favourable Treatment of 28 November 1979, also called the 'Enabling Clause'.[166] This clause, one of the outcomes of the Tokyo Round negotiations, 'enabled' the developed countries to grant non-reciprocal tariff preferences to developing countries, which did not need to be extended to all

---

[165] This provision should be read in conjunction with the Decision on Safeguard Action for Development Purposes, L/4897, 28 November 1979; the Declaration on Trade Measures Taken for Balance-of-Payments Purposes, L/4904, 28 November 1979 and the Understanding on Balance-of-Payments Provisions of the General Agreement on Tariffs and Trade 1947.

[166] Decision on Differential and More Favourable Treatment, Reciprocity and Fuller Participation of Developing Countries, 26S/203, done in Geneva on 28 November 1979.

other Contracting Parties on the basis of MFN. It should be noted that the clause only applies to trade in *goods*. It is also important that it *imposes no obligation* on developed countries to accord differential treatment to developing countries.[167] The legal status of the Enabling Clause is up to discussion. At first sight, it seems logical to say that the clause is an exception to Article I GATT (MFN). The legal basis for such 'exception' is not entirely clear, however. Would this imply that the clause is a 'waiver' in the sense of Article XXV.5 GATT?[168] The text of the Enabling Clause lacks any reference to this article. Moreover, the clause is not mentioned in the list of GATT 1947 waivers, which is attached to the GATT 1994.[169] Neither does the clause comply with the conditions for waivers. There are no 'exceptional circumstances' mentioned and it is not limited to a particular Member. A reputed scholar concluded that "the Enabling Clause does not function as a waiver".[170] On the contrary, the Enabling Clause is an integral part of GATT 1994. It is indeed one of the *'other decisions of the Contracting Parties to GATT 1947'*, as mentioned in the GATT 1994[171] and fits perfectly into Part IV (Trade and Development)[172] of the GATT.[173] Nevertheless, the Appellate Body has now stated unambiguously that "the Enabling Clause operates as an 'exception' to Article I.1".[174]

89. The Enabling Clause contains four main measures. First of all, it provides a legal basis for the Generalized System of Preferences.[175] An important tool for fostering development in developing countries is the Generalized System of Preferences (GSP). The idea of such system has emerged from the United Nations Conference on Trade And Development (UNCTAD). It involves a "general, non-

---

[167] UNCTAD, *1982 Report by the Secretary-General of UNCTAD, Assessment of the Results of the Multilateral Trade Negotiations*, UNCTAD Doc. T/B/778/Rev. 1, para. 176.
[168] Note that the Enabling Clause has been adopted long before the establishment of the WTO. Thus, art. IX.3 WTO Agreement cannot be a legal basis for the clause.
[169] See L. BARTELS, 'The WTO Enabling Clause and Positive Conditionality in the European Community's GSP Program', *Journal of International Economic Law* (2003), pp. 514–515. On 'waivers', see *infra* para. 253.
[170] R. HOWSE, 'India's WTO Challenge to Drug Enforcement Conditions in the European Community Generalized System of Preferences: A Little Known Case with Major Repercussions for "Political" Conditionality in US Trade Policy', *Chicago Journal of International Law* (2003), p. 390.
[171] Para. 1 (b) (iv) GATT 1994; L. BARTELS, *supra* note 169, p. 515.
[172] This part has been added on the impulse of UNCTAD in February 1965. It entered into force in June 1966. Art. XXXVI.3 and 4 GATT (included in Part IV) call for "positive efforts designed to ensure that less-developed Contracting Parties secure a share in the growth in international trade commensurate with the needs of their economic development." Therefore, "[…] there is a need to provide in the largest possible measure more favourable and acceptable conditions of access to world markets for these products." The developed countries did not expect reciprocity for these preferential commitments.
[173] R. HOWSE, *supra* note 170, p. 390.
[174] Appellate Body Report: European Communities – Conditions for the Granting of Tariff Preferences to Developing Countries, WT/DS246/AB/R (7 April 2004), paras. 90 and 99.
[175] Para. 2 (a) Enabling Clause.

reciprocal, non-discriminatory system in favour of developing countries, including special measures in favour of the least-developed countries among the developing countries".[176] It is intended that industrialized nations grant trade advantages (e.g. lower import tariffs) to developing countries, which are not extended to other industrialized countries. This would give developing countries a competitive advantage with regard to their exports, which in turn is advantageous to their economic development. Nevertheless, this Generalized System conflicted with one of the basic principles of the GATT, the principle of Most Favoured Nation.[177] As indicated earlier, this principle requires a GATT Contracting Party (today: 'Member of the WTO') to extend to all other Contracting Parties any advantage granted to one State. Thus, it is not allowed to discriminate between the different Contracting Parties. Yet, this was exactly what the Generalized System was proposing: industrialized countries would give advantages to developing countries, which would not be extended to other countries. Therefore, the Generalized System could not be implemented by the Contracting Parties of the GATT without an exception being made on the principle of Most Favoured Nation. In June 1971, the GATT Contracting Parties approved a 'waiver'[178], which makes preferential treatment of developing countries possible. This waiver initially applied for ten years, but became permanent with the adoption of the 'Enabling Clause'. The Enabling Clause is still the basis of the present-day tariff preferences. Each country can adopt its own Generalized System of Preferences, hence the GSPs of, for instance, the EC, the US or Canada differ. Since States often link conditions to the granting of these preferences, the Appellate Body has set out a number of conditions under which differential treatment *among* developing countries is possible.[179]

---

[176] UNCTAD Res. 21 (II), van 26 March 1968.
[177] Art. I GATT.
[178] Decision on the Generalized System of Preferences, 18S/24, done in Geneva on 25 June 1971.
[179] States are allowed to grant Least Developed Countries better treatment than other developing countries (Para 2 (d) Enabling Clause). Yet, it was unclear to what extent other distinctions could be drawn within the group of developing countries. A Panel and the Appellate Body have reprimanded the EC in a case where the EC had granted tariff preferences to twelve explicitly listed developing countries in order to allow them to take measures to reduce the traffic in illegal drugs. The advantageous trade conditions would give the countries an additional income to take such measures. India (who was not included in the list of benefiting countries) claimed that these tariff preferences violated the principle of MFN and were not exempted by the Enabling Clause. The Appellate Body found that the special drug arrangements violated the Enabling Clause. The term non-discrimination in the Enabling Clause requires that 'similarly situated' developing countries are treated similarly. Differentiation among the developing countries would thus be possible if some countries have other development needs than others. Nevertheless, this differentiation needs to comply with a number of conditions, some of them substantive, other procedural. First, the criteria used by the developed country that grants the preferences should be linked to development, financial and trade needs. Not all needs are acceptable. They should concern 'development, financial or trade' issues and an objective standard should be used. These needs may change over time and may be particular to certain countries. Second, the measures taken by the preference-granting country should

90. Second, the Enabling Clause allows non-reciprocal differential and more favourable treatment of developing countries with regard to non-tariff measures.[180]

91. Third, it also addresses the special situation of South-South Free Trade Areas.[181] Since Article XXIV GATT is often not appropriate to accommodate for such arrangements, a specific basis with less stringent conditions was necessary. Under the Enabling Clause, it is permitted to agree upon a mutual reduction or elimination of tariffs and non-tariff measures, notwithstanding Article I GATT. This is similar to what is allowed under Article XXIV GATT. Also similar to Article XXIV is the requirement that such arrangements must not raise barriers to or create undue difficulties for the trade of the other WTO Members.[182] In addition, such arrangements must not constitute an impediment to the reduction or elimination of tariff and non-tariff barriers on an MFN basis.[183] Nevertheless, the Enabling Clause is much more flexible for these South-South trade agreements than what would be the case under Article XXIV. It does not prescribe a specific form of trade arrangement, neither does it include the requirement to cover 'substantially all trade'.[184] These provisions are much more "ambiguous and loose [...] than Article XXIV". [185]

92. Finally, the Enabling Clause also allows special treatment of a specific category of developing countries: the least-developed countries (LDCs).[186] Countries are labelled LDCs according to specific criteria set out by the Economic and Social Council of the UN.[187] Since they are a well-specified group, these countries can easily receive different treatment to other developing countries.

---

respond positively to these needs. This means that there should be a sufficient nexus between the preference granted and the likelihood that it will address the relevant need. Third, the measures cannot impose unjustifiable burdens on other WTO Members. Finally, a procedural condition needs to be complied with: the preferences should be available to all beneficiaries that share this need. There should be an objective mechanism that allows for the inclusion of additional States that share these needs and the removal of States that do not share this need any more. See Appellate Body Report: European Communities – Conditions for the Granting of Tariff Preferences to Developing Countries, WT/DS246/AB/R (7 April 2004), paras. 146–167 and 179–183.

[180] Enabling Clause, para. 2 (b).
[181] Ibid. para. 2 (c).
[182] Ibid. para. 3 (a).
[183] Ibid. para. 3 (b).
[184] See supra para. 84.
[185] See S.-H. Park, 'Regionalism, Open Regionalism and Article XXIV GATT: Conflicts and Harmony', in F. Snyder (ed.), Regional and Global Regulation of International Trade, (Oxford, Hart 2002), p. 276.
[186] Para. 2 (d) Enabling Clause.
[187] See infra para. 232.

B. AGREEMENT ON SANITARY AND PHYTOSANITARY MEASURES

93. It is an essential task of a State to ensure that safe and healthy products are offered to its citizens. Moreover, States want to decide themselves to what extent they are willing to accept certain risks.[188] Yet, at the same time these health and safety regulations cannot be an excuse to protect the domestic producers. Normally, in the absence of any further specific agreements, if they are *de jure* or *de facto* discriminatory, these measures would need to be addressed under Articles I and III GATT. This may often be the case because, as explained (*supra* para. 66), the intent underlying a distinction between products is not formally taken into account when determining 'likeness'. Moreover, even if a measure is not discriminatory, it may form a trade barrier mainly by the fact that it exists and differs from the rules with which importers have to comply in their home country. During the Uruguay Round, the GATT Contracting Parties desired clearer rules regulating this specific situation of non-tariff barriers. The Agreement on Technical Barriers on Trade (TBT Agreement) and the Agreement on Sanitary and Phytosanitary Measures (SPS Agreement) provide basic rules to ensure that such measures are adopted in conformity with the principles of GATT. Although these Agreements provide increased trade scrutiny on national measures, they may also provide more guidance than the general GATT principles on how to perform this scrutiny, especially by referring to international standards.

The difference between technical regulations and sanitary measures lies in the objective that they pursue. The objectives of sanitary and phytosanitary measures are clearly specified. On the other hand, technical standards and regulations can have diverse objectives (open list). In this section, we will discuss the SPS Agreement.[189] In the next Section, the TBT Agreement will be addressed. It

---

[188] A good example of this problematic is the infamous trade dispute between the US, Canada and the EC concerning hormones. Indeed, the EC holds on to a regulation that restricts the sale of meat that is treated with hormones. Therefore, hormone-treated meat from the US or Canada cannot be sold in the EC. This regulation was found to be violating art. III GATT. See Appellate Body Report: European Communities – Measures Concerning Meat and Meat Products (Hormones), WT/DS26 and 48/AB/R (16 January 1998).

[189] See on this subject: M. IYNEDJIAN, *L'accord de l'Organisation mondiale du commerce sur l'application des mesures sanitaires et phytosanitaires: une analyse juridique*, (Paris, L.G.D.J. 2002), xiv + 262 p.; D. MACLAREN, *Trade Barriers and Food Safety Standards*, (Melbourne, University of Melbourne 2003), 11 p.; G. MARCEAU and J. TRACHTMAN, 'The Technical Barriers to Trade Agreement, the Sanitary and Phytosanitary Measures Agreement, and the General Agreement on Tariffs and Trade: a Map of the World Trade Organization Law of Domestic Regulation of Goods', *Journal of World Trade* (2002), pp. 811–881; M.M. SLOTBOOM, 'The Hormones Case: an Increased Risk of Illegality of Sanitary and Phytosanitary Measures', *C.M.L. Rev.* (1999), pp. 471–491.; G. STANTON, *The Multilateral Trading System and the SPS Agreement*, (Geneva, WTO 2000), p. 19; P. VERGANO, 'The Sanitary and Phytosanitary

should be noted that the SPS Agreement is a *lex specialis* when compared to the TBT Agreement. Article 1.5 of the TBT Agreement clearly states that the provisions of that agreement do not apply to sanitary and phytosanitary measures, as they are defined under the SPS Agreement.

94. The SPS Agreement covers measures a Member adopts (a) to protect animal and plant life or health from pests, diseases, disease-carrying and -causing organisms; (b) to protect human and animal life against additives, contaminants, toxins or disease-causing organisms in food; (c) to protect human life or health from risks from diseases that can be carried by plants or animals or (d) from the spread of pests.[190] SPS measures that conform to the disciplines in the SPS Agreement are presumed to comply with the GATT provisions, especially Article XX (b) GATT.[191] The disciplines that the SPS Agreement imposes can be considered twofold. On the one hand, there are provisions that contain a prohibition to discriminate. On the other hand, there are provisions that go beyond discrimination.

SPS measures cannot arbitrarily or unjustifiably discriminate between Members where identical conditions prevail or can be applied in a manner which would constitute a disguised restriction on international trade.[192] There is thus first of all an obligation that such measures cannot discriminate. What is more, the SPS Agreement also requires WTO Members to be consistent in their policies to protect human life or health and animal and plant life or health.[193] Although the preamble of the SPS Agreement seems to support the claim that no Member should be prevented from setting the own level of acceptable risk and the Appellate Body has confirmed this in the context of Article XX(b) (also concerning health),[194] it seems that WTO Members are nevertheless required to choose this level in a consistent way in separate situations. It is indeed feared that such distinctions in the levels of protection would lead to discrimination or disguised restrictions of trade. However, the Appellate Body stated that this requirement can go too far. Requiring that a Member takes measures in *every* situation where there is a comparable risk would require "such a comprehensive and massive

---

Agreement', *ERA Forum* (2001), pp. 118–128.; P. WALKENHORST, *The SPS Process and Developing Countries*, (Paris, OECD 2003), 20 p. and M. WYNTER, 'The Agreement on Sanitary and Phytosanitary Measures in the Light of the WTO Decisions on EC Measures Concerning Meat and Meat Products (Hormones)', in P. MENGOZZI (ed.), *International Trade Law on the 50th Anniversary of the Multilateral Trading System*, (Milan, A. Guiffrè 1999), pp. 471–526.

[190] Annex A.1 SPS Agreement.
[191] Art. 2.4 SPS Agreement.
[192] *Ibid.* art. 2.3.
[193] *Ibid.* art. 5.5.
[194] Appellate Body Report: European Communities – Measures Affecting Asbestos and Asbestos-Containing Products, WT/DS135/AB/R, (5 April 2001), para. 168.

governmental intervention [...] as to reduce the comparison itself to an absurdity".[195] It would indeed require too much of a government if the fact that it is trying to protect its citizens in one area (e.g. hormones in beef), would mean that it has to do so consistently in *every* other area where there is a risk (e.g. natural hormones in milk, or even added hormones in pork).

Nevertheless, contrary to the GATT, the SPS Agreement is not solely a regime that is based on the prohibition of discrimination. The Agreement imposes positive obligations upon Members, thereby going beyond a system of 'negative integration'. In order to be in compliance with the SPS Agreement, the measures can only be applied to the extent that they are (i) necessary to protect health; (ii) based on scientific principles and (iii) not maintained without sufficient scientific advice.[196] With regard to the *first aspect*, it seems that a so-called 'necessity test' becomes thus part of the claim challenging the SPS measure. The SPS measures must not be "more trade restrictive than required to achieve their appropriate level of protection, taking into account technical and economic feasibility".[197] With regard to the division of the burden of proof, the necessity test in the SPS Agreement stands in contrast with Article XX GATT. Whereas for the latter, necessity is part of the *defence* by the challenged Party, for the SPS Agreement, a *complaining* Party has the burden to prove that the defendant has not complied with its obligations under the SPS Agreement. The complainant has to show three elements: (a) a significantly[198] less trade-restrictive measure was (b) reasonably available taking into account technical and economic feasibility and (c) would be able to achieve the appropriate level of protection.[199] It is not entirely clear whether a Panel or the Appellate Body is allowed to question the level of protection chosen by the WTO Member. As has been stated above, WTO Members are free to choose the appropriate level of protection as long as this is done in a consistent way. It therefore does not seem possible that the level that is chosen is called into question. Nevertheless, it has been stated above with regard to the test in Article XX GATT (*supra* para. 75) that the Appellate Body introduced a test of weighing and balancing of the vitality of the interest against the trade effects. For the same reason as stated there (too large a leeway for WTO Members makes the test nugatory), the test under the SPS Agreement may also involve the questioning of

---

[195] Appellate Body Report: European Communities – Measures Concerning Meat and Meat Products (Hormones), WT/DS26 and 48/AB/R (16 January 1998), para. 221.
[196] Art. 2.2 SPS Agreement.
[197] *Ibid.* art. 5.6.
[198] This reference to the fact that an alternative must be 'significantly' less restrictive, gives WTO Members some leeway in selecting the appropriate measure to pursue the objective. See F. ORTINO, 'From 'non-discrimination' to 'reasonableness': a paradigm shift in international economic law?', *Jean Monnet Working Paper* 01/05 (April 2005), pp. 42–43, available at www.jeanmonnetprogram.org.
[199] Footnote 3 SPS Agreement.

the vitality of the objective and thus the level of protection.[200] Still, given the fact that SPS measures pursue objectives (health) the vitality of which may in many cases be relatively more obvious than for some other measures under Articles XX or TBT measures (e.g. the prevention of deceptive practices), it may be argued that the intensiveness of the scrutiny into the level of protection may be much less under the SPS Agreement than under Article XX GATT or the TBT Agreement.

The *second and third aspects* introduce the element of scientific evidence, which plays an essential role in the SPS Agreement. In principle, Members must base their sanitary or phytosanitary measures on existing international standards, guidelines and recommendations[201] that are drafted by international organizations in which they should play a full part.[202] This should result in a wide harmonization of these measures while, at the same time, the right and duty of Members to protect the life and health of their people are recognized and safeguarded.[203] The reference to international standards makes a link between the WTO and the work of international standard-setting organizations. If the measures are not solely based on international standards, but are conform to them[204], they are (refutably) presumed to be consistent with the provision of the SPS Agreement as well as those of GATT.[205] However, if a Member wants to impose a higher standard, it has to justify this with sufficient scientific justification.[206] Providing such scientific justification is often difficult, especially for developing countries. This contributes to the importance of the international standards and may indeed lead to regulatory convergence among WTO Members. Annex A.3 of the SPS Agreement indicates the specific international standards, guidelines and recommendations to which

---

[200] See J. TRACHTMAN, 'Lessons for GATS Article VI from the SPS, TBT and GATT Treatment of Domestic Regulation' (29 January 2002), available at http://papers.ssrn.com/sol3/papers.cfm?abstract_id=298760, p. 13.

[201] *Ibid.* art. 3.1.

[202] *Ibid.* art. 3.4. This is why the EC has acceded the '*Codex Alimentarius Commission*' in 2003. This Commission, which is based in Rome, develops standards for food safety. See Council Decision 2003/822/EC of 17 November 2003 on the accession of the European Community to the Codex Alimentarius Commission, O.J., 2003, L 309/14. Note that Annex A.3(d) of the SPS Agreement requires only that the relevant international organizations are "open for membership to all Members". It is thus not required that all WTO Members are in fact members of this organization. See also, for TBT: Annex 1.4.

[203] Appellate Body Report: European Communities – Measures Concerning Meat and Meat Products (Hormones), WT/DS26 and 48/AB/R (16 January 1998), para. 177.

[204] To underline the difference, the Appellate Body stated that: "A measure that 'conforms to' and incorporates a Codex standard is, of course, 'based on' that standard. A measure, however, based on the same standard might not conform to that standard, as where only some, not all, of the elements of the standard are incorporated into the measure." Appellate Body Report: European Communities – Measures Concerning Meat and Meat Products (Hormones), WT/DS26 and 48/AB/R (16 January 1998), para. 163.

[205] Art. 3.2 SPS Agreement.

[206] *Ibid.* art. 3.3.

the national measures should conform in order to be presumed consistent. This list is exhaustive[207], but the SPS Committee can identify other international organizations that promulgate appropriate standards if their membership is open to all WTO Members.[208] Three international standard-setting agencies are listed: the Codex Alimentarius Commission[209], the International Office of Epizootics[210] and the Secretariat of the International Plant Protection Convention.[211][212] Furthermore, a Member has to perform a *risk assessment* in order to define the appropriate level of protection.[213] In this assessment, Members must take into account available scientific evidence.[214] If the State cannot find sufficient scientific evidence for its measure, but still thinks a serious risk is possible, it may provisionally adopt sanitary or phytosanitary measures on the basis of the available pertinent information.[215] It concerns an application of the precautionary principle.[216]

95. Whereas under the TBT Agreement, technical regulations always have to be applied on an MFN basis, measures can be adopted under the SPS Agreement that are more or less stringent according to the origin of the good. The criterion is indeed the presence of a specific disease or pest in a country or a specific region of this country.[217]

C. AGREEMENT ON TECHNICAL BARRIERS TO TRADE

96. Because of the numerous agreements and concessions that have been made in the framework of GATT and the WTO over the years, it is much more difficult for Members to protect their own production. Quantitative restrictions are in principle prohibited and tariffs are gradually being reduced to a minimum.

---

[207] M. IYNEDJIAN, *supra* note 189, p. 60.
[208] Annex A.3 (d) SPS Agreement.
[209] See www.codexalimentarius.net.
[210] See www.oie.int
[211] International Plant Protection Convention, done at Rome on 6 December 1951, *UNTS* no. 1963, 13742.
[212] Annex A.3 (a)–(c) SPS Agreement.
[213] Art. 5 SPS Agreement.
[214] *Ibid.* art. 5.2.
[215] *Ibid.* art. 5.7.
[216] Yet, the precautionary principle "has not been written into the SPS Agreement as a ground for justifying SPS measures that are otherwise inconsistent with the obligations of Members set out in the particular provisions of that Agreement." It is also unclear whether the precautionary principle is a rule of customary international law. See Appellate Body Report: European Communities – Measures Concerning Meat and Meat Products (Hormones), WT/DS26 and 48/AB/R (16 January 1998), para. 123.
[217] Art. 6 SPS Agreement.

Therefore, Members adopt ever more often measures that set certain requirements for products and by which certain foreign products are (on purpose or not) shielded from the domestic market. It concerns technical regulations and standards that fix specific characteristics of a product, such as the size, shape, design, functions and performance or the way it is labelled or packaged before it is put on sale. Whereas compliance with standards is voluntary, technical regulations are obligatory: when they are not followed, the product cannot be sold on the market.[218] The Agreement on Technical Barriers to Trade (TBT Agreement) contains the basic rules for such measures. The TBT Agreement and the SPS Agreement are two different agreements with a distinct scope. The provisions of the TBT Agreement do not apply to sanitary and phytosanitary measures.[219]

97. In principle, each State has the right to adopt technical regulations and standards, ensuring a protection level as it considers appropriate. Nevertheless, the TBT Agreement reiterates the obligations of National Treatment and Most Favoured Nation[220] and thus first of all imposes a prohibition of discrimination. Yet, as is the case for the SPS Agreement, this regime is not solely one of non-discrimination. Even if they are non-discriminatory, the technical measures cannot be more trade restrictive than necessary to fulfil a legitimate objective[221] and can only be adopted after an assessment of the risks. Again, a 'necessity test' will need to be performed. Like for the SPS Agreement, a complainant will need to show that (a) a less trade restrictive measures is (b) reasonably available and (c) fulfils the WTO Member's legitimate objective.[222] In performing the test, a Panel or the Appellate Body needs to take account of the "risks non-fulfilment [of the objective] would create". This may point to the fact that a 'weighing and balancing' of interests will take place. The vitality of the legitimate objective that is pursued is then determined by the magnitude and probability of the risk.[223] In this respect, scientific evidence is only one of the relevant elements that should be considered next to, among others, technical information, technology or end-uses of products.

---

[218] See Annex 1.1 and 1.2 TBT Agreement.
[219] Art. 1.5 TBT Agreement. For the difference between the types of measures, see *supra* para. 93.
[220] *Ibid.* art. 2.1.
[221] *Ibid.* art. 2.2. Technical regulations cannot be maintained if there is a less trade-restrictive measure available because of the changed circumstances or objectives. See art. 2.3.
[222] Although the wording of art. 2.2 TBT Agreement differs from that of art. 2.2 *juncto* art. 5.6 SPS Agreement, we agree with DESMEDT and ORTINO that the basic three pillars of the test are the same. See A. DESMEDT, 'Proportionality in WTO Law', *Journal of International Economic Law* (2001), pp. 441–480, at pp. 458–459 and F. ORTINO, 'From 'non-discrimination' to 'reasonableness': a paradigm shift in international economic law?', *Jean Monnet Working Paper* 01/05 (April 2005), pp. 42–43, available at www.jeanmonnetprogram.org.
[223] See J. TRACHTMAN, 'Lessons for GATS Article VI from the SPS, TBT and GATT Treatment of Domestic Regulation' (29 January 2002), available at http://papers.ssrn.com/sol3/papers.cfm?abstract_id=298760, p. 13.

Indeed, scientific evidence plays a less prominent role under the TBT Agreement than under the SPS Agreement. This is also apparent in the provisions on international standards, where no mention is made of scientific justification. Members must use relevant existing international standards (or those of which completion is imminent) as a basis for[224] their technical regulations, except when these would be ineffective or inappropriate[225] to achieve the legitimate objective.[226] If the regulation is in accordance with relevant international standards, it must be rebuttably presumed not to create an unnecessary obstacle to international trade.[227]

98. The wording of the 'necessity test' in the TBT Agreement is somewhat different from the SPS Agreement in the sense that it is stated that the measure in question must be necessary to fulfil a legitimate objective. As has been stated above (*supra* para. 93), SPS measures can only pursue the 'human life or health' – and 'animal and plant life or health' – objectives that are explicitly stated in the SPS Agreement. On the other hand, the TBT Agreement has an open list of legitimate objectives. Because of this reference, it seems that the legitimacy of the objective that is pursued by a TBT measure may be called into question.[228] It recognizes several legitimate objectives for a technical regulation or standard. Most regulations are designed to protect human safety or health, but also animal and plant life and health as well as the environment in general can be protected by technical regulations. Furthermore, these regulations often try to avoid confusion with consumers.

99. Since a new regulation may often have important consequences for the export to other Members, Article 2.9 TBT Agreement requires WTO Members to notify their technical regulations as clearly as possible.

---

[224] Similar to what was said in the Hormones case (*supra* note 204) a Panel held that 'as a basis for' means that "Members are to use a relevant international standard as "the principle constituent… or fundamental principle" and does not mean that Members must conform to or comply with that relevant international standard." See Panel Report: European Communities – Trade Description of Sardines, WT/DS231/R, (29 May 2002), para. 7.78. This was confirmed by the Appellate Body.

[225] The effectiveness is "the capacity of a measure to accomplish the stated objectives"; the appropriateness is "the suitability of a measure for the fulfillment of the stated objectives." See Appellate Body Report: European Communities – Trade Description of Sardines, WT/DS231/AB/R, (26 September 2002), para. 289.

[226] Art. 2.4 TBT Agreement.

[227] *Ibid.* art. 2.5.

[228] It has been noted, however, that this is difficult to reconcile with the 6th paragraph of the Preamble of the TBT Agreement, which states that each WTO Member can set the protection "at the levels it considers appropriate." See A. DESMEDT, *supra* note 222, at pp. 458–460.

100. An important aspect of technical regulations is the 'conformity assessment procedures'. At the time of importation of a product, it has to be assessed whether a product complies with the technical regulations that apply in the importing country. These procedures may constitute a sizeable cost to the import, both in time and money. Therefore, members have to ensure that their conformity assessment procedure is not applied more stringently than necessary to assure that the product complies with the regulations. In this way, the procedure no longer constitutes an unnecessary barrier to trade. In this respect, the risks of non-conformity must be taken into account.[229] To this end, the European Community has concluded several agreements for mutual recognition of conformity assessment procedures.[230]

D. AGREEMENT ON SAFEGUARDS

101. If, because of the concessions Members have made, unforeseen developments result in such increased imports of certain products that domestic producers of like or directly competitive products suffer or threaten to suffer serious injury, the importing Member is allowed to adopt measures to prevent or remedy such injury.[231] This is the so-called GATT 'escape clause' in Article XIX GATT. Safeguard Measures may seem outright protectionist. However, it has been argued that the GATT and WTO law on safeguards is a way to ensure that such measures at least are disciplined and only temporary. Thus they function as a 'safety valve' to ensure that the unavoidable protectionist pressure within States is channelled through measures that are controlled. Moreover, States are more willing to commit themselves to trade concessions if they know they can in certain cases adopt safeguard measures.[232]

---

[229] Art. 5.1.2 TBT Agreement.
[230] It concerns agreements that accept examinations in order to define to what extent a product, process or service complies with specific requirements as equivalent. These agreements, concluded because of art. 6 TBT, remove an important barrier to trade. See especially the Agreement on Mutual Recognition between the European Community and the United States of America, done at London on 18 May 1998, O.J., 1999, L 31/4; Agreement on Mutual Recognition between the European Community and Canada, done at London on 14 May 1998, O.J., 1998, L 280/3; Agreement on Mutual Recognition in relation to Conformity Assessment between the European Community and New Zealand, done at Wellington on 25 June 1998, O.J., 1998, L 229/62 and Agreement on Mutual Recognition in relation to Conformity Assessment, Certificates and Markings between the European Community and Australia, done at Canberra on 24 June 1998, O.J., 1998, L 229/3.
[231] Art. XIX GATT.
[232] See the extensive discussion in A. SYKES, 'Protectionism as a "Safeguard": A Positive Analysis of the GATT "Escape Clause" with Normative Speculations', *University of Chicago Law Review* (1991), pp. 255–299 and A. SYKES, 'The Persistent Puzzles of Safeguards: Lessons from the Steel Dispute', *Journal of International Economic Law* (2004), pp. 523–564, at pp. 524–525.

102. In principle, a Member must do this in accordance with the Most Favoured Nation principle. This implies that the measures (*inter alia* the suspension of concessions) have to be applied to all WTO Members (also the ones that do not export so intensively to the country concerned). This was one of the reasons why during the GATT era, States preferred to make use of other instruments to protect their markets against such import surges, thereby circumventing the MFN principle. States often used 'voluntary export restraints', where an exporting country agreed not to export above a certain threshold. Voluntary export restraints not only violate Article XIX GATT, but also Article XI and Article I. Moreover, Article XIX required the State that wanted to impose a safeguard to negotiate compensation with the affected countries.[233] If such negotiations were unsuccessful, the affected States could themselves suspend their own concessions to an equivalent level.[234] This was another reason why countries preferred to rely on voluntary export restraints. Nevertheless, no dispute occurred in which a GATT Party challenged such export restraints. This was due to the fact that, during the GATT era, there was a need for consensus to establish a Panel. What is more, States that voluntarily restrict their exports obtain 'monopoly rents' because, in that way, they keep the prices of their products high. In order to curtail this evolution, the Agreement on Safeguards has made it possible to adopt safeguards that only target a Member that exports a large volume to the country concerned.

103. The Safeguards Agreement explicitly prohibits voluntary export restraints.[235] In order to adopt safeguards, four requirements must be fulfilled. A domestic investigating authority must show that (i) as a result of unforeseen developments (ii) imports in increased quantities (iii) have caused or threatened to cause (iv) injury to the domestic industry producing the like product.[236] The requirement of 'unforeseen developments' does not figure anywhere in the Agreement on Safeguards, but is mentioned in Article XIX GATT, with which the safeguard measures also have to comply.[237] The requirement of 'unforeseen developments' stipulates that the injury to domestic producers must have been 'unexpected'.[238] This means that it would not be reasonable to expect at the time

---

[233] Art. XIX.2 GATT.
[234] *Ibid.* art. XIX.3.
[235] Art. 11.1 (b) Agreement on Safeguards.
[236] *Ibid.* art. 2.1.
[237] Appellate Body Report: Korea – Definitive Safeguard Measures on Imports of Certain Dairy Products, WT/DS98/AB/R (14 December 1999), para. 80 and Appellate Body Report: Argentina – Safeguard Measures on Imports of Footwear, WT/DS121/AB/R, (14 December 1999), paras. 83-84.
[238] Appellate Body Report: Korea – Definitive Safeguard Measure on Imports of Certain Dairy Products, WT/DS98/AB/R, (14 December 1999), para. 84.

of the last negotiation[239] of tariff concessions that such a development could occur in the future. Second, as a result of these unforeseen developments, there have to be imports in increased quantities. The determination of whether this is the case is "not a merely mathematical or technical determination. In other words, it is not enough for an investigation to show simply that imports of the product this year were more than last year – or five years ago".[240] The increase needs to be recent, but it is unclear how recent it has to be.[241] Linked to this and pointing to the level of increase, as a third condition, the increase in imports must be *such as to* cause *serious injury or threat* of serious injury. The standard of 'serious injury' is very high and connotes a much higher standard of injury than in the Agreement on Subsidies and Countervailing Measures (*infra* Section III.1.E).[242] A 'threat of serious injury' must be 'clearly imminent', *i.e.* "on the very verge of occurring".[243] The injury has to be done to the domestic industry producing the like or directly competitive product. Article 4.2, a) of the Safeguards Agreement lists a number of factors to consider when one determines what constitutes a serious injury. A State that is willing to impose a safeguard needs to have discussed one or more of these factors in its report on the safeguard action.[244] The fourth, and final, condition for safeguard actions is the requirement of a causal link between the increased imports and the serous injury. It is not required that the "increased imports must be 'sufficient' to cause, or threaten to cause, serious injury". Nor is it required that "increased imports 'alone' be capable of causing, or threatening to cause, serious injury".[245] However, if the increased imports have not contributed to the injury at all, no case for safeguards can be made. The causation condition implies that the injury would not have occurred *but for* the import surge.

The domestic investigating authorities can impose safeguard measures only to redress the extent of the injury caused by imports.[246] A Member can apply the safeguard measures only for the time necessary to prevent or remedy the serious

---

[239] See Panel Report: United States – Definitive Safeguard Measures on Imports of Certain Steel Products, WT/DS248-49, 251-54 and 258-59/R (11 July 2003), para. 10.74.
[240] Appellate Body Report: Argentina – Safeguard Measures on Imports of Footwear, WT/DS121/AB/R, (14 December 1999), para. 129.
[241] See P. MARTIN RODRIGUEZ, 'Safeguards in the World Trade Organization Ten Years After: A Dissociated State of the Law?', *Journal of World Trade* (2007), pp. 159–190, at p. 163.
[242] Appellate Body Report: United States: Safeguard Measures on Imports of Fresh, Chilled or Frozen Lamb Meat from New Zealand and Australia, WT/DS177 and 178/AB/R, (1 May 2001), para. 124.
[243] *Ibid.* para. 125.
[244] Appellate Body Report: Argentina – Safeguard Measures on Imports of Footwear, WT/DS121/AB/R, (14 December 1999), para. 139.
[245] *Ibid.* para. 170.
[246] Art. 5.1 Agreement on Safeguards. See Appellate Body Report: United States – Definitive Safeguard Measures on Imports of Circular Welded Carbon Quality Line Pipe from Korea, WT/DS202/AB/R, (15 February 2002), paras. 241–260.

injury and for a maximum of four years. Yet, this maximum period can be extended for an additional period of maximum four years.[247] Like Article XIX.2 GATT, the Safeguards Agreement requires the Member that wants to impose a safeguard measure to negotiate trade compensation.[248] Nevertheless, contrary to what is the case under Article XIX.3 GATT, if these negotiations are unsuccessful, the affected Members can only adopt equivalent suspension of concessions after three years in which the safeguard measure was in effect.[249] This is an important incentive for Members to agree to compensation, at least at a lower level than what was the case under Article XIX GATT.[250]

Safeguards have to be applied on an MFN basis. However, safeguards in the form of quantitative restrictions can be allocated according to the market shares of the exporters in the previous representative period.[251] Moreover, it is even possible to address specifically those imports from countries that affect the domestic industry disproportionately.[252]

E. AGREEMENT ON SUBSIDIES AND COUNTERVAILING MEASURES

104. The GATT does not prevent the payment of subsidies exclusively to domestic producers.[253] When the WTO was established in 1994, Members also adopted a multilateral agreement on Subsidies and Countervailing Measures (SCM Agreement), targeting trade distortive subsidies as well as regulating the response by other countries on subsidization (imposition of countervailing duties).[254] Contrary to what is the case for safeguards, where 'fair trade' measures

---

[247] Art. 7.1 and 7.3 Agreement on Safeguards.
[248] *Ibid.* art. 8.1.
[249] *Ibid.* art. 8.3.
[250] See A. Sykes, 'The Persistent Puzzles of Safeguards: Lessons from the Steel Dispute', *Journal of International Economic Law* (2004), pp. 523–564, at p. 537.
[251] See Art. 5.2 a) Agreement on Safeguards.
[252] *Ibid.* art. 5.2 b).
[253] Art. III.8 (b) GATT. This is an exception to the principle of National Treatment. Note that the GATT 1947 was very lenient towards subsidies: Art. XVI only required the GATT Contracting Parties to notify subsidies that were export stimulating or import reducing. Upon request, the State was required to "discuss" with the other Contracting Parties concerned the possibility of limiting the subsidization where it may cause serious prejudice to the other Parties. It was possible that affected Parties imposed countervailing duties up to the amount of the subsidy when it was determined that the subsidy caused material injury to the domestic industry. See art. VI.6, a) GATT. The exact procedures for such determination were not defined, however.
[254] See *inter alia* T. Becker, *Das WTO Subventionsübereinkommen: Einfluß auf die Rechtsschutzmöglichkeiten Dritter gegen Beihilfen im Rahmen des EG Rechts*, (Frankfurt am Main, Lang 2001), 292 p.: M. Bénitah, The Law of Subsidies under the GATT/WTO System, (The Hague, Kluwer Law International 2001), xii + 424 p.; J. Bourgeois, *Subsidies and*

could be tackled in emergency situations, but similar to the Agreement on Antidumping (see *infra* para. 108), the SCM Agreement addresses 'unfair' trade measures.[255] Again it was clear that subsidies could not – and should not – be entirely abolished. Only trade distortive subsidies are targeted. Neither could and should the use of countervailing measures be eliminated. It was therefore decided to regulate their use.[256]

105.   A subsidy can be described as a financial contribution by a government which confers a benefit to a recipient.[257] Moreover, in order to be subject to the SCM Agreement such a subsidy should be specific, in the sense that it must be granted to an enterprise, or industry, or group of enterprises or industries.[258] One can thus discern two elements in the definition: first a financial contribution by a government is made, second a benefit is conferred. In addition, the benefit must be specific. As to the first element, it should be noted that the requirement of a financial contribution by a government prevents any government measure from which some actors benefit and others not and thereby distort trade from coming under scrutiny of the SCM Agreement. Still, the concept of '*financial contribution by a government*' is broad and consists of three situations: (i) a direct transfer of funds by the government; (ii) government revenue that is otherwise due is foregone or not collected and (iii) the government provides goods or services other than general infrastructure, or purchase of goods.[259] In particular, situation (ii) is

---

International Trade: A European Lawyer's Perspective, (Deventer, Kluwer 1991), ix + 214 p.; C. Grave, *Der Begriff der Subvention im WTO-Übereinkommen über Subventionen und Ausgleichsmaßnahmen*, (Berlin, Dunker & Humblot 2002), 306 p.; R. Luja, *Assessment and Recovery of Tax Incentives in the EC and the WTO: A View on State Aids, Trade Subsidies and Direct Taxation*, (Antwerp, Intersentia 2003), xii + 311 p.; A. Reich, 'Institutional and Substantive Reform of the Antidumping and Subsidy Agreements: Lessons from the Israeli Experience', *Journal of World Trade* (2003), pp. 1037–1061; T. Rice, 'Farmgate: the Developmental Impacts of Agricultural Subsidies', *in* H. Katrak and R. Strange, *The WTO and Developing Countries*, (Basingstoke, Palgrave Macmillan 2004), pp. 233–256; M. Sánchez Rydelski, *EG und WTO Antisubventionsrecht: ein konzeptioneller Vergleich der EG Antisubventions-Verordnung mit den Beihilfevorschriften des EG-Vertrages unter Berücksichtigung des Subventionsübereinkommens der WTO*, (Baden-Baden, Nomos 2001), 355 p. and T.P. Stewart and A.S. Dwyer, *WTO Antidumping and Subsidy Agreements: a Practitioner's Guide to "Sunset" Reviews in Australia, Canada, the European Union, and the United States*, (The Hague, Kluwer 1998), xv + 268 p.

[255] Appellate Body Report: United States – Definitive Safeguard Measures on Imports of Circular Welded Carbon Quality Line Pipe From Korea, WT/DS202/AB/R, (15 February 2002), para. 80.
[256] Appellate Body Report: United States – Final Countervailing Duty Determination with Respect to Certain Softwood Lumber from Canada, WT/DS257/AB/R (19 January 2004), para. 64.
[257] Art. 1 SCM Agreement.
[258] *Ibid.* art. 2. This is an exhaustive list: See Panel Report: United States – Measures Treating Export Restraints as Subsidies, WT/DS194/R (29 June 2001), para. 8.28–8.29.
[259] Art. 1.1 (a)(1) SCM Agreement.

contentious. If a Member levies duties or imposes taxes on certain foreign goods while exempting other goods from these charges, this can be qualified as a subsidy under the SCM Agreement if it provides a benefit.[260] Hence, there is a subsidy if the tax would be due *but for* the exemption that is granted. Yet, because of the complexity of tax systems, it is not always possible to define the general rule and the exception.[261] This leads to a different test: a comparison should be made between the situation at hand (where allegedly a subsidy is granted) and the fiscal treatment of legitimately comparable income.[262] Indeed, in cases where it is not possible to compare the exceptional situation at hand with the more general legal situation, it would be necessary to compare the situation at hand with the situation that would have been at hand if the State had not made the policy decision to apply a different tax rule to this situation.[263] It then in fact concerns an examination on the appropriateness of the categorization a State makes of the different situations.[264] The financial contribution should be granted *by a government* or by *private bodies that are entrusted or directed by the government to perform one of the actions in (i)-(iii)*. The subsidies can thus also be granted through private bodies, but some government control will need to be established.[265] As to the

---

[260] It has to be established that the latter goods would normally be subjected to the charges, thus that revenue is foregone that is 'otherwise due' (see art. 1.1 (a)(1), (ii) SCM Agreement). This will be determined on the basis of the tax rules applied by Member in question. See Appellate Body Report: United States – Tax Treatment of Foreign Sales Corporations, WT/DS108/AB/R, (24 February 2000), paras. 88-92. Importantly, a subsidy that is exclusively granted to domestic industries is only exempted from the National Treatment obligation (pursuant to Article III.8 (b) GATT) if it involves *direct* government expenditure. In contrast, tax that is foregone by the State will qualify as a subsidy under the SCM Agreement, but will still have to comply with the National Treatment obligation of Article III GATT. Consequently, such subsidies cannot be limited to domestic industries. Appellate Body Report: Canada – Certain Measures Concerning Periodicals, WT/DS31/AB/R, (30 July 1997), pp. 32-35. See S. DE BOER, 'Trading Culture: The Canada-US Magazine Dispute', *in* J. CAMERON and K. CAMPBELL (eds.), *Dispute Resolution in the WTO*, (London, Cameron May 1998), p. 246. See, on the relation between Article III and the SCM Agreement, Panel Report: Indonesia – Certain Measures Affecting the Automobile Industry, WT/DS54, 55, 59 and 64/R, (2 July 1998), paras. 14.33-14.36 and 14.39-14.40.
[261] Appellate Body Report: United States – Tax Treatment of Foreign Sales Corporations, WT/DS108/AB/R, (24 February 2000), para. 91.
[262] Appellate Body Report: United States – Tax Treatment of Foreign Sales Corporations, Recourse to Article 21.5 of the DSU by the European Communities, WT/DS108/AB/RW, (14 January 2002), para. 91.
[263] *Ibid.* paras. 98-102.
[264] See J. TRACHTMAN: "In the final analysis, it involves panels and the Appellate Body in determining whether to respect or disrespect regulatory categories established by government, with few guiding principles." J. TRACHTMAN, 'United States – Tax Treatment of Foreign Sales Corporations – Recourse to Article 21.5 of the DSU by the European Communities', *European Journal of International* (2002), available on http://www.ejil.org/journal/curdevs/sr32.html.
[265] See Panel Report: Korea – Measures Affecting Commercial Vessels, WT/DS273/R (7 March 2005), paras. 7.352-7.356 and Appellate Body Report: United States – Countervailing Duty Investigations on Dynamic Random Access Memory Semiconductors (DRAMS) From Korea, WT/DS296/AB/R (27 June 2005), para. 116.

second element in the definition, there will be a *benefit* for a "person, natural or legal, or a group of persons"[266], if this person or group of persons would not be able to achieve this under the same conditions on the market. This is the so-called 'private investor' test. The conduct of the State is compared with that of a private investor. If the government behaves in the same way, the recipient of the alleged benefit is not better off than it would have been otherwise.[267] Nevertheless, if no such comparison can be made (for instance because there exists no market on which the contribution could be obtained or because the market is distorted due to the presence of the government), the Appellate Body stated that other than private prices in the country of provision may be used.[268] Such alternative benchmarks "could include proxies that take into account prices for similar goods quoted on world markets, or proxies constructed on the basis of production costs". The Appellate Body emphasized, however, "that where an investigating authority proceeds in this manner, it is under an obligation to ensure that the resulting benchmark relates or refers to, or is connected with, prevailing market conditions in the country of provision, and must reflect price, quality, availability, marketability, transportation and other conditions of purchase or sale, as required by Article 14(d) [of the SCM Agreement]".[269]

In order to be subject to obligations of the SCM Agreement, such a financial contribution by the government that confers a benefit should also be *'specific'* to an 'enterprise or industry or group of enterprises or industries'.[270] The category of *prohibited subsidies* (*i.e.* export subsidies and local content subsidies) is presumed to be specific.[271] Article 2 of the SCM Agreement sets out a number of principles to define whether a subsidy is specific.

Subsidies are *prohibited* only if they are contingent upon export performance or upon local content requirements.[272] These two types of prohibited subsidies are considered to be 'specific' and should thus not pass the specificity test.[273] The contingency implies that the subsidy is 'conditional' or 'depending for its existence on' export or local content.[274] An illustrative (*i.e.* non-exhaustive) list of export

---

[266] Appellate Body Report: Canada – Measures Affecting the Export of Civilian Aircraft, WT/DS70/AB/R (2 August 1999), para. 156.
[267] *Ibid.* para. 157.
[268] Appellate Body Report: United States: Final Countervailing Duty Determination with Respect to Certain Softwood Lumber from Canada, WT/DS236/AB/R (19 January 2004), para. 103.
[269] *Ibid.* para. 106.
[270] Art. 2.1 SCM Agreement.
[271] *Ibid.* art. 2.3.
[272] *Ibid.* art. 3.
[273] *Ibid.* art. 2.3.
[274] Appellate Body Report: Canada – Measures Affecting the Export of Civilian Aircraft, WT/DS70/AB/R (2 August 1999), para. 166. The conditionality can be *de jure* or *de facto*. With

subsidies is included in Annex I of the SCM Agreement. Local content subsidies are subsidies contingent on the use of domestic input and therefore create trade distortion of the input industry. Other specific subsidies are not prohibited, but are *'actionable'* by Members that experience 'adverse effects' because of this subsidy. The 'adverse effects' may be demonstrated in three ways[275]: (i) there is an injury[276] to the domestic industry; (ii) there is nullification or impairment of benefits accruing to WTO Members[277] or (iii) there is serious prejudice to the interests of another Member.[278] A third category of *'non-actionable'* subsidies was deleted from the SCM Agreement in March 2000.[279]

106. WTO Members may *challenge* actionable and prohibited subsidies *through the WTO dispute settlement system.* There are specific dispute settlement procedural rules for prohibited subsidies[280] and for actionable subsidies.[281] If a subsidy is found to be prohibited, the subsidy must be withdrawn without delay.[282] If this is not done, appropriate countermeasures can be taken.[283] These can be higher than normal under the DSU. Under Article 22.4 DSU, it is required that the countermeasures are equivalent to the level of nullification and impairment. The level of countermeasures may be up to the amount of the subsidy and is not limited to the actual injury suffered.[284] With regard to actionable subsidies, the

---

regard to export subsidies, the elements of *de facto* conditionality are defined in art. 3.1 (a) SCM Agreement. *De jure* conditionality should be 'demonstrated on the basis of the words of the relevant legislation, regulation or other legal instrument'. *Ibid.* para. 167.

[275] Art. 5 SCM Agreement.
[276] This involves material injury as well as threat of material injury. *Ibid.* art. 15, footnote 45.
[277] Contrary to what is the case for (i) (injury to the *domestic industry* of other States), this involves the adverse effects that the exporting industry of other WTO Members experiences *within the market of the subsidizing State.* Because of the subsidy to the exporting industry in the subsidizing State, the reciprocity in tariff bindings will be undermined. Indeed, tariff bindings are made with the expectation that certain trade volumes will occur. If a subsidy is allowed, the volumes will alter, and therefore also the reciprocity.
[278] The concept of 'serious prejudice' is clarified in art. 6 SCM Agreement. Art. 6.1 SCM Agreement included a rebuttable presumption of serious prejudice. Nevertheless, this provision expired in 1999, because WTO Members could not agree on the continuation (see art. 31 SCM Agreement). Even in the absence of any prior tariff commitment, WTO Members could cause adverse effects through subsidization if this results in displacing or impeding imports of another Member into the market of the subsidizing State. See A. HODA and R. AHUJA, 'Agreement on Subsidies and Countervailing Measures: Need for Clarification and Improvement', *Journal of World Trade* (2005), p. 1018. There is also prejudice if the subsidization causes the replacement of imports from one WTO Member into the subsidizing Member by imports of another Member. (See art. 6.3 SCM Agreement)
[279] *Ibid.* art. 31.
[280] *Ibid.* art. 4.
[281] *Ibid.* art. 7.
[282] *Ibid.* art. 4.7.
[283] *Ibid.* art. 4.10.
[284] See Arbitration Report: Brazil – Export Financing Programme for Aircraft, Recourse to Arbitration by Brazil under Article 22.6 of the DSU and Article 4.11 of the SCM Agreement,

subsidizing Member must take appropriate steps to remove the adverse effects or must withdraw the subsidy.[285]

Alternatively,[286] Members may, after an investigation into whether the criteria of the SCM Agreement[287] are fulfilled, impose *countervailing duties (CVDs)* on imports originating from the subsidizing Member.[288] Importantly, these CVDs can only be imposed in cases where the domestic industry of a WTO Member suffers injury because of the increased imports of the subsidized product. Obviously, countervailing duties cannot be imposed to respond to the harm of the subsidy to the exporting industries of WTO Members in a third Member. This harm is caused because they are now competing with the subsidized exports of the subsidizing Member in that third Member. Neither can CVDs be imposed when the exporting industries of WTO Members suffer from the subsidy because they have to compete with subsidized goods in the subsidizing Member. Even if no CVDs can be imposed, recourse to dispute settlement is possible in all these cases.[289] CVDs can be lawfully imposed if the Member, which is willing to impose them, shows (i) the existence of a specific subsidy; (ii) the existence of injury to its domestic industry producing the like product and (iii) a causal link between (i) and (ii).[290] An investigation must be initiated the object of which will be to demonstrate the existence of these three elements. Moreover, the investigating Member must consult with Members on the products that may be subject to investigation[291] and further during the whole investigation.[292] Article 12 SCM Agreement has specific provisions on the gathering and use of evidence. The SCM Agreement prescribes modes to be used by WTO Members in order to properly calculate the amount of the subsidy granted.[293]

WT/DS64/ARB (28 August 2000), para. 3.54. The countermeasure is indeed intended to induce States to withdraw the subsidy.

[285] Art. 7.8 SCM Agreement.

[286] Members are not allowed to impose *at the same time* countervailing measures and apply countermeasures in cases where a Member has failed to withdraw its subsidy. Challenging a subsidy is generally a more lengthy process than applying a countervailing measure. See B. HOEKMAN and P. MAVROIDIS, *supra* note 103, p. 50.

[287] Art. 5 SCM Agreement.

[288] These countervailing duties can be imposed on prohibited and actionable subsidies. Prohibited subsidies only have to be withdrawn if a Panel believes that the subsidy scheme at hand is indeed prohibited. *Ibid.* art. 4.7.

[289] Nevertheless, this is a more lengthy process. Countries that see their exports replaced on third markets by subsidized goods thus have no other choice than to engage in such lengthy process.

[290] Art. 5 and 7 SCM Agreement.

[291] *Ibid.* art. 13.1.

[292] *Ibid.* art. 13.2.

[293] *Ibid.* art. 14.

All countervailing measures may remain in force as long as necessary to counteract the subsidization[294] and have to be withdrawn no later than five years after their imposition unless the WTO Member can show the removal would amount to recurrence of injury. [295]

107. Article 27 of the SCM Agreement recognizes that 'subsidies may play an important role in economic development programmes of developing countries'[296] and spells out special and differential treatment of developing countries in the case of subsidies. Special and differential treatment is granted for one type of prohibited subsidies: export subsidies. The provisions in Article 3.1 (a) SCM Agreement that discipline such subsidies are not applicable to Least Developed Countries[297] and some specific low-income countries listed in Annex VII until their Gross National Product per capita has reached USD 1000 per annum during three consecutive years.[298] Other developing countries had eight years to phase out their export subsidies. There is a possibility, however, of requesting the SCM Committee to extend this period. The SCM Committee will then consider all relevant economic, financial and development needs and, if extension is granted, annually the necessity of maintaining these subsidies.[299] Some special and differential treatment is also provided in case of actionable subsidies. In order to stimulate privatization programmes, direct forgiveness of debts and subsidies to cover social costs directly linked to privatization cannot be challenged as actionable subsidies.[300]

It should finally be noted that the Agreement on Agriculture needs to be taken into account in the specific case of agricultural subsidies (see *infra* paras. 112–119).

---

[294] *Ibid.* art. 21.1.
[295] *Ibid.* art. 21.3.
[296] *Ibid.* art. 27.1.
[297] Annex VII (a) SCM Agreement. On the definition by the United Nations of Least Developed Countries, see *infra* para. 232.
[298] Annex VII (a) SCM Agreement *juncto* WTO Ministerial Conference Decision, Implementation-Related Issues and Concerns, WT/MIN(01)/17, 14 November 2001, para. 10.1. (the condition in Annex VII (a) is thus modified by the Doha Ministerial Conference). If the Gross National Product falls below USD 1000, the country is again allowed to maintain export subsidies. *Ibid.* para. 10.4.
[299] Art. 27.4 SCM Agreement. In its extension decision, the SCM Committee has to avoid differential treatment of countries in the same circumstances. Moreover, certain small developing countries were granted annual extensions to 2007 for export subsidy programmes in force in 2001 that provided full or partial exemptions from import duties and internal taxes. See WTO Ministerial Conference Decision, Implementation-Related Issues and Concerns, WT/MIN(01)/17, 14 November 2001, para. 10.6 *juncto* Committee on Subsidies and Countervailing Measures, Procedures for Extensions under Article 27.4 for Certain Developing Country Members, G/SCM/39, 20 November 2001.
[300] They shall be granted for a limited period of time and eventually the privatization must result. See Art. 27.13 SCM Agreement.

F. AGREEMENT ON ANTIDUMPING

108. Article VI GATT and the Agreement on Implementation of Article VI of the General Agreement on Tariffs and Trade ('Antidumping Agreement') allow WTO Members to impose 'countervailing duties' on products that are imported at less than their normal value if these imports cause injury to the domestic market.[301] Similar to the SCM Agreement, the Antidumping Agreement addresses 'unfair' trade practices. It concerns price discrimination between national markets in which a producer sells at a lower price abroad than on his home market.[302] Even if there is no home market, there may still be dumping when there is discrimination between the national markets where the product is sold.[303]

109. A product is 'dumped' if it is introduced into the commerce of another country at less than its normal value.[304] The determination of dumping depends thus on the determination of this *'normal value'*. The lower the normal value, the lower the chance that dumping will be found. The 'normal value' of the product is the comparable price, in the ordinary course of trade, for the like product when

---

[301] See *inter alia* A. BUAT, *L'antidumping: quelles améliorations pour cet instrument de défense nécessaire aux entreprises?: rapport présenté au nom de la Commission du Commerce International et adopté à l'Assemblée générale du 4 décembre 2003*, (chambre de commerce et de l'industrie de Paris, 2003), 26 p.; R. CUNNINGHAM and T. CRIBB, 'Dispute Settlement through the Lens of Free Flow of Trade: a Review of WTO Dispute Settlement of US Antidumping and Countervailing Duty Measures', *Journal of International Economic Law* (2003), pp. 155–170; J. CZAKO and J. HUMAN, *A Handbook on Antidumping Investigations*, (Cambridge, Cambridge University Press 2003), xx + 543 p.; N. DISALVO, 'Let's Dump the 1916 Antidumping Act: Why the 1994 GATT Provides Better Price Protection for the US Industries', *Vanderbilt Journal of Transnational Law* (2004), pp. 791–826; R. GREY, 'Politiques antidumping et concurrence', in UNDP, *Les initiatives des pays en développement pour les futures négociations commerciales*, (New York, United Nations 2000), pp. 517–548; J. JACKSON and E. VERMULST, *Antidumping Law and Practice: a Comparative Study*, (New York, Harvester Wheatsheaf 1990), xi + 520 p.; M.M. KOSTECKI, 'Le système antidumping et l'Uruguay Round', *Droit et Pratique du commerce international* (1991), Vol. 17 no. 2, pp. 206–225; D. Palmeter, 'A Commentary on the WTO Antidumping Code', *Journal of World Trade* (1996), pp. 43–69; E.U. PETERSMANN, 'Settlement of International and National Trade Disputes through the GATT; the Case of Antidumping Law', *Adjudication of International Trade Disputes in International and National Economic Law; Pupil*, vol. 7, 1992, pp. 77–138; B. RICHEZ, 'L'OMC et la pratique antidumping', *Revue de droit des affaires internationales* (2003), pp. 79–89; I. VAN BAEL, 'Improving GATT Disciplines relating to Antidumping Measures', *in A new GATT for the nineties and Europe '92*, (Baden-Baden, Nomos Verlag 1991), pp. 171–185; E. VERMULST and P. MIHAYLOVA, 'EC Commercial Defence Actions against Textiles from 1995 to 2000: Possible Lessons for Future Negotiations', *Journal of International Economic Law* (2001), pp. 527–555 and E. VERMULST and F. GRAAFSMA, *WTO Disputes: Antidumping, Subsidies and Safeguards*, (London, Cameron May 2002), 878 p.

[302] See E. VERMULST, *The WTO Antidumping Agreement*, (Oxford, Oxford University Press 2005), p. 1.

[303] See J. VINER, *Dumping: A Problem of International Trade*, (New York, Kelley 1966), p. 4.

[304] Art. VI.1 GATT and art. 2.1 Antidumping Agreement.

destined for consumption in the exporting country. Four elements can be discerned in this definition. First, the sales that are relied on to define the normal value must be made *in the ordinary course of trade*. Sales made to affiliated parties may[305] be considered as outside the ordinary course of trade. This may result in prices that are either higher or lower than the 'ordinary course' price, and both may distort normal value.[306] Also sales below cost may be discarded as being outside the ordinary course of trade.[307] Second, the sales that are relied on must be for *like products*. According to Article 2.6 of the Antidumping Agreement, a like product is 'a product which is identical, *i.e.* alike in all respects to the product under consideration, or in the absence of such product, another product which, although not alike in all respects, has characteristics closely resembling those of the product under consideration'. Third, the like products that are considered must be *destined for consumption in the exporting country*. Fourth, the prices in the exporting and importing Member must be *comparable*. This often means that they need to be adjusted to be at the same level (mostly *ex factory*).

If there is no such local price in the country of export[308], two alternative methods for calculating the 'normal value' are available. First, there is dumping when the import price is lower than the comparable price of the like product when exported to a relevant third country, provided that this price is representative.[309] Second, when such price is also not available, the import price has to be compared with the cost of production in the country of origin plus a reasonable amount for administrative, selling and any other costs and for profits.[310] These two methods (relying on prices in third countries and constructed normal value) are alternatives and there is no requirement to rely on one instead of the other. The *normal value* has to be *compared* with the *export price* to determine whether there is dumping. This is difficult because the price at which the product is sold in the importing country is also determined by transport costs, administrative costs, by profit

---

[305] Still, it has to be demonstrated that they are effectively not in the ordinary course of trade.
[306] Appellate Body Report: United States – Antidumping Measures on Certain Hot-Rolled Steel Products from Japan, WT/DS184/1B/R (21 July 2001), para. 157. If the sales to affiliated parties are made at a lower level and would be included in the calculation of 'normal value', this would mean that dumping would less quickly be found. If the sales to affiliated parties are made at a higher level, this would mean that dumping would more quickly be found. In both cases they are not adequate to calculate correctly the normal value.
[307] See the conditions in art. 2.2.1 Antidumping Agreement.
[308] Because there are no sales 'in the ordinary course of trade' or because there are no domestic sales or there is a low volume of sales (this is the so-called 'home-market viability test': see Footnote 2 to the Antidumping Agreement). Finally this may also be the case because of a 'particular market situation' in the home market. (See 2.2 of the Antidumping Agreement).
[309] This is logical, since also price discrimination among third countries is considered as dumping. See *supra* note 303 and accompanying text.
[310] Art. 2.2 Antidumping Agreement. Art. 2.2.1.1 sets out conditions for the calculation of the cost of production and the administrative, selling and other costs.

margins realized by different resellers etc. The prices must be compared at the same level of trade (at the time the goods leave the producer) and in respect of sales made at the same time.[311] Also this export price may need to be constructed because there is no export price or because the price is unreliable because of the relation between the importer and exporter.[312] Moreover, the prices have to be compared in the same currency.[313] The comparison may be made according to three methods: (i) weighted average of the normal value compared with the weighted average of the export prices during the period on consideration; (ii) the normal value and export price on or around the same day of transaction and (iii) the weighted average normal value compared with the export price on each transaction.

110. Not all dumping may be addressed by countervailing measures. It is necessary that the dumped imports cause material injury to domestic industry, threaten to cause such injury or are such as to retard materially the establishment of a domestic industry.[314] The 'material' injury standard is less stringent than the 'serious' injury standard under the SCM Agreement (see *supra* Section III.1.D). Whether there is material injury must be based on positive evidence and involve an objective examination of both (a) the volume of dumped imports and the effect of the dumped imports on prices in the domestic market for like products, and (b) the consequent impact of these imports on domestic producers of such products.[315] The injury must be caused to the domestic industry, meaning the domestic producers as a whole of the like products or those whose collective output of the products constitutes a major proportion of the total domestic production of those products.[316]

111. The determination whether there is dumping is a fact-intensive process. Detailed procedures are set out on how antidumping cases are to be initiated, how the investigations are to be conducted[317], and lay down the conditions for ensuring that all interested parties are given an opportunity to present evidence.[318]

---

[311] See H. VAN HOUTTE, *The Law of International Trade*, (London, Sweet & Maxwell 2002), p. 121.
[312] In such cases the selling price to the first independent buyer is used or another constructed price. See art. 2.3 and 2.4 Antidumping Agreement. See also Panel Report: United States – Antidumping measures on stainless steel plate in coils and stainless steel sheet and strips from Korea, WT/DS179/R (22 December 2000), paras. 6.91–6.94.
[313] Art. 2.4.1 Antidumping Agreement sets out rules for currency conversions. The rates of exchange on the day of sale need to be used and traders must be allowed 60 days to adjust their prices in response to currency fluctuations.
[314] Art. VI.6 (a) GATT and art. 3.1 Antidumping Agreement.
[315] *Ibid.* art. 3.1.
[316] *Ibid.* art. 4.1.
[317] *Ibid.* art. 5.
[318] *Ibid.* art. 6.

Antidumping measures can remain in force only as long as to the extent necessary to counteract the dumping that causes injury[319] and must expire five years after the date of imposition, unless an investigation shows that ending the measure would lead to injury.[320]

G. AGREEMENT ON AGRICULTURE

112. The treatment of agricultural products is a contentious issue in the WTO.[321] The Agreement on Agriculture[322], which was negotiated during the Uruguay Round, is aimed at reforming trade in this sector and at making policies fair and more market-oriented.[323] This would improve predictability and security for importing and exporting countries alike. Indeed, agricultural quotas, domestic support and export subsidies seriously distort international trade in agricultural products. At the same time, it was necessary to take into account the specific

---

[319] *Ibid.* art. 11.1.
[320] *Ibid.* art. 11.3.
[321] The GATT 1947 also applied to trade in agricultural goods. Nevertheless, art. XI on the prohibition on quantitative restrictions exempted import restrictions on agricultural goods. See art. XI.2 (c) GATT. Also the provisions on subsidies were quite limited and provided for an exception for 'primary products'. Subsidies for primary products were allowed, as long as this did not result in the subsidizing state having 'more than an equitable share of world export trade in that product'. Interpreting the concept 'more than an equitable share' was extremely difficult. See art. XVI GATT. For a discussion, see M. TREBILCOCK and R. HOWSE, *The Regulation of International Trade*, (London, Routledge 2005), pp. 322–324.
[322] See *inter alia* R. BHALA, 'World Agricultural Trade in Purgatory: the Uruguay Round Agriculture Agreement and its Implications for the Doha Round', *North Dakota Law Review* (2003), pp. 691–830; D. DIAKOSAVVAS, 'The Uruguay Round Agreement on Agriculture in Practice: How Open Are the OECD Markets?', *in* M. INGCO and A. WINTERS (eds.), *Agriculture and the New Trade Agenda: Creating a Global Trading Environment for Development*, (Cambridge, Cambridge University Press 2004), pp. 37–73; J. MAH, 'Reflections on the Special Safeguard Provision in the Agreement on Agriculture of the WTO, *Journal of World Trade* (1999), pp.197–204; J.A. MCMAHON, *Agricultural Trade, Protectionism and the Problems of Development: a Legal Perspective*, (Leicester, Leicester University Press 1992), ix + 278 p.; J. MACMAHON, *The WTO Agreement on Agriculture: A Commentary*, (Oxford, Oxford University Press 2006), xxi + 333 p.; S. MODWEL, 'The WTO and Agriculture: Why is India so Furious?', *The Journal of World Investment & Trade* (2004), pp. 289–319; M. MONTAÑÀ I MORA, *The US-E.C. Agricultural Export Subsidies Dispute: a GATT Perspective*, (Bellaterra, Institut Universitari d'Estudis Europeus 1993), 55 p.; S. MURPHY, *The Uruguay Round Agreement on Agriculture and its Renegotiation*, (Berlin, Friedrich Ebert Stiftung 2003), 35 p.; B. O'CONNOR, 'A Note on the Need for More Clarity in the World Trade Organization Agreement on Agriculture', *Journal of World Trade* (2003), pp. 839–846; I. STURGESS, 'The Agenda 2000 CAP Reform and the "Millennium Round": Negotiations on Agriculture', *in Negotiating the Future of Agricultural Policies*, (The Hague, Kluwer Law International 2000), pp. 97–111 and T. STEWART and C. SCHENEWERK, 'The Conflict between Facilitating International Trade and Protecting US Agriculture from Invasive Species: APHIS, the US Plant Protection Laws and the Argentine Citrus Dispute', *Journal of Transnational Law and Policy* (2004), pp. 305–346.
[323] Second Preliminary Consideration Agreement on Agriculture.

situation of developing and least-developed countries.[324] To this end, many deadlines for the implementation of the Agreement on Agriculture are longer and tariff-reduction targets are less important. Moreover, several exceptions were provided for least-developed countries.

113. Three topics are central in the Agreement on Agriculture. First, the Agreement addresses the various trade restrictions confronting imports, thus improving market access. Second, programmes of domestic support should be disciplined and, third, export subsidies and other methods used to make exports artificially competitive should be tackled.

114. The Agreement purports to achieve improved *market access* by requiring that all quantitative restrictions or other non-tariff measures have to be replaced by tariffs.[325] This has been done in schedules of each Member. Initially, these tariffs could provide the same level of protection as their non-tariff predecessor. However, WTO Members undertook commitments to reduce these tariff levels substantially within certain periods of time. The developed countries were obliged to cut their tariffs by an average of 36% over 6 years. The developing countries had to reduce their tariffs with 24% over 10 years. Least-developed countries are not required to undertake reduction commitments.[326] Members could indicate in their schedules that they regarded certain products potentially subject to 'special safeguard provisions'. These 'special safeguards' can be used to prevent import surges or price drops.[327]

115. There are three different regimes in the Agreement on Agriculture to tackle *domestic support* measures, depending on the degree to which they are deemed to distort markets.[328] Domestic support directly distorts trade and production. These subsidies are called *'amber-box'* subsidies. They had to be reduced by developed countries by 20% by 2000. Developing countries were obliged to make a 13% cut by 2004.[329] Least-developed countries again have no reduction

---

[324] There is no definition for 'developing countries' in the WTO Agreement. There exists, however, a definition of 'least-developed countries' by the Economic and Social Council of the UN. This definition is also used by the WTO. See *infra* paras. 231–232.

[325] Art. 4.2 and footnote 1, Agreement on Agriculture. Annex 5 to the Agreement provides certain 'special treatment' provisions, allowing for restriction of imports of particularly sensitive products during the implementation periods.

[326] *Ibid.* art. 15.2. The exact percentages are included in the schedules of commitments made by Members.

[327] *Ibid.* art. 5.

[328] *Ibid.* art. 3.1, 3.2 and Part IV.

[329] Again, these percentages are included in the schedules. To calculate the amount of subsidies that has to be reduced, the Agreement on Agriculture makes use of the concept of 'Aggregate Measurement of Support' (AMS), *i.e.* the sum of all non-exempted (see *infra* on exempted domestic support) annual support for individual products and the annual support which is not

commitments. New reductions of domestic support are supposed to be agreed in the Doha Round, but are in fact a main reason for the stalled negotiations. Certain domestic support measures are excluded from reduction commitments because they would not distort trade. These are the so-called *'green box'* measures. These domestic support measures must be provided through a publicly funded government programme[330] and must pursue specific policy goals. It concerns *inter alia* support for research, disease control, infrastructure and food security, direct payments to producers that are 'decoupled'[331] from production, measures to ensure income, disaster relief, structural adjustment programmes and environmental and regional assistance programmes.[332] For certain types of direct payments, further specific criteria need to be fulfilled in order to fall within the 'green box' and thus not be subject to reduction commitments. Certain support measures are trade-distortive (and thus would normally fall in the 'amber box'), but are nevertheless exempt from the reduction commitments because they concern assistance measures provided by developing countries to encourage agricultural and rural development[333] or because they are *de minimis* (5% or less of a developed Member's total value of production of basic agricultural products; 10% or less in the case of developing countries).[334] A specific third box of subsidies (in fact a sub-category of the 'amber box') concerns direct payments under production-limiting programmes.[335] These *'blue box'* subsidies are trade-distortive and thus normally subject to the reduction commitments of the 'amber box', yet since they are linked to a programme of production limiting, they would still be allowed. The idea is that such subsidies would decrease over time, as production decreases. All domestic support that is not exempted (because in the 'green box', in the 'blue box', assistance by developing countries to encourage agricultural and rural development or *de minimis*) is subject to reduction commitments.[336]

---

product-specific. The reduction of the total AMS of a WTO Member then needs to be calculated with reference to the Base Total AMS, *i.e.* the average amount of non-exempted subsidies over the years 1986–1988. Annex 3 Agreement on Agriculture. It should be noted that during the period 1986–1988, developed countries had maintained a high level of domestic support. This implies that the reduction commitments are calculated with reference to a high base level. The commitments of the developed countries were thus in practice not as ambitious as they would seem.

[330] Annex 1.1 Agreement on Agriculture.
[331] This means that the amount of the payments is not related to the type or volume of production. See *Ibid.* Annex 2.6.
[332] *Ibid.* Annex 2.2–2.13.
[333] *Ibid.* art. 6.2.
[334] *Ibid.* art. 6.4.
[335] *Ibid.* art. 6.5.
[336] *Ibid.* art. 6.1.

116. *Export subsidies* are prohibited, unless they are specified in a Member's schedule of commitments.[337] Export subsidies are (i) subsidies contingent upon export and (ii) the subsidies listed (non-exhaustively) in Article 9 of the Agreement on Agriculture.[338] Non-scheduled subsidies that are listed in Article 9 are prohibited as such. The listed subsidies that are scheduled have to be reduced by 36% in value terms and 21% in volume terms from a 1986–1990 base over six years by developed countries. Developing countries have to reduce their subsidies by 14% over 10 years. The latter countries could, however, for a period of 6 years use export subsidies to reduce the costs of marketing and transporting exports.[339] Least-developed Members have no obligations in this respect. Export subsidies that are not listed in Article 9 of the Agreement on Agriculture are only subject to the anti-circumvention principle in Article 10.1 of the Agreement on Agriculture: the non-listed types of export subsidies[340] may not be applied in a manner which results in, or threatens to lead to, circumvention of export subsidy commitments.

117. Article 13 of the Agreement on Agriculture contains the so-called 'peace clause'. This provision states that the modes of action that are included in Part III of the SCM Agreement and in Article XXIII GATT cannot be used to challenge domestic support measures.[341] What is more, due restraint has to be exercised when applying 'countervailing measures' to offset the possible consequences of the subsidy.[342] However, the peace clause expired on 31 December 2003. An attempt to agree upon an extension at the Ministerial Conference in Cancún failed. This opened the door to several challenges of domestic support subsidies that were not yet subject to the obligation to reduce.[343]

118. The Agreement on Agriculture envisaged further reform in trade in agricultural products. One year before the end of the implementation process (*i.e.* in 2000) new negotiations were started.[344] In the Doha Declaration of 14 November 2001, WTO Members committed themselves to 'comprehensive negotiations aimed at: substantial improvements in market access; reductions of, with a view

---

[337] *Ibid.* art. 3.1, 3.3 and Part V.
[338] *Ibid.* art. 1 (e).
[339] *Ibid.* art. 9.4.
[340] Such non-listed subsidies include subsidizing export credits, export credit guarantees or insurance programmes. See Appellate Body Report: United States – Subsidies on Upland Cotton, WT/DS267/AB/R (21 March 2005), paras. 608–628.
[341] Art. 13 (a) and (b) Agreement on Agriculture.
[342] *Ibid.* art. 13 (c).
[343] See, for challenges of subsidies that were already subject to challenge *before* the expiration of the peace clause, *inter alia* Appellate Body Report: United States – Subsidies on Upland Cotton, WT/DS267/AB/R, (18 June 2004) and Appellate Body Report: European Communities – Export Subsidies on Sugar, WT/DS265, 266 and 283/AB/R, (28 April 2005).
[344] Art. 20 Agreement on Agriculture.

Overview of the WTO Agreements

to phasing out, all forms of export subsidies; and substantial reductions in trade-distorting domestic support. [They agreed] that special and differential treatment for developing countries shall be an integral part of all elements of the negotiations'.[345] Nonetheless, negotiations in this field have proven extremely difficult. Before the Cancún Ministerial Conference in September 2003 the European Communities and the United States had made a proposal to transform all domestic support measures for which reduction commitments were made, into direct payments to farmers, 'decoupled' from the level of production. Hence, in principle, these payments would not distort trade. Export subsidies would be reduced for products that are of particular interest to developing countries. This proposal was seen by developing countries as not ambitious enough. This was one of the reasons why no consensus could be achieved at the Cancún Ministerial Conference. After the failure of Cancún, WTO Members still managed to agree upon the so-called 'July Decision'[346] (named after the compromise achieved in July 2004) on 1 August 2004. In this Decision, the developed countries committed themselves to reducing domestic support and export subsidies. In return, an agreement could be reached with the developing countries to further open up their markets and make new steps in liberalizing the services sector. Despite some optimism, the July Decision was only a framework.

119. More concrete commitments had to be made on the sixth WTO Conference in Hong Kong in December 2005. Shortly before the Ministerial Conference, the Chairman of the Committee on Agriculture noted in his Status Report that the "agriculture negotiations are stalled – there is no way to conceal that reality".[347] He could do no more than highlight the essential decisions that needed to be made. At the Ministerial Conference, WTO Members reaffirmed their commitments in the Doha Declaration and the July Decision.[348] With regard to *domestic support*, they agreed to negotiate reductions according to three categories ('bands') of Members. The Member with the highest level of permitted support would be in the top band, subject to the highest commitments. Members with the second and third highest levels of support would be in the second band, subject to a second category of commitments. All other WTO Members are in the third band, which thus includes all developing countries. In addition, developed-country Members would make additional reduction commitments. Further, all *export subsidies* and measures with equivalent effect would be eliminated by 2013.

---

[345] Ministerial Declaration of Doha, 14 November 2001, *supra* note 138, para. 13.
[346] Decision Adopted by the General Council of the WTO on 1 August 2004, WT/L/579. Annex A to the Decision sets out the modalities in agriculture.
[347] Committee on Agriculture, Special Session, Agriculture Negotiations. Status Report II. Looking Forward to the Hong Kong Ministerial, TN/AG/19, 1 August 2005, par. 4.
[348] See Ministerial Declaration of Hong Kong, done on 22 December 2005, WT/MIN(05)/DEC, available on http://www.wto.org/English/thewto_e/minist_e/min05_e/final_text_e.pdf, para. 4.

Market access for agricultural products would also be improved by agreeing further tariff cuts within four 'bands' and developing countries would be able to identify 'sensitive products' that would escape high tariff reduction and apply a 'special safeguard mechanism'. Yet, the thresholds still needed to be agreed upon. It may be clear that the Hong Kong Ministerial did not provide much progress. It certainly kept the negotiations going, but did not result in concrete commitments, except for the elimination of export subsidies by 2013.

H. AGREEMENT ON TEXTILES AND CLOTHING

120. The Agreement on Textiles and Clothing of 1995[349] was intended to abolish the high number of restrictions that had been imposed on trade in textiles and clothing during the period that the Multi-Fibre Arrangement was operational. The latter Arrangement, to which not all GATT Contracting Parties were party, allowed for bilateral quotas in order to restrict exports, which would normally have violated Article XI GATT. In four stages, all textiles products were integrated into the GATT rules. At each stage (1995-1998-2002-2005), products amounting to a certain minimum percentage of the volume of the country's imports in 1990 were to be included in the integration process.[350] The Agreement also required Members to phase out their quantitative restrictions that were adopted outside the framework of the Multi-Fibre Arrangement.[351] During the implementation period, Members were allowed, under very strict conditions, to take special

---

[349] See *inter alia* I. DICKSON, 'China's Interest in the World Trade Organization's Deregulation of International Textiles Trade', *in* D.Z. CASS, B.G. WILLIAMS and G. BAKER (eds.), *China and the World Trading System: Entering the New Millennium*, (Cambridge, Cambridge University Press 2003), pp. 175-201; J.M. JENNINGS, 'In Search for a Standard: "Serious Damage" in the Agreement on Textiles and Clothing', *Northwestern Journal of International Law and Business* (1996), pp. 272-319; S.J. KIM, K.A. REINERT and G.C. RODRIGO, 'The Agreement on Textiles and Clothing: Safeguard Actions from 1995 to 2001', *Journal of International Economic Law* (2002), pp. 445-468; J. MAYER, 'Not Totally Naked: Textiles and Clothing Trade in a Quota-Free Environment', *Journal of World Trade* (2005), pp. 393-426; H.K. NORDÅS, *The Global Textiles and Clothing Industry Post the Agreement on Textiles and Clothing*, (Geneva, WTO Publications 2004), 37 p.; M. SMEETS, 'Main Features of the Uruguay Round Agreement on Textiles and Clothing and Implications for the Trading System', *Journal of World Trade* (1995), pp. 97-109; R. STRANGE and J. NEWTON, 'From Rags to Riches? China, the WTO and World Trade in Textiles and Clothing', *in* H. KATRAK (ed.), *The WTO and Developing Countries*, (Basingstoke, Palgrave MacMillan 2004), pp. 233-256; E. VERMULST and P. MIHAYLOVA, 'EC Commerce Defence Actions Against Textiles from 1995 to 2000: Possible Lessons for Future Negotiations', *Journal of International Economic Law* (2001), pp. 527-555; M. WILLIAMS, Y-C CHOI and Y. SHEN, 'Bonanza or Mirage? Textiles and China's Accession to the WTO', *Journal of World Trade* (2002), pp. 577-591 and A. J-H WOHN, 'Towards GATT Integration: Circumventing Quantitative Restrictions on Textiles and Apparel Trade under the Multi-Fiber Agreement', *University of Pennsylvania Journal of International Economic Law* (2001), pp. 375-419.
[350] Art. 1 Agreement on Textiles and Clothing.
[351] *Ibid.* art. 3.

safeguard actions in respect of textile and clothing products that were not subject to quotas and not integrated into the GATT.[352]

121. On 1 January 2005, the implementation of the Agreement on Textiles and Clothing was finalized. In principle, no restrictions can be imposed on trade in textiles, other than the safeguard measures that comply with the Agreement on Safeguards (*supra* Section III.1.D). China seems to be the country that benefited most from the expiration of the Agreement, although the smaller developing countries appear to be the main losers. These developing countries are unable to compete with the Chinese textiles industry.[353] Countries that are afraid that their textiles industries will be harmed by the Chinese imports may try to recur to GATT-consistent trade measures (antidumping, countervailing measures or safeguards). What is more, China's terms of accession to the WTO included a 'textile product-specific safeguard clause' that allows, until 2008[354], WTO Members to impose quantitative restrictions on imports of Chinese textiles and clothing products[355] if they are found to disrupt[356] markets.[357] Members are therefore allowed to limit the increase of imports of specific products to 7.5%[358] above the level of imports in the preceding year.[359] On 23 May 2005, the US imposed temporary quotas on Chinese imports of textiles. On 10 June 2005, the

---

[352] *Ibid.* art. 6.
[353] Many of these countries benefited from previously existing preferential quota access. An attempt by Tunisia at the WTO Council for Trade in Goods of 10 May 2005 to discuss the competitive position of developing countries with regard to trade in textiles was blocked by China.
[354] It may be possible that even after the end of 2008, special safeguards can be applied on the basis of the 'Transitional Product-Specific Safeguard' Mechanism. Like the 'textile product-specific safeguard measure', this is a deviation from the normal rules on safeguard, applying a lower injury standard (market disruption), excluding the principle of MFN, allowing for voluntary export restrictions by China and restricting China's ability to retaliate. This Transitional Product-Specific Safeguard Mechanism may be applied until 2013. See art. 16 Protocol on the Accession of the People's Republic of China to the WTO. For a discussion of the differences, see H. LIU and L. SUN, 'Beyond the Phase-out of Quotas in the Textile and Clothing Trade: WTO-Plus Rules and the Case of US Safeguards Against Chinese Exports in 2003', *Asia-Pacific Development Journal* (2004), pp. 57–60.
[355] Thus, the safeguard can be limited to Chinese products, and does not need to be applied on a non-discriminatory basis. This is a deviation from the principle of MFN, which normally needs to be complied with when applying safeguards.
[356] This is a significant lower standard than the 'serious injury' standard that is normally required for safeguard measures.
[357] See para. 242 of the Report of the Working Party on the Accession of China to the World Trade Organization, WT/ACC/CHN/49, 1 October 2001, available on http://www.uschina.org/public/documents/2005/05/workingpartyreport.doc.
[358] 6% for wool product categories.
[359] The European Commission has published Guidelines to clarify under what circumstances it would be using the textile specific safeguard clause. See Guidelines for the Use of Safeguards on Chinese Textiles Exports to the EU, MEMO/05/110, Brussels, 6 April 2001.

EC and China agreed upon a bilateral deal to limit the volumes of Chinese imports into the EC.

I. AGREEMENT ON TRADE-RELATED INVESTMENT MEASURES

122. Foreign direct investment (FDI) is seen as an important driving force behind globalization. FDI is defined as "an investment involving a long-term relationship and reflecting a lasting interest and control by a resident entity in one economy (foreign direct investor or parent enterprise) in an enterprise resident in an economy other than that of the foreign direct investor (FDI enterprise or affiliate enterprise or foreign affiliate)".[360] FDI flows mainly from developed to developing countries, although certain developing countries (Malaysia, Singapore, South Korea, Chile, Mexico, South Africa, Brazil, China and India) also have become important sources of FDI.[361]

123. FDI is beneficial for receiving countries (promoting transfer of technology), but also entails risks. Receiving countries may become locations for simple assembly operations, foreign direct investors may quickly withdraw their investment because of changing economic and political factors or foreign firms may exercise undue political influence.[362] Therefore, States often impose limits on FDI, which in turn may hamper economic development. It is therefore essential to create international rules that foster a better investment environment. Often, countries conclude bilateral investment treaties for the protection and promotion of investment.[363] These treaties provide for a right of access of investors and investments to a host country and include Most Favoured Nation (an investor from a country that has concluded a bilateral investment treaty is entitled to the best treatment that is given in the receiving country to investors from other countries) and National Treatment (an investor from a country that has concluded a bilateral investment treaty is entitled to the same protection as the domestic

---

[360] See UNCTAD, *World Investment Report 2004. The Shift towards Services*, (Geneva, United Nations Publications 2004), p. 345.
[361] *Ibid.* pp. 19–21.
[362] INTERNATIONAL TRADE CENTER/COMMONWEALTH SECRETARIAT, *supra* note 2, p. 282.
[363] See R. DOLZER and M. STEVENS, *Bilateral Investment Treaties*, (The Hague, Nijhoff 1995), 352 p.; H. FRICK, *Bilateraler Investitionsschutz in Entwicklungsländern*, (Berlin, Duncker & Humblot 1975), 296 p.; A.T. GUZMAN, 'Why LDCs Sign Treaties that Hurt Them: Explaining the Popularity of Bilateral Investment Treaties', *Virginia Journal of International Law* (1998), pp. 639–688; G. SACERDOTI, 'Bilateral Treaties and Multilateral Instruments on Investment Protection', 269 *Rec. Cours* (1997), pp. 251–460 and K.J. VANDEVELDE, 'Investment Liberalization and Economic Development: the Role of Bilateral Investment Treaties', *Columbia Journal of Transnational Law* (1998), pp. 501–527.

Overview of the WTO Agreements

investors) obligations. Attempts to establish a Multilateral Agreement on Investment by the OECD countries[364] failed because developing countries (traditional receivers of FDI) were not involved and because of serious differences among the participating countries on the inclusion of special provisions on labour, environment and cultural industries.

124. The Agreement on Trade-Related Investment Measures (TRIMS)[365] applies to investment measures related to trade in goods only.[366] It prohibits at least[367] five types of trade-related investment measures. In fact, the listed measures were already prohibited by Article III.4 and Article XI GATT[368], but TRIMS clearly identified these measures. The 'illustrative list' of GATT-inconsistent measures, in Annex to TRIMS, mentions measures that demand a certain local content in the products of the enterprise concerned[369], measures that require a balance between the volume of imports used and exports realized[370] and measures that

---

[364] See C. HUIPING, *OECD's Multilateral Agreement on Investment: a Chinese Perspective*, (The Hague, Kluwer Law International 2002), xiii + 156 p.; J. HUNER, 'The Multilateral Agreement on Investment and the Review of the OECD Guidelines for Multinational Enterprises', in M.T. KAMMINGA and S. ZIA-ZARIFI (eds.), *Liability of Multinational Corporations under International Law*, (The Hague, Kluwer Law International 2000), pp. 197–205; G. KELLEY, 'Multilateral Investment Treaties: a Balanced Approach to Multinational Corporations', *Columbia Journal of Transnational Law* (2001), pp. 483–532; P.T. MUCHLINSKI, 'The Rise and Fall of the Multilateral Agreement on Investment: Where Now?', *Int. Law.* (2000), pp. 1033–1053; E.C. NIEUWENHUYS (ed.), *Multilateral Regulation of Investment*, (The Hague, Kluwer Law International 2001), vi + 244 p. and SOCIÉTÉ FRANÇAISE POUR LE DROIT INTERNATIONAL (ed.), *Un accord multilateral sur l'investissment: d'un forum de négociation à l'autre?*, (Paris, Pedone 1999), 140 p.

[365] See C. CURTISS, 'Agreement on Trade-Related Investment Measures: a Five-Year Review', *Comparative Law Yearbook of International Business* (2004), pp. 233–255; J.F. DENNIN and V.M. ROUTHIER, 'Trade-Related Investment Measures', *Comparative Law Yearbook of International Business* (2001), pp. 129–191; R.H. EDWARDS and S.N. LESTER, 'Towards a More Comprehensive World Trade Organization Agreement on Trade Related Investment Measures', *Stanford Journal of International Law* (1997), pp. 169–214; W.A. FENNELL and J.W. TYLER, *Trade-Related Investment Measures*, (Deventer, Kluwer Law and Taxation Publishers 1993), xii + 250 p; S.N. LESTER, 'Update on TRIMs: the Development of a TRIMS Jurisprudence in the WTO Panel Report on Indonesia: Certain Measures affecting the Automobile Industry', *World Competition*, (1998), pp. 85–97; M. ROY, 'Implications for the GATS of Negotiations on a Multilateral Investment Framework: Potential Synergies and Pitfalls', *The Journal of World Investment* (2003), pp. 963–986; J. STEINBACH, 'Einfluβ des TRIMs-Abkommens auf das chinesische Recht für ausländische Direktinvestionen', *in* R. HEUSER and R. KLEIN (eds.), *Die WTO und das neue Ausländerinvestitions- und Aussenhandelsrecht der VR China: Gesetze und Analysen*, (Hamburg, Institut für Asienkunde 2004), pp. 67–77 and A. TANKOANO, 'Le projet d'accord relative aux mesures concernant les investissements et liées au commerce (TRIM)', *Droit et Pratique du Commerce International* (1993), pp. 264–289.

[366] Art. 1 TRIMS.
[367] The list is not exhaustive.
[368] Art. 2 TRIMS.
[369] *Ibid.* Annex 1 (a) and 2 (a).
[370] *Ibid.* Annex 1 (b) and 2 (b).

restrict the exportations of products by the enterprise concerned.[371] WTO Members were required to notify all inconsistent trade-related investment measures within 90 days after the entry into force of the WTO Agreement.[372] They had to be eliminated within 2 years (5 years for developing countries and 7 years for least-developed countries). Nevertheless, trade-related investment measures may benefit from the exceptions that exist under GATT.[373]

125. The TRIMS has a limited coverage.[374] It also mainly imposes obligations upon the host countries towards foreign corporations. It does not impose any obligations on the home country of a corporation with regard to the conduct of this corporation in the host country. The Agreement notes that the Council for Trade in Goods would review the Agreement after 5 years and consider whether the Agreement should be complemented with further provisions on investment policy and competition policy.[375] A Working Group on the Relationship between Trade and Investment was established during the 1996 Ministerial Conference in Singapore to examine the relationship between trade and investment. However, this Working Group does not negotiate on new rules or commitments.[376] In 2001, the Ministerial Conference in Doha merely urged the Goods Council 'to consider positively' possible requests for extension by least-developed countries of the seven-year transition period given to them under the TRIMs Agreement to eliminate inconsistent trade-related investment measures.[377] In July 2004, the General Council agreed that no further work towards negotiations on the relation between trade and investment would take place within the WTO during the Doha Round.[378]

J. AGREEMENT ON CUSTOMS VALUATION

126. As explained, customs duties can be levied on an *ad valorem* basis or as specific duties on some products. Since most countries prefer to levy *ad valorem* duties, it is essential that the valuation of the goods on which the duties are levied is based on fair, uniform and neutral criteria, precluding the use of arbitrary or

---

[371] *Ibid.* Annex 2(c).
[372] *Ibid.* art. 5.1.
[373] *Ibid.* art. 3.
[374] It should be noted that, with regard to services, the fact that 'commercial presence' is one of the modes of supply included in GATS, makes the GATS also a tool for disciplining measures that limit foreign direct investment.
[375] Art. 9 TRIMS.
[376] See for its latest report: Report (2003) of the Working Group on the relation between Trade and Investment to the General Council, WT/WGTI/7, 11 July 2003.
[377] Ministerial Declaration of Doha, 14 November 2001, *supra* note 138, para. 6.
[378] Decision Adopted by the General Council of the WTO on 1 August 2004 ('July Decision'), WT/L/579, para. 1 (g).

fictitious customs values.[379] Indeed, a higher valuation of the products leads to a higher duty and therefore creates a barrier for the imported products.

127. Due to the controversial nature of customs valuation, a Customs Valuation Code was developed and adopted in the Tokyo Round (formally the 'Agreement on Implementation of Article VII of the GATT'[380]). Goods were to be valued on the basis of the price actually paid or payable for the imported goods ('transaction value'). This Code was replaced in the Uruguay Round by the WTO Agreement on Implementation of Article VII of the GATT 1994 (hereinafter 'Agreement on Customs Valuation'). The provisions of this agreement are the same as for the Tokyo Code. They relate only to the valuation of goods for the purpose of levying *ad valorem* duties. *Six alternative methods of valuation* are established. If the first method is not adequate to apply, one has to shift to the second method and so on. The primary basis for customs valuation is the 'transaction value'. This is the "price actually paid or payable for the goods when sold for export to the country of importation"[381] adjusted to include specified costs, charges and expenses that are not reflected in the price actually paid or payable for the goods.[382] The transaction value cannot be used if the transaction in question is between related parties,[383] except when, after consultations with the importer and after examination of the circumstances surrounding the transaction and whether the relationship has influenced the price, the customs authorities find that the relationship has not influenced the declared transaction value.[384] In case of related parties, the importer may demonstrate that the value approximates the customs value of past import transactions between unrelated buyers and sellers of identical or similar goods or deductive or computed values calculated for identical or similar goods.[385]

128. The customs authorities can reject the transaction value if it has reason to doubt the truth or accuracy of the value declared by the importer or the documents that are submitted.[386] The authorities have to give the importer the opportunity to justify the price. If the customs authorities are still not satisfied, they will have to give the importers in writing its reasons for not accepting the transaction value they have declared.[387] If the transaction value cannot be determined or used, the 'customs value shall be the transaction value *of identical goods* sold for export to

---

[379] Fourth Preliminary Consideration, Agreement on Customs Valuation.
[380] Agreement on Implementation of Article VII & Protocol, GATT, BISD 26S/116 (1980).
[381] Art. 1.1 Agreement on Customs Valuation.
[382] *Ibid.* art. 8.
[383] *Ibid.* art. 1.1 (d).
[384] *Ibid.* art. 1.2.
[385] *Ibid.* art. 1.2 (b).
[386] Uruguay Round Decision Regarding Cases where Customs Administrations have Reasons to Doubt the Truth or Accuracy of the Declared Value, para. 1.
[387] *Ibid.*

the same country of importation and exported at or about the same time as the goods being valued'.[388] If the transaction for identical goods cannot be determined either, one must use the 'transaction value *of similar goods* sold for export to the same country of importation and exported at or about the same time as the goods being valued'.[389] If this is not possible either, the value 'shall be based on the unit price at which the imported goods or identical or similar imported goods are so sold in the greatest aggregate quantity, at or about the same time as the goods being valued, to persons who are not related to the persons from whom they buy the goods'.[390] From this value, deductions have to be made for commissions or profit, general expenses, transport and insurance costs, customs duties and certain other costs. The resulting value is called the 'deducted value'. A fifth way to determine the value of a good is to make the sum of the costs of producing the article in the country of exportation, an amount for profit and general expenses and the cost or value of all other expenses necessary to reflect the valuation option chosen by the party.[391] This value is the 'computed value'. The importer can request to use the fifth method before the fourth is applied.[392] If it is still not possible to determine the customs value, it 'shall be determined using reasonable means consistent with the principles and general provisions of [the Agreement on Customs Valuation] and of Article VII of GATT 1994 and on the basis of data available in the country of importation'.[393]

K. AGREEMENT ON PRESHIPMENT INSPECTION

129. Preshipment inspection is mainly used by developing countries whose customs authorities do not have the technical capacities yet to verify prices. Importers may indeed try to undervalue or misclassify their imports into a country in order to pay lower customs duties. Preshipment inspection takes place on behalf of the country of importation in the country of exportation. Because there is no obligation for a WTO Member to allow a government entity of another country to operate on its territory[394], importing countries make use of private preshipment inspection companies. However, the criteria used by these companies are often regarded as insufficiently transparent. Moreover, there is no opportunity for appeal against the inspection report and procedures would unduly delay the shipment. Therefore, the preshipment inspection procedures would constitute a

---

[388] Art. 2.1 (a) Agreement on Customs Valuation (emphasis added).
[389] *Ibid.* art. 3.1 (a) (emphasis added).
[390] *Ibid.* art. 5.1 (a).
[391] *Ibid.* art. 6.1.
[392] This choice cannot be made on the discretion of the customs officer. *Ibid.* art. 4.
[393] *Ibid.* art. 7.1.
[394] Art. 1.4, footnote Agreement on Preshipment Inspection.

serious barrier to trade. To solve these problems and at the same time take into account the need of developing countries to make use of these procedures, the Agreement on Preshipment Inspection imposes a number of obligations upon both importing and exporting countries.

130. Preshipment inspection activities are defined as 'all activities relating to the verification of the quality, the quantity, the price, including currency exchange rate and financial terms, and/or the customs classification of goods to be exported to the territory of the user Member'.[395] The importing countries are obliged to apply all procedures and criteria for preshipment inspection on an equal basis to all exporters (MFN)[396] and cannot apply them in a manner that will result in less favourable treatment of the goods that are inspected, in comparison with like domestic products (National Treatment).[397] They must ensure that the preshipment activities are conducted in a transparent manner[398], that confidential information is treated appropriately and that unreasonable delays are avoided.[399] Exporting Members also have an obligation of non-discrimination[400] and transparency.[401] One of the objectives of the Agreement is to regulate the use of preshipment inspection activities by developing countries 'for as long and in so far as it is necessary to verify the quality, quantity or price of imported goods'.[402] In order to enable the developing countries to develop the required technical skills to do such verifications themselves, the exporter Members must offer to provide these countries technical assistance.[403]

131. Finally, the Agreement is also aimed at facilitating review procedures in case the decisions of preshipment inspection procedures are disputed. Preshipment inspection entities must designate officials to whom exporters may appeal against decisions.[404] Furthermore, the Agreement establishes an independent review entity that can deal with disputes between exporters and preshipment inspection entities.[405] This review entity became operational on 1 May 1996 and is constituted by the WTO, the International Chamber of Commerce and the International

---

[395] *Ibid.* art. 1.3.
[396] *Ibid.* art. 2.1.
[397] *Ibid.* art. 2.2 *juncto* art. III.4 GATT.
[398] *Ibid.* art. 2.5.
[399] *Ibid.* art. 2.15.
[400] *Ibid.* art. 3.1.
[401] *Ibid.* art. 3.2.
[402] *Ibid.* third preliminary consideration.
[403] *Ibid.* art. 3.3.
[404] *Ibid.* art. 2.21.
[405] *Ibid.* art. 4.

Federation of Inspection Agencies.[406] If Members have a dispute concerning the provisions of the Agreement on Preshipment Inspection, they can invoke WTO dispute settlement procedures.[407]

L. AGREEMENT ON IMPORT LICENSING PROCEDURES

132. The Agreement on Import Licensing Procedures lays down rules for the adoption and implementation of national procedures for issuing import licences. Governments use import licensing to administer quantitative or other import restrictions or as a means of keeping track of imports for statistical purposes.[408] The Agreement distinguishes automatic (approval of the application is granted in all cases) and non-automatic (approval of the application is dependent upon the authorities' discretion) import licensing. All licensing procedures should be not more burdensome than necessary (they should not have trade-distorting effects additional to those caused by the imposition of the restriction for which the licence is used), be transparent and predictable and protect importers and foreign suppliers from unnecessary delays and arbitrary actions.[409] Automatic licences must be granted immediately, on receipt of the application, and in any case within a maximum period of 10 working days.[410] Non-automatic licences must be issued within 30 days of the receipt of application, when they are issued on a first-come first-served basis and no longer than 60 days if all applications are considered simultaneously.[411] The Members have the obligation to publish quota volumes and modes of allocation.[412]

M. AGREEMENT ON RULES OF ORIGIN

133. Determining the origin of a good is often essential to apply international trade rules. In principle, no distinction can be made according to the origin of a good. Yet, in the cases where this is still possible, the determination of the origin will be crucial. The Agreement on Rules of Origin sets requirements for rules of

---

[406] General Council Decision of 13 December 1995, Operation of the independent entity established under Article 4 of the agreement on preshipment inspection, WT/L/125/Rev.1, 9 February 1996.
[407] Art. 8 Agreement on Preshipment Inspection.
[408] J. Croome, *supra* note 8, p. 121.
[409] Tenth, Eleventh and Twelfth Preliminary Consideration of the Agreement on Import Licensing Procedures. See, more in detail, *ibid.* art. 1.4–1.11.
[410] *Ibid.* art. 2.2.
[411] *Ibid.* art. 3.5 (f).
[412] *Ibid.* art. 3.5 (b) and (c).

origin in a broad range of commercial policy instruments.[413] Thus, there are no separate provisions on rules of origin for purposes of MFN treatment, safeguard measures, antidumping and countervailing duties, or government procurement. The Agreement includes a process to reach a harmonization of the different rules of origin of Members.[414] In the transition period before harmonized rules of origin apply, Members can apply different rules of origin depending on the purpose of the rules. However, these rules must be based on a positive standard. This means that they should specify what is required to achieve origin and not what is insufficient.[415] Moreover, they must include clearly defined requirements[416] and cannot create 'restrictive, distorting, or disruptive effects on international trade'.[417] They have to be 'administered in a consistent, uniform, impartial and reasonable manner'.[418] The Agreement also requires MFN and national treatment with regard to rules of origin. The determination of the origin of imported or exported goods cannot be more stringent than the determination of the domestic origin. The rules cannot discriminate otherwise between Members.[419]

134. After the transition period, *i.e.* when all the rules of origin of Members are harmonized, the rules will apply equally for MFN, antidumping, countervailing duty and safeguard purposes.[420] As a basic rule, origin will be determined on the basis of the location where the last substantial transformation[421] has been carried out.[422] The same requirements for consistency, uniformity, impartiality and reasonability of the administration of rules are set.[423] The harmonization of the rules of origin had to be completed three years after the initiation of the work programme on harmonization.[424] This difficult work is performed by the Committee on Rules of Origin and the Technical Committee on Rules of Origin[425]

---

[413] Art. 1.2 Agreement on Rules of Origin.
[414] *Ibid.* Part IV.
[415] Negative standards can only form a clarification of the positive standard. *Ibid.* art. 2 (f).
[416] *Ibid.* art. 2 (a).
[417] *Ibid.* art. 2 (c).
[418] *Ibid.* art. 2 (e).
[419] *Ibid.* art. 2 (d).
[420] *Ibid.* art. 3 (a).
[421] The meaning of 'substantial transformation' is unclear. The Technical Committee on Rules of Origin is requested to draft a definition of this concept. It would mean that there is a change in tariff classification or, supplementary, that there is a certain percentage of value added or that there is a specific manufacturing or processing operation. *Ibid.* art. 9.2 (c).
[422] *Ibid.* art. 3 (b).
[423] *Ibid.* art. 3 (d).
[424] *Ibid.* art. 9.2 (a).
[425] The Technical Committee on Rules of Origin is created under the auspices of the World Customs Organization (formerly the Customs Cooperation Council). Its main functions are (a) to carry out the harmonization work; and (b) to deal with any matter concerning technical problems related to rules of origin. (For a description of both Committees, see *infra* para. 287). *Ibid.* art. 4.2. See also D. LUFF, *supra* note 41, pp. 371-372.

and had to be finished initially on July 1998.[426] This deadline was extended several times. The last deadline was July 2005. The work had to be finalized by 31 December 2005.[427] Eventually, the deadline for finalization was again extended to December 2007.[428] The final harmonized rules must be approved by the Ministerial Conference and eventually annexed to the Agreement.[429]

§ 2. GATS

1. Services

135. The international trade in services is growing in importance[430] and the GATS offers a multilateral legal framework for this ever expanding field.[431] The GATS is a framework agreement, which to a large extent takes over the GATT principles, but which to a large extent has to wait for further negotiations to make these principles operational.[432] The agreement has a remarkably large scope of

---

[426] The work should proceed in three stages: (i) first, developing a definition of 'goods wholly obtained in one country' and of minimum operations and processes that not by themselves are enough to confer origin on a good; (ii) second, requirements for a good to qualify as 'substantially transformed' because having changed from tariff heading; (iii) finally additional criteria for defining whether a good is 'substantially transformed' should be developed.

[427] WTO, Committee on Rules of Origin, Tenth annual review of the implementation and operation of the agreement on rules of origin, G/RO/59, 10 December 2004.

[428] Report (2006) of the Committee on Rules of Origin to the Council of Trade in Goods, G/L/790, 27 October 2006.

[429] Art. 9.4 Agreement on Rules of Origin.

[430] It counts for 30% of world employment and for 60% of the global trade. See WTO Website, Services: Rules for Growth and Investment, http://www.wto.org/english/thewto_e/whatis_e/tf_e/agrm6_e.htm. In the richest countries, the trade in services has in the meantime become much more important than the trade in goods. Trade in services counts for more than 70% of total economic activity. The service sector does not only flourish in rich countries. In the countries with the lowest income, it counts already for a third of the GDP. See B. HOEKMAN and M. KOSTECKI, *supra* note 5, p. 237. This increase is partly due to swift evolutions in communication technology.

[431] See *inter alia* P. MENGOZZI, 'Le GATS: un accord sans importance pour la Communauté européenne?', *Revue du Marché Unique Européen* (1997/2), pp. 19–44; C. PITSCHAS, 'Die Liberalisierung des internationalen Dienstleistungshandels im Rahmen des GATS', *Recht der Internationalen Wirtschaft* (2003), pp. 676–689; K.P. SAUVANT and J. WEBER, 'The International Legal Framework for Services', in *Law and Practice under the GATT and Other Trading Arrangements*, (New York, Oceana 1992–1996), 3 vol.; P. SAUVÉ and R.M. STERN (eds.), *GATS 2000: New Directions in Services Trade Liberalization*, (Washington, Brookings Institution 2000), xi + 544 p.; WTO SECRETARIAT (ed.), *Guide to the GATS: An Overview of Issues for Further Liberalization of Trade in Services*, (London, Kluwer Law International 2001), xxix + 704 p. See also several specific contributions in P. SAUVÉ (ed.), *Trade Rules Behind Borders: Essays on Services, Investment and the New Trade Agenda*, (London, Cameron May 2003), 541 p., as well as in B. HOEKMAN, A. MATTOO and PH. ENGLISH (eds.), *Development, Trade and the WTO: A Handbook*, (Washington D.C., World Bank 2002), 641 p.

[432] See WTO SECRETARIAT, *Guide to the GATS, supra* note 431, p. 3.

application, covering 'any service in any sector *except* services supplied in the exercise of governmental authority'.[433] Services supplied in the exercise of governmental authority are services which are supplied neither on a commercial basis nor in competition with one or more service suppliers. It should also be noted that the GATS Annex on Air Transport Services excludes some services from the GATS.[434]

136. The GATS does not define precisely what a 'service' is, or where the exact difference with 'good' lies.[435] It only defines forms ('modes') of 'trade in services'. The GATS applies to four different ways of providing services[436]: (i) Mode 1: cross-border supply of services, *i.e.* the service crosses the border without any movement of the service provider or consumer[437]; (ii) Mode 2: consumption abroad, *i.e.* the reception of services abroad by which the service consumer moves

---

[433] Art. I.3 (b) GATS (emphasis added). The exact definition of this exception is also subject to discussion. See E. LEROUX, 'What is a "Service supplied in the exercise of governmental authority" under art. I:3(b) and (c) of the General Agreement on Trade in Services?', *Journal of World Trade* (2006), pp. 345–385.

[434] It concerns air traffic rights and services directly related to the exercise of such traffic rights (except aircraft repair and maintenance services and computer reservation services). See paras. 2 and 3 of the GATS Annex on Air Transport Services.

[435] Would it then be possible that at the same time the WTO rules relating to services and to goods are applicable? That is at least what a WTO Panel has suggested in one case and which was confirmed by the Appellate Body. The Panel stated that "[t]he ordinary meaning of the texts of GATT 1994 and GATS [...] indicates that the obligations under GATT 1994 and GATS can co-exist and that one does not override the other". (See Panel Report: Canada – Certain Measures concerning Periodicals, WT/DS43/R, (14 March 1997), at para. 5.17; confirmed by the Appellate Body in Appellate Body Report: Canada – Certain Measures concerning Periodicals, WT/DS43/AB/R, (30 June 1997), p. 19). In a later case, the Appellate Body further clarified that, depending on the measure in question, there can be discerned three situations of applicability of the GATT and the GATS. Some measures affect only trade in goods, implying that they fall exclusively within the scope of GATT (or the other Multilateral Agreements on Trade in Goods). Other measures affect only trade in services, implying that they fall exclusively within the scope of GATS. Yet, there exists also a third situation where measures affect both goods and services: they "involve a service relating to a particular good or service supplied in conjunction with a particular good." The Appellate Body stated that in all such cases in this third category, the measure in question could be scrutinized under both the GATT 1994 and the GATS. (See Appellate Body Report: European Communities – Regime for the Importation, Distribution and Sale of Bananas, WT/DS27/AB/R, (9 September 1997), para. 221.) Nevertheless, in that case the GATT and the GATS will each affect separate aspects of the measure in question. This would avoid that GATT and GATS apply simultaneously and therefore avoids conflicts between the Agreements. M. MATSUSHITA, T. SCHOENBAUM and P. MAVROIDIS, *supra* note 60, pp. 609–611. Yet, it is a fact that the lack of clear definitions for goods and services leads to almost insuperable discussions on the applicable trade rules. A case-by-case delimitation provides no solution in the long term and fails to provide necessary legal certainty. For an extensive discussion, see F. SMITH and L. WOODS, 'A Distinction without a Difference: Exploring the Boundary between Goods and Services in the World Trade Organization and the European Union', *Columbia Journal of European Law* (2005), pp. 1–60.

[436] *Ibid.* art. I.2. See J. CROOME, *supra* note 8, pp. 163–165.

[437] *E.g.* a financial service or legal advice.

abroad[438]; (iii) Mode 3: commercial presence, *i.e.* the service provider has commercial presence abroad (*legal* person), no matter what form the subsidiary or branch takes; and (iv) Mode 4: the presence of a *natural* person in the territory of another Member in order to offer services.[439]

It should also be noted that, because of the 'immaterial' nature of a service, the provisions in the GATS not only apply to services, but also to service providers. Indeed, although Modes 1 and 2 still focus on the movement of the service, Modes 3 and 4 rather concern the movement of the service provider (legal or natural person). As will be explained below (*infra* para. 138), this has some implications for addressing the problem of 'likeness'.

137. The GATS contains two types of obligations. There are, first, general obligations and principles, which apply in principle immediately to all service sectors and providers of all Members of the WTO. These obligations are included in Part II of the GATS.[440] Second, there are obligations that only apply if a WTO Member has made specific commitments, indicating that these obligations apply to the national services sectors upon which, and to the extent that, the country has inscribed a specific commitment in its Schedule of Commitments.[441] These obligations are included in Part III of the GATS. We will address the most important obligations here.

---

[438] *E.g.* receiving medical treatment abroad.

[439] *E.g.* an architect or contractor. This mode of supply might have been very important for developing countries who see this as an important tool for labour migration. Nevertheless, the GATS Annex on Movement of Natural Persons Supplying Services under the Agreement stipulates that the GATS 'shall not apply to measures affecting natural persons seeking access to the employment market of a Member, nor shall it apply to measures regarding citizenship, residence or employment on a permanent basis' (para. 2 of this Annex). Moreover, the GATS does not prevent a Member from applying measures to regulate the entry of natural persons into, or their temporary stay in, its territory, including those measures necessary to protect the integrity of, and to ensure the orderly movement of natural persons across, its borders. Yet, such measures cannot be applied in such manner as to nullify of impair the benefits under a specific commitment (see para. 4 of this Annex). The footnote to this paragraph notes that the "sole fact of requiring a visa for natural persons of certain Members and not for those of others shall not be regarded as nullifying or impairing benefits." HOEKMAN and MAVROIDIS argue that this Annex does not prevent WTO Members from making specific commitments under Mode 4 that would involve long term (thus non-temporary) stay of natural persons. See B. HOEKMAN and P. MAVROIDIS, *supra* note 103, p. 67.

[440] However, some obligations spelled out in Part II only apply to sectors in which a Member has taken specific commitments.

[441] In contrast to trade in goods, trade in services is not protected by tariffs. Service providers in a certain WTO Member will thus experience a sharp competition if foreign service providers in the territory of that Member, are receiving immediately the same treatment as them: M. DJORDEVIC, 'Domestic Regulation and Free Trade in Services – A Balancing Act', *Legal Issues of Economic Integration* (2002), p. 306.

2. General Obligations and Disciplines

138. Article II GATS contains the general principle of *Most Favoured Nation*. It is a general obligation that applies from the start. It prohibits both *de jure*[442] and *de facto*[443] discrimination.[444] Nevertheless, practical effect of the principle of Most Favoured Nation is different from GATT. It was possible for WTO Members to inscribe exemptions on its application when the GATS was drafted (or upon accession to the WTO).[445] The GATS Annex on Article II exemptions notes that abolition of the exemptions is subject to negotiation.[446] In principle, these exemptions could not have a duration of more than 10 years (Article II.2 GATS) and would thus have expired in December 2005. Yet, because their expiration is subject to negotiations and the Hong Kong Ministerial Conference could not agree upon this, the exemptions are still applicable. Some countries already indicated that they are not willing to give up some of their exceptions in the current negotiations.

As with any provision on non-discrimination, also for the MFN principle in GATS it needs to be defined whether the services or service suppliers are 'like' and whether they are treated differently. The criteria that are used to determine the likeness of *services* are not much elaborated upon in dispute settlement on trade in services. A Panel mentioned the nature and characteristics of the services as criteria.[447] This seems to suggest that the same criteria are used as for goods, namely end-uses, consumer tastes and habits and product characteristics. Nevertheless, several authors argue that some criteria for goods are of limited use

---

[442] A measure discriminates *de jure* if it is based on the difference in origin of a service or a service supplier.
[443] A measure discriminates *de facto* if it is formally origin-neutral but nevertheless has a discriminatory effect.
[444] This was indeed stated by the Panel in Panel Report: European Communities – Regime for the Importation, Sale and Distribution of Bananas, WT/DS27/R/ECU, WT/DS27/R/MEX and WT/DS27/R/USA, (22 May 1997), paras. 7.301–304. The Panel referred to the explicit reference in art. XVII.2 GATS (National Treatment) to the fact that either formally identical or formally different treatment may be required to comply with the non-discrimination standard in art. XVII GATS. The Appellate Body agreed that the MFN principle in art. II GATS extends both to formally identical and formally different treatment and thus to *de jure* and *de facto* discrimination, but suggested that rather reference should be made to the MFN principle in art. I GATT, which applied to both *de jure* and *de facto* discrimination. See Appellate Body Report: European Communities – Regime for the Importation, Sale and Distribution of Bananas, WT/DS27/AB/R, (9 September 1997), paras. 232–234.
[445] It was decided during the Uruguay Round that "liberalization subject to some temporary MFN exceptions would be preferable to no liberalization at all." J. CROOME, *supra* note 8, p. 166.
[446] Para. 6 GATS Annex on Article II exemptions.
[447] See Panel Report: European Communities – Regime for the Importation, Sale and Distribution of Bananas, WT/DS27/R/ECU, WT/DS27/R/MEX and WT/DS27/R/USA, (22 May 1997), para. 7.322.

for services.[448] It may be submitted that in defining likeness, one should mainly focus on the interchangeability of the services (determined by their end-uses) by applying a cross-price elasticity test. It seems even less clear what criteria should be applied for determining whether *service suppliers* are like. A Panel has merely noted with regard to 'likeness' of service suppliers in Article II GATS (MFN) that "to the extent that the service suppliers concerned supply the same services, they should be considered 'like'".[449] Despite its concise formulation, the impact of this statement may be wide-sweeping.[450] As soon as services are like, the service providers are also considered like. In an extreme reading, this would limit to a great extent the regulatory autonomy of WTO Members: if the likeness of services determines the likeness of the providers, any regulation which draws distinctions between providers because they have *e.g.* different qualifications, would be outlawed. Some authors have therefore argued that a 'disjunctive' test should be applied: if the measure in question concerns services, the likeness of services should be considered; if the measure concerns suppliers, the likeness of service suppliers should be examined.[451] Other authors argue that it is difficult to separate the characteristics of services and service suppliers because they are so much intertwined. Likeness of the service providers will then be defined as a "function of the likeness of the services".[452] The question is then what characteristics of the providers are relevant to decide that the providers are not 'like'. The relevance of the characteristics is determined by considering which characteristics influence consumer decisions on interchangeability of services.

139. A second important general obligation is the obligation of *transparency* (Article III GATS). Lack of knowledge of the diverse national regulations applicable to services may strongly discourage services providers to offer their

---

[448] Indeed, it makes often no sense to define the physical characteristics of something immaterial as a service. Neither is the classification of a service in the Central Product Classification System of much use since this System is much less developed than the Harmonised System for goods. See M. MATTOO, 'National Treatment in the GATS: Corner-Stone or Pandora's Box?', *Journal of World Trade* (1997), pp. 107–136, at p. 127–128 and W. ZDOUC, 'WTO Dispute Settlement Practice Relating to the General Agreement on Trade in Services', in F. ORTINO and E.-U. PETERSMANN (eds.), *The WTO Dispute Settlement System 1995–2003*, (Antwerp, Kluwer 2004), pp. 395–397.

[449] Panel Report: Canada – Certain Measures Affecting the Automotive Industry, WT/DS193 and 142/R, (11 February 2000), para. 10.248.

[450] W. ZDOUC, *supra* note 448, at p. 398.

[451] See K. NICOLAIDIS and J. TRACHTMAN, 'From Policed Regulation to Managed Recognition: Mapping the Boundary of GATS', in J. TRACHTMAN, *The International Economic Law Revolution and the Right to Regulate*, (London, Cameron May 2006), pp. 294–295. See also, approving this approach, M. KRAJEWSKI, *National Regulation and Trade Liberalization in Services: The Legal Impact of the General Agreement on Trade in Services (GATS) on National Regulatory Autonomy*, (The Hague, Kluwer 2003), pp. 106–107.

[452] See G. VERHOOSEL, *National Treatment and WTO Dispute Settlement*, (Oxford, Hart Publishing 2000), p. 63.

services to consumers in other WTO Members. The obligation of transparency is designed to address this problem. Each WTO Member must publish all relevant measures of general application which pertain to or affect the provision of services.[453] Hence national legislation (and international agreements if relevant) concerning *inter alia* legal services, accountancy services, telecommunications etc. must be made public to enable foreign service providers to take them into account. What is more, each WTO Member must promptly and at least annually inform the Council for Trade in Services of the introduction of new (or of changes to existing) laws, regulations or administrative guidelines which significantly affect trade in services covered by its specific commitments.[454] It must also respond to requests for information on these measures of general application. WTO Members are obliged to provide inquiry points where other Members can collect all necessary information on the national regulation that is applicable in a certain service sector.[455]

140. A third important obligation concerns Article VI on *domestic regulation*.[456] National services regulations that do not lay down quantitative or maximum limitations (and therefore are not caught by Article XVI on Market Access (see *infra* para. 144)) and are not discriminatory (and therefore not caught by Art. II (MFN) or by Art. XVII (National Treatment (see *infra* para. 145))[457] may still

---

[453] If prompt publication is not practicable, the information must be made otherwise publicly available (Article II.2 GATS).
[454] So, this obligation is subject to a specific commitment made by the WTO Member concerned.
[455] In case of the request for information by developing countries, the GATS goes even further. Developed countries have to install inquiry points where service providers from developing countries (and not only their governments) can collect all necessary information. See art. IV GATS.
[456] For a more in-depth analysis on this contentious issue, see *inter alia* M. DJORDEVIC, *supra* note 441, pp. 305–322; J.H. JACKSON, 'The WTO: Domestic Regulation and the Challenge of Shaping Trade: Presentation Summary and Comments', *International Lawyer* (2003), pp. 809–816; M. KRAJEWSKI, *National Regulation and Trade Liberalization in Services: the Legal Impact of the General Agreement on Trade in Services (GATS) on National Regulatory Autonomy*, (The Hague, Kluwer 2003), xxii + 245 p.; A. MATTOO and P. SAUVÉ (eds.), *Domestic Regulation and Services Trade Liberalization*, (Washington, World Bank and Oxford University Press 2003), 236 p.; D.A. OSIRO, 'GATT/WTO Necessity Analysis: Evolutionary Interpretation and Its Impact on the Autonomy of Domestic Regulation', *Legal Issues of Economic Integration* (2002), pp. 123–141; P. SAUVÉ and A. MATTOO, 'Domestic Regulation and the Gats: Untangling the Issues', in P. SAUVÉ (ed.), *Trade Rules Behind Borders: Essays on Services, Investment and the New Trade Agenda*, (London, Cameron May 2003), pp. 113–130; W. WARREN, 'The WTO: Domestic Regulation and the Challenge of Shaping Trade', *International Lawyer* (2003), pp. 677–695 and J. WOUTERS and D. COPPENS, 'Domestic Regulation within the Framework of GATS', in K. BYTTEBIER, K. VAN DER BORGHT (eds.), J. WOUTERS and F. ZIA MANSOOR (ass. eds.), *WTO Obligations and Opportunities: Challenges of Implementation* (London, Cameron May 2007), pp. 25–84.
[457] It seems that nothing in the GATS explicitly excludes that also discriminatory measures may fall within the scope of art. VI.4–5. It may be useful to clarify this issue since, in the case of overlap of scope, even if a WTO Member has made no commitments under art. XVII GATS,

result in double regulatory burdens for service suppliers that want to provide their services in several WTO Members at the same time. Hence, regulatory diversity may lead to obstacles to the cross-border provision of services. Fully removing this regulatory diversity would require harmonization of the national regulation on services. Article VI GATS lays down some provisions to make sure that these diverse national regulations do not impede the cross-border provision of services. Some of the paragraphs of Article VI apply to all services sectors. Other paragraphs only apply to services sectors where specific commitments have been made. There are first of all a number of procedural requirements set out in domestic regulations.[458] Article VI.1 requires that, for sectors where specific commitments have been made, measures of general application affecting trade in services be administered in a reasonable, objective and impartial manner. Again, in sectors where specific commitments have been made, when it is necessary to obtain an authorization to provide services, Article VI.3 requires that such authorization be decided upon by the Member's authorities within a reasonable period of time after the request for authorization. In sectors where specific commitments have been made, Members must also provide for adequate procedures to verify the competence of professionals from another Member (Art. VI.6). Article VI.2 requires WTO Members to maintain or institute as soon as practicable judicial, arbitral and administrative tribunals or procedures to provide appropriate remedies to challenge administrative decisions affecting trade in services. Such procedures must provide for an objective and impartial review. Article VI.2 applies to *all service sectors*, regardless whether a specific commitment has been made or not.

The remaining paragraphs of Article VI GATS (VI.4 and VI.5) go beyond merely procedural requirements. They apply to a limited set of domestic regulations (specifically: qualification requirements and procedures, technical standards and licensing requirements). Similar to the desire of States to monitor the sale of goods so as to protect consumers, health, the environment etc., it may be necessary to guarantee the quality of service delivery. It is therefore possible that degrees, certificates or licences are required.[459] Articles VI.4 and 5 GATS are intended to

---

the measure may still violate the disciplines of art. VI.4. In Paragraph 1 of the Accountancy Disciplines, it was explicitly indicated that they do not apply to measures subject to scheduling under Articles XVI and XVII of the GATS, See para. 1 Working Party on Professional Services, Disciplines on Domestic Regulation in the Accountancy Sector, S/WPPS/W/21, 30 November 1998, adopted by the Council on Trade in Services Decision S/L/63 of 14 December 1998. If no commitments were made under art. XVII GATS, art. VI.5 would not apply anyway, since it only applies as far as specific commitments were made.

[458] See Panel Report: United States – Measures Affecting the Cross-Border Supply of Gambling and Betting Services, WT/DS285/R (10 November 2004), para. 6.432.

[459] Paragraph 4 of the Preamble of GATS recognizes the right of 'Members to regulate and to introduce new regulations, on the supply of services within their territories in order to meet

prevent the three specific types of domestic regulations from constituting unnecessary barriers to trade. To that end, the Working Party on Domestic Regulation (see *infra* para. 296) tries to develop so-called 'disciplines'. These disciplines should ensure that the mentioned national regulations are (a) based on objective and transparent criteria; (b) not more burdensome than necessary to ensure the quality of the service and (c) in case of licensing procedures not in themselves a restriction on the supply of the service. It should be noted, however, that negotiations on such disciplines in the Working Party on Domestic Regulation are still on-going and have not produced any concrete results. Only under its predecessor, the Working Party on Professional Services (which had a more limited mandate), *Disciplines on Domestic Regulation in the Accountancy Sector* were developed.[460] An important element of these Disciplines is the so-called necessity test. Paragraph 2 of the Disciplines states that Members must ensure that regulatory measures for accountancy shall not be more trade-restrictive than necessary to fulfil the legitimate objective they pursue. It is clear that this necessity test may potentially provide a serious limitation of the national regulatory autonomy of WTO Members in the field of services. It is intended that these disciplines are fully integrated in the GATS before the end of the Doha Negotiation Round. As has been said, the current negotiations on further disciplines are still on-going. There is much disagreement on how they should be designed (horizontal or sector-specific, including a necessity test or not). It is also unclear what their legal status will be: will they become a part of the GATS, as is intended with the Disciplines on Accountancy Services, or will they merely form additional commitments that can be voluntarily undertaken by Members (as is possible under Article XVIII GATS)?

Pending the entry into force of new disciplines developed under Article VI.4, Members cannot, in sectors *where specific commitments have been made*, apply licensing and qualification requirements and technical standards that nullify or impair the specific commitments (Article VI.5 (a) GATS). This would be the case if they are nontransparent, more burdensome than necessary and (in case of

---

national policy objectives [...]'. See J. WOUTERS and D. COPPENS, 'GATS and Domestic Regulations: Balancing the Right to Regulate and Trade Liberalization', in M. ANDENAS and K. ALEXANDER (eds.), *The World Trade Organization and Trade in Services*, (The Hague, Nijhoff 2008), pp. 207–262.

[460] Working Party on Professional Services, Disciplines on Domestic Regulation in the Accountancy Sector, S/WPPS/W/21, 30 November 1998, adopted by the Council on Trade in Services Decision S/L/63 of 14 December 1998. They have not yet entered into force. In the Decision by which the Council on Trade in Services adopted the Disciplines, it was stated that they are meant to become integral part of the GATS "no later than at the conclusion of the forthcoming round of services negotiations."

licensing procedures) in themselves a restriction on the supply of a service.[461] Yet, it would in addition be necessary that these new measures could not reasonably have been expected by other WTO Members at the time that the specific commitments were made by the Member who is now adopting the measures.[462] The existence of the latter condition may be very difficult to prove. Indeed, if the measures that are now challenged existed when the commitments were made, they cannot lead to nullification and impairment because they could reasonably be expected. On the contrary, for measures that are adopted *after* the commitments are made, it is (rebuttably) presumed that they could not reasonably be anticipated.[463] Only newly adopted measures are thus subject to the discipline of Article VI.5. With regard to existing measures, the focus lies much more on eliminating them at the time that the concessions were made. It should finally be noted that Article VI.5 (b) GATS indicates that when determining whether a Member is in conformity with the obligations under Article VI.5 (a), account shall be taken of international standards of relevant international organizations, applied by that Member. Thus, like for the TBT and the SPS Agreements, a link is made to the work of international standard-setting organizations.

141. A fourth general obligation worth mentioning is Article VII concerning *recognition* by one WTO Member of the education or experience obtained, requirements met or licences or certifications granted in another WTO Member. This can be done through harmonization (as is done in the European Community) or on the basis of an agreement of mutual recognition. If a mutual recognition agreement is concluded, other WTO Members must have an adequate opportunity to negotiate their accession to such an agreement. It may also be possible that a Member unilaterally recognizes the equivalence of such requirements in certain other Members. In that case, any WTO Member must have the opportunity to demonstrate the equivalence of its requirements. Such recognition may not amount to discrimination between WTO Members or a disguised restriction of trade (Article VII.3). In order that such recognition does not become a way to discriminate between WTO Members, Article VII.5 notes that WTO Members must cooperate with intergovernmental and non-governmental organizations to

---

[461] In fact, the three ways in which domestic regulation would constitute an unnecessary barrier to trade, as mentioned in art. VI.4, are repeated here.

[462] TRACHTMAN and NICOLAIDIS have stated that this means that art. VI.5 is in fact only a 'standstill' obligation. See K. NICOLAIDIS and J. TRACHTMAN, 'From Policed Regulation to Managed Recognition: Mapping the Boundary of GATS', *in* J. TRACHTMAN, *The International Economic Law Revolution and the Right to Regulate*, (London, Cameron May 2006), pp. 281–321, at p. 299.

[463] See Panel Report: Japan – Measures Affecting Consumer Photographic Film and Paper, WT/DS44/R, (31 March 1998), para. 10.61. In this report, the Panel addressed the condition of nullification and impairment to bring a non-violation complaint under art. XXIII.1 (b) GATT.

establish common international standards on the basis of which such mutual recognition can take place.[464]

142. Finally, there are some general provisions relevant to competition law and subsidies. The obligations relevant to competition law concerns monopolies/ exclusive service suppliers as well as restrictive business practices. To guarantee the quality of service provision in sensitive sectors, States also provide regulations that grant particular service providers exclusive rights. WTO Members must assure in such cases that *exclusive service providers* do not abuse their monopoly position or exclusive rights.[465] WTO Members have also recognized that certain business practices, other than those by the mentioned exclusive service providers, may restrain competition and thereby restrict trade in services (Article IX.1 GATS). WTO Members must enter into consultations to eliminate such practices.

At present, there is no regime in the GATS that disciplines *subsidies* in favour of service providers. Article XV GATS states that Members must enter into negotiations with a view to developing the necessary multilateral disciplines to avoid trade-distorting effects of service subsidies and to address the appropriateness of countervailing measures.[466] If certain Members experience adverse effects, they may request consultations with the subsidising Member.[467] Remarkably, contrary to the GATT, the GATS provision on national treatment (*infra* para. 145) does not contain an exception for subsidies granted to domestic producers (service providers). If a WTO Member has made a commitment to provide national treatment in a service sector, and has made no exception for subsidies, subsidies to service providers must be granted in the same way to foreign service providers.

3. *Specific Commitments*

143. The second category of obligations in the GATS apply only as far as specific commitments have been undertaken by a WTO Member. These specific commitments are inscribed in Member's *schedules of specific commitments*. Not unlike what is the case for GATT, WTO Members have made liberalization

---

[464] An important forum for doing so is the Working Party on Domestic Regulation. Yet, also outside the WTO, many fora may be relevant. For financial services, the standards developed by the Basel Committee on Banking Supervision, the International Organization for Securities Commissions, the International Association for Insurance Supervisors and the International Accountants Standards Board (a non-governmental organization) may be relevant. For telecommunications services, the standards set by the International Standardization Organization and the International Telecommunications Union should be considered.
[465] Art. VIII.1-2 GATS.
[466] For the latest state of play, see Working Party on GATS Rules – Report of the Meeting of 21 June 2006, WTO Doc. S/WPGR/M/56, 4 July 2006, paras. 2–26.
[467] Art. XV.2 GATS.

commitments (removing regulatory barriers) according to the Services Classification List[468] (which is based on the United Nations Central Product Classification System).[469]

144. The specific commitments concern first of all the principle of *Market Access* (Article XVI GATS). If WTO Members make specific commitments on Market Access in specific sectors, they cannot maintain or adopt certain measures that impede the access to these sectors unless otherwise specified in its Schedule. It seems that the measures that are prohibited by this provision may be either of a discriminatory or non-discriminatory nature (which may distinguish it from the National Treatment obligation in Article XVII GATS, which only prohibits discriminatory measures).[470] Nevertheless, only *quantitative* measures or, in the

---

[468] WTO Secretariat, Services Sectoral Classification List, Note by the Secretariat, MTN.GNS/W/120, 10 July 1990. The use of the Services Sectoral Classification List is not obligatory, yet it is encouraged to use it in the Guidelines for Trade in Services of 2001. See Council for Trade in Services, Guidelines for the Scheduling of Specific Commitments under the General Agreement on Trade in Services, S/L/92, 28 March 2001.

[469] United Nations Central Product Classification System, Version 1.1, UN Doc ST/ESA/STAT/SER.M/77/Ver.1.1, March 2002, available on http://unstats.un.org/unsd/cr/registry/regcst.asp?Cl=16&Lg=1.

[470] See E. LEROUX, 'Eleven Years of GATS Case Law: What Have We Learned?', *Journal of International Economic Law* (2007), advance access 24 July 2007, doi:10.1093/jiel/jgm014, p. 20. As ORTINO argues, it may be necessary to make a distinction between the scope of application of the provisions and the normative content of the provisions. F. ORTINO, 'Treaty Interpretation and the WTO Appellate Body Report in *US-Gambling*: A Critique', *Journal of International Economic Law* (2006), pp. 117–148, at p. 137. With regard to the *scope of application* of art. XVI, PAUWELYN argues that art. XVI covers measures that apply only to imported services and foreign suppliers as well as measures that apply to imports and foreign suppliers at the same time as to domestic services and suppliers. Art. XVII on National Treatment would cover the same measures as art. XVI on Market Access, but would of course have a broader scope of application since art. XVI applies only to the limited list of measures in art. XVI ?, whereas art. XVII applies to all measures affecting the supply of a service. See J. PAUWELYN, '*Rien ne Va Plus?* Distinguishing Domestic Regulation from Market Access in GATT and GATS', *World Trade Review* (2005), pp. 131–170, at pp. 148–149. On the contrary, MAVROIDIS sees the scope of application of art. XVI more restricted as covering measures that apply only to imported services and foreign suppliers and not to domestic services or suppliers. Art. XVII would then cover measures that apply only to imported services and foreign suppliers as well as measures that apply to imported services and foreign suppliers as well as to domestic services and suppliers. See P. MAVROIDIS, 'Highway XVI Re-Visited: The Road from Non-discrimination to Market Access in GATS', *World Trade Review* (2007), pp. 1–23, at p. 9. The specific scope of application is important because the normative content of art. XVI and XVII differs. Art. XVI imposes an absolute prohibition to adopt one of the listed measures in art. XVI. In contrast, art. XVII imposes a more nuanced test: the measures falling within art. XVII are only prohibited if they are discriminatory. This means that, under PAUWELYN's approach, measures that apply to imported services or foreign suppliers as well as to domestic services or suppliers that are of the type listed in art. XVI.2 will be immediately prohibited (of course as far as art. XVI commitments have been made and unless justified under one of the GATS exceptions). These measures may at the same time also violate art. XVII, if they are discriminatory. In that case, they violate both art. XVI and XVII. Other authors seem to take a similar approach on

Overview of the WTO Agreements

view of some authors, measures that impose maximum limitations[471] are caught by the prohibition to limit market access as provided in a Member's schedules of specific commitments.[472] The enumeration of the measures in Article XVII.2 is exhaustive.[473] It concerns (a) limitations on the number of services suppliers;[474] (b) limitations on the total value of service transactions or assets; (c) limitations on the total number of service operations or the total quantity of the service output[475] expressed in terms of designated numerical units; (d) limitations on the total number of natural persons that may be employed in a particular service sector or that a service supplier may employ and who are necessary for, and directly related to, the supply of a specific service[476]; (e) measures which restrict

---

the scope of art. XVI and XVII, but derive from art. XX.2 GATS (which states that measures inconsistent with both articles and for which a Member wants to ensure their maintenance even though commitments are made, must be inscribed in the column relating to art. XVI), that once a measure falls within the scope of art. XVI, art. XVII does not apply. See M. KRAJEWSKI, *supra* note 456, p. 115. On the contrary, under MAVROIDIS' approach, such measures will not fall under art. XVI (which only applies to measures that apply only to imported services or foreign suppliers) but need to be considered under art. XVII. If they are *de jure* or *de facto* discriminatory, they violate art. XVII. Moreover, these measures may also violate art. VI.4 or 5 GATS, depending on whether they fall within the scope of application of these provisions and fail to satisfy the test set out. Measures that violate art. XVI (*i.e.* measures that apply only to imported services or foreign suppliers) violate at the same time art. XVII (since they treat imported services or foreign suppliers less favourably). According to MAVROIDIS, because of the overlap between the scope of art. XVI and XVII, art. XVI becomes only relevant if no commitments were made under art. XVII.

[471] See P. DELIMATSIS, 'Don't Gamble with GATS—The Interaction between Articles VI, XVI, XVII and XVIII GATS in the Light of the US-Gambling Case', *Journal of World Trade* (2006), pp. 1059-1080, at pp. 1070-7071. See also J. PAUWELYN, *supra* previous note, at pp. 152-153. ORTINO argues that the distinction between measures falling within the scope of art. XVI and those within art. VI is not so much their 'quantitative' nature, but rather the fact that the measures that fall within the scope of art. XVI are (rebuttably) *presumed* to have no legitimate public policy justification. See F. ORTINO, *supra* previous note, at p. 142.

[472] See Appellate Body Report: United States – Measures Affecting the Cross-Border Supply of Gambling and Betting Services, WT/DS285/AB/R, (7 April 2004), para. 232.

[473] *Ibid.* para. 238. It should be noted that the Panel and the Appellate Body agreed that a prohibition to provide services may amount to a zero quota and thus also be such quantitative limitation (more specifically as mentioned in art. XVI.2 (a) and (c)). The interpretation by the Panel and Appellate Body that the list in art. XVI.2 is limitative is not uncontested. See M. MATSUSHITA, T. SCHOENBAUM and P. MAVROIDIS, *supra* note 60, pp. 655-657. The Appellate Body did not adhere to a strict interpretation of the listed measures in art. XVI.2. Neither did the Appellate Body agree that all measures that have the *effect* of limiting the number of service suppliers would fall within the scope of art. XVI.2. Appellate Body Report: United States – Measures Affecting the Cross-Border Supply of Gambling and Betting Services, WT/DS285/AB/R, (7 April 2004), paras. 231-232. For a critique on this approach, indicating the uncertainty resulting from the ambiguous statements of the Appellate Body, see P. DELIMATSIS, *supra* note 471, at pp. 1067-1068 and note 49.

[474] This can be in the form of numerical quotas, monopolies, exclusive service suppliers or on the basis of an economic needs test (whereby the national authority decides whether there is a 'need' for the foreign supplier being present on the market, *e.g.* on the basis of market saturation).

[475] Measures that limit the total quantity of services output are not prohibited under art. XVI.2 (c).

[476] The measures prohibited under (b)-(d) will take the form of quotas or an economic needs test.

or require specific types of legal entity or joint venture through which a service supplier may supply a service and (f) limitations on the participation of foreign capital in terms maximum percentage limit on foreign shareholding or the total value of individual or aggregate foreign investment.

145. A second obligation that only applies as far as a WTO Member has made a specific commitment concerns the *National Treatment* obligation. This principle has the same meaning as in Article III GATT: a WTO Member cannot discriminate between foreign services and service suppliers, on the one hand, and like domestic services and domestic service suppliers, on the other hand. Again, a determination of 'likeness' of the services and service suppliers needs to be made, on the basis of the criteria set out above for the MFN principle (see *supra* para. 138). Article XVII.3 GATS explicitly extends the national treatment requirement to formally identical treatment. It therefore covers both *de jure*[477] and *de facto*[478] discrimination. In case of *de jure* discrimination, the fact that a regulatory distinction is based on the specific national origin may suggest that there is obviously a violation of the principle of National Treatment. Yet, as it has been stated for trade in goods, it is always necessary to show that because of the distinction the conditions of competition are less favourable.[479] Hence, formally different treatment does not *per se* violate Article XVII GATS.[480] Article XVII.2 GATS has an explicit reference to the fact that either formally identical or formally different treatment may be required to comply with the non-discrimination standard in Article XVII GATS. The Appellate Body has clarified on the basis of Article XVII.2 that the National Treatment principle in the GATS applies also to *de facto* discrimination.[481] Footnote 10 to Article XVII GATS puts a limit to the scrutiny of the National Treatment provision. It provides that the commitments under the National Treatment provision of the GATS made by WTO Members 'shall not be construed to require any Member to compensate for any inherent competitive disadvantages which result from the foreign character of the relevant services or service suppliers'. This footnote makes clear what the obligation of National Treatment is *not* about.[482] WTO Members that made a specific commitment are not required to compensate for disadvantages that are merely due to the foreign character of the

---

[477] A measure discriminates *de jure* if it is based on the difference in origin of a service or a service supplier.
[478] A measure discriminates *de facto* if it is formally origin-neutral but nevertheless has a discriminatory effect.
[479] See Appellate Body Report: Korea – Measures Affecting Imports of Fresh, Chilled and Frozen Beef, WT/DS161 and 169/AB/R (11 December 2000), paras. 135–137.
[480] There is an explicit reference in art. XVII.3 to the fact that treatment is less favourable if it modifies the conditions of competition in favour of domestic services or service suppliers.
[481] Appellate Body Report: European Communities – Regime for the Importation, Sale and Distribution of Bananas, WT/DS27/AB/R, (9 September 1997), para. 233.
[482] See M. KRAJEWSKI, *supra* note 456, p. 111.

service or service supplier. It "does not provide cover for actions which might modify the conditions of competition against services and service suppliers which are already disadvantaged due to their foreign character".[483] The problem is of course how to distinguish in practice the inherent competitive disadvantages from those created by the regulatory measure.[484]

Finally, WTO Members can even go beyond their Market Access and National Treatment commitments and make *additional commitments* (Article XVIII GATS). Such commitments can include (but are not limited to) undertakings with respect to qualifications, technical standards, licensing procedures and other domestic regulations that are consistent with Article VI[485] and with Article XVI and Article XVII GATS.

4. *Exceptions*

146. As in the GATT, the GATS contains a number of exceptions to the obligations. The main, general exception concerns Article XIV GATS. Article XIV GATS has the same structure as Article XX GATT: there are a number of specific policy goals that 'trump' the goal of free trade in services and there is an introductory paragraph ('chapeau') that sets conditions to the way the particular national measure is applied. Therefore, the case-law on Article XX GATT is also relevant for Article XIV GATS.[486] As in case of Article XX GATT, the Panels and Appellate Body first consider whether the measure pursues one of the goals listed in Article XIV (a)-(e). In a second step, they consider whether the way the measure is applied satisfies the conditions of the chapeau.

147. Some of the *specific policy goals* enumerated in Article XIV (a)-(e) are similar to GATT; others are different. There are also a number of goals that are mentioned in GATT but are absent under the GATS. Nothing in the GATS prevents WTO Members from taking measures (a) necessary to protect public

---

[483] Panel Report: Canada – Certain Measures Affecting the Automotive Industry, WT/DS193 and 142/R, (11 February 2000), para. 10.300.
[484] ZDOUC has elaborated a theoretical test on how to compare, on the one hand, the restrictive impact of the measure on the foreign service or provider with, on the other hand, the restrictive effect of the regulation on the domestic service or provider *plus* the inherent competitive advantages from being a foreign service or provider. This test is difficult to apply in practice because the restrictive impact needs to be quantified somehow. This is recognized by ZDOUC himself. W. ZDOUC, *supra* note 448, p. 412.
[485] See 2001 Scheduling Guidelines.
[486] See Appellate Body Report: United States – Measures Affecting the Cross-Border Supply of Gambling and Betting Services, WT/DS285/AB/R, (7 April 2004), para. 305 *et seq.*

morals or to maintain public order[487] (the latter goal is absent in Article XX GATT); (b) necessary to protect human, animal or plant life or health and (c) necessary to secure compliance with laws or regulations which are not inconsistent with the provisions of the GATS. (This includes measures relating to (i) the prevention of deceptive and fraudulent practices or to deal with the effects of a default on services contracts, (ii) the protection of privacy of individuals in relation to the processing and dissemination of personal data and the protection of confidentiality of individual records and accounts, (iii) safety.) Two exceptions are made to particular GATS provisions (and not to *all* obligations): (d) measures that are inconsistent with the National Treatment obligation, provided that the difference in treatment is aimed at ensuring the equitable or effective imposition or collection of direct taxes in respect of services or service suppliers of other WTO Members and (e) measures that are inconsistent with the MFN principle, provided that the difference in treatment is the result of an agreement on the avoidance of double taxation or provisions on the avoidance of double taxation in any other international agreement or arrangement.

Once it is determined that the measure in question falls within one of the paragraphs of Article XIV (a)-(e), it should be defined whether the way the measure is applied constitutes a means of *arbitrary* or *unjustifiable* discrimination between Members where the like conditions prevail, or a *disguised restriction on trade* in services (chapeau of Art. XIV). There would be discrimination if a WTO Member does not behave consistently across comparable situations.[488]

Furthermore, Article XIV*bis* GATS provides for exceptions for measures that pursue essential security interests.

---

[487] In the first and, until now, only case relating to Article XIV(a) GATS, the Panel noted that "'public order' refers to the preservation of the fundamental interests of a society, as reflected in public policy and law." Nevertheless, a WTO Member that relies on this provision to defend its measures will have to prove that his trade-restrictive measure was 'necessary' to protect public order. This involves a 'weighing and balancing' of (a) the importance of the interests that are protected; (b) the extent to which the measures contribute to achieve the end pursued and (c) the respective trade impact of the measures. Complying with this test is often very difficult. See Panel Report: United States – Measures Affecting the Cross-border Supply of Gambling and Betting Services, WT/DS285/R, (10 November 2004), paras. 6.467 and 6.475–6.477. On the 'weighing and balancing' see also Appellate Body Report: Korea – Measures Affecting Imports of Fresh, Chilled and Frozen Beef, WT/DS161/AB/R and WT/DS169/AB/R, (10 January 2001), para. 178 and Appellate Body Report: European Communities – Measures Affecting Asbestos and Asbestos-Containing Products, WT/DS135/AB/R, (5 April 2001), para. 172. In its report on the 'Gambling case', the Appellate Body stressed that the alternative measure should be 'reasonably available'. It thereby showed that one should assess carefully in every case whether indeed such alternative is really attaining the objective that is pursued. See Appellate Body Report: United States – Measures Affecting the Cross-Border Supply of Gambling and Betting Services, WT/DS285/AB/R, (7 April 2004), para. 326.

[488] *Ibid.* paras. 351 and 356.

148. Moreover, Article V GATS provides an exemption for economic integration agreements. There are a number of differences between Article V GATS and Article XXIV GATT. The differences with Article XXIV start already with the heading of the article. It does not refer to customs unions or free trade areas. Instead, it states that Members may enter into an 'agreement liberalizing trade in services between or among the parties to such an agreement'. This is probably because, generally, there are no customs duties or tariffs levied on imports and exports of services.[489] A more fundamental difference concerns the formulation of the '*internal trade requirement*' in Article V.1(a) GATS. The provision indeed states that the regional agreements must have 'substantial sectoral coverage'. This condition should be 'understood in terms of number of sectors, volume of trade affected and modes of supply. In order to meet this condition, agreements should not provide for the a priori exclusion of any mode of supply'.[490] There is thus no requirement for the regional agreements to cover substantially all trade. They can be limited to certain sectors or sub-sectors. In the sectors that are covered in the agreement, substantially all discrimination has to be eliminated between or among the parties.[491] No new or more discriminatory measures can be introduced.[492] This obligation is narrower than in case of Article XXIV GATT, where all duties and other restrictive trade regulations must be eliminated. The '*external trade requirement*' specifies that the agreement should in respect of any WTO Member outside the regional agreement not raise the overall level of barriers to trade in services within the respective sectors or subsectors compared to the level applicable prior to the agreement.[493] Yet, if a WTO Member modifies its schedule of specific commitments because of the establishment of the regional trade agreement, it has to offer compensation.[494] Planned economic integration agreements must be notified to the Council for Trade in Services, who may then establish a Working Party to examine the agreement.[495] Contrary to what is the case for Article XXIV GATT, the GATS allows for some special flexibility for north–south regional agreements in the application of the mentioned conditions.[496] In case of south–south trade agreements, the degree of flexibility can even be greater.[497]

---

[489] See H. RUIZ FABRI, 'Les accords externes de la Communauté européenne sous le contrôle de l'Organisation Mondiale du commerce', in M.-F. CHRISTOPHE TCHAKALOFF, *Le concept d'association dans les accords passés par la Communauté: Essai de clarification*, (Bruxelles, Bruylant 1999), p. 258.
[490] Note to art. V.1 (a) GATS.
[491] *Ibid*. art. V.1 (b) (i).
[492] *Ibid*. art. V.1 (b) (ii).
[493] *Ibid*. art. V.4.
[494] *Ibid*. art. V.5.
[495] *Ibid*. art. V.7 (a).
[496] *Ibid*. art. V.3.
[497] *Ibid*. art. V.3 (b).

Chapter III

149. Article XII GATS also contains an exception for measures taken in case of balance-of-payments and external financial difficulties.[498] In that case, a WTO Member may adopt or maintain restrictions on trade in services on which it has undertaken commitments, subject to a number of conditions.[499] Such restrictions may include restrictions on payments and transfers for transactions related to such commitments. In those cases, Members are required to consult promptly with the Committee on Balance-of-Payments Restrictions.[500] In such consultations, all findings and other facts presented by the IMF relating to foreign exchange, monetary reserves and balance of payments must be accepted and conclusions of the Committee on Balance-of-Payments Restrictions must be based on the assessment by the IMF of the balance-of-payments and financial situation of the WTO Member (on these links between the IMF and the WTO, see *infra* paras. 174–180).[501]

Remarkably, the GATS does not contain an *Enabling Clause*, as exists for the GATT. Non-reciprocal preferences that are specifically granted to developing countries are thus only possible if a WTO Member has made MFN exceptions to this extent, or if these preferences are granted in the framework of an Article V GATS-compatible economic integration agreement.

It should finally be remembered that a WTO Member could make exceptions to Article II (MFN) upon accession (no new exceptions can be scheduled). As long as the Doha Round is not concluded, these exceptions will remain in place.

§ 3. TRIPS

150. The regulation of intellectual property[502] is greatly influenced today by WTO law. The TRIPS Agreement[503] (TRIPS) seeks equilibrium between the

---

[498] *Ibid.* art. XII.
[499] They (a) must not discriminate among Members; (b) must be consistent the Articles of Agreement of the IMF; (c) must avoid unnecessary damage to the commercial, economic and financial interests of other Members; (d) must not exceed those necessary to deal with the balance-of-payments difficulties and (e) must be temporary and be phased out progressively as the difficulties decrease. See Art. XII.2 GATS.
[500] *Ibid.* art. XII.5 (a).
[501] *Ibid.* art. XII.5 (e).
[502] It concerns copyrights and related rights, trademarks, geographic indications, industrial designs, patents, topographies of integrated circuits and the protection of undisclosed information. Part II TRIPS.
[503] See on TRIPS *inter alia* M. BRONCKERS, 'The impact of TRIPS: intellectual property protection in developing countries', *Common Market Law Review* (1994), pp. 1245–1281; D. GERVAIS, *The TRIPS Agreement. Drafting History and Analysis*, (London, Sweet and Maxwell 2003), xlvi + 580 p.; C.-J. HERMES, *TRIPS im Gemeinschaftsrecht: zu den innergemeinschaftlichen Wirkungen*

protection of intellectual property and the need to prevent national rules on intellectual property from distorting or impeding international trade. The holder of an intellectual property right can indeed bar the production of goods in a certain country or stop the sale and export of a good under a certain name.[504] The TRIPS Agreement does not derogate from the provisions of the existing agreements on intellectual property rights that were concluded within the World Intellectual Property Organization (WIPO).[505] Moreover, TRIPS incorporates Articles 1–12 and 19 of the Paris Convention.[506] Thus, these provisions bind WTO Members, even if they were not Party to the Paris Convention.

151. The provisions of Part II of the TRIPS introduce minimum standards of protection that WTO Members must respect concerning the availability, scope and use of copyrights, trade marks, geographic indications, industrial designs, patents, integrated circuits and undisclosed information, taking into account the basic principles of national treatment and Most Favoured Nation, which are included in Article 1 TRIPS. Article 3 TRIPS contains the principle of national treatment: every Member 'shall accord to the nationals of other Members treatment no less favourable than that it accords to its own nationals with regard to the protection of intellectual property'. Furthermore, the principle of Most Favoured Nation must be respected.[507] When a Member accords *e.g.* a more favourable procedure for the enforcement of property rights for economic operators from a certain WTO Member, this advantage has to be accorded to economic operators from all other WTO Members. It is important to note that all

---

  von WTO-Übereinkünften, (Berlin, Duncker & Humblot 2002), 374 p; INTERNATIONAL CHAMBER OF COMMERCE, *Intellectual Property and International Trade. A Guide to the Uruguay Round TRIPS Agreement*, (Paris, ICC Publishing 1996), 140 p.; S. KREIBICH, *Das TRIPS-Abkommen in der Gemeinschaftsordnung: Aspekte der Kompetenzverteilung zwischen WTO, Europäischer Gemeinschaft und ihren Mitgliedstaaten*, (Frankfurt am Main, Lang 2003), 322 p.; M. NOLFF, *TRIPS, PCT and Global Patent Procurement*, The Hague, Kluwer Law International, 2001, x + 301p.; K.-N. PFEIFER, 'Brainpower and Trade: The Impact of TRIPS on Intellectual Property', *Jahrbuch für internationales Recht* (1996), pp. 100–133 and P. ROTT, *Patentrecht und Sozialpolitik unter dem TRIPS-Abkommen*, (Baden-Baden, Nomos 2002), 385 p.

[504] D. GERVAIS, *supra* note 503, 1.08. See also M. BUYDENS, 'L'accord ADPIC (TRIPS) et les dispositions destinées à assurer la mise en oeuvre effective des droits de propriété intellectuelle', *Droit Intellectuel* (1997), 1.2.
[505] See 2.2 TRIPS. It concerns the Paris Convention for the Protection of Industrial Property, done in Paris on 20 March 1883, last reviewed in Stockholm on 14 July 1967; the Berne Convention for the Protection of Literary and Artistic Works, done in Paris on 24 July 1971; International Convention for the Protection of Performers, Producers of Phonograms and Broadcasting Organizations, done in Rome on 26 October 1961; Treaty on Intellectual Property in Respect to Integrated Circuits, done in Washington on 26 May 1989, available on http://www.jus.uio.no/lm/ip.integrated.circuits.treaty.washington.1989/toc.html.
[506] Art. 2.1 TRIPS.
[507] *Ibid.* art. 4.

EU Member States are seen together as one State. More favourable treatment of intellectual property rights between EU Member States can therefore not be invoked by a non-EU Member State as a basis for MFN treatment.[508]

152. TRIPS touches certain sensitive chords in the relation between industrialized nations and developing countries. Article 7 TRIPS provides that the objective of the protection and enforcement of intellectual property rights is the 'promotion of technological innovation and [...] the transfer and dissemination of technology, to the mutual advantage of producers and users of technological knowledge'. This *'transfer of technology'* was an important reason why developing countries decided to approve the TRIPS, aside from the fact that this agreement was part of the 'package' of the Uruguay Round and therefore was used as an amendment to favour developed countries in exchange for concessions in the fields of textiles and agriculture, which in turn favoured developing countries. However, there is a fear that the TRIPS does not benefit the numerous AIDS patients in developing countries. The holder of a patent on a medical drug can decide not to make it available or to grant a licence to possible producers only on unreasonable terms. The TRIPS tried to resolve this problem by providing the option of compelling a patent holder to give a licence at a reasonable price.[509] At the Ministerial Conference in Doha in 2001, the ministers declared that TRIPS does not prevent measures that protect *public health*.[510] On 30 August 2003, the General Council finally adopted a decision that clarifies the conditions for compulsory licences and makes the import of cheap drugs, made under compulsory licence, in poorer countries possible.[511] This concerned a waiver of the (limiting) conditions for exports made under compulsory licence to countries that are unable to manufacture the drugs themselves. On 6 December 2005, the Ministerial Conference adopted an amendment to the TRIPS, making this

---

[508] Art. 4 TRIPS provides for a number of exemptions from the obligation of MFN, *inter alia* for advantages that flow from international agreements on the protection of intellectual property rights that entered into force prior to the entry into force of the WTO Agreement, on the condition that they are notified to the Council for TRIPS and do not constitute an arbitrary or unjustifiable discrimination against nationals of other Members (art. 4 (d) TRIPS). It has been stated that the EC therefore has to notify the EC Treaty to the Council for TRIPS, because it has implications for intellectual property rights: See G. GLAS, 'Algemene bepalingen en vraagstukken van TRIPS', *Intellectuele Eigendom* (1996), p. 192, with reference to J. COHEN, 'Auteursrecht in TRIPS', *Informatierecht/AMI* (1995), p. 124.

[509] So called 'compulsory licensing': see art. 31 TRIPS.

[510] Ministerial Declaration of Doha, 14 November 2001, *supra* note 138, para. 17; Ministerial Declaration on the TRIPS Agreement and Public Health, adopted in Doha on 20 November 2001, WT/MIN(01)/DEC/2, para. 6, available on http://www.wto.org/english/thewto_e/minist_e/min01_e/mindecl_trips_e.htm.

[511] Implementation of paragraph 6 of the Doha Declaration on the TRIPS Agreement and Public Health, Decision of the General Council, adopted on 30 August 2003, available on http://www.wto.org/english/tratop_e/trips_e/implem_para6_e.htm.

Overview of the WTO Agreements

decision permanent. The amendment will take effect when two thirds of Members have accepted it. The goal is to have this done by 1 December 2007.

§ 4. DISPUTE SETTLEMENT UNDERSTANDING [p.m.]

See Chapter IV. § 3. Dispute Settlement.

§ 5. TRADE POLICY REVIEW MECHANISM [p.m.]

See Chapter IV. § 2. Decision-Making.

§ 6. PLURILATERAL TRADE AGREEMENTS

153. As explained, contrary to the other WTO Agreements, adherence to the plurilateral agreements is not obligatory for WTO Members: they can choose whether or not to become a Party. Four plurilateral trade agreements were concluded, two of which are still in force.

A. AGREEMENT ON TRADE IN CIVIL AIRCRAFT

154. The Agreement on Trade in Civil Aircraft is one of the 'Tokyo Round Agreements'. It was concluded on 12 April 1979 and entered into force on 1 January 1980. Attempts during the Uruguay Round to negotiate a new, multilateral, agreement on trade in civil aircraft failed. It is the Agreement from 1979 that was included in Annex IV to the Marrakesh Agreement.[512]

155. The Agreement on Trade in Civil Aircraft applies to all civil aircraft, civil aircraft engines and their parts and components, all other parts components and sub-assemblies of civil aircraft and all ground flight simulators and their parts and components, whether used as original or replacement equipment in the manufacture, repair, maintenance, rebuilding, modification or conversion of civil

---

[512] The Committee on Civil Aircraft (established in art. 4 Agreement on Civil Aircraft) set up a sub-committee to negotiate such new Agreement during the Uruguay Round. Committee on Civil Aircraft Decision of 16 July 1992, AIR/M/32, para. 35. The failure to achieve such new agreement leaves the legal status of the Agreement on Civil Aircraft "highly unsatisfactory". See Report (1995) of the Committee on Trade in Civil Aircraft, WT/L/107 and L/7665, 24 November 1995, para. 3.

aircraft.[513] The aim is to establish free trade in civil aircraft and parts thereof. The Signatories had to remove their import duties on these products and on civil aircraft repairs by 1 January 1980.[514] Furthermore, the Agreement explicitly notes that the TBT Agreement applies to civil aircraft[515], prohibits government intervention in the freedom of choice of aircraft purchasers[516] and prohibits trade restrictions, except in cases where the GATT allows this.[517] An important issue concerns the granting of *subsidies* to aircraft producers. Such subsidies are not prohibited, though these subsidies are not allowed to cause adverse effects on trade in civil aircraft, assessed according to the criteria of the SCM Agreement.[518] Yet, when one performs such assessment, 'the special factors which apply in the aircraft sector should be taken into account, in particular the widespread governmental support in this area, their international economic interests, and the desire of producers of all Signatories to participate in the expansion of the world civil aircraft market'.[519] If a Signatory wants to impose countervailing duties because of another Signatory's aircraft subsidies, it first has to engage in consultations with the other Signatories in the Committee on Trade in Civil Aircraft.[520] This Committee may be requested to review the matter.[521] Disputes can finally be brought before the Dispute Settlement Body of the WTO.[522]

---

[513] Art. 1 and Annex to Agreement on Civil Aircraft.
[514] *Ibid.* art. 2.
[515] *Ibid.* art. 3.
[516] *Ibid.* art. 4.
[517] *Ibid.* art. 5.
[518] *Ibid.* art. 6.1. See *supra* paras. 104–111.
[519] *Ibid.*
[520] *Ibid.* art. 8.6.
[521] *Ibid.* art. 8.7.
[522] *Ibid.* art. 8.8. Nevertheless, as Appendix 1 of the DSU indicates, the application of the dispute settlement procedures is subject to the adoption of a decision of the parties of the plurilateral agreement setting out the conditions for the application of the DSU. This has not happened yet for the Agreement on Civil Aircraft. On 6 October 2004, the European Community and the United States both filed a complaint against each other before the Dispute Settlement Body of the WTO. The claims are based on alleged violations of the GATT and the SCM Agreement. On 31 May 2005, the EC and the US requested the establishment of a Panel. See European Communities – Measures Affecting the Trade in Large Civil Aircraft, WT/DS316/2, 3 June 2005 and United States – Measures Affecting the Trade in Large Civil Aircraft, WT/DS317/2, 3 June 2005. Note that the US and the EC also have a bilateral agreement on trade in large civil aircraft carriers. This agreement prohibits the granting of direct subsidies to large aircraft producers, but allows subsidies for the development of new aircraft construction programmes, under certain conditions. This bilateral agreement is not part of the WTO package, thus cannot be subject to WTO dispute settlement. Bilateral Agreement on Trade in Large Civil Aircraft, done on 17 July 1992, O.J., 1992, L301/31. See D. Luff, *supra* note 41, pp. 765–766.

B. AGREEMENT ON GOVERNMENT PROCUREMENT

156. The Agreement on Government Procurement is the second plurilateral agreement still in force. Because the GATT and the GATS do not apply to purchases of goods and services by governments for their own use[523], there was a need for a separate agreement. The present Agreement on Government Procurement was concluded in 1994. It covers both trade in goods and services and applies to procurement by central and sub-central government entities, public utilities, services and construction services.[524] Procurement can be performed by any contractual means.[525] Nonetheless, the value of the contracts has to exceed a certain threshold level.[526]

157. The Agreement imposes the obligation of National Treatment and Most Favoured Nation upon the Signatories.[527] Each Signatory must provide to the products, services and suppliers of the other Signatories treatment no less favourable than (a) that accorded to domestic products, services and suppliers and (b) that accorded to products, services and suppliers of any other Party. Furthermore, the Agreement promotes the principle of transparency in government procurement. The technical specifications laying down the characteristics of the products or services to be procured must not be prepared, adopted or applied with a view to, or with the effect of, creating unnecessary obstacles to international trade.[528] Tendering procedures[529], the qualification of suppliers[530], the invitation to tender[531], selection procedures[532], time limits[533], documentation requirements[534], procedures for the award of contracts[535] and negotiations with tenderers[536] must all conform to the principle of transparency. Specific procedural obligations are laid down in the Agreement. The Agreement provides for special and differential treatment of developing countries. The

---

[523] See art. III.8 (a) and art. XVII.2 GATT and art. XIII GATS.
[524] Art. I.1 and Appendix I Agreement on Government Procurement. Appendix I differs for every Signatory of the Agreement. The Appendix contains the specific national commitments the Signatory has made. Therefore, the procuring entities that are listed in the Appendix and thus are covered by the Agreement also differ.
[525] *Ibid.* art. I.2.
[526] *Ibid.* art. I.4 and Appendix I.
[527] *Ibid.* art. III.
[528] *Ibid.* art. VI.1.
[529] *Ibid.* art. VII.
[530] *Ibid.* art. VIII.
[531] *Ibid.* art. IX.
[532] *Ibid.* art. X.
[533] *Ibid.* art. XI.
[534] *Ibid.* art. XII.
[535] *Ibid.* art. XIII.
[536] *Ibid.* art. XIV.

Signatories must duly take into account the development, financial and trade needs of developing countries[537] and facilitate, with regard to government procurement, increased imports from developing countries.[538]

158. At the Singapore Ministerial Conference, a Working Group on Transparency in Government Procurement was established.[539] This Working Group has identified the possible main elements for an Agreement on Transparency in Government Procurement.[540] Nevertheless, in the 'July Decision' of August 2004, it was decided that no further work would be performed on this issue during the Doha Round.[541]

C. INTERNATIONAL DAIRY AGREEMENT

159. In order to stabilize the fluctuating trade in dairy products, several efforts were made from 1970, including the International Dairy Agreement of 1994, which was the last multilateral instrument adopted to do so. Its governing body, the International Dairy Council, monitored the trends in the world market of dairy products. If necessary, prices could be adjusted. Nevertheless, the Agreement was terminated on 30 September 1997. The monitoring of the world market of dairy products is now performed by the Committee on Agriculture and the Committee on Sanitary and Phytosanitary Measures. However, price adjustments can no longer be made.

D. INTERNATIONAL BOVINE MEAT AGREEMENT

160. Like the International Dairy Agreement, the International Bovine Meat Agreement established a Council to monitor the trends in the market for bovine meat. However, contrary to the previous agreement, the International Bovine Meat Council was not intended to influence the trade flows. This agreement was also terminated on 30 September 1997. These functions are now performed by the Committee on Agriculture and the Committee on Sanitary and Phytosanitary Measures.

---

[537] *Ibid.* art. V.1.
[538] *Ibid.* art. V.2.
[539] Ministerial Declaration of Singapore, *supra* note 139, para. 21. See also Ministerial Declaration of Doha, *supra* note 138, para. 26.
[540] See the latest report: Report (2003) of the Working Group on Transparency in Government Procurement to the General Council, WT/WTGP/7, 15 July 2003.
[541] July Decision, *supra* note 378, para. 1 (g).

CHAPTER IV
INSTITUTIONAL FRAMEWORK

161. As indicated above[1], it proved impossible to establish an ITO in 1948. Also efforts to establish an Organization for Trade Cooperation (OTC) failed. It was immediately decided in 1947 that GATT should be applied provisionally. For decades, the international trade system did not have a full-fledged intergovernmental organization, only a *de facto* organization in the form of GATT.[2] The following sections address the institutional framework of the WTO. In a first section, the WTO will be situated in the international legal field. The WTO has international legal personality and interacts with several other international organizations. Remarkably, the WTO is independent from the United Nations and is not a part of the UN system. At the time of writing, the WTO has 151 Members, the majority of which are developing countries. The Members have to provide annual contributions to the WTO, which form the budget of the organization. The next two sections respectively deal with the decision-making and the dispute settlement in the organization. From the discussion in these sections, it should be apparent how the decision-making processes seem to lag behind the dispute settlement processes.

§ 1. THE WTO AS AN INTERNATIONAL ORGANIZATION

A. INTERNATIONAL LEGAL PERSONALITY

162. In contrast with GATT 1947, the WTO is a full-fledged international organization with international legal personality explicitly attributed to it.[3] According to the International Court of Justice, being an international legal person implies being "capable of possessing international rights and duties and [having] capacity to maintain its rights by bringing international claims".[4] This

---

[1] See *supra* paras. 14–15.
[2] It should be noticed that when the Uruguay Round was launched, it was not immediately planned to establish an international organization: Ministerial Declaration, done in Punta del Este on 20 December 1986, available on http://www.sice.oas.org/trade/Punta_e.asp.
[3] Art. VIII.1 WTO Agreement.
[4] ICJ Advisory Opinion of 11 April 1949, *Reparation for Injuries Suffered in the Service of the United Nations*, I.C.J. Rep. 1949, 174.

legal personality is functional and therefore limited to the necessities for the exercise of the functions of the organization.[5]

163. The organization enjoys privileges and immunities accorded by Members. Moreover, also the officials of the WTO and the representatives of Members enjoy the privileges and immunities in the same way as is the case for the Specialized Agencies of the United Nations and its officials.[6] The immunities are functionally limited, since they are accorded as far as 'necessary for the exercise of [the Organization and its officials'] functions'. They help guarantee the independence of the WTO officials and are closely linked with the obligation of Members to refrain from instructing the Director-General and WTO staff. Indeed, Members must respect the international character of their duties.[7] Yet, the officials of the WTO Secretariat must also respect the laws of the host State. It is the Director-General who can decide to waive the immunity of these officials.

164. The WTO has its headquarters in Geneva. During the Uruguay Round, Germany offered to host the WTO in Bonn, but this was not considered desirable given the fact that many organizations that work in the same field as the WTO have their headquarters in Geneva. Moreover, also the old GATT 1947 Secretariat was based in Geneva.[8] The WTO has concluded a headquarters agreement with Switzerland.

B. RELATIONSHIP WITH OTHER INTERGOVERNMENTAL ORGANIZATIONS

165. The Marrakesh Agreement imposes an obligation on the General Council of the WTO to make appropriate arrangements for cooperation with intergovernmental organizations that operate in the same field as the WTO.[9] The objective of this cooperation is to achieve greater coherence in global economic policymaking.

---

[5] H.G. Schermers and N.M. Blokker, *International Institutional Law*, (The Hague, Nijhoff 1995), para. 1570.
[6] Art. VIII.4 WTO Agreement. The Privileges and Immunities of UN Specialized Agencies are laid down in a Convention approved in the UN General Assembly Resolution 179(III) of 21 November 1947, 33 *UNTS*, p. 261. This is also the case for WTO Members who are not parties to this Convention.
[7] Art. VI.4 WTO Agreement.
[8] P. Van den Bossche, 'The Establishment of the World Trade Organization: The Dawn of a New Era in International Trade?', *Maastricht Journal of European and Comparative Law* (1994), p. 424.
[9] Art. V.1 WTO Agreement. The main partners in this field are the International Monetary Fund and the World Bank. (Art. III.5 WTO Agreement). During the GATT 1947 years, the relationship with international organizations was merely informal. There was only institutionalized involvement of the IMF in the Balance of Payments Committee. See *infra*

1. Observer Status

166. Seven international organizations currently have observer status in the WTO General Council.[10] Observer status has to be requested for each individual WTO body. Consequently, the international organizations that have observer status differ for each body. In the following discussion, the intergovernmental observers are indicated as appropriate for each body. There is no access for observers to the Committee on Budget, Finance and Administration and the Dispute Settlement Body. An exception is made for the IMF, which has some limited access to the Dispute Settlement Body.[11] The WTO has developed guidelines on the basis of which requests for observer status have to be considered.[12] Observer status can only be granted to organizations that have competence and direct interest in trade policy matters or that have responsibilities related to those of the WTO.[13] Observers have the right to attend meetings, but cannot participate in decision-making or speak during these meetings unless they are invited to do so.[14] They have no right to circulate papers or make proposals without consent. An observer organization which fails to attend the meetings of a body for more than one year loses its status as observer in that body. This period is extended to two years with regard to meetings in the Ministerial Conference.[15] The various WTO bodies may always invite any organization to attend a specific meeting, even if this organization has no formal observer status.[16]

2. Cooperation Agreements

167. Furthermore, the WTO has concluded cooperation agreements with the two other main pillars of international economic policy: the IMF[17] and the World Bank.[18] Indeed, the desire of WTO Members for greater coherence in global economic policymaking through closer cooperation between the WTO, World

---

para. 178 and B. HOEKMAN and M. KOSTECKI, *The Political Economy of the World Trading System*, (Oxford, Oxford University Press 2001), p. 68.

[10] This concerns in the General Council: the UN, UNCTAD, IMF, World Bank, FAO, WIPO and OECD.
[11] See *infra* para. 178
[12] Observer Status for International Intergovernmental Organizations in the WTO, WT/L/161, Annex 3, Adopted by the General Council on 31 January 1995 (WT/L/28).
[13] *Ibid.* para. 2.
[14] *Ibid.* para. 8.
[15] *Ibid.* para. 10. The aim is to avoid an 'overkill' of observers that only attend the occasional meeting.
[16] *Ibid.* para. 5.
[17] See *infra* paras. 174–180.
[18] Agreement between the International Bank for Reconstruction and Development, the International Development Association and the World Trade Organization, done at Singapore, 9 December 1996, WT/L/195, Annex II. See *infra* paras. 181–183.

Bank and IMF is expressed in a number of Agreements, Ministerial Declarations and Decisions, most recently in the Hong Kong Ministerial Declaration.[19] Cooperation agreements are also concluded with the United Nations, the World Intellectual Property Organization, the International Office for Epizootics and the International Telecommunications Union, be it that the links with these organizations are not very elaborated.[20]

a.   United Nations

168.   Already during the GATT 1947 era there existed some indirect linkages with the UN through the International Trade Centre (ITC). The ITC was created by the GATT 1947 in 1964[21] and has been operated jointly by the GATT 1947 (now WTO) and the UN (through UNCTAD) since 1968. Therefore, the ITC is a 'joint subsidiary organ' of UN and WTO. Both organizations contribute to the budget of the ITC. The ITC helps developing countries and countries in transition to expand their import and export operations. This happens *inter alia* through the collection of trade information or the provision of services to these countries. The focus is mainly on the business sector of these countries and only occasionally touches upon other UN issues, such as food security (through coordination with the UN Food and Agriculture Organization (FAO)) or sustainable development (through coordination with the UN Development Programme (UNDP)[22]). The ITC is also one of the six international agencies participating in the Integrated Framework for Trade-Related Technical Assistance to Least-developed Countries ('Integrated Framework').[23]

169.   Moreover, in 1976 the UN General Assembly adopted a document on the relations of GATT 1947 and the UN.[24] Its provisions require the exchange of relevant documents between the GATT and the UN and call upon the Contracting Parties to take any UN resolution relating to GATT into consideration. Upon request, the GATT had to report on the action taken as a result of its consideration.

---

[19]   Ministerial Declaration of Hong Kong, done on 22 December 2005, WT/MIN(05)/DEC, available on http://www.wto.org/English/thewto_e/minist_e/min05_e/final_text_e.pdf, para. 56.
[20]   A proposal of formal links with the World Customs Organization was dismissed. See WT/GC/W/421, para. 26 (a).
[21]   GATT 1947 Contracting Parties decision SR.21/9 of 19 March 1964.
[22]   The ITC nonetheless operates as an executive agency of UNDP, being directly responsible for implementing UNDP-financed projects.
[23]   The Integrated Framework, launched in 1997, is a process established to support LDC governments in trade capacity building and integrating trade issues into overall national development strategies. It is a joint programme between the six main international agencies in this field: World Bank, IMF, UNDP, UNCTAD, ITC and WTO.
[24]   UN General Assembly document A/AC.179/5 of 9 March 1973, Relations of the General Agreement on Tariffs and Trade with the United Nations.

Moreover, the UN Secretary-General could attend the sessions of the GATT Contracting Parties, the GATT Council and all regular GATT committees and working parties. The GATT Director-General for his part was invited to the General Assembly plenary meetings (and its committees and meetings) and meetings of the Economic and Social Council (and its subsidiary bodies). The GATT Director-General was also part of the Administrative Committee on Co-ordination.[25] The document also deals with coordination between the secretariats and cooperation in personnel and administrative matters.

170. The World Trade Organization and the United Nations concluded an agreement on 29 September 1995.[26] This cooperation agreement establishes that the previously mentioned UN General Assembly Document continues to guide relations between the UN and the WTO. The provisions on reciprocal participation between the WTO and the UN in each other's meetings continue to apply, as well as the provisions on exchange of information, cooperation in personnel and administrative matters. The agreement finally also envisages further regulations that would strengthen the cooperation between the WTO and UNCTAD. It did not, however, establish *formal institutional links* with the UN. The Preparatory Committee for the WTO saw "no grounds for formal institutional links between the WTO and the United Nations".[27] Diverse reasons may have played a part in this decision: the specificity of the issues the WTO deals with[28], the sceptical position of some Members towards the budgetary and personnel policies of the UN and their alleged inefficiencies[29], and the fear for the politicization of issues in the UN.[30]

---

[25] This UN Committee was established by the Economic and Social Council in 1946 in order to supervise the implementation of the relationship agreements between the United Nations and the then existing three specialized agencies. See UN Economic and Social Council Resolution 13(III) of 21 September 1946, UN DOC. E/231. Over the years its mandate evolved and it became the main instrument for executive heads of the UN system to coordinate their actions and policies. However, its activities were criticized as being highly unsatisfactory. See K. IDRIS and M. BARTOLO, *A Better United Nations for the New Millennium*, (The Hague, Kluwer Law International 2000), p. 84 and pp. 115–118. In 2001, it was transformed into the 'United Nations System Chief Executives Board of Coordination', see *infra* para. 173.

[26] The Agreement was concluded via an exchange of letters between the Director-General of the World Trade Organization and the United Nations Secretary-General. For the text, see WT/GC/W/10, Annex, 3 November 1995.

[27] Arrangements for effective cooperation with other intergovernmental organizations. Relations between the WTO and the United Nations, WT/GC/W/10, 3 November 1995, 1. Report of the Preparatory Committee for the World Trade Organization, PC/R, 31 December 1994.

[28] T. FLORY, *L'Organisation Mondiale de Commerce. Droit institutionnel et substantiel* (Brussels, Bruylant 1999), para. 22.

[29] J. JACKSON, *The World Trade Organization. Constitution and Jurisprudence* (London, The Royal Institute of International Affairs 1998), p. 52.

[30] P. VAN DEN BOSSCHE, *The Law and Policy of the World Trade Organization* (Cambridge, Cambridge University Press 2005), p. 423.

Chapter IV

171. Nonetheless, on several occasions the UN called for the WTO and the UN system to come closer. UN Secretary-General Boutros Boutros-Ghali indicated at the first WTO Ministerial Conference in 1996 that one of the main steps[31] to take for the WTO in order to achieve its endeavour of promoting economic growth and sustainable development through trade was to "further reinforce its cooperation with the United Nations system to respond effectively to the evolving requirements of the new international environment".[32] He even pleaded for a full integration of the WTO in the UN system.[33] He also recognized the already existing cooperation with UNCTAD.

172. As has been said, the mentioned cooperation agreement also acknowledged the need for further specific arrangements for cooperation between the WTO and UNCTAD. These two organizations cooperate especially on technical assistance. On 16 April 2003, the WTO and UNCTAD finally institutionalized their cooperative relations in a Memorandum of Understanding.[34] The Memorandum aims 'to deepen and give practical effect to the strategic partnership' between the WTO and UNCTAD.[35] It also provides for regular meetings between the Director-General of the WTO and Secretary-General of UNCTAD (every 6 months) to review this partnership.[36] Until now, no other formal arrangements have been drawn up between the WTO and the United Nations. UNCTAD as well as UNDP also participate in the Integrated Framework (*supra* para. 168).

173. It is remarkable that the WTO is not a specialized agency of the United Nations. Indeed, its origins lie with the UN[37] and in many respects, the WTO pursues similar objectives as the UN. The preamble of the WTO Agreement states that the organization should aim at 'raising standards of living, ensuring full employment and a large and steadily growing volume of real income and effective demand, […] while allowing for the optimal use of the world's resources in accordance with the objective of sustainable development […]'.[38] Using partially the same words, Chapter IX of the UN Charter states that the UN should promote

---

[31] Next to the strengthening of developing-country participation and the achievement of universal membership.
[32] Message to the Ministerial Conference from Dr. Boutros Boutros-Ghali, Secretary General of the UN, Singapore, 11 December 1996, WT/MIN(96)/ST/82.
[33] Boutros Boutros-Ghali, An Agenda for Development: recommendations. Report of the Secretary-General, UN DOC A/49/665, para. 60.
[34] Memorandum of Understanding between the World Trade Organization and the United Nations Conference on Trade and Development, done at Geneva on 16 April 2003. Hereinafter 'WTO-UNCTAD Memorandum of Understanding'.
[35] Art. I WTO-UNCTAD Memorandum of Understanding.
[36] *Ibid.* art. I.2.
[37] See *supra* para. 14.
[38] First preliminary consideration WTO Agreement.

'higher standards of living, full employment, and conditions of economic and social progress and development'.[39] The different declarations of both organizations also seem to overlap. The WTO trade ministers expressed in the 2001 Ministerial Declaration of Doha their strong conviction that "the aims of upholding and safeguarding an open and non-discriminatory multilateral trading system, and acting for the protection of the environment and the promotion of sustainable development can and must be mutually supportive".[40] At the UN's 2002 Johannesburg summit on sustainable development, ministers committed themselves to promoting "open, equitable, rules-based, predictable and nondiscriminatory multilateral trading and financial systems that benefit all countries in the pursuit of sustainable development".[41] It should be noted, however, that these declarations express a wish rather than a reality.[42] What is more, the WTO is increasingly faced with issues that are not part of the traditional territory of trade, but that should rather be dealt with by the UN. The Helms-Burton Act of the US, for instance, which applies sanctions to (American and other) companies that are engaged in trade relations with Cuban companies, was challenged before the dispute settlement system of the WTO.[43] The US defended its measure on the basis of reasons of national security.[44] The WTO was thus confronted with a difficult balancing act, that could better be done by the UN Security Council.[45] Another well-known example concerns the French prohibition to sell products that contain asbestos.[46] Canada brought the dispute on this prohibition to the Dispute Settlement Body of the WTO. Once more, the WTO had to express itself on the acceptability of a measure that certainly had an impact on trade, but still belonged mainly to the domain of the World Health Organization (WHO), a specialized agency of the UN. There are numerous other examples of disputes where the WTO had to rule on a measure that pursued other objectives

---

[39] Art. 55 (a) UN Charter.
[40] Ministerial Declaration of Doha, done on 14 November 2001, WT/MIN(01)/DEC/1, available on http://www.wto.org/english/thewto_e/minist_e/min01_e/mindecl_e.htm, para. 6.
[41] Report of the World Summit on Sustainable Development, Johannesburg, 26 August to 4 September 2002, A/CONF.199/20, Resolution 2, Annex, para. 47, a). Compare the 2005 World Summit Outcome Document, UN General Assembly, 20 September 2005, A/60/L.1, para. 27: "A universal, rule-based, open, non-discriminatory and equitable multilateral trading system, as well as meaningful trade liberalization, can substantially stimulate development worldwide, benefiting countries at all stages of development."
[42] See G.P. SAMPSON, 'Is there a Need for Restructuring the Collaboration among the WTO and UN Agencies so as to Harness their Complementarities?', *Journal of International Economic Law* (2004), p. 718.
[43] United States – The Cuban Liberty and Democratic Solidarity Act, WT/DS38 (13 May 1996). Eventually, the US and the EU reached a settlement.
[44] See art. XXI GATT.
[45] See A.F. PEREZ, 'WTO and UN Law: Institutional Comity in National Security', *The Yale Journal of International Law* (1998), p. 379.
[46] European Communities – Measures Affecting Asbestos and Asbestos-Containing Products, WT/DS 135.

than the regulation of trade and in fact only touched upon trade in a limited way. Unfortunately, the UN bodies and agencies fail to tackle such issues. It is said that the weakness of other multilateral institutions has increased the expectations that the WTO should address issues that initially fell outside its mandate.[47] This is chiefly due to the fact that the WTO has an effective enforcement mechanism, through its dispute settlement system. States may try to use WTO-approved trade sanctions to enforce measures on which the UN remains silent. Nevertheless, the WTO often has insufficient expertise to settle such disputes. Therefore, the dispute settlement Panels[48] tend to rely on existing international instruments concerning public health[49] or the protection of the environment.[50]

Since the WTO regularly takes into account the UN instruments to make a well-considered decision in areas where the Organization lacks the expertise, one may wonder whether the WTO should not become part of the UN family. This would strengthen the linkages with the UN and streamline the policies. Still, making the WTO a UN specialized agency as is the case for the IMF or the World Bank, does not solve many problems. The content of the present UN–WTO cooperation agreement is largely similar to the agreements that made the IMF and World Bank specialized UN agencies. What is more, those organizations are in fact 'independent specialized agencies', since they are not obliged to comply with the recommendations of ECOSOC. Granting such status to the WTO is indeed of no use. Still, it may be an important symbolic step to stress the linkages between both organizations. Furthermore, there is also some clear potential in the possibility of the UN adopting resolutions concerning the WTO, after which the WTO can be asked to indicate how it has implemented those resolutions. Thus, the status of a 'real' specialized agency seems desirable. It would help to guide WTO policymaking in a UN-consistent manner. It would also stimulate the WTO dispute settlement Panels or Appellate Body to request information to the competent UN bodies in case of trade disputes that relate also to other fields (*e.g.* environment, human rights, public health etc.). The expertise that exists in the UN can help a well-balanced decision be reached. Finally, it would be desirable to strengthen the functioning of the 'United Nations System Chief Executives Board of Coordination', which is the successor of the Administrative Committee on

---

[47] D. LUFF, *Le droit de l'Organisation mondiale de commerce: analyse critique* (Brussels, Bruylant 2004), pp. 6–7 and J.E. ALVAREZ and D.W. LEEBRON, 'Symposium: The Boundaries of the WTO: Linkages', *American Journal of International Law* (2002), pp. 5–27.
[48] See *infra* para. 338.
[49] See for instance the GATT Panel Report: Thailand – Restriction on the Importation of and internal taxes on Cigarettes, BISD 37S/200 (7 November 1990), where the World Health Organization was asked to provide advice on the health effects of smoking (see para. 50).
[50] See for instance the Appellate Body Report: United States – Import Prohibition of Certain Shrimp and Shrimp Products, WT/DS58/AB/R (12 October 1998), para. 168.

Coordination (*supra* para. 169)[51] in order to make it a better vehicle for policy coordination between the WTO and the UN.

b. IMF

174. The IMF was established following the Conference of Bretton Woods in 1944 and has as primary responsibility the promotion of international monetary cooperation and the guarding of exchange rate stability. Yet, the Articles of Agreement of the IMF already indicate that trade issues are not entirely outside the scope of the IMF. Indeed, one of the purposes of the IMF is to 'facilitate the expansion and balanced growth of international trade'.[52] These same Articles of Agreement also call for cooperation with other international organizations that have responsibilities in related fields.[53] Obviously, the provision does not refer *nominatim* to the GATT or the WTO, since neither existed at the time of its drafting. When a few years later an ITO Charter was drafted, working arrangements between the ITO and the IMF[54] were prepared.

175. Nevertheless, this ITO never came into existence. As has been explained, only the GATT 1947 entered into force through a Protocol of Provisional Application. Article XV.2 of GATT 1947 includes some provisions that explicitly oblige the GATT Contracting Parties to consult the IMF for matters relating to monetary reserves, balance of payments and exchange rate issues. The GATT (and now also the GATS[55]) indeed provides some exceptions to its principles for situations where States impose trade restrictions to safeguard the balance of payments[56] or adopt exchange measures in accordance with the Articles of Agreement of the IMF.[57] In order to organize consultation on these three matters, the Contracting Parties had to establish an agreement on procedures of consultation. Initially, the IMF had no obligation to respond to such requests for consultation.[58] Furthermore, the IMF was included in the Balance-of-Payments Committee, which monitors the trade restrictions States are allowed to impose as

---

[51] Despite the transformation in 2001, the Chief Executives Board for Coordination did not undergo any substantial changes. See also *supra* note 19 in Chapter II.
[52] Art. I(2) Articles of Agreement of the IMF.
[53] Art. X Articles of Agreement of the IMF.
[54] See the Provisional Working Arrangements between the ITO and the IMF, UN Doc. ICITO/EC.2/2/Add.2, Rev. 1, 14 August 1948 and the Agreement on Relations between ITO and IMF, UN Doc. ICITO/EC.2/SC.3/6, 4 September 1948. See D. AHN, 'Linkages between International Financial and Trade Institutions: IMF, World Bank and WTO', *Journal of World Trade* (2000), pp. 1–36.
[55] See Art. XII GATS.
[56] See Art. XII GATT and art. XVIII, section B (specifically addressing developing countries) GATT.
[57] See Art. XV.9 GATT.
[58] But, see *infra* para. 178, the obligation included in the WTO-IMF Cooperation Agreement.

quantitative restrictions[59] to tackle balance of payment difficulties (see Article XII or XVIII, section B GATT 1947).[60] Specific consultation procedures for balance-of-payments purposes were established in the 1970s.[61]

176. The WTO Agreement establishes cooperation with the IMF and the World Bank as one of the five basic functions of the WTO.[62] In this regard, cooperation is not merely seen as useful (which is the case for cooperation with other intergovernmental organizations[63]), but as indispensable to ensure harmony in international economic policies. This has been recognized in the 1994 Ministerial Declaration on the Contribution of the World Trade Organization to Achieving Greater Coherence in Global Economic Policymaking.[64] Paragraph 5 of this declaration called for "consistent and mutually supportive policies". At the same time, the Declaration tried to respect the different mandates of the IMF and the WTO and the confidentiality requirements and autonomy of their decision-making procedures. In addition, developing countries feared that close cooperation between the WTO and the IMF (and World Bank) would deliver more influence to the latter two institutions in the trade policy decisions in the WTO and lead to 'cross-conditionality'. It was believed that the more the two financial institutions were involved, the more their 'conditionality' policies would also contaminate the WTO.[65]

---

[59] Although Articles XII and XVIII GATT refer to quantitative restrictions, the 'Declaration on Trade Measures taken for Balance of Payments Purposes', L/4904, 28 November 1979 allowed for the practice of Contracting Parties to impose non-quantitative restrictions for balance-of-payments purposes. The 'Understanding of the Balance-of-Payments Provisions of the General Agreement on Tariffs and Trade 1994', as part of the Uruguay Round Final Act, even obliges Members to give preference to 'price-based measures' (e.g. import surcharges) instead of quantitative restrictions.

[60] At the time the GATT was established, fixed exchange rates existed, monitored by the IMF. Thus, States could not freely modify their exchange rates to resolve balance of payments problems. (A devaluation would mean that imports would become more expensive and exports cheaper.) Since today, most exchange rates are no longer fixed, the use of these provisions is much more limited.

[61] See the 'Full Consultation Procedures', BISD 18S/45–49, 29 December 1972. 'Simplified Consultation Procedures' were provided for the least-developed countries, and with some limitations for developing countries in general: BISD, 20S/47–49, 29 December 1972.

[62] Art. III.5 WTO Agreement.

[63] Art. V WTO Agreement.

[64] Ministerial Declaration on the Contribution of the World Trade Organization to Achieving Greater Coherence in Global Economic Policymaking, approved in Marrakesh on 15 April 1994. This Declaration is part of the Final Act Embodying the Results of the Uruguay Round, LT/UR/A/1.

[65] See D. AHN, *supra* note 54, p. 7 and W. BENEDEK, 'Relations of the WTO with other International Organizations and NGOs', in F. WEISS, E. DENTERS and P. DE WAART (eds.), *International Economic Law with a Human Face*, The Hague, Kluwer Law International, (1998), p. 489.

177. In 1996, the WTO and the IMF signed a formal cooperation agreement.[66] Consultation between the secretariats and staffs should take place on matters of mutual interest.[67] The Agreement provides observer status for the secretariats or staffs of both institutions in each other's relevant meeting.[68] More specifically, the WTO Secretariat has a standing invitation to ordinary meetings of the Fund's Executive Board on general and regional trade policy issues and on the discussions of the IMF's World Economic Outlook Report which involve trade issues. The WTO Secretariat may also be invited, on recommendation of the Managing Director, to send an observer to the Executive Board meetings each time a matter of common interest is dealt with. The IMF, from its part, has a standing invitation to attend all meetings of the Ministerial Conference, General Council, Trade Policy Review Body, the three sectoral councils (Councils on Trade in Goods, on Trade in Services and on Trade-Related Aspects of Intellectual Property Rights), the Committee on Trade and Development, Committee on Regional Trade Agreements, Committee on Trade-Related Investment Measures, and Committee on Trade and Environment and their subsidiary bodies provided that matters of jurisdictional relevance to the IMF are under consideration.[69] Since the Committee on Budget, Finance and Administration and the Dispute Settlement Body[70] have no jurisdictional relevance to the IMF, the IMF has no observer status in these bodies. Yet, it is possible that the IMF receives an *ad hoc* invitation to attend a meeting of the Dispute Settlement Body and the other WTO bodies for which there is no standing invitation, if the WTO, after consultation with the WTO Secretariat and the IMF staff, finds that such would be in the common interest of both organizations. Still, such *ad hoc* invitation is not possible for the meetings of the Committee on Budget, Finance and Administration and the dispute settlement Panels. The IMF has not (yet) been granted observer status in the Trade Negotiations Committee that was set up by the Doha Declaration.[71] In order to make such mutual attendance useful, both organizations must make available to

---

[66] Agreement between the International Monetary Fund and the World Trade Organization, signed at Singapore, 9 December 1996, WT/L/195, Annex I, 18 November 1996 (hereinafter 'WTO-IMF Cooperation Agreement').
[67] Para. 2 WTO-IMF Cooperation Agreement.
[68] Paras. 5 and 6 WTO-IMF Cooperation Agreement.
[69] Para. 6 WTO-IMF Cooperation Agreement.
[70] This includes the Panels, arbitrators and the Appellate Body established under the DSU, the Textiles Monitoring Body established under the Agreement on Textiles and Clothing, the Permanent Group of Experts established under the Agreement on Subsidies and Countervailing Measures, the Panels appointed by the independent entity established pursuant to the Agreement on Preshipment Inspection and any other bodies with restricted membership constituted for the settlement of disputes. See the Agreed Commentary on the Agreement between the International Monetary Fund and the World Trade Organization, WT/L/195, Annex III, 18 November 1996.
[71] WTO Secretariat, Coherence in Global Economic Policy-Making: WTO Cooperation with the IMF and the World Bank, WT/TF/COH/S/9, 11 October 2004, p. 6.

each other in advance the agendas, and relevant documents, for the meetings to which they are invited.[72] The cooperation agreement also provides for mutual documentation exchange between the institutions.[73] They have access to each other's databases. The IMF can also provide the WTO, for the confidential use of its Secretariat, the staff reports on Article IV Consultations, subject to the consent of the Member concerned.[74]

178. The Fund undertakes the obligation to inform the WTO of any decisions approving restrictions on payments or transfers or discriminatory currency agreements.[75] Both organizations have agreed to share views on matters of mutual interest to the other organization or any of its organs or bodies. These views form part of the official record of these organs and bodies.[76] WTO dispute settlement Panels are excluded from this exchange of views. Yet, the Fund is obliged to inform in writing the relevant WTO body (including dispute settlement Panels) considering exchange measures within the Fund's jurisdiction whether such measures are consistent with the Articles of Agreement of the Fund. As explained, Article XV GATT already provided an obligation for the WTO to consult fully with the IMF 'with regard to problems concerning monetary reserves, balance-of-payments or foreign-exchange arrangements'.[77] The cooperation agreement now imposes an obligation on the IMF to respond to this request for consultation[78] (but includes no corresponding obligation for WTO dispute settlement Panels to share their views with the IMF).[79] The IMF informs the WTO in writing.[80] Under Article XV GATT, the WTO is obliged to accept the Fund's views. Some of the Fund's views may concern factual determinations (such as information on the monetary reserves). This factual information is necessary for the WTO to decide upon exceptions for balance-of-payment purposes.[81] On the other hand, when

---

[72] Para. 7 WTO-IMF Cooperation Agreement.
[73] *Ibid*, para. 9.
[74] *Ibid.*, para. 11.
[75] *Ibid.*, para. 3.
[76] *Ibid.*, para. 8.
[77] Art. XV.2 GATT.
[78] Para. 4 (concerning balance of payments issues) and para. 8 (concerning questions whether exchange measures within the Fund's jurisdiction are consistent with the Articles of Agreement of the Fund) WTO-IMF Cooperation Agreement. See D.E. SIEGEL, 'Legal Aspects of the WTO-IMF Relationship: the Fund's Articles of Agreement and the WTO Agreements', *American Journal of International Law* (2002), p. 569.
[79] See D. AHN, *supra* note 54, p. 18.
[80] This intends to clarify that the IMF has no full role in dispute settlement proceedings, but will only submit a written report. See D.E. SIEGEL, *supra* note 78, p. 570.
[81] It should be noted that the WTO and the IMF are developing criteria for assessing the adequacy of reserves and the justification of trade restrictions, under Article XVIII.B GATT. See WTO Secretariat, Coherence in Global Economic Policymaking and Cooperation between the WTO, the IMF and the World Bank, WT/TF/COH/S/7, 29 April 2003, para. 48 and Committee

Institutional Framework

the IMF determines whether a trade measure is consistent with the Articles of Agreement of the IMF, it concerns a legal ruling, which the WTO has to accept.[82] There has been some discussion on whether this consultation requirement also extends to dispute settlement by the Panels. Some authors viewed this as compromising the Panel's independence[83] and the confidentiality of the procedure.[84] Article XV.2 GATT, drafted in 1947, refers to the obligation of the Contracting Parties to consult the IMF. It was thus unclear whether this included the dispute settlement Panels. Indeed, in the first case concerning the balance-of-payments exception (which is explicitly referred to in Art. XV.2 GATT)[85], the Panel consulted the IMF based on Article 13 DSU (which involves a right of the Panel to seek information[86]), rather than on Article XV.2 GATT.[87] It also implied that the Panels were not required to accept the determination provided by the IMF. This stands in clear contrast with the obligation to consult the IMF and to accept its determination, when Article XV.2 GATT is applied. The Appellate Body confirmed that the Panel could critically assess the information from the Fund if the IMF is consulted on the basis of Article 13 DSU.[88] This issue now seems to be settled. In a recent Panel decision, it was confirmed that Panels are indeed obliged, pursuant to Article XV.2 GATT, to consult the IMF and accept its determinations when addressing problems concerning monetary reserves, balance-of-payments or foreign-exchange arrangements, but the Panel in this case still made its own determination whether there was a violation of Article XV.9 GATT.[89] It is important to note that this consultation requirement is limited to these three

---

on Balance-of-Payments Restrictions, Work on Implementation Issues in Accordance with Paragraph 12(b) of the Doha Declaration, WT/BOP/R/66, 19 November 2002.

[82] D.E. SIEGEL, *supra* note 78, p. 571. See also art. XI and XII GATS.

[83] Panels would not be able to make an 'objective assessment of the facts', as required in art. 11 DSU.

[84] See W. BENEDEK, *supra* note 65, p. 488.

[85] Panel Report: India – Quantitative Restrictions on Imports of Agricultural, Textile and Industrial Products, WT/DS90/R (6 April 1999).

[86] See *infra* para. 178.

[87] Panel Report: India – Quantitative Restrictions on Imports of Agricultural, Textile and Industrial Products, WT/DS90/R (6 April 1999), paras. 5.12–5.13.

[88] Appellate Body Report: India – Quantitative Restrictions on Imports of Agricultural, Textile and Industrial Products, WT/DS90/AB/R, (23 August 1999), paras. 149–150. Interestingly, however, the Appellate Body stated that it did not take position on "the question whether Article XV.2 of the GATT 1994 requires panels to consult with the IMF and to consider *as dispositive* specific determinations of the IMF" because this issue was not appealed. *Ibid.* para. 152.

[89] Panel Report: Dominican Republic – Measures Affecting the Importation and Internal Sale of Cigarettes, WT/DS302/R, (26 November 2004), paras. 7.138–7.142. No appeal was made with regard to the decision of the Panel to consult the IMF on the basis of art. XV.2 GATT. It was the question whether a 'foreign exchange fee' constituted a 'foreign exchange restriction' under the Articles of Agreement of the IMF. If so, art. XV.9 GATT would apply and this restriction could not be precluded by the GATT. The IMF responded by stating that the fee was not a foreign exchange restriction.

The World Trade Organization

mentioned problems. Measures that are taken by the State in the light of the conditions the IMF attaches to the financing it grants to this State are not considered to be such a problem.[90] In those cases, the IMF may be consulted on the basis of the voluntary right of Panels to seek information, pursuant to Article 13 DSU.

179. The WTO's interactions with the IMF are not limited to the GATT. In the Declaration on the Relationship of the World Trade Organization with the International Monetary Fund, it was stressed that 'unless otherwise provided for in the Final Act [of the Uruguay Round], the relationship of the World Trade Organization with the International Monetary Fund, with regard to the areas covered by the Multilateral Trade Agreements in Annex 1A of the WTO Agreement, will be based on the provisions that have governed the relationship of the Contracting Parties to the GATT 1947 with the International Monetary Fund'.[91] It was thus confirmed that the provisions in Article XV GATT governing the relationship with the IMF, also apply to the other Multilateral Agreements on Trade in Goods, unless one of these agreements contains an explicit exception to this principle. Concerning trade in services, the GATS also contains a number of provisions that take into account Fund jurisdiction. Article XI.2 GATS preserves the rights and obligations under the Articles of Agreement of the IMF for IMF Members that are also Members of the WTO.[92] Nevertheless, restrictions on capital transactions that are inconsistent with the specific commitments a Member undertook under the GATS will always be prohibited unless these measures are requested by the IMF or if these measures concern restrictions to safeguard balance of payments.[93] If a State applies the latter measures, it is obliged to consult with the Committee on balance-of-payments restrictions.[94] In such consultations, the factual findings relating to foreign exchange, monetary reserves and balance of payments, provided by the IMF must be accepted and conclusions must be based

---

[90] Appellate Body Report: Argentina – Measures Affecting Imports of Footwear, Textiles, Apparel and Other Items, WT/DS56/AB/R & Corr. 1 (27 March 1998), para. 84. The Appellate Body decided that the commitments of a Member State of the IMF, which is also a Member of the WTO, do not prevail over the commitments of this Member under the WTO Agreement and its annexes, unless in the specific cases set out in art. XII, XIV, XV and XVIII GATT. Adjustment measures in a Fund-supported programme would not fall within the scope of these articles. *Ibid.*, paras. 70–73.

[91] Declaration on the Relationship of the World Trade Organization with the International Monetary Fund, included in the Final Act Embodying the Results of the Uruguay Round of Multilateral Trade Negotiations, done at Marrakesh on 15 April 1994, 33 ILM at 1252.

[92] Concerning payments and transfers for currency transactions, this is an exception to the prohibition, inscribed in art. XI.1 GATS, to apply restrictions on international transfers for currency transactions relating to its specific commitments (except for restrictions to safeguard its balance of payments under Article XII GATS).

[93] Art. XII GATS.

[94] *Ibid.* art. XII.5, (b).

on the Fund's assessment of the balance-of-payments and financial situation of the consulting Member.[95]

180. The IMF also cooperates with the WTO on technical assistance through the Integrated Framework[96], the WTO Training Institute and the Joint Vienna Institute (also providing training).[97] The IMF has also set up a Trade Integration Mechanism in April 2004 to assist developing countries that face balance-of-payments shortfalls that result from trade liberalization.

c.   World Bank

181. In the GATT 1947 era, there were only informal links between the WTO and the World Bank. Yet, the WTO Agreement requires the WTO to establish cooperative relationships with the World Bank, in the same way as the Agreement requires this for relations with the IMF.[98] The objective is to achieve coherence in global economic policymaking.

182. The WTO and the World Bank concluded a cooperation agreement on 28 April 1997.[99] The Agreement first of all provides the basis for carrying forward the WTO's ministerial mandate to achieve greater coherence in global economic policymaking by cooperating with the World Bank.[100] This is to be achieved through consultation, exchange of views and data, and cooperative actions. Both organizations have observer status in each other's meetings at different levels. The WTO has the right to attend meetings of the World Bank's Board of Governors, of the Executive Directors on general and regional trade issues, as well as any meeting with potential common interest for the organizations.[101] Similarly, the World Bank has the right to attend as an observer the meetings of the Ministerial Conferences, the General Council and the different trade councils. The cooperation agreement excludes World Bank attendance in the Dispute Settlement Body, the Committee on Budget, Finance and Administration and the dispute settlement

---

[95] *Ibid.* art. XII.5, (e).
[96] See www.integratedframework.org.
[97] www.jvi.org.
[98] Art. III.5 WTO Agreement.
[99] Agreement between the International Bank for Reconstruction and Development, the International Development Association and the World Trade Organization, 28 April 1997, WT/L/195, Annex II, 18 November 1996 (hereinafter 'World Bank-WTO Cooperation Agreement').
[100] Para. 1–2 World Bank-WTO Cooperation Agreement.
[101] *Ibid.* para. 4. The invitation of such *ad hoc* attendance will be issued after consultation between the WTO and the World Bank.

Panels.[102] Both organizations will exchange information[103], share access to databases, undertake joint research and technical cooperation activities and exchange views on policy issues.[104] This will ensure that the interests of Members are integral to the thinking of each organization and that policies will be consistent and mutually supportive.[105] Contrary to the IMF-WTO Cooperation Agreement, this cooperation agreement has no provision for written communications on matters of mutual interest. Therefore, the rights of participation and access to documentation are more limited than for relations with the IMF, where there is a legal basis provided for both organizations to actively seek information.[106]

183. Some examples of this attempt to achieve greater coherence in the policymaking of both organizations are available. The WTO drew the World Bank's attention in the Poverty Reduction Strategy Papers and Country Assistance Strategies[107] to trade issues.[108] An initiative of the WTO Director-General and the President of the World Bank has established a six-month, renewable strategy for staff cooperation between the WTO and the World Bank. There are also close links between the World Bank Institute[109] and WTO Institute for Training and Technical Cooperation. Since 1997, they have maintained a joint website. The World Bank also participates in the Integrated Framework and the Standard and Trade Development Facility (STDF).[110]

d. World Intellectual Property Organization

184. The World Intellectual Property Organization (WIPO), a UN specialized agency, aims 'to promote the protection of intellectual property throughout the world through cooperation among States and, where appropriate, in collaboration

---

[102] *Ibid.* para. 5.
[103] *Ibid.* para. 9.
[104] *Ibid.* para. 7.
[105] *Ibid.* para. 8.
[106] Para. 8 IMF-WTO Cooperation Agreement.
[107] These documents form the basis of the conditions attached to loans provided by the World Bank.
[108] Coherence in Global Economic Policymaking and Cooperation between the WTO, the IMF and the World Bank, WT/TF/COH/S/7, 29 April 2003, para. 9.
[109] This is the learning arm of the World Bank. In 1955, the World Bank established the Economic Development Institute, in order to train government officials of developing countries in economic analysis and implementation of development projects. After expanding its focus more and more, the Institute merged in 1999 with the Bank's Learning and Leadership Centre. From then on, the Institute also trained World Bank Staff. In 2000, it was renamed the World Bank Institute.
[110] The STDF was established in 2002 by the World Bank, the WTO, the FAO, the World Organization for Animal Health and the WHO, to provide developing countries with capacity-building and technical assistance in shaping and implementing sanitary and phytosanitary (SPS) standards.

with any other international organization'.[111] WIPO also ensures administrative cooperation between the Paris Union and Berne Union.[112] Several treaties on intellectual property have been developed within the framework of this organization.

185. One of the reasons why developed countries pushed for the inclusion of intellectual property in the Uruguay Round negotiations was the lack of enforceability of the agreements that were developed within WIPO. Indeed, in contrast with the WTO, the WIPO has no enforcement mechanism. In the end, the Agreement on Trade-Related Aspects of Intellectual Property Rights (TRIPS) was established as Annex 1C to the WTO Agreement. The inclusion of an agreement on intellectual property in the WTO caused some eyebrows to be raised and provoked some fears that the WIPO would become redundant. The opposite has turned out to be the case.[113] WIPO saw the number of Members increase significantly. Moreover, the TRIPS incorporated the provisions of WIPO's fundamental treaties, the Paris and Berne Conventions. Members of the WTO automatically become party to these Agreements. The applauded synergy of WTO and WIPO[114] lies in the fact that where one organization seems to fail, the other one fills the gap. Whereas, because of decision-making by consensus, the WTO is slow at developing new agreements, this organization nevertheless has an effective dispute settlement and enforcement mechanism. In contrast, WIPO has no such enforcement mechanism, but nonetheless can decide in the absence of consensus.[115]

186. The WTO and WIPO concluded a cooperation agreement on 22 December 1995.[116] This agreement first of all provides for an exchange of information

---

[111] Art. 3 (i) Convention Establishing the World Intellectual Property Organization, signed at Stockholm on 14 July 1967, as amended on 28 September 1979 (hereinafter 'WIPO Agreement').

[112] These two Unions were bureaux monitoring the implementation of respectively the Paris Convention for the Protection of Intellectual Property, done in Paris on 20 March 1889, last amended in Stockholm on 14 July 1967, UNTS no. 11851 and the Berne Convention for the Protection of Literary and Artistic Works, done in Paris on 24 July 1971, UNTS no. 11850.

[113] P. SALMON, 'Cooperation between the World Intellectual Property Organization (WIPO) and the World Trade Organization (WTO)', *Saint John's Journal of Legal Commentary* (2003), p. 429.

[114] See J. ALVAREZ and D. STEGER, 'Afterword: The "Trade and ..." Conundrum – A Commentary', *American Journal of International Law* (2002), p. 136 and W.T. FRYER, 'Global IP Development: A Recommendation to Increase WIPO and WTO Cooperation', *University of Baltimore School of Law Intellectual Property Law Journal* (2001), p. 171.

[115] Voting in the General Assembly of WIPO takes place by two-thirds majority (art. 6.3 (d) WIPO Agreement), unless in specific cases, where a higher majority is required (art. 6.3 (e)-(f) WIPO Agreement).

[116] Agreement between the World Intellectual Property Organization and the World Trade Organization, done at Geneva on 22 December 1995, IP/C/6 (hereinafter 'WIPO-WTO Cooperation Agreement').

between the two organizations. WIPO in particular has an extensive collection of laws and regulations that have been notified by its Members. The computerized databases should be accessible to Members of both organizations.[117] The WIPO also administers the procedures for communication of emblems, flags and seals as well as the transmittal of objections under TRIPS[118] in accordance with Article 6*ter* Paris Convention.[119] Finally, the cooperation agreement provides for information exchange between the International Bureau of WIPO and the WTO Secretariat[120] and for assistance by each organization to Members of the other organization, even if these Members are not part of WIPO.[121] In this regard, the two organizations have launched two joint technical cooperation initiatives. The first programme was aimed at helping developing countries to adopt their intellectual property regimes in order to comply with the TRIPS by the 1 January 2000 deadline. A second initiative was launched in 14 June 2001 for least-developed countries. These countries had until 1 January 2006 to comply with TRIPS.[122] The technical assistance available under the joint initiative includes cooperation with preparing legislation, training, institution building, modernizing intellectual property systems and enforcement.

187. It should finally be noted that, under TRIPS, the TRIPS Council should establish cooperation arrangements with the bodies of WIPO.[123] This provision may conflict with the general right of the General Council to make arrangements for cooperation with other intergovernmental organizations.[124] Nevertheless, pursuant to Article XVI.3 WTO Agreement, in case of conflict between the provisions of any of the multilateral agreements and the WTO Agreement, the provisions of the WTO Agreement prevail.[125]

e. International Office of Epizootics

188. Article 12.3 SPS requires the Committee on Sanitary and Phytosanitary Measures to 'maintain close contact with the relevant international organizations in the field of sanitary and phytosanitary protection, especially [...] the International Office of Epizootics [...]'.[126] This relation is particularly important since SPS aims

---

[117] Art. 2 WIPO-WTO Cooperation Agreement.
[118] Art. 2.2 TRIPS.
[119] Art. 3 WIPO-WTO Cooperation Agreement.
[120] *Ibid.* art. 4.3.
[121] *Ibid.* art. 4.1.
[122] Art. 66 TRIPS.
[123] *Ibid.* art. 68.
[124] Art. V.1 WTO Agreement.
[125] See WTO Analytical Index: Marrakesh Agreement, available on http://www.wto.org/english/res_e/booksp_e/analytic_index_e/wto_agree_03_e.htm#fntext207, para. 144.
[126] Art. 12.3 SPS.

Institutional Framework

to harmonize sanitary and phytosanitary measures between Members on the basis of international standards, guidelines and recommendations developed by *inter alia* the International Office of Epizootics.[127] The WTO and the International Office of Epizootics concluded on 4 May 1998 a cooperation agreement through an exchange of letters.[128]

The *Office international des épizooties* (International Office for Epizootics, hereinafter 'OIE') coordinates studies of animal diseases, informs governments of animal diseases, and assists in the harmonization of regulations involving the trade of animals and animal products.[129] The OIE is the oldest veterinary association in the world and has a long history of establishing international standards.[130]

189. The mentioned cooperation agreement established cooperation and consultation between the WTO and OIE.[131] Representatives of OIE may attend meetings of the Committee on Sanitary and Phytosanitary Measures of the WTO and even participate in deliberations.[132] Similarly, the WTO representatives have the right to attend Annual General Sessions of the International Committee of the OIE and participate in deliberations.[133] Both organizations have to keep each other informed and exchange technical documents.[134]

f.   International Telecommunication Union

190. The International Telecommunication Union (ITU), a UN specialized agency, is an organization within which governments and the private sector work together to coordinate the operation of telecommunication networks and services and to advance the development of communications technology.[135] One of the

---

[127] Preamble of SPS, sixth preliminary consideration and art. 3 SPS.
[128] Agreement between the World Trade Organization and the Office International des Epizooties, done at Geneva on 4 May 1998, WT/L/272, approved by the Committee on Sanitary and Phytosanitary Measures on 1–2 July 1997, G/SPS/R/8, the Council for Trade in Goods on 21 July 1997, G/C/M/22 and the General Council on 22 October 1997, WT/GC/M/23.
[129] Art. 3 Organic Statutes of the Office International des Epizooties, Appendix to the International Agreement for the Creation of an Office International des Epizooties in Paris, done in Paris on 25 January 1924 (hereinafter 'OIE-WTO Cooperation Agreement').
[130] T.P. STEWART and D.S. JOHANSON, 'The SPS Agreement of the World Trade Organization and International Organizations: the Roles of the Codex Alimentarius Commission, the International Plant Protection Convention, and the International Office of Epizootics', *Syracuse Journal of International Law and Commerce* (1998), p. 49.
[131] OIE-WTO Cooperation Agreement, para. 1.
[132] Except when limited to the delegates of WTO Members. *Id.* para. 2.
[133] *Ibid.* para. 3.
[134] *Ibid.* paras. 4–5.
[135] For an overview, see G.A. CODDING, 'The International Telecommunications Union: 130 Years of Telecommunications Regulation', *Denver Journal of International Law and Politics* (1995), p. 501.

main activities of the ITU is the standardization of telecommunication networks and services.[136] Taking into account the fact that telecommunications is an important driving force behind economic development, the ITU also provides technical assistance to developing countries in order to enable them to take full advantage of the possibilities of telecommunication networks.[137] The GATS and its Annex on telecommunications recognize the importance of cooperation with the ITU.

191. Telecommunication services are addressed specifically in an Annex to the GATS. Trade in telecommunication services is not only an important economic activity on itself, but also supports economic development. Therefore, the Annex on Telecommunications addresses specifically measures affecting the access to and the use of telecommunications transport networks and services.[138] The provisions of this annex have also great relevance to the work of the ITU. The Members of the WTO recognized that an 'efficient, advanced telecommunications infrastructure in countries, particularly developing countries is essential to the expansion of their trade in services'.[139] Technical cooperation projects, such as those developed by the ITU, may help achieve this end.[140] The importance of standardization by relevant international bodies, such as the ITU, is stressed.[141]

192. In line with these provisions[142], the WTO and the International Telecommunication Union concluded a formal cooperation agreement.[143] Staff of both organizations are to cooperate and information, reports and documents of mutual interest to be exchanged.[144]

Similar to other cooperation agreements, this agreement grants the right to the Secretariat of each organization to attend, as an observer, the meetings of the bodies of the respective organizations.[145] Each Secretariat will make available its agenda to the other Secretariat if this agenda includes a telecommunications matter of interest to the other organization, as well as the documents for the meetings to which they

---

[136] Art. 1.1 (f) and 1.2 (c) Constitution of the International Telecommunication Union.
[137] Ibid. art. 1.1 (b)–(d) and 1.2 (d).
[138] Annex on Telecommunications, para. 1.
[139] Ibid. para. 6 (a).
[140] Ibid. para. 6 (c).
[141] Ibid. para. 7.
[142] Also having regard to art. V WTO Agreement and art. XXVI GATS.
[143] Agreement Between the International Telecommunication Union and the World Trade Organization, signed at S/C/11, approved by the Council for Trade in Services on 26 May 2000 and by the General Council on 10 October 2000, (hereinafter 'ITU-WTO Cooperation Agreement').
[144] ITU-WTO Cooperation Agreement, paras. 7 and 9.
[145] Ibid. para. 3–4.

are invited.[146] Importantly, the WTO and ITU cooperate in technical assistance and technical cooperation activities for developing countries.[147]

g. ILO

193. The relationship between core labour standards, as recognised in the conventions of the International Labour Organization (ILO),[148] and the law of the WTO is a controversial topic.[149] ILO conventions are legally binding on Member States that have ratified them, but there is no enforcement mechanism in case of grave and persistent breaches of the principles and obligations within these Conventions. WTO Members that had ratified the core conventions were eager to include a social clause in the agenda of the Uruguay Round multilateral trade negotiations. Yet, this was rejected, especially by developing countries, who believed that the insistence on respect for core labour standards would deprive these countries of their comparative advantage of having low labour costs and

---

[146] *Ibid.* para. 5.
[147] *Ibid.* para. 6.
[148] Eight ILO conventions have been identified by the Governing Body of the ILO as 'core conventions': 1. Convention No. 29 concerning Forced and Compulsory Labour, 1930; 2. Convention No. 105 concerning the Abolition of Forced Labour, 1957; 3. Convention No. 87 concerning Freedom of Association and Protection of the Right to Organise, 1948; 4. Convention No. 98 concerning the Application of the Principles of the Right to Organise and to Bargain Collectively, 1949; 5. Convention No. 100 concerning Equal Remuneration for Men and Women Workers for Work of Equal Value, 1951; 6. Convention No. 111 concerning Discrimination in Respect of Employment and Occupation, 1951; 7. Convention No. 138 concerning Minimum Age for Admission to Employment, 1973; 8. Convention No. 182 concerning the Prohibition and Immediate Action for the Elimination of the Worst Forms of Child Labour, 1999.
[149] See *inter alia*: B. BURGOON, 'The Rise and Stall of Labor Linkage in Globalization Politics', *International Politics* (2004), pp. 196–220; L. COMPA and S. F. DIAMOND (eds.), *Human Rights, Labour Rights, and International Trade*, (Philadelphia, University of Pennsylvania Press 1996), 311 p.; K. DE FEYTER, 'The Prohibition of Child Labour as a Social Clause in Multilateral Trade Agreements', in E. VERHELLEN (ed.), *Monitoring Children's Rights*, (The Hague, Nijhoff 1996), pp. 431–444; H.J. FRUNDT, *Trade Conditions and Labour Rights: US Initiatives, Dominican and Central American responses* (Gainesville, University Press of Florida 1998), 385 p.; K. GRAY, 'Labour Rights and International Trade: a Debate Devolved', in M. IRISH, *The Auto Pact: Investment, Labour and the WTO*, (The Hague, Kluwer 2004), pp. 277–300; V. LEARY and D. WARNER (eds.), *Social Issues, Globalization and International Institutions: Labour rights and the EU, ILO, OECD and WTO*, (Leiden, Nijhoff 2005), 418 p.; C. LOPEZ-HURTADO, 'Social Labelling and WTO Law', *Journal of International Economic Law* (2002), pp. 719–746; G. SHAFFER, 'WTO Blue-Green Blues: the Impact of US Domestic Policies on Trade-Labor, Trade-Environment Linkages for the WTO's Future', *Fordham International Law Journal* (2000), pp. 608–651; A. SUKTHANKAR and S. NOVA, 'Human and Labour Rights under the WTO', in L. WALLACH and P. WOODALL, *Whose Trade Organization? A Comprehensive Guide to the WTO*, (New York, New Press 2004), pp. 219–238; A. VANDAELE and S. WILLIAMS, 'The WTO and Labour Rights Revisited', *Sri Lanka Journal of International Law* (2002), pp. 135–164.

would have resulted in the WTO being able to block products originating in countries where fundamental labour rights are not respected.

194. Nevertheless, the debate remained alive after the entry into force of the WTO agreements. At the 1996 Singapore Ministerial Conference, the US proposed establishing a Working Group on Trade and Labour. The EC favoured a joint ILO/WTO Standing Working Forum on the issue and Canada suggested a WTO Working Group on the relationship between appropriate trade, developmental, social and environmental policy choices in the context of adjusting to globalization. In the Final Ministerial Declaration, Members noted "that the secretariats of the WTO and the ILO will continue to collaborate as they do at present".[150] Members reiterated their commitment to fundamental norms relating to labour, but stressed that the "ILO is the competent organ for establishing these norms".[151] There is currently no work on this issue in the WTO. Moreover, even though the Singapore Ministerial declaration mentions collaboration between the WTO and the ILO, there are only loose relations between the Secretariats of the two organizations. The ILO does not have the status of observer in any of the WTO bodies, except for the WTO Ministerial Conferences. Nevertheless, the ILO and WTO Secretariats did cooperate in the deliberations of the ILO's Working Party on the Social Dimension of Globalization, which established the World Commission on the Social Dimension of Globalization in November 2002. This World Commission produced a report in February 2004[152], for which the WTO Secretariat provided input. On 19 February 2007, the WTO Secretariat and the ILO issued a Joint Study on Trade and Employment in which the WTO Director-General and ILO Director-General noted that "the multilateral trading system has the potential to contribute to increasing global welfare and to promote better employment outcomes".[153]

h. Advisory Centre on WTO Law

195. The Advisory Centre on WTO Law (ACWL) was established in 2001 in order to create 'a source of legal training, expertise and advice on WTO law readily accessible to developing countries, in particular the least developed among

---

[150] Ministerial Declaration of Singapore, done on 13 December 1996, WT/MIN(96)/DEC, available on http://www.wto.org/english/thewto_e/minist_e/min96_e/wtodec_e.htm, para. 4.
[151] *Ibid.*
[152] *See* World Commission on the Social Dimension of Globalization, *A Fair Globalization: Creating Opportunities for All* (February 2004), available on http://www.oit.org/public/english/wcsdg/docs/report.pdf.
[153] INTERNATIONAL LABOUR OFFICE and SECRETARIAT OF THE WORLD TRADE ORGANIZATION, *Trade and Employment. Challenges for Policy Research*, (Geneva, WTO Secretariat 2007), viii + 105 p.

them, and countries with economies in transition'.[154] The ACWL was created because some WTO Members realised that even if the creation of the Dispute Settlement System of the WTO had as its underlying idea that international trade disputes would no longer be resolved on the basis of the economic strength of the Parties involved, in practice developing countries were rarely able to effectively enforce their rights under the WTO agreements. Developing countries often do not possess the specialist legal expertise that is necessary to assess whether their rights are being infringed, to prepare submissions and participate effectively in dispute settlement proceedings.[155]

196. It is true that the Understanding on the Settlement of Disputes has specific provisions that are meant to support developing countries in WTO dispute settlement.[156] More specifically, Article 27.2 states that the WTO Secretariat must make available a qualified legal expert from the WTO technical cooperation services to any developing country Member which so requests. The WTO

---

[154] *See* Agreement establishing the Advisory Centre on WTO Law, done at Seattle on 13 November 1999, fifth preliminary consideration, available on www.acwl.ch (hereinafter ('ACWL Agreement').

[155] It has been observed, however, that because of the Most Favoured Nation basis of the dispute settlement proceedings, developing countries have benefited from many dispute settlement proceedings in which they were not complainants. P. GALLAGHER, *Guide to the WTO and Developing Countries*, (The Hague, Kluwer 2000), p. 185.

[156] Apart from art. 27, which will be discussed further here, there are a number of specific provisions in the Understanding on the Settlement of Disputes that take into account the particular situation of developing countries. Art. 3.12 states that a developing-country Member that wants to bring a complaint may decide not to rely on the normal WTO dispute settlement procedures, but rather rely on the good offices of the Director-General and make use of a Panel procedure with shorter time limits. Further, art. 4.10 calls upon WTO Members to give special attention to the particular problems and interests of developing countries during consultations. When a dispute is between a developing country and a developed country, the Panel includes at least one panelist from a developing country, if the developing country member so requests (art. 8.10). If consultations are on-going on a measure taken by a developing country, the parties to these consultations may agree to extend the normal period for consultation and in examining a complaint against a developing country Member, the Panel will accord sufficient time for the developing country to prepare and present its argumentation (art. 12.10). When the Panel eventually adopts its Report and one of the Parties to the dispute is a developing country, the Report should indicate how any special and differential provisions raised by the developing country have been taken into account (art. 12.11). Also in the surveillance and implementation of recommendations and rulings, the interests of developing countries should be taken into account (art. 21.2). In cases that have been brought by a developing country, the Dispute Settlement Body needs to consider what further action might be taken when surveillancing the implementation of recommendations to take into account the trade coverage of the measures complained of and their impact on the developing country (art. 21.7-8). If a Least-Developed Country is involved in a dispute, particular consideration will be given to the special situation of that country (Members must exercise due restraint in raising matters in dispute settlement procedures, asking for compensation or seeking authorization for retaliation) (art. 24.1). Least-Developed Countries that are involved in a dispute where consultations fail may request the Director-General or the Dispute Settlement Body Chairman to offer his good offices before the request for a Panel is made (art. 24.2).

Secretariat has indeed made two legal affairs officers available and has engaged two consultants.[157] The last sentence of Article 27.2 notes, however, that the expert must ensure the impartiality of the Secretariat. It is clear that this may be difficult. Being part of the WTO Secretariat, it is unlikely that the two legal affairs officers are able to act as council or assist in drafting submissions, since this would be irreconcilable with the impartiality of the Secretariat.

197. To address these problems, a far-reaching proposal on Article 27.2 was submitted by Venezuela. Venezuela suggested creating an independent legal unit in the WTO Secretariat, consisting of five consultants. The fact that this unit would be independent within the Secretariat would allow it to assist Members in dispute settlement procedures, without endangering the neutrality of the Secretariat. Nevertheless, when the Advisory Centre on WTO Law was finally created, it became an international organization, independent from the WTO. Still, the ACWL must cooperate with the WTO (and other international organizations) to further the objectives of the ACWL. The Director-General of the WTO or its delegate is invited to participate in the meetings of the Managing Board of the ACWL. The Centre is situated in Geneva, Switzerland and has international legal personality.[158] Membership to the ACWL is open to all WTO Members.[159] Nevertheless, only developing countries and economies in transition can make use of the services of the ACWL.[160]

198. The functions of the ACWL are threefold.[161] It provides legal advice on WTO law concerning measures taken or contemplated by a Member. This is to avoid inconsistencies with WTO obligations. Legal advice is also given on matters that arise in WTO decision-making and negotiations. Second, the ACWL provides advice when a Member considers challenging under WTO dispute settlement procedures. The Centre assesses the chances of prevailing in a proceeding and provides legal support in all stages of the proceeding, even in the negotiation and drafting of a settlement agreement. The third task of the Centre is to train government officials in WTO law, through seminars or internships. The General Assembly of the ACWL can add any further tasks.

---

[157] See K. Van der Borcht, 'The Advisory Center on WTO Law: Advancing Fairness and Equality', *Journal of International Economic Law* (1999), p. 724.
[158] Art. 10 ACWL Agreement.
[159] *Ibid.* art. 16. ACWL Members entitled to the services of the ACWL are: Bolivia, Colombia, Dominican Republic, Ecuador, Egypt, El Salvador, Guatemala, Honduras, Hong Kong China, India, Indonesia, Jordan, Kenya, Nicaragua, Oman, Mauritius, Pakistan, Panama, Paraguay, Peru, Philippines, Taiwan, Thailand, Tunisia, Turkey, Uruguay and Venezuela. The Developed-Country Members (not entitled to the ACWL services) are: Canada, Denmark, Finland, Ireland, Italy, Netherlands, Norway, Sweden, Switzerland and United Kingdom.
[160] *Ibid.* art. 6.1.
[161] *Ibid.* art. 2.2.

199. Legal advice on WTO law is free for Members of the Centre and for all Least-Developed Countries (subject to a maximum number of hours). Developing countries that are non-Members of the Centre can also request legal advice on WTO law, but have to pay a fee, depending on the category in which they are classified. These categories are defined on the basis of a country's share in world trade, with an upward correction reflecting the per capita income of a country. The hourly rate is 350 USD for category A, 300 USD for category B and 250 USD for category C. The ACWL charges fees for its legal advice in dispute settlement proceedings. In that case, Members of the Centre also have to pay fees. The hourly rate for non-Members is the same as previously mentioned for legal advice on WTO law. Nonetheless, Members pay a lower fee (fixed on 250 USD) and get a discount on this fee, depending on the category of country. This means in practice that Category A countries pay an hourly rate of 200 USD, Category B of 150 USD, Category C of 100 USD and Least-Developed Countries 25 USD.[162] This is a clear incentive to become a Member of the Centre. The Centre provides a time budget in order to make sure that the country knows in advance what the approximate cost of the services will be. It is possible that two developing countries are involved in the same WTO dispute settlement proceedings. Because of the conflicts of interests that this will create within the Centre, a priority needs to be defined. Legal support will in first order be given to Least-Developed Countries. If such countries are not involved, Members that have accepted the ACWL Agreement ('Founding Members') will benefit from legal support. In final order, Members that acceded to the ACWL Agreement will obtain support.[163]

200. The Members of the ACWL have to make a contribution to the Centre's Endowment Fund upon accession and thereafter annual contributions. The contributions are determined in the instrument of accession of Member.[164] Least-Developed Countries do not have to make contributions to the Endowment Fund. Both developing and developed country members make contributions to the Centre. Again, the contributions differ according to the category of each country (Developed, Category A, B and C). Also the World Bank makes a contribution to the costs of the operations of the ACWL.

201. The organizational structure of the ACWL consists of a General Assembly, a Management Board and an Executive Director. The General Assembly, in which all Members are represented, is the highest decision-making body and oversees the functioning of the Centre. The Management Board consists of six persons

---

[162] Annex IV to the ACWL Agreement.
[163] *Ibid.* art. 8.
[164] *Ibid.* art. 6.2.

acting in their personal capacity.[165] One of the Members of the Management Board is the Executive Director, who is responsible for the day-to-day management of the Centre.

C. RELATIONSHIP WITH NON-GOVERNMENTAL ORGANIZATIONS

202. The WTO is an intergovernmental organization. In principle, actors other than government representatives have no legal standing in the organization. However, there is a widespread call for NGO involvement in the WTO. Many actors that feel affected by the agreements that exist and emerge within the WTO want their voice to be heard at Geneva. According to Daniel Esty "NGOs offer the promise of serving as 'connective tissue' that will help bridge the gap between WTO decision-makers and the distant constituencies which they are meant to serve, thereby ensuring that the WTO's actions are perceived as responsive and fair".[166] They can indeed make the WTO aware of the concerns of the very subjects of its decisions and help fine-tune policies. As WTO competence touches increasingly more on issues where the WTO lacks expertise, the input by experts from the field may prove extremely useful. Moreover, input by civil society may add fairness to WTO decisions. Possibly affected parties will be able to express their views and will ensure that rules and principles are applied even-handedly over time and issues.[167] It is also said that governments often only represent the position of the majority of a certain country. NGOs may collect minority views in separate countries and hence show that these views in fact enjoy a plurality of support at a global level and therefore represent voices which would otherwise not be heard. Finally NGOs may be an additional source of ideas for policymaking and provide fruitful intellectual competition to the governments in the WTO.[168]

203. Article V.2 of the WTO Agreement provides that the General Council may make appropriate arrangements for consultation and cooperation with non-governmental organizations. In contrast with Article V.1 (cooperation arrangements with intergovernmental organizations), this is not an obligation but merely an option. The 1996 Guidelines for Arrangements on Relations with

---

[165] These members are selected on the basis of their professional qualifications. One of them has to be nominated by the Least-Developed Countries. Art. 3.3 ACWL Agreement.
[166] See D.C. Esty, 'Non-Governmental Organizations at the World Trade Organization: Cooperation, Competition or Exclusion', *Journal of International Economic Law* (1998), pp. 125–126, available on http://www3.oup.co.uk/jielaw/hdb/Volume_01/Issue_01/pdf/010123.pdf.
[167] *Ibid.* p. 127.
[168] *Ibid.* p. 136.

Non-Governmental Organizations gave the task to the WTO Secretariat to establish actively contacts with NGOs. Paragraph 4 of the Guidelines reads: '[...] this interaction [...] should be developed through various means such as inter alia the organization on an ad hoc basis of symposia on specific WTO-related issues, informal arrangements to receive the information NGOs may wish to make available for consultation by interested delegations and the continuation of past practice of responding to requests for general information and briefings about the WTO'.[169] In pursuit of the objectives set out in the 1996 Guidelines, the Secretariat has been giving consideration to activities that might be carried out with NGOs. The basic objective of this programme of activities is to facilitate and encourage substantive and responsible discussion with NGOs on issues falling within the WTO's mandate.[170] The Secretariat has allowed the NGOs to participate in technical seminars and has organized stand-alone workshops. Large numbers of NGOs also try to attend WTO Ministerial Conferences.[171]

Table 1. NGO Attendance at Ministerial Conferences

Ministerial	No. of eligible NGOs	NGOs who attended	No. of participants
Singapore 1996	159	108	235
Geneva 1998	153	128	362
Seattle 1999	776	686	approx. 1500
Doha 2001	651	370	370
Cancún 2003	961	795	1578
Hong Kong, China 2005	1065	811	1596

Source: WTO Annual Report 2006, p. 60.

D. MEMBERSHIP

1. Procedure

204. Membership of the WTO is open to any State or separate customs territory possessing the full autonomy in the conduct of its external commercial relations.[172]

---

[169] Guidelines For Arrangements on Relations With Non-Governmental Organizations adopted on 18 July 1996, para. 4, WT/L/162, 23 July 1996.
[170] See http://www.wto.org/english/thewto_e/minist_e/min01_e/min01_ngo_activ_e.htm
[171] At the first conference in Singapore in 1996, only a modest 108 NGOs attended the conference. In 2003, on the other hand, the request for accreditation for the Cancún conference was so large that the WTO decided to severely limit access of NGOs. NGOs could send by mail a request for registration indicating how they are concerned with matters related to those in the WTO. Selected NGOs could register three representatives. Of these three, only one was allowed at the convention centre at any one time. In the end, 795 NGOs participated in the conference. See WTO, *Annual Report 2004*, (Geneva, WTO Publications 2004), p. 76, available on http://www.wto.org/english/res_e/booksp_e/anrep_e/anrep04_e.pdf.
[172] Art. XII.1 WTO Agreement.

The WTO Agreement makes a distinction between 'original Members' and other ('new') Members. The term 'original Members' applies to the Contracting Parties of GATT 1947 and the European Communities, on the condition of accepting the WTO Agreement, all Multilateral Trade Agreements, the Schedules of Concessions annexed to the GATT 1994 and the Schedules of Specific Commitments annexed to GATS.[173] There are no consequences linked to the distinction. The term 'original Members' is only used to distinguish between Members that have acceded through the previously described procedure and Members that accede through the normal procedure.[174]

205. Becoming a Member of the WTO is a lengthy process.[175] All candidate Members have observer status in the WTO before joining the organization.[176] Candidates have to submit to the Director-General of the WTO a formal written request for accession. The first step of the accession process is the establishment of a working party by the General Council. The working party is open to all interested WTO Members. This working party will examine the applicant's trade regime. To this end, the candidate has to submit a memorandum describing among others its trade rules, tariffs and policies. The proposed memorandum contains seven main headings[177]: (1) Introduction; (2) Economy, Economic Policies and Foreign Trade; (3) Framework for Making and Enforcing Policies Affecting Foreign Trade in Goods and Trade in Services; (4) Policies Affecting Trade in Goods; (5) Trade-Related Intellectual Property Regime; (6) Trade-Related Services Regime; (7) Institutional Base for Trade and Economic Relations with Third Countries. The working party's focus is especially on the consistency of this regime with the WTO rules. If measures are found inconsistent, they have to be adjusted or removed. Next, parallel bilateral talks start.[178] Candidate Members will negotiate with each existing Member commitments and concessions to ensure market

---

[173] *Ibid.* art. XI.1.
[174] P. Van den Bossche, *supra* note 30, p. 413.
[175] The accession of China lasted more than fifteen years. The average accession time for the first 16 new Members to accede to the WTO was six years. See Technical Note on the Accession Process, WT/ACC/10, 21 December 2001, pp. 10-11.
[176] With the exception of the Holy See, observers must start accession negotiations within five years of becoming observers. See Guidelines on Observer Status for Governments in the WTO, WT/L/61, Annex II, 25 July 1996, para. 4.
[177] Outline Format for a Memorandum on the Foreign Trade Regime, Attachment to Accession to the World Trade Organization. Procedures for Negotiations under art. XII, WT/ACC/1, 24 March 1995.
[178] World Trade Organization, *Understanding the WTO*, (Geneva, WTO Publications, 2007), available on www.wto.org, p. 105.

access.[179] Members can take this opportunity but are not obliged to negotiate with the candidate.[180] Much depends on the trade interests of Members.

These engagements imply a far-reaching liberalization of the candidate's economy, which is sometimes criticized as going too far.[181] Nevertheless, the WTO Agreement recognizes that, in principle, developed and least-developed countries 'should only be required to undertake commitments and concessions to the extent consistent with their individual development, financial and trade needs or their administrative and institutional capabilities'.[182]

Eventually, the working party submits a report on accession to the General Council, together with a draft decision, a protocol of accession and the resulting tariff schedules. It is possible that specific (temporary) derogations from the principles of the WTO agreements are included in the accession protocol or working party report.[183] The Ministerial Conference must approve the agreement on the terms of accession by a two-thirds majority of WTO Members.[184] The Protocol of Accession enters into force thirty days after the acceptance by the candidate Member either by signature or by deposit of the instrument of ratification, if parliamentary approval is required.[185] The new Member accedes to the WTO Agreement and the Multilateral Agreements as a 'single undertaking'.[186]

[179] This is sometimes referred to as 'negotiating the ticket of admission'. See J. JACKSON, *The World Trade Organization. Constitution and Jurisprudence, supra* note 29, p. 48. The GATT 1947 included a provision stating that customs territories that are dependent on a GATT 1947 Contracting Party and for which this Contracting Party has accepted the GATT, gain automatic membership of GATT (*i.e.* without negotiating concessions) when they acquire full autonomy. The responsible Contracting Party had to sponsor the membership (art. XXVI.5 (c) GATT). This concerned colonies that became independent and thus joined without schedules of concessions. This provision still exists in the GATT. Nevertheless, art. XII.1 WTO Agreement states that accession requires the negotiation of an agreement with the WTO. This provision prevails over art. XXVI.5 (c) GATT (see art. XVI.2 WTO Agreement).
[180] B. HOEKMAN and M. KOSTECKI, *supra* note 9, p. 66.
[181] Cambodia acceded as least-developed country to the WTO on 13 October 2004. Much criticism was heard about powerful developed nations pressuring the smaller, poorer country into an inequitable arrangement. Yet, counterarguments are also heard, namely that, ultimately, Cambodia will benefit from the WTO accession. See R. POVARCHUK, 'Cambodia's WTO Accession: A Strenuous but Necessary Step for a Poor Nation Seeking Economic Prosperity', *Pacific Rim Law and Policy Journal* (2004), pp. 645-671.
[182] Art. XI.2 WTO Agreement, which is titled 'Original Membership'. Nevertheless, the principle applies also for newly acceding countries. See Preamble of the WTO Agreement, para. 1 *in fine*. See also, on the position of developing countries in the WTO, *infra* paras. 231-234.
[183] See, for instance, the Working Party report and Protocol of Accession of China, in which specific safeguard measures were included. See *supra* note para. 121.
[184] Art. XII.2 WTO Agreement.
[185] Accession to the World Trade Organization. Procedures for Negotiations under art. XII, WT/ACC/1, 24 March 1995, para. 15.
[186] Art. XII.1 WTO Agreement. See Appellate Body Report: Brazil – Measures Affecting Desiccated Coconut, WT/DS22/AB/R, (14 February 1997), p. 12.

Although it is possible that the Protocol of Accession specifies some transition periods, pressure is put on the candidate Member to implement the WTO obligations immediately. Moreover, the general practice in accession protocols is to state that also the transition periods that are already provided for in the WTO agreements should be calculated for the acceding Member from the entry into force of the WTO Agreement (1 January 1995). The acceding Member should thus ensure that it is able to comply with all WTO obligations upon accession. The duration of the accession process is essentially its transition period.[187]

206. Remarkably, there is a possibility for Members to invoke the non-application of the WTO Agreement or Annexes 1 (Multilateral Trade Agreements) or 2 (DSU) vis-à-vis a new Member when it joins. Similarly, the new Member may declare the non-application of any of the mentioned agreements vis-à-vis any existing Member. This option already existed under the GATT 1947.[188] Pre-WTO cases of this 'opt-out' still apply.[189] The Member that invokes non-application has to notify the Ministerial Conference before the approval of accession by the Conference.[190] Such cases of 'opt-out' are provoked by political reasons and may lead to a situation where a new Member is approved for accession, but still has no treaty rights vis-à-vis some other Members who have opted out.[191] It was not possible for the 'original Members' of the WTO to choose for opt-out vis-à-vis other 'original Members' on the occasion of the 'transition' from GATT to WTO.[192]

207. Being a democratic State is not a condition for WTO membership. It has been suggested that requiring a minimal level of democratic practice from its membership could possibly help further democratize the WTO.[193] This would, however, be problematic if applied to some present Members. It also remains a question whether a Member should be sanctioned when it violates democratic standards.[194]

---

[187] See W. DAVEY, "Institutional Framework", in P. MACRORY, A. APPLETON and M. PLUMMER (eds.), *The World Trade Organization: Legal, Economic and Political Analyses*, (New York, Springer 2005), Volume I, p. 77.
[188] Art. XXXV GATT.
[189] Art. XIII.2 WTO Agreement.
[190] *Ibid.* art. XIII.3.
[191] See J. JACKSON, *The World Trade Organization. Constitution and Jurisprudence*, supra note 29, p. 49. JACKSON mentions the invocation of India of the GATT 1947 provision when South Africa acceded in 1948. He also points out the fact that the US may have used the provision against certain 'communist' countries.
[192] Already existing opt-outs remained applicable. Art. XIII.2 WTO Agreement. See J. CROOME, *Guide to the Uruguay Round Agreements*, (The Hague, Kluwer 1999), p. 13.
[193] G. FOX, 'Strengthening the State', *Indiana Journal of Global Legal Studies* (1999), p. 63.
[194] J. ATIK, 'Democratizing the WTO', *George Washington International Law Review* (2001), p. 466.

208. The WTO Agreement imposes only two obligations on Members. First of all there is the obligation for a Member to contribute promptly its share of the expenses of the WTO.[195] There is also a general obligation to ensure that a Member's laws, regulations and administrative procedures are in conformity with the WTO package of agreements.[196] A Member may not invoke its own constitution or laws as a reason for not complying with its WTO obligations.[197] This conformity obligation does not seem to imply that there is an obligation to make the WTO Agreement self-executing in domestic law.[198] Specific substantive obligations are imposed by the agreements in the annexes to the WTO Agreement. Acceding Members cannot make any reservations to the WTO Agreement. Reservations in respect of any of the provisions of the Multilateral Trade Agreements and in respect of a provision of a Plurilateral Trade Agreement are governed by the provision of the Agreement in question.[199]

209. Members have the right to withdraw at any time from the WTO Agreement and the Multilateral Trade Agreements. However, if a Member wants to withdraw, it has to do so from the whole 'package'. One cannot withdraw from just one provision or one agreement.[200] The WTO Agreement does not provide for a general procedure for the expulsion of a Member. Nonetheless, Article X.5 of the Agreement provides for the possibility of expulsion of a Member that refuses to approve an amendment to the Agreement. The Ministerial Conference may judge (by three-fourths majority) that an amendment, which will alter the rights and obligations of Members, is of such importance that this refusing Member can only stay in the organization if the Ministerial Conference consents to this.[201]

210. Accession to and withdrawal from the plurilateral agreements is governed by the provisions of these agreements.[202] Whether an acceding Member adheres to the plurilateral agreement is indicated in its Accession Protocols.

---

[195] Art. VII.4 WTO Agreement.
[196] *Ibid.* art. XVI.4. Note that under the GATT 1947, the Protocol of Provisional Application indicated that Part II of the GATT only applied as far as this was consistent with existing legislation.
[197] Panel Report: United States – Sections 301–310 of the Trade Act 1974, WT/DS152/R (22 December 1999), para. 7.41. See E. MCGOVERN, *International Trade Regulation*, (Exeter, Globefield Press 2005), p. 1.13–4.
[198] E. MCGOVERN, *ibid.*
[199] Art. XVI.5 WTO Agreement.
[200] To this end, States should rather apply for a 'waiver'. See *infra* para. 253.
[201] Art. X.5 WTO Agreement. The article formulates this diplomatically by stressing the freedom of the refusing Member to withdraw from the organization.
[202] Art. XII.3 and art. XV.2 WTO Agreement.

211. The General Council has adopted Guidelines on the accession of Least-Developed Countries.[203] The Doha Ministerial Declaration called for the acceleration and facilitation of the accession process with Least-Developed Countries.[204] The General Council noted the need for further positive efforts designed to assist LDCs in participating in the rules-based multilateral trading system and decided that a streamlined and simplified accession process was necessary. The rules include the obligation of Members to exercise restraint when seeking market access commitments from Least-Developed Countries; the principle that special and differential treatment in WTO agreements should apply to them; the granting of transitional periods and arrangements; and the principle that these countries should not be required to accede to the plurilateral agreements.

Table 2. Table of Members of the WTO

Albania 8 September 2000	Chile 1 January 1995
Angola 23 November 1996	China 11 December 2001
Antigua and Barbuda 1 January 1995	Chinese Taipei 1 January 2002
Argentina 1 January 1995	Colombia 30 April 1995
Armenia 5 February 2003	Congo 27 March 1997
Australia 1 January 1995	Costa Rica 1 January 1995
Austria 1 January 1995	Côte d'Ivoire 1 January 1995
Bahrain, Kingdom of 1 January 1995	Croatia 30 November 2000
Bangladesh 1 January 1995	Cuba 20 April 1995
Barbados 1 January 1995	Cyprus 30 July 1995
Belgium 1 January 1995	Czech Republic 1 January 1995
Belize 1 January 1995	Democratic Republic of the Congo 1 January 1997
Benin 22 February 1996	Denmark 1 January 1995
Bolivia 12 September 1995	Djibouti 31 May 1995
Botswana 31 May 1995	Dominica 1 January 1995
Brazil 1 January 1995	Dominican Republic 9 March 1995
Brunei Darussalam 1 January 1995	Ecuador 21 January 1996
Bulgaria 1 December 1996	Egypt 30 June 1995
Burkina Faso 3 June 1995	El Salvador 7 May 1995
Burundi 23 July 1995	Estonia 13 November 1999
Cambodia 13 October 2004	European Communities 1 January 1995
Cameroon 13 December 1995	Fiji 14 January 1996
Canada 1 January 1995	Finland 1 January 1995
Central African Republic 31 May 1995	Former Yugoslav Republic of Macedonia (FYROM) 4 April 2003
Chad 19 October 1996	

---

[203] Accession of Least-Developed Countries, WT/L/508, 20 January 2003.
[204] Ministerial Declaration of Doha, *supra* note 40, para. 42.

France 1 January 1995	*Moldova* 26 July 2001
Gabon 1 January 1995	*Mongolia* 29 January 1997
Georgia 14 June 2000	*Morocco* 1 January 1995
Germany 1 January 1995	*Mozambique* 26 August 1995
Ghana 1 January 1995	*Myanmar* 1 January 1995
Greece 1 January 1995	*Namibia* 1 January 1995
Grenada 22 February 1996	*Nepal* 23 April 2004
Guatemala 21 July 1995	*Netherlands — For the Kingdom in Europe and for the Netherlands Antilles* 1 January 1995
Guinea Bissau 31 May 1995	
Guinea 25 October 1995	*New Zealand* 1 January 1995
Guyana 1 January 1995	*Nicaragua* 3 September 1995
Haiti 30 January 1996	*Niger* 13 December 1996
Honduras 1 January 1995	*Nigeria* 1 January 1995
Hong Kong, China 1 January 1995	*Norway* 1 January 1995
Hungary 1 January 1995	*Oman* 9 November 2000
Iceland 1 January 1995	*Pakistan* 1 January 1995
India 1 January 1995	*Panama* 6 September 1997
Indonesia 1 January 1995	*Papua New Guinea* 9 June 1996
Ireland 1 January 1995	*Paraguay* 1 January 1995
Israel 21 April 1995	*Peru* 1 January 1995
Italy 1 January 1995	*Philippines* 1 January 1995
Jamaica 9 March 1995	*Poland* 1 July 1995
Japan 1 January 1995	*Portugal* 1 January 1995
Jordan 11 April 2000	*Qatar* 13 January 1996
Kenya 1 January 1995	*Romania* 1 January 1995
Korea, Republic of 1 January 1995	*Rwanda* 22 May 1996
Kuwait 1 January 1995	*Saint Kitts and Nevis* 21 February 1996
Kyrgyz Republic 20 December 1998	*Saint Lucia* 1 January 1995
Latvia 10 February 1999	*Saint Vincent & the Grenadines* 1 January 1995
Lesotho 31 May 1995	*Saudi Arabia* 11 December 2005
Liechtenstein 1 September 1995	*Senegal* 1 January 1995
Lithuania 31 May 2001	*Sierra Leone* 23 July 1995
Luxembourg 1 January 1995	*Singapore* 1 January 1995
Macao, China 1 January 1995	*Slovak Republic* 1 January 1995
Madagascar 17 November 1995	*Slovenia* 30 July 1995
Malawi 31 May 1995	*Solomon Islands* 26 July 1996
Malaysia 1 January 1995	*South Africa* 1 January 1995
Maldives 31 May 1995	*Spain* 1 January 1995
Mali 31 May 1995	*Sri Lanka* 1 January 1995
Malta 1 January 1995	*Suriname* 1 January 1995
Mauritania 31 May 1995	*Swaziland* 1 January 1995
Mauritius 1 January 1995	*Sweden* 1 January 1995
Mexico 1 January 1995	*Switzerland* 1 July 1995

Tanzania 1 January 1995	*United Arab Emirates* 10 April 1996
Thailand 1 January 1995	*United Kingdom* 1 January 1995
The Gambia 23 October 1996	*United States of America* 1 January 1995
Togo 31 May 1995	*Uruguay* 1 January 1995
Tonga 27 July 2007	*Venezuela (Bolivarian Republic of)* 1 January 1995
Trinidad and Tobago 1 March 1995	*Viet Nam* 11 January 2007
Tunisia 29 March 1995	*Zambia* 1 January 1995
Turkey 26 March 1995	*Zimbabwe* 5 March 1995
Uganda 1 January 1995	

Source: WTO website.

2. Groupings and Alliances in the WTO

212. Within the WTO, Members with common interests form groupings and alliances. The most cohesive and formalized group is the European Union (EU) or, legally more correctly, the European Community (EC).[205] The European Commission represents the EC and EU Member States (of course after preliminary consultation with the latter) at almost every WTO meeting. Yet, there are also less formal groups.

a. ASEAN

213. A regional grouping, until now much less integrated than the EC but often taking common positions, is the Association of Southeast Asian Nations (ASEAN).[206] ASEAN is based in Jakarta and has ten Members.[207] The Association wants to further economic growth, social progress and cultural development in

---

[205] See *infra* paras. 220–222.
[206] See *inter alia* A. FABBRICOTTI, 'The ASEAN Free Trade Area (AFTA) and its Compatibility with GATT/WTO', *Asean Yearbook of International Law* (2003), pp. 37–58; A. FUKUSHIMA, 'The ASEAN Regional Forum', in M. WESLEY (ed.), *The Regional Organizations of the Asia-Pacific*, (Basingstoke, Palgrave Macmillan 2003), pp. 76–93; J. HENDERSON, *Reassessing ASEAN*, (New York, Oxford University Press 1999), 85 p.; Q. KONG, 'China's WTO Accession and the ASEAN-China Free Trade Area: the Perspective of a Chinese Lawyer', *Journal of International Economic Law* (2004), pp. 839–861; H. NESADURAI, *Globalization, Domestic Politics and Regionalism: the ASEAN Free Trade Area*, (London, Routledge 2003), 226 p.; H. NESADURAI, 'Cooperation and Institutional Transformation in ASEAN: Insights from the AFTA Project', in R. THAKUR and E. NEWMAN (eds.), *Broadening Asia's Security Discourse and Agenda: Political, Social, and Environmental Perspectives*, (Tokyo, United Nations University Press 2004), pp. 279–305; S. SRIVASTAVA, 'What does the Economic Rise of China Imply for ASEAN and India?: Focus on Trade and Investment Reforms', in H.S. KEHAL (ed.), *Foreign Trade and Investment in Developing Countries* (Basingstoke, Palgrave MacMillan 2004), pp. 171–204 and L.H. TAN, 'Will ASEAN Economic Integration Process Beyond a Free Trade Area?', *The International and Comparative Law Quarterly* (2004), pp. 935–967.
[207] It concerns the following 10 countries: Brunei, Cambodia, Philippines, Indonesia, Laos, Malaysia, Myanmar, Singapore, Thailand and Vietnam.

the region, as well as regional peace and stability.[208] Tariff preferences have been accorded between the ASEAN Members[209] and in 1995, it was decided to work towards an ASEAN Free Trade Area (AFTA).[210] The AFTA should be finalized by 2010.[211]

214. ASEAN Vision 2020, a declaration by the leaders of the ASEAN Member States, envisaged a central role for ASEAN in the international community.[212] To support the conduct of its external relations, the Association has established committees composed of heads of diplomatic missions in several capitals in the world. ASEAN has indeed often played an active role in the WTO. For instance, ASEAN diplomats rejected a United States proposal to open up the WTO dispute settlement mechanism by allowing Panels and the Appellate Body to accept *amicus curiae* briefs (see *infra* paras. 396-363).[213] ASEAN also opposed the Belgian labelling law for Socially Responsible Production.[214] The aim of this law is to create a label which companies can affix to their products only if the products meet, among others, certain criteria and standards of certain specified ILO Conventions. According to the Association, "this amounts to a blatant discrimination of products and services based on non-trade criteria which goes against multilaterally agreed WTO rules and practices". ASEAN was also concerned about the "impact of this law on companies in developing countries. Companies in developing countries [would have] difficulties in meeting these unilaterally imposed criteria."[215] ASEAN strongly supported the accession of China. China and ASEAN are also negotiating a Free Trade Area (ACFTA), which would complement the WTO obligations of the countries that are involved.[216]

---

[208] See the ASEAN Declaration, done at Bangkok on 8 August 1967.
[209] Agreement on ASEAN Preferential Trading Arrangements, done at Manila on 24 February 1977 (Amended by Protocol, done at Bangkok on 15 December 1995).
[210] Agreement on the Common Effective Preferential Tariff (CEPT) for the ASEAN Free Trade Area (AFTA), done at Singapore on 28 January 1992.
[211] See ASEAN, *Southeast Asia: A Free Trade Area*, (Jakarta, ASEAN Secretariat 2002), p. 2, available on http://www.aseansec.org/viewpdf.asp?file=/pdf/afta.pdf.
[212] ASEAN Vision 2020, done at Kuala Lumpur on 15 December 1997.
[213] See Minutes of the Meeting held in the Centre William Rappard on 25 September 1997, WT/DSB/M/37, 4 November 1997, p. 27.
[214] Law of 27 February 2002 for the Promotion of Socially Responsible Production, *Moniteur Belge* 26 March 2002. See Chapter 15 of A. VANDAELE, *International Labour Rights and the Social Clause: Friends or Foes?*, (London, Cameron May 2004).
[215] ASEAN Concerns Regarding the Proposed Belgian Law for the Promotion of Socially Responsible Production, G/TBT/W/159, 28 May 2001, paras. 3-4.
[216] Framework Agreement on Comprehensive Economic Cooperation between the Association of Southeast Asian Nations and the People's Republic of China, done at Phnom Penh on 4 November 2002, eighth Preliminary Consideration and art. 9.

Chapter IV

b.   Cairns Group

215.   A well-known organization of a different nature is the 'Cairns Group'[217], which is made up of 19 countries from four continents[218] who account for over 23 per cent of the world's agricultural exports. Remarkably, contrary to other groupings in the WTO, this group unites both developing and developed countries. Their common aim is to liberalize international trade in agricultural products.

The Cairns Group's ambition and broad objectives for the agriculture negotiations were set out in its 'Vision Statement'. The Vision Statement outlines the Cairns Group's objectives in each of the three key reform areas within the framework for agricultural trade. These include deep cuts to all tariffs and removal of tariff escalation, the elimination of all trade-distorting domestic subsidies; the elimination of export subsidies and clear rules to prevent circumvention of export subsidy commitments.[219]

216.   The Cairns Group Members maintain little or no agricultural support measures. The Group played an active role during the Uruguay Round. They refused to "accept a cosmetic outcome on agriculture".[220] As is known, eventually the negotiations resulted in an Agriculture Agreement with numerous exceptions.

---

[217]   The Group is named after the place where it was formed (Cairns, Australia), early in the Uruguay Round negotiations. See *inter alia* K. ANDERSON, 'Developing Country Interest in Agricultural Trade Reform: A Cairns Group Perspective', in J.A. MACMAHON (ed.), *Trade & Agriculture: Negotiating a New Agreement?*, (London, Cameron May 2001), pp. 89–120; R.A. HIGGOTT and A. COOPER, 'Middle Power Leadership and Coalition Building: Australia, the Cairns Group and the Uruguay Round of Trade Negotiations', in K. ANDERSON and T. JOSLING (eds.), *The WTO and Agriculture*, (Cheltenham, Elgar 2005), pp. 53–96; D. KENYON, 'Position of the Cairns Group of the New Round', in S. BILAL and P. PEZAROS (eds.), *Negotiating the Future of Agricultural Policies: Agricultural Policies: Agricultural Trade and the Millennium Round*, (The Hague, Kluwer Law International 1999), pp. 243–249; C. REUTTER, 'Critical Role of the Cairns Group in Liberalizing Farm Trade', in Rural INDUSTRIES RESEARCH AND DEVELOPMENT COOPERATION (ed.), *Reason versus Emotion: Requirements for a Successful WTO Round* (1999), pp. 1–20; I. TAILOR, 'The Cairns Group and the Commonwealth: Bridge-Building for International Trade', *The Round Table: A Quarterly Review of the Politics of the British Empire* (2000), pp. 375–386 and S. TUCKER, 'Lessons from Implementation of the Uruguay Round Agreement on Agriculture: A Cairns Group Perspective', in M.D. INGCO (ed.), *Agriculture, Trade and the WTO: Creating a Trading Environment for Development*, (Washington D.C., World Bank 2002), pp. 60–64.
[218]   Namely Argentina, Australia, Bolivia, Brazil, Canada, Chile, Columbia, Costa Rica, Guatemala, Indonesia, Malaysia, New Zealand, Pakistan, Paraguay, Peru, Philippines, South Africa, Thailand and Uruguay.
[219]   Cairns Group 'Vision' for the WTO Agriculture Negotiations. Completing the Task, done at Sydney on 3 April 1998.
[220]   See L. HEGGY, 'Free Trade Meets US Farm Policy: Life after the Uruguay Round', *Law and Policy in International Business* (1994), p. 1394.

At the Doha conference, the Cairns Group threatened to block any consensus as long as no commitment was made by the EU and others to the objective of phasing out agricultural export subsidies.[221] In the present negotiation round, they use the fact that the Peace Clause has expired and – consequently – the possibility of challenging all types of agricultural support measures (see *supra* paras. 105-106) as a leverage tool in the agriculture negotiations in the WTO.[222] In the run-up to the Ministerial Conference in Cancún, the Cairns Group issued a communiqué, stating that a date should be fixed for eliminating all export subsidies for agricultural products; substantial reductions in trade-distorting support had to be made as well as substantial improvements in access for their exporters. Finally, new operational measures should be adopted with respect to key elements of special and differential treatment.[223] During the Ministerial Conference itself, however, less unity was shown, since several members of the Group sought alliances along other lines. This is probably due to the fact that opening up all markets for agricultural goods would mainly benefit the larger and wealthier members of the group (e.g. Australia), whereas it would seriously hurt the smaller members. Hence, the latter are more favourable towards special and differential treatment for developing countries. It was therefore no surprise that some Cairns Members united with other developing countries in the G20+ (*infra* para. 218). At the Hong Kong Ministerial Conference, the Cairns Group held a joint ministerial meeting with the G20+.

c.   The Quad

217.   Finally, there is a group that is called the 'Quad' (from *quadrilaterals*). It comprises Canada, the EC, Japan and the United States (US). Especially in the case of extremely difficult negotiations, a breakthrough among those four Members is necessary. Therefore, it is often said that "[a]lthough theoretically the WTO operates by consensus, the reality is generally different". Some critics state that "[u]ntil the Ministerial Conference in Seattle in 1999, the Quad had traditionally functioned as an informal steering committee for the WTO system".[224] Nevertheless, the accession to the WTO of new major players such as China, as well as the formation of new alliances and groupings, may slowly

---

[221] J. CLARKE, 'WTO: Now the Hard Work Really Begins', *International Trade Law and Regulation* (2002), p. 40. CLARKE states: "In the end a Solomonic solution was found: the phasing out of export subsidies would indeed be an objective, but the negotiations would begin without prejudice to any outcome. The devil, as always, lies in the details."

[222] See T.E. JOSLING, 'When the Peace Ends: The Vulnerability of EC and US Agricultural Subsidies to WTO Legal Challenge', *Journal of International Economic Law* (2003), p. 414.

[223] Cairns Group Communiqué, Cancún: A Moment of Choice, done at Cancún on 9 September 2003.

[224] D.K. DAS, *Global Trading System at the Crossroads: A Post-Seattle Perspective*, (London, Routledge 2001), § 4.3, p. 39.

Chapter IV

counterbalance the power of the Quad. This became quite apparent at the Ministerial Conference in Cancún in 2003 and may be even more obvious in the years to come. Therefore, reference is now sometimes made to the 'New Quad' countries: China, Brazil, India and South Africa.[225] Pascal Lamy, the present Director-General of the WTO, used the term 'new Quad' in yet another sense to refer to a coalition between the US, the EU, the G20 (with India, Brazil, South Africa, and China at its core), and the G90[226] (centred on the African group).[227]

d.   G20+

218.   It appears that a new coalition of primarily developing countries emerged during the Ministerial Conference in Cancún in September 2003. This 'G20+'[228], led by Brazil, China, India and South Africa formed a front against the (richer) industrialized nations. Even though it was thought that the Group would collapse after the Ministerial Conference, it is still active.[229] It made its own proposal for the introduction of certain modalities with regard to market access for agricultural products.[230] On 12 June 2004, it convened again, on the initiative of Brazil, in São Paulo to prepare the 11th conference of the United Nations Conference on Trade and Development (UNCTAD). The Members stressed their belief in the importance of the WTO and the multilateral trading system and reaffirmed that progress on agricultural issues is essential to avoid a failure of the Doha Round.[231] Yet, now criticism is being voiced that the initial resistance of the G20+ was overcome in the 'July Decision' by bringing the G20+'s main leaders, Brazil and India centre stage in the agriculture negotiations with the Quad. The July Decision

---

[225]   See M. BRONCKERS and N. VAN DEN BROECK, 'Financial Compensation in the WTO: Improving the Remedies of WTO Dispute Settlement', *Journal of International Economic Law* (2005), p. 120.

[226]   The Group of 90 Developing Countries.

[227]   See P. DRAPER, 'A French Twist for Trade', *Bangkok Post* (31 August 2005), available on http://www.saiia.org.za/modules.php?op=modload&name=News&file=article&sid=697.

[228]   One speaks also about 'G20' or 'G22'. In order not to confuse with the G20, an international forum of Finance Ministers and Central Bank Governors representing 19 countries, the European Union and the Bretton Woods Institutions (the International Monetary Fund and the World Bank), we will use the term G20+. It includes Argentina, Bolivia, Brazil, Chile, China, Cuba, Egypt, India, Indonesia, Mexico, Nigeria, Pakistan, Paraguay, the Philippines, South Africa, Thailand, Venezuela and Zimbabwe. Ecuador, Guatemala and Peru left, but joined again in the meantime. Costa Rica left the group: 'Seeds of anger take root', *Guardian* (14 December 2003), http://www.guardian.co.uk/wto/article/0,2763,1106544,00.html.

[229]   C. GRANT, 'The WTO Ten Years On: Trade and Development', *Tralac Working Paper No5/2006*, http://www.tralac.org/pdf/20060518_wto_trade_dev_grant.pdf#search=%22G20%2B%20 and%20%22Hong%20Kong%20ministerial%20conference%22%22, p. 15.

[230]   See G-20 Proposal on a Framework for Establishing Modalities in Agriculture. Market Access, 28 May 2004, http://www.ictsd.org/issarea/ag/resources/G-20_Ag_tariff_Proposal.pdf.

[231]   See G-20 ministerial communiqué on the occasion of UNCTAD XI, Communication from Brazil, WT/L/575, 18 June 2001.

indeed includes a commitment of developed countries to phase out all export subsidies, an issue which was of particular importance for Brazil. Nevertheless, the Decision also includes some issues that favour the smaller developing countries (e.g. the idea of establishing a 'Special Safeguard Mechanism' for developing countries.) Still, in all cases the proposals had to be made more concrete in a decision with clear binding commitments. On 9 and 10 September 2005, the Group met in Bhurban (Pakistan) to map its strategy for the sixth Ministerial Conference in Hong Kong.[232] One month before the Ministerial Conference, on 9 November 2005, the Group met in Geneva and noted that both the EU proposal and US proposal on agriculture fell short of responding to the Group's proposals. It was also concluded that the proposals by the developed members did not adequately incorporate special and differential treatment for developing countries.[233] At the start of the Ministerial Conference, the G20+ indeed made a joint declaration, calling for substantial reductions in trade-distorting domestic support and the elimination of all forms of export subsidies.[234] During the conference, the G20+, G33[235] and G90 cooperated and acted as G-110, which contributed to a number of clear references in the Ministerial Declaration to development and special and differential treatment.[236] The G20+ met again in Geneva on 29 June 2006 to discuss further steps in the liberalization of trade in agriculture.[237]

---

[232] See the Bhurban G-20 Ministerial Declaration, done at Bhurban on 10 September 2005, available on http://www.g-20.mre.gov.br/conteudo/ministerials_Bhurban01.htm.
[233] See the Geneva G-20 Ministerial Declaration, done at Geneva on 9 November 2005, available on http://www.g-20.mre.gov.br/conteudo/ministerials_Genebra01.htm.
[234] See the Hong Kong G-20 Ministerial Declaration, done at Hong Kong on 13 December 2005, available on http://www.g-20.mre.gov.br/conteudo/ministerials_HongKong01.htm; see also Statement by H.E. Mr. Celso Amorim, Minister of External Relations of Brazil, WT/MIN(05)/ST/8, 14 December 2005.
[235] The Group of 33 comprises 42 countries, mainly developing countries, which are concerned about food security, livelihood security and rural development needs.
[236] See for instance Hong Kong Ministerial Declaration, done on 22 December 2005, WT/MIN(05)/DEC, available on http://www.wto.org/English/thewto_e/minist_e/min05_e/final_text_e.pdf, paras. 35–38.
[237] See the Geneva G-20 Ministerial Statement, done at Geneva on 29 June 2006, available on http://www.g-20.mre.gov.br/conteudo/ministerials_Genebra03.htm.

Chapter IV

Figure 1. Groups and Alliances in the WTO for Agriculture Negotiations

There exist many more groups and alliances that are formed to further all kinds of objectives. The following scheme gives an impression of the different alliances in agriculture negotiations.

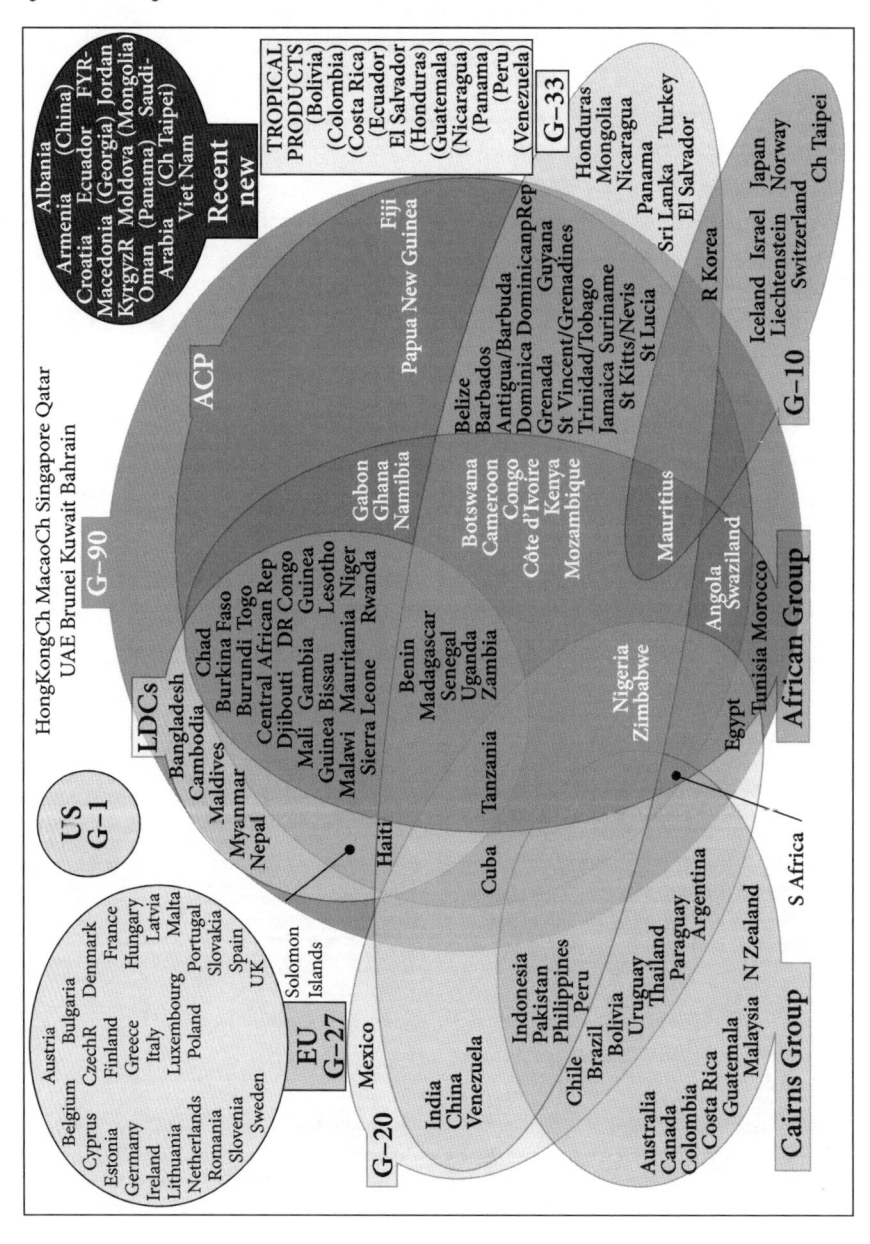

Source: Mr. Peter Ungphakorn, WTO Information Officer.

(Names in parentheses in the "Recent New" group are members who are also in other coalitions, except Georgia, which has signed some papers but not the latest, TN/AG/GEN/24. All members of the Tropical Products Group are members of other coalitions, except El Salvador.)

The complexity of the alliances has one virtue: all interested countries are members of at least one group. When small group talks are organized e.g. 20-30 delegations, all members can be represented by their group co-ordinators.

Cairns Group (19): Argentina, Australia, Bolivia, Brazil, Canada (opting out of some proposals), Chile, Colombia, Costa Rica, Guatemala, Indonesia, Malaysia, New Zealand, Pakistan, Paraguay, Peru, Philippines, South Africa, Thailand, Uruguay.

Commodities Group (6): Côte d'Ivoire, Kenya, Rwanda, Tanzania, Uganda, Zimbabwe.

Cotton-4: Benin, Burkina Faso, Chad, Mali.

G–10 (9): Iceland, Israel, Japan, Korea, Liechtenstein, Mauritius, Norway, Switzerland, Chinese Taipei.

G-20 (22): Argentina, Bolivia, Brazil, Chile, China, Cuba, Egypt, Guatemala, India, Indonesia, Mexico, Nigeria, Pakistan, Paraguay, Peru, Philippines, South Africa, Tanzania, Thailand, Uruguay, Venezuela, Zimbabwe.

G-33 (46): Antigua and Barbuda, Barbados, Belize, Benin, Bolivia, Botswana, China, Congo, Côte d'Ivoire, Cuba, Dominica, Dominican Republic, El Salvador, Grenada, Guatemala, Guyana, Haiti, Honduras, India, Indonesia, Jamaica, Kenya, Rep. Korea, Madagascar, Mauritius, Mongolia, Mozambique, Nicaragua, Nigeria, Pakistan, Panama, Peru, Philippines, St Kitts and Nevis, St Lucia, St Vincent and the Grenadines, Senegal, Sri Lanka, Suriname, Tanzania, Trinidad and Tobago, Turkey, Uganda, Venezuela, Zambia, Zimbabwe.

G-90 (64 WTO members of the African Union/Group, ACP and least-developed countries): Angola, Antigua and Barbuda, Bangladesh, Barbados, Belize, Benin, Botswana, Burkina Faso, Burundi, Cambodia, Cameroon, Central African Republic, Chad, Congo, Côte d'Ivoire, Cuba, Democratic Republic of the Congo, Djibouti, Dominica, Dominican Republic, Egypt, Fiji, Gabon, The Gambia, Ghana, Grenada, Guinea (Conakry), Guinea Bissau, Guyana, Haiti, Jamaica, Kenya, Lesotho, Madagascar, Malawi, Maldives, Mali, Mauritania, Mauritius, Morocco, Mozambique, Myanmar, Namibia, Nepal, Niger, Nigeria, Papua New Guinea, Rwanda, Saint Kitts and Nevis, Saint Lucia, Saint Vincent and the Grenadines, Senegal, Sierra Leone, Solomon Islands, South Africa, Suriname, Swaziland, Tanzania, Togo, Trinidad and Tobago, Tunisia, Uganda, Zambia, Zimbabwe.

Least-developed countries (LDCs) (32): Angola, Bangladesh, Benin, Burkina Faso, Burundi, Cambodia, Central African Republic, Chad, Congo, Democratic Republic of the, Djibouti, Gambia, Guinea, Guinea Bissau, Haiti, Lesotho, Madagascar, Malawi, Maldives, Mali, Mauritania, Mozambique, Myanmar, Nepal, Niger, Rwanda, Senegal, Sierra Leone, Solomon Islands, Tanzania, Togo, Uganda, Zambia.

Recently Acceded Members (15): Albania, Armenia, China, Croatia, Ecuador, FYR of Macedonia, Jordan, Kyrgyz Republic, Moldova, Mongolia, Oman, Panama, Saudi Arabia, Chinese Taipei, Viet Nam.

"Small and vulnerable economies" (14): Barbados, Bolivia, Cuba, Dominican Republic, El Salvador, Fiji, Guatemala, Honduras, Mauritius, Mongolia, Nicaragua, Papua New Guinea, Paraguay, and Trinidad and Tobago.

Tropical and Alternative Products Group (11): Bolivia, Colombia, Costa Rica, Ecuador, El Salvador, Honduras, Guatemala, Nicaragua, Panama, Peru, Venezuela.

3. Separate Customs Territories as Member of the WTO

219. As explained, besides States, any 'separate customs territory possessing the full autonomy in the conduct of its external commercial relations'[238] can join the WTO. Remarkably, full nation-state sovereignty is not a condition of Membership.[239] Indeed, in 1995, the European Community joined the WTO, next to the individual EU Member States. Hong Kong and Macao were already Contracting Parties to the GATT 1947 and therefore were 'original Members' of the WTO from its establishment in 1995. In 2002, Chinese Taipei became WTO Member.

a. European Community

220. Special attention should be paid to the place of the European Community in the WTO.[240] During GATT 1947, the EC was not a treaty party. Nevertheless, the EC did replace in many issues EU Member States (exclusive competences) or acted together with them (shared competences), on the basis of the important competences in the field of the common commercial policy that have been accorded to it in the EC Treaty.[241] When the WTO was established, the EC became a Member of the organization, together with the individual EU Member States.[242]

---

[238] Art. XII.1 WTO Agreement.
[239] See J. JACKSON, *The World Trade Organization. Constitution and Jurisprudence*, supra note 29, p. 48.
[240] See *inter alia* F. ABBOTT, 'GATT and the European Community, a Formula for Peaceful Coexistence', *Michigan Journal of International Law* (1990), pp. 1–58; F. CASTILLO DE LA TORRE, 'The Status of GATT in EEC Law', *Journal of World Trade* (1992), pp. 35–43; G. DE BÚRCA and J. SCOTT, *The EU and the WTO: Legal and Constitutional Issues*, (Oxford, Hart 2001), x + 332 p.; P. DIDIER, *WTO Trade Instruments in EU Law: Commercial Policy Instruments: Dumping, Subsidies, Safeguards, Public Procurement*, (London, Cameron May 1999), 844 p.; S. DILLON, *International Trade and Economic Law and the European Union*, (Oxford, Hart 2002), xviii + 391 p; A. MURPHY, *The European Community and the International Trading System, Vol I Completing the Uruguay Round of the GATT, Vol. II The European Community and the Uruguay Round*, (Brussels, Centre for European Policy Studies 1990), vol. I, 166 p., vol. II, 140 p.; E.-U. PETERSMANN, 'The Uruguay Round of Multilateral Trade Negotiations and the Single European Market 1992', in *EG und Drittstaatsbeziehungen nach 1992*, (1991), pp. 195–212; L.S. ROSSI, *Commercio internazionale sostenibile?: WTO e Unione europea*, (Bologna, Il Mulino 2003), 343 p; R. SENTI, 'The Role of the EU as an Economic Actor within the WTO', *European Foreign Affairs Review* (2002), 7, p. 111–117 and J.H.H. WEILER (ed.), *The EU, the WTO, and the NAFTA: Towards a Common Law of International Trade?*, (Oxford, Oxford University Press 2001), xx + 238 p.
[241] ECJ, Joint Cases 21–24/72, *International Fruit Company*, [1972] ECR 1219, paras. 11–15. See also E.-U. PETERSMANN, 'Die EWG als GATT-Mitglied – Rechtsconflikte zwischen GATT-Recht und Europäischem Gemeinschaftsrecht', in M. HILF and E.U. PETERSMANN (eds.), *GATT und EG*, (Baden-Baden, Nomos Verlag 1986), pp. 119–174.
[242] K. LENAERTS and P. VAN NUFFEL, *Constitutional Law of the European Union*, (London, Sweet & Maxwell 2005), p. 841.

In the case of voting, the EC has as many votes as all EU Member States together.[243] Until the Treaty of Nice[244], the Community could only act on the basis of Article 133 EC Treaty when it concerned agreements on trade in goods. Other trade agreements were part of the shared competences of the Community and EU Member States.[245] Therefore, the Community could not act on the basis of Article 133 EC Treaty when it concerned agreements on trade in services or trade-related aspects of intellectual property rights. The negotiation and conclusion of such agreements was only possible on the basis of Article 300 EC Treaty, implying a necessary unanimity in the Council. Since the Treaty of Nice, Article 133.5, first paragraph of the EC Treaty provides that sections 1 to 4 of Article 133 are also applicable to the negotiations on and conclusion of agreements in the field of trade in services (GATS) and the trade-related aspects of intellectual property rights (TRIPS). Thus, in principle, in these fields the Commission can negotiate and the Council decides by qualified majority. There are, however, several exceptions to this principle, where the Council has to decide by unanimity.[246] First of all, unanimity is required when the agreement concerns subject matters for which internal EC provisions require unanimity.[247] Further unanimity is required as well when the Community has not yet exercised its competences on the basis of the EC Treaty. Finally, unanimity is required for agreements that relate, apart from trade in services or intellectual property, to cultural and audiovisual services, educational services or social and public health services.[248] These agreements are concluded by the Community and EU Member States together.

221. As one of the most important international trade partners[249], the EC (with the EU Member States) is a leading Member of the WTO. Taking into account its

---

[243] K. Van de Casteele, 'Internationale handel', in X., *Handels en Economisch recht. Commentaar met overzicht van rechtspraak en rechtsleer*, (Antwerp, Kluwer 1995), p. 273.
[244] Treaty of Nice amending the Treaty on the European Union, the Treaties establishing the European Communities and certain related acts and Final Act, done at Nice on 26 February 2001, O.J., 2001, C80/1.
[245] P. Van Nuffel, 'Le traité de Nice – Un commentaire', *Revue du Droit de l'Union Européenne* (2001), p. 368.
[246] See for a more detailed analysis J. Wouters, 'De Europese Unie als internationale actor na het Verdrag van Nice', *Nederlands Tijdschrift voor Europees Recht* (2002), pp. 62–70. For a comparison between the present state of play and the EU Constitution, see J. Wouters and D. Coppens, 'A Global Actor in the Making? Reforming the EU's External Relations Machinery with or without the Constitution', *Institute for International Law Working Paper No 79* (June 2005), available on http://law.kuleuven.be/iir/nl/wp/WP/WP79e.pdf.
[247] This is a logical application of the principle '*in foro interno, in foro externo*'. This principle of parallelism in voting procedures within the Council for internal and external competences is also included in art. 300(2), first paragraph EC Treaty.
[248] Art. 133(5), third paragraph EC Treaty. These are the so-called 'horizontal agreements'.
[249] The EC accounts for 18.8% of the world trade in goods (after the US with 20.8%) and 23.8% of world trade in services (preceding the US with 21.2%) See European Commission, 'Making Globalization Work for Everyone. The European Union and World Trade' in *Europe on the*

Chapter IV

broad competences, it is more than often confronted with its WTO obligations. In the field of health and consumer protection, the Community has to take into account the law of the WTO, especially the TBT and SPS Agreements.[250] Therefore, it concluded several agreements on mutual recognition of conformity assessments.[251] Because of the SPS Agreement, the EC also acceded to the Codex Alimentarius Commission.[252] This agreement encourages Members to base their policies on the food safety standards developed by this Commission.[253] The weight of the EC within the WTO is also relevant for the further negotiations within the WTO. It proved impossible in Cancún, where it was hoped to proceed on the 'Doha Development Agenda', to strike an agreement on the so-called 'Singapore issues'[254] – which the EC values as highly important – and on agriculture. After the failure of the Ministerial Conference, the (then) WTO Director-General called upon the EC several times to reactivate the Doha Round with concrete proposals. The EC has expressed its preference for multilateralism[255] but wished to reflect on its role in the negotiations and in the current negotiation system.[256] Furthermore, the EC plays an important role in the WTO Dispute Settlement Mechanism.[257]

Move, (Brussels, Directorate-General Press and Communication Publications 2002), p. 10, available on http://europa.eu.int/comm/publications/booklets/move/37/en.pdf.

[250] The notorious Hormones dispute (European Communities – Measures Concerning Meat and Meat Products (Hormones), WT/DS26 and 48) shows sufficiently how strong the impact of WTO rules can be in this field.

[251] It concerns agreements that accept examinations in order to define to what extent a product, process or service complies with specific requirements as equivalent. These agreements, concluded because of art. 6 TBT, remove an important barrier to trade. See especially Agreement on Mutual Recognition between the European Community and the United States of America, done at London on 18 May 1998, O.J., 1999, L31/4; Agreement on Mutual Recognition between the European Community and Canada, done at London on 14 May 1998, O.J., 1998, L280/ 3; Agreement on Mutual Recognition in relation to Conformity Assessment between the European Community and New Zealand, done at Wellington on June 25, 1998, O.J., 1998, L229/62; Agreement on Mutual Recognition in relation to Conformity Assessment, Certificates and Markings between the European Community and Australia, done at Canberra on June 24, 1998, O.J., 1998, L229/3.

[252] Council Decision 2003/822/EG of 17 November 2003 on the accession of the European Community to Codex Alimentarius Commission, O.J., 2003, L309/14.

[253] Art. 3.4 and Annex A.3.a) SPS Agreement.

[254] Namely foreign investment, competition policy, transparency in government procurement and trade facilitation. The EC eventually was willing to drop competition policy and investment.

[255] See the speech by (former) Commissioner P. LAMY to the European Parliament on the occasion of the failure of the summit in Cancún, 24 September 2003 and his speech to the International Chamber of Commerce Conference in Dhaka, 18 January 2004, both available on http://europa.eu.int/comm/commissioners/lamy/speeches_articles.

[256] See the evaluation of the Ministerial summit in Cancún by the Commission in 'The Doha Development Agenda After Cancún', available on http://rorg.no/rorg/aktuelt/samle/0302/cancun/brudd/carl.pdf.

[257] The EC has, in the framework of the WTO dispute settlement mechanism, already acted 76 times as complainant and 58 times as defendant. It is at present involved in thirty disputes before the WTO: fifteen as complainant, in fifteen as defendant. The majority of the EC's active

Natural and legal persons that act on behalf of an industry in the Community[258], individual enterprises in the EC[259] and also the EU Member States themselves[260] can alert the Commission to trade barriers by non-EC states that cause them harm. The Commission can decide to initiate an investigation, take provisional measures and eventually file a complaint with the DSU.

222. It is finally also important to note that the European Court of Justice has not accepted the direct effect of the WTO agreements in general and of the dispute settlement reports produced within the WTO.[261] There are two exceptions: (i) if the Community wanted to execute a specific obligation within the framework of the WTO[262]; and (ii) if the EC rules refer explicitly to specific GATT/WTO rules.[263] The absence of direct effect does not waive the national courts' obligation to apply the national rules as much as possible in the light of the wording and objectives of these provisions, if it concerns a subject matter for which the EC has already exercised its regulatory powers.[264] When it concerns a subject matter

---

disputes are against the US. COMMISSION OF THE EUROPEAN COMMUNITIES, 'WTO Dispute Settlement. State of play of 20 July 2007', available on http://trade-info.cec.eu.int/doclib/docs/2007/may/tradoc_134652.pdf.

[258] Art. 3 Council Regulation (EC) No 3286/94 of 22 December 1994 laying down Community procedures in the field of the common commercial policy in order to ensure the exercise of the Community's rights under international trade rules, in particular those established under the auspices of the World Trade Organization, O.J., 1994, L349/71.

[259] *Ibid.* art. 4.

[260] *Ibid.* art. 6.

[261] See the decisions: ECJ Case C-149/96, *Portugal v. Council*, [1999] ECR I-8395, paras. 34–52; ECJ Joint Cases C-300/98 and C-392/98, *Perfumes Christian Dior*, [2000] ECR I-11307, paras. 41–44; ECJ Case C-89/99, *Schieving-Nijstadt e.a.*, [2001] ECR I-5851, paras. 54–73; ECJ Case C-377/98, *Netherlands v. European Parliament*, [2001] ECR I-7079, para. 52. See, concerning the review of legality, ECJ Case C-93/02P, *Biret International v. Council*, [2003] ECR I-10479, para. 52. See *inter alia* A. DESMEDT, 'Rechtstreekse werking van WTO-akkoorden via de achterdeur? De bevoegdheid van de nationale rechter tot de interpretatie van het TRIPS-akkoord na de Dior-zaak', *Nederlands Tijdschrift Europees Recht* (2001), pp. 79–83; M. MENDEZ, 'The Impact of WTO Rulings in the Community Legal Order', *European Law Review* (2004), pp. 517–529; P. VAN NUFFEL and V. VANOVERMEIRE, 'Over de bevoegdheid van het Hof van Justitie tot uitlegging van TRIPS en de directe werking van art. 50 lid 6 TRIPS', *Tijdschrift Belgisch Handelsrecht* (2001), pp. 445–454; J. WIERS, 'One Day, You're Gonna Pay: The European Court of Justice in *Biret*', *Legal Issues of Economic Integration* (2004), pp. 143–151; J. WOUTERS and D. VAN EECKHOUTTE, 'Enforcement of Customary International Law through European Community Law' in J.M. Prinssen and A. Schrauwen (eds.), *Direct effect. Rethinking a Classic of EC Legal Doctrine*, (Groningen, European Law Publishing 2002), pp. 183–234 and G. ZONNEKEYN, 'De directe werking van de TRIPs Overeenkomst – Een stand van zaken', *I.R.D.I.* (2002), pp. 132–147.

[262] See ECJ Case 69/89, *Nakajima*, [1991] ECR I-2069, para. 31. See recently ECJ, judgment of 27 September 2007 in Case C-351/04 Ikea Wholesale, not yet published, para. 35.

[263] See ECJ Case 70/87, *Fediol*, [1989] ECR 1781, paras. 19–22.

[264] See ECJ Case C-61/94, *Commission v. Germany*, [1996] ECR I-3989, para. 10.

Chapter IV

where the EC has not yet exercised its regulatory powers, it is up to EU Member States whether or not to accord direct effect to the WTO obligations.[265]

b. Hong Kong, China

223. After the United Kingdom handover of Hong Kong to China in 1997, Hong Kong became a Special Administrative Region of China with a high degree of autonomy in respect of its economic and financial policies. This has been established according to a 'one country – two systems' regime, implying a 50-year commitment by China to allow Hong Kong to maintain the existing free and open market system.[266] Yet, Hong Kong is an inalienable part of the People's Republic of China.

224. Hong Kong was already a GATT 1947 Contracting Party. Indeed, according to Article XXVI.5 (c) GATT, a separate customs territory could become a Party to the GATT if another GATT Contracting Party sponsored this accession. This 'sponsorship' was provided to Hong Kong by the United Kingdom in 1986, when Hong Kong became a separate Contracting Party to GATT 1947. Hence, when the WTO was established in 1995, Hong Kong was an 'original Member' of the WTO. It remained a Member in its own right after it became a Special Administrative Region of China. Indeed, according to the 'Basic Law' – Hong Kong's post-handover mini-constitution – Hong Kong has a high degree of autonomy and is a separate customs territory that can manage its own public finance, monetary, trade, industry and commerce affairs. It is explicitly recognized that Hong Kong can participate in relevant international organizations.[267] As explained, the WTO Agreement provides for such Membership since any 'separate customs territory possessing full autonomy in the conduct of its external commercial relations and of the other matters provided for in [the WTO Agreement] and the Multilateral

---

[265] See ECJ Case C-392/98, *Parfums Christian Dior*, [2000] ECR I-11307, para. 48; ECJ, judgment of 11 September 2007 in Case C-431/05 *Merck Genéricos*, not yet published.

[266] See art. 5 of the Basic Law of the Hong Kong Special Administrative Region of the Peoples' Republic of China, Adopted on 4 April 1990 by the Seventh National People's Congress of the People's Republic of China at its Third Session (hereinafter 'Basic Law'). See R.H. WEBER, 'Repositioning Hong Kong as a Regional and International Financial Centre in View of China's Imminent Accession to the WTO', *Hong Kong Law Journal* (2001), p. 123. The Trade Policy Review Report of 2002 notes in this respect: "Hong Kong's reversion to the People's Republic of China in 1997 has not altered the Territory's trade and investment regime. However, [Hong Kong] has had to face considerable structural adjustment associated with its growing integration into the rest of China." See Trade Policy Review of Hong Kong, China – Report by the Secretariat, WT/TPR/S/109, 18 November 2002, p. vii.

[267] Art. 116 of the Basic Law.

Trade Agreements' can join the WTO.[268] This membership will most likely remain until at least 2047.[269]

225. On 29 June 2003, the People's Republic of China and Hong Kong signed the 'Mainland and Hong Kong Closer Economic Partnership Arrangement' (CEPA).[270] With the perspective of China becoming a WTO Member in 2001, several enterprises in Hong Kong feared that they would lose their competitive advantage over foreign companies once China's market was fully opened up. Therefore, they pressed the governments of Mainland China and Hong Kong to negotiate on special preferential treatment from the mainland.[271] The CEPA is a Free Trade Area and covers (i) trade in goods, (ii) trade in services and (iii) trade and investment facilitation. Remarkably, the CEPA Parties have both recognized that Mainland China has a market economy. They also agreed that the specific safeguards WTO Members are entitled to apply against China, pursuant to its Working Party Report and Accession Protocol (see *supra* para. 121), will not be applicable to trade between the CEPA Parties.[272] It is stated that it is unlikely that Hong Kong would apply such measures against goods from Mainland China even without such explicit provision in the CEPA and, therefore, that this provision is mainly symbolic.[273] Nevertheless, it is also recognized that Mainland China may rely on this provision to circumvent textiles product-specific safeguards that would be applied by other WTO Members.[274]

c. Macao, China

226. After several centuries as a Portuguese colony Macao became a Special Administrative Region under Chinese Sovereignty in December 1999. As is the case for Hong Kong, the principle of 'one country, two systems' applies also to Macao. The People's Republic of China agreed in the 'Basic Law' of Macao, not to apply the socialist system and policies in Macao and not to affect the present way

---

[268] Art. XII.1 WTO Agreement.
[269] R.H. WEBER, *supra* note 266, p. 123.
[270] Mainland and Hong Kong Closer Economic Partnership Arrangement, signed in Hong Kong on 28 July 2003. English (non-authentic) version available on http://www.tid.gov.hk/english/cepa/files/main_e.pdf (hereinafter 'CEPA Arrangement').
[271] H.S. GAO, 'Legal Issues under WTO Rules on the Closer Economic Partnership Arrangement (CEPA) Between Mainland China and Hong Kong', *Chinese Journal of International Law* (2003), p. 629.
[272] Art. 4 CEPA Arrangement.
[273] H.S. GAO, *supra* note 271, p. 631.
[274] It is also suggested that China may use the explicit recognition that it is a market economy as a counterargument in 'unfair-trade' disputes such as antidumping and antisubsidy cases. H.S. GAO, *ibid.*

of life for 50 years. It is a separate customs territory[275] and has been, under such status, an original Member of the WTO since its establishment in 1995. Macao became a GATT 1947 Contracting Party on 11 January 1991.

d.   Chinese Taipei (Taiwan)

227.   The relationship between the People's Republic of China and Taiwan is a politically complicated one. Both the governments of the People's Republic of China and of Taiwan claim that they are the true representative of the whole of China. This would supposedly be the consensus that would have been reached in 1993 and is called the principle of 'One China, Separate Interpretations'.[276] However, economic relations between both have also been tense. In principle, since Taiwan is considered as part of China, Chinese laws and regulations govern Taiwanese business actions. Yet, Taiwan has for many years imposed several barriers on economic and trade relations with China.[277]

228.   In early 1965 Taiwan requested and was granted observer status at sessions of the General Agreement on Tariffs and Trade (GATT 1947). In 1971, this status was removed, following a decision by the UN General Assembly that recognized the People's Republic as the only legitimate government of China.[278]

229.   Taiwan acceded to the WTO in 2002 as the 'Separate Customs Territory of Taiwan, Penghu, Kinmen and Matsu'. The WTO is the only international organization of which Taiwan is a full Member. To Taiwan, WTO Membership is seen as a confirmation that it is internationally on an equal footing with China. China, in contrast, stresses that Taiwan is a Member of the WTO as a separate customs territory (in the same way as Hong Kong and Macao) and that the WTO

---

[275]   Art. 112 of the Basic Law of the Macao Special Administrative Region of the People's Republic of China, adopted on 31 March 1993 by the Eighth National People's Congress at its First Session on 31 March 1993.
[276]   The present ruling party of Taiwan disputes the existence of such consensus and would prefer independence from Mainland China. See Q. KONG, 'Cross-Taiwan Strait Relations: What are the Legitimate Expectations from the WTO?', *Minnesota Journal of Global Trade* (2004), p. 95, note 15.
[277]   See Q. Kong, 'Can the WTO Dispute Settlement Mechanism Resolve Trade Disputes between China and Taiwan?', *Journal of International Economic Law* (2002), pp. 751–756. On 15 February 2002, for instance, Taiwan adopted mechanisms for special safeguard measures against goods and textiles from China. These are similar to the special product-specific safeguards that have been included in China's accession documents (*supra* note 183). It is doubtful whether Taiwan would be entitled to invoke the latter provisions, since Taiwan was not a Member of the WTO when China joined. *Ibid.* p. 756, note 38.
[278]   UNGA Res. 2758 (XXVI) of 25 October 1971.

Institutional Framework

is not an international organization based on statehood.[279] It is reluctant to engage in direct talks with Taiwan in the WTO framework. Nevertheless, China was hesitant to block Taiwan's accession to the WTO. Two reasons have been suggested for this. First, the People's Republic of China needed to compromise with the existing WTO Members if it wanted to join the WTO. Second, China was satisfied with the fact that Taiwan would be identified as a 'Separate Customs Union'.[280] Even so, the WTO Agreements do not treat relations between States and Separate Customs Territories that are Members of the WTO differently from relations between the other Members.[281] Taiwan also refuses to accept any difference.[282]

230. Thus, even though the relationship between China and Taiwan is far from settled, both sides have to accept that they are equal WTO Members, between which the WTO rights and obligations apply. In fact, China could have avoided this by invoking the non-application clause of Article XIII WTO Agreement at the time of Taiwan's accession. As a consequence, it would not have been possible to invoke the WTO Agreement and its Annexes 1 and 2 between China and

---

[279] J. SHIJIAN MO, 'Settlement of Trade Disputes between Mainland China and the Separate Customs Territory of Taiwan within the WTO', *Chinese Journal of International Law* (2003), p. 145.

[280] See Q. KONG, 'Cross-Taiwan Strait Relations: What are the Legitimate Expectations from the WTO?', *supra* note 276, p. 96, note 19. During its accession negotiations (and before the accession of Taiwan), China requested that Taiwan would be categorized as a 'Separate Customs Territory *of China*'. Nonetheless, this was rejected by the US Deputy Trade Representative. *Ibid.* p. 98.

[281] Nevertheless, it may be argued that the GATT 1947 Contracting Parties took an ambiguous position towards the relationship between China and Taiwan. In 1992, the Contracting Parties and China (who filed its application to join the GATT in 1986) reached an understanding implying that the GATT Council should examine the Working Party Report and adopt the Accession Protocol of China before examining the Report and adopting the Protocol for Taiwan (who applied to join the GATT in 1990). This gives the impression that Taiwan was indeed seen as linked to China and therefore acceding as a customs territory under old art. XXXIII GATT 1947. Nonetheless, the Chairman of the GATT Council also noted that the Working Party Reports should be examined independently, which may point to the other direction: Taiwan as separate from China. See Q. KONG, 'Can the WTO Dispute Settlement Mechanism Resolve Trade Disputes Between China and Taiwan?', *supra* note 277, p. 747, note 2.

[282] When China requested consultations on exports of cold-rolled steel in November 2002 and referred to Taiwan's Economic and Trade *Office* in Geneva, Taiwan refused to hold talks, unless China requested consultations by referring to Taiwan's *Mission* in Geneva. *Office* is indeed the title used by Hong Kong and Macau, two other 'Separate Customs Territories', which are, however, undisputedly part of China. Also when the former Director-General of the WTO, Supachai Panitchpakdi, requested Taiwan in February 2003 to change the title of Taiwan's Mission to Office, Taiwan refused to do so. The Director-General had based its request on a 1992 agreement by the General Council of GATT 1947, in which it was decided that the representation of Chinese Taipei in GATT would "be along the same lines as that of Hong Kong and Macau" and "titles carried by its representatives would not have any implication on the issue of sovereignty." See Q. KONG, 'Cross-Taiwan Strait Relations: What are the Legitimate Expectations from the WTO?', *supra* note 276, p. 92, note 3 and p. 97, note 23.

Taiwan. Still, China decided not to invoke Article XIII WTO Agreement.[283] Therefore, in theory, all provisions of the WTO agreements apply between them. In practice, however, it is said that Taiwan puts its security concerns above its economic and trade policy towards China. In fact, such would only be possible as far as this fits into the security exceptions of Article XXI GATT and XIV*bis* GATS. China, from its side, is hesitant to make use of the Dispute Settlement System of the WTO to challenge certain Taiwanese measures, since this could be seen as recognizing Taiwan's position on the international plane.

4. *Developing Countries in the WTO*

231. There are no WTO definitions of 'developed' or 'developing' country. Members can decide for themselves to be considered as 'developing' country. This implies that they can freely choose to benefit from the special provisions for developing countries in the WTO agreements.[284] Nevertheless, the other WTO Members can always challenge the decision of a Member to make use of these special provisions. Resolving such issues is often a matter of negotiation between the country that claims developing-country status and the other countries that will be affected by this decision.[285] As explained above some WTO provisions recognize the interest of developing countries in a general matter. Others ease the rules or number of obligations to be met. Still others provide longer time frames for the implementation of certain obligations. Finally, developing countries can benefit from technical assistance. All these provisions are especially important from a substantive-law perspective (see *supra* paras. 84-92). Yet, also institutionally, the specific situation of developing countries is taken into account. In principle, the system of decision-making by consensus would guarantee equal power for large industrial Members, like the US, and for small developing countries. However, it is clear that, in practice, this power balance is not equal. As explained, alliances such as the Quad often dominate the decision-making in the WTO. Nevertheless, new emerging coalitions such as the G20+ may rebalance power relations in the WTO. Also the larger developing countries, including China,

---

[283] It is unclear why China did not do this. KONG suggests that this may have been part of the compromise with the other WTO Members or perhaps because China hoped to induce and engage Taiwanese businessmen and Taipei with business opportunities in China in exchange for compromise on certain issues on the Taiwanese side. Perhaps China merely showed its good will and true adherence to the objectives of the WTO. Q. KONG, *ibid.*, p. 99.

[284] Note that, for the Generalized System of Preferences (see *supra* para. 89), it is the preference-giving Member that decides which countries qualify for the preferential tariff treatment.

[285] See A. NARLIKAR, *The World Trade Organization. A Very Short Introduction*, (Oxford, Oxford University Press 2005), p. 9. The 'self-election' of a developing country has never been subject to challenge before a WTO Panel, but this does not seem to be excluded.

Brazil, India and South Africa, are said to be "formidable champions of the cause of the developing-country Members within the WTO".[286]

232. Contrary to what is the case for the category of 'developing countries', there is an accepted definition of 'least-developed' countries. The WTO recognizes as least-developed countries those countries which have been designated as such by the United Nations. In order to qualify as a 'least-developed country', a country has to fit the following three criteria: 1) a low-income criterion, based on a three-year average estimate of the gross domestic product per capita (under $750 for inclusion); 2) a human resource weakness criterion, involving a composite Augmented Physical Quality of Life Index (APQLI) based on indicators of: (a) nutrition; (b) health; (c) education; and (d) adult literacy; and 3) an economic vulnerability criterion, involving a composite Economic Vulnerability Index (EVI) based on indicators of: (a) the instability of agricultural production; (b) the instability of exports of goods and services; (c) the economic importance of non-traditional activities (share of manufacturing and modern services in GDP); (d) merchandise export concentration; and (e) the handicap of economic smallness (as measured through the population in logarithm); and the percentage of population displaced by natural disasters.[287] The UN has included 50 countries on the list of least-developed countries, 32 of which are also WTO Members.[288]

233. In the Committee on Trade and Development, WTO Members consider broad issues relating to the trade of developing countries. The Committee on Trade and Development serves as a focal point for consideration and coordination of technical assistance work on development in the WTO and its relationship to development-related activities in other multilateral agencies. At the Doha Ministerial Conference, in November 2001, Trade Ministers mandated the Committee on Trade and Development to identify which special and differential treatment provisions are mandatory, and to consider the implications of making mandatory those which are currently non-binding. The Committee on Trade and Development also holds dedicated sessions on the special challenges of small

---

[286] P. VAN DEN BOSSCHE, *supra* note 30, p. 106.
[287] See ECOSOC, Advance, unedited copy of the Report of the Committee for Development Policy on its Sixth Session (29 March–2 April 2004), E/2004/33, available on http://www.un.org/special-rep/ohrlls/ldc/E-2004-33_2004advcdpreport.pdf.
[288] These countries are: Angola, Bangladesh, Benin, Burkina Faso, Burundi, Cambodia, Central African Republic, Chad, Democratic Republic of the Congo, Djibouti, Gambia, Guinea, Guinea Bissau, Haiti, Lesotho, Madagascar, Malawi, Maldives, Mali, Mauritania, Mozambique, Myanmar, Nepal, Niger, Rwanda, Senegal, Sierra Leone, Solomon Islands, Tanzania, Togo, Uganda, Zambia.

economies in the WTO. On 13 September 2005, the Committee presented a Report on the Development Aspects of the Doha Round of Negotiations.[289]

234. The Sub-Committee on Least-Developed Countries is a subsidiary body to the Committee on Trade and Development. The mandate of the Sub-Committee on Least-Developed Countries is to look specifically at issues of particular importance to least-developed countries such as: ways of integrating least-developed countries into the multilateral trading system and technical cooperation for least-developed countries, including the Integrated Framework for Trade-Related Technical Assistance to Least-Developed Countries.

E. BUDGET

235. Members contribute to the budget of the WTO. Their contributions should reflect their share in international trade in goods, services and intellectual property.[290] The Committee on Budget, Finance and Administration[291] has developed Financial Regulations to guide the distribution of the expenses among Members and the measures in respect of Members in arrears.[292] Each calendar year, the Director-General of the WTO prepares a budget estimate for the WTO. This estimate is submitted to the Committee on Budget, Finance and Administration for review.[293] The Committee prepares a report, which it submits together with the budget estimate to the General Council for approval.[294] The Committee also proposes financial regulations on (a) the scale of Members' contributions to the WTO's expenses; and (b) measures to be taken in respect of Members in arrears.[295] Since a Member's contribution will depend on its average share in international trade in the past three years, an estimate of that Member's (or separate Customs Territory's) volume of international trade (imports plus exports) in relation to the total volume of international trade of all Members has

---

[289] Committee on Trade and Development, Developmental Aspects of the Doha Round of Negotiations, WT/COMTD/W/143, 13 September 2005.
[290] P. VAN DEN BOSSCHE, *supra* note 30, p. 411.
[291] This is one of the three Committees that the Ministerial Conference had to establish, pursuant to art. IV.7 WTO Agreement.
[292] Art. VII.2 WTO Agreement; Financial Regulations of the World Trade Organization, WT/L/156, 5 August 1996, approved by the General Council (by two-thirds majority comprising more than half of Members of the WTO (art. VII.3 WTO Agreement)) on 15 November 1995, WT/GC/M/8, section 7 (c). The Director-General has developed rules to carry out the Regulations (Financial Regulation 3): See Financial Rules of the World Trade Organization, WT/L/157, 5 August 1996.
[293] Art. VII.1 WTO Agreement.
[294] *Ibid.* and Financial Regulations 10–11. This decision requires a two-thirds majority, comprising more than half of Members of the WTO. Art. VII.3 WTO Agreement.
[295] E. MCGOVERN, *supra* note 197, p. 1.25–2.

to be made.[296] The source of these data is the balance of payment statistics of the IMF.[297] If these data are not available, the WTO will use data of the best alternative resource.[298] There is a minimum contribution of 0.03 per cent of the WTO budget.[299] In addition to the contributions of Members, there is also some miscellaneous income for the WTO.[300] It concerns *inter alia* income generated from publications and receipts from the rental of meeting rooms and offices.[301] The WTO also manages a number of trust funds, which have been contributed by Members. These are used in support of special activities for technical cooperation and training intended to enable least-developed and developing countries to make better use of the WTO and draw greater benefit from the multilateral trading system. The Financial Regulations require that an internal control[302] and an external audit[303] is performed on the WTO budget.

236. In 2006, the WTO budget amounted to 175 000 150 Swiss Francs (CHF). The WTO Secretariat received CHF 170,274,150 of this total and the Appellate Body and its Secretariat CHF 4,726,000. The largest cost was the salary of the staff: CHF 78,071,000 for the Secretariat and CHF 1,956,500 for the Appellate Body and its Secretariat.[304]

§ 2. DECISION-MAKING BODIES

237. The WTO provides the 'common institutional framework for the conduct of trade relations among its Members in matters related to the agreements and associated legal instruments included in the Annexes of [the WTO Agreement]'.[305] With the WTO, an intergovernmental, but by no means supranational organization was established. Rather, it is a so-called 'member-driven' organization. It is Members and not the WTO Secretariat or the Director-General who define the agenda of the WTO and make decisions.[306] The Director-General and the

---

[296] Financial Regulation 12.2.
[297] *Ibid.* 12.4. See on the website of the IMF: http://www.imf.org/external/np/sta/bop/bop.htm.
[298] *Ibid.* 12.6.
[299] *Ibid.* 12.7. The minimum contribution applies to Members with a share of less than 0.03 per cent of world trade.
[300] Financial Regulation 18.
[301] For an enumeration, see Financial Rule 3.3.
[302] This will be performed by the Director-General. Financial Regulation 41 (d).
[303] Financial Regulations 46–49.
[304] See WTO, *Annual Report 2006*, (Geneva, WTO Publications 2006), p. 107, available on http://www.wto.org/english/res_e/booksp_e/anrep_e/anrep06_e.pdf.
[305] Art. II.1 WTO Agreement.
[306] This led to the sneering remark of one diplomat during the Uruguay-Round negotiations, addressed to the Director-General: "*Sir, there is a difference between you and me; I am a Contracting Party and you are a Contracted Party.*"

Secretariat can only try to facilitate and steer the negotiations in the right direction.[307] This indicates again the extreme importance States attach to their sovereignty. It stands in sharp contrast to the dispute settlement mechanism of the WTO, which can impose direct obligations on Members.

238. Economic policymaking in the WTO happens through elaborate procedures at several levels (A). The highest level of decision-making in the WTO is the Ministerial Conference (B). Since this Ministerial Conference is not permanently in session, its tasks are performed by the General Council, supported by three subsidiary councils and numerous committees, subcommittees, bodies and working groups (C). A relatively small Secretariat in Geneva has no decisive powers, but nevertheless plays an invaluable role in the organization (D). Even though the decision-making procedures may appear to guarantee equality between all WTO Members, several concerns have been raised as to the legitimacy and democracy of the WTO (E).

A. DECISION-MAKING AND VOTING PROCEDURES

239. Decision-making within the WTO takes place along the same lines as in GATT 1947, in principle by *consensus*.[308] This means that an agreement is reached when no Member that is present opposes.[309] Absence of Members does not prevent

---

[307] This became for instance clear after the failed Ministerial Conference in Cancún. In several declarations, (then) Director-General S. PANITCHPAKDI called upon Members to relaunch the negotiations.

[308] This should give enough protection and influence to all Members. In practice, it has often turned out that Members were confronted with a *fait accompli* when the Quad (*supra* para. 217) had reached an agreement. It should be noted that the GATT did not mention anywhere explicitly the consensus practice. Indeed, GATT was not meant to be an institutional agreement and provided only loose wording on decision-making. The Contracting Parties therefore rather recurred to negotiation to achieve a decision by consensus. This consensus was built by negotiating in small groups, during so-called 'green room' meetings. These meetings were only accessible upon invitation and the list of invitees was confidential. These meetings were still common during the early WTO years, but have been heavily criticized, especially after the Seattle Ministerial Conference. The meetings are now announced and WTO Members that want to participate can do so. Yet, it has been noted by NARLIKAR that developing countries often feel insufficiently capable to identify their interests and decide upon the usefulness of participating in the small group meetings. Moreover, they feel unable to credibly threaten to block consensus if they have not participated in the meetings. Finally, she argues that this places considerable discretion in the hands of the chairmen of meetings. Participation in the decision-making process becomes a "daunting task for the smaller and newer members of the WTO". See A. NARLIKAR, *supra* note 285, p. 47.

[309] See footnote 1 to art. IX.1 WTO Agreement. This process is sometimes known as 'passive consensus', as opposed to the process or procedure of 'building a consensus', which is known as 'active consensus'. See M. FOOTER, *An Institutional and Normative Analysis of the World Trade Organization*, (The Hague, Nijhoff 2005), p. 138–139.

consensus.³¹⁰ The fact that there are no objections by Members who are present does not necessarily mean that a majority of countries agrees.³¹¹ This process of decision-making matters for all WTO bodies: Ministerial Conference, General Council, specialized Councils, Committees, Sub-committees and Working Parties. In building consensus formal and especially informal negotiation processes are crucial. It has been suggested that in these processes, the diplomatic culture of the GATT era is still prevalent, which may lead to nontransparent decision-making that fails to be inclusive.³¹² Consensus is achieved through bargaining on the basis of reciprocal tariff concessions, which are multilateralized through the MFN principle. Furthermore, separate issues are linked to each other to create a 'package' that would contain something advantageous for everyone.³¹³

240. For certain decisions, an *explicit' consensus* is required. This is the case for further steps to be taken with regard to the so-called 'Singapore Issues'. The Singapore Ministerial Declaration states that "further negotiations, if any, regarding multilateral disciplines in these areas, will take place only after an explicit consensus is taken among WTO Members regarding such negotiations".³¹⁴ Explicit consensus is also mentioned in the Ministerial Declaration of Doha, regarding the same issues.³¹⁵ The exact meaning of this type of consensus has been subject of discussion. Developing countries see it as a way to decide upon the prior approval to negotiate. Yet, it has been argued that developed countries seemed to consider the inclusion of explicit consensus in the Declaration of Doha as an indication that there was an agreement on the starting of the negotiations on the Singapore issues and that the explicit consensus would only be required for agreeing on the modalities of the negotiations.³¹⁶ An explicit consensus is finally

---

310 There is nevertheless a quorum of a simple majority of Members. (Rules of Procedure for Sessions of the Ministerial Conference, WT/L/161, 25 July 1996, rule 16.) JACKSON states that, even when present, Members that do not completely agree with a proposed decision will nevertheless remain silent out of deference to countries with more important economic interests in the decision. J. JACKSON, *The World Trade Organization. Constitution and Jurisprudence, supra* note 29, p. 46.
311 This is particularly problematic for developing countries, which often have insufficient resources to have their civil servants attend all WTO meetings.
312 See A. NARLIKAR, *supra* note 285, p. 51. See also *infra* §2.E on legitimacy, democracy and efficiency.
313 Still, such issue linkages may have as an effect that developed countries manage to convince developing countries by offering them further development assistance or other advantages. It may be questioned whether such deals are in the long term advantageous to developing countries.
314 Ministerial Declaration of Singapore, *supra* note 150, para 20.
315 Ministerial Declaration of Doha, *supra* note 40, paras. 20, 23, 26 and 27.
316 A. NARLIKAR, *supra* note 285, pp. 49–50.

also needed in order to add or remove an agreement to the Plurilateral Trade Agreements.[317]

241. Certain decisions are made according to a further type of consensus: *'reverse consensus'*. Such decisions will be deemed to be adopted, unless there is consensus not to adopt the decision. This means that all WTO Members need to agree *not to adopt* the decision. This type of consensus is used in the area of WTO dispute settlement.[318]

242. WTO Members have agreed that for decisions on waivers and on accessions, there can be consensus decision-making *in lieu of voting*.[319] Both decisions normally have to be put to a formal vote.[320] Nevertheless, an individual Member may always request to put the matter to a vote, but has to be present at the meeting in which the matter is considered.

243. It has recently been noted by civil society organizations and trade unions that the concept of consensus is being redefined, at least in the practice of the Council for Trade in Services.[321] Whereas normally, an item is included in a negotiation text after consensus has been built among Members, the Chair of the Council for Trade in Services has been including items, even if there was no consensus among Members. The item can thereafter only be removed if there is a consensus to do so. This may indeed speed up the negotiation process, but is hardly democratic and gives extensive power to the Chair. This would mean in practice that "the chairs can propose what they think should be the consensus, and countries must openly declare their opposition in order to block a consensus"[322] and thus lead to a generalization of 'reverse consensus' (which normally applies only in specific circumstances[323]) in all negotiations. In a reply, Director-General

---

[317] Art. X.9 WTO Agreement.
[318] See *infra* § 3.
[319] Decision-making procedures under Article IX and XII of the WTO Agreement, WT/L/93 (24 November 1995).
[320] See art. IX.3 WTO Agreement ('Waivers are granted by a majority of three fourths of Members, except when it concerns waivers from obligations that are subject to a transition period or a period for staged implementation. If in the latter case a Member has not performed its obligations at the end of the stated period, a waiver can only be granted by consensus') and art. XII.2 WTO Agreement ('Approval of accession requires a two-thirds majority of Members').
[321] "Open Letter to WTO Director-General Pascal Lamy. Redefining what 'Consensus' Means in the WTO?", 27 October 2005, available on http://www.wto.org/English/news_e/news05_e/dg_openletter_nov05_e.htm.
[322] R. STUMBERG, 'The WTO Moves on Domestic Regulation', *Forum on Democracy and Trade*, 18 November 2005, available on http://www.forumdemocracy.net/trade_negotiations/forum_news_domestic_regulation_intro_111805.html#RET20.
[323] See *supra* para. 241.

Pascal Lamy noted that nowhere was there a requirement that consensus would be required to delete any of the elements. The purpose of a Chairman's text in the preparatory process of negotiations would be "to provide delegations with a common basis for discussing their proposals and pursuing their interests in an equitable and transparent manner".[324] NGOs maintained that the Chair was in fact overreaching its mandate and only selectively included objections of Members in draft negotiation texts.[325] The Director-General noted that all Members have the opportunity to comment on the texts and that they remain in the driving seat.[326]

244. When it proves impossible to reach a consensus [327], decisions are made, according to the WTO Agreement, by *voting*. Each Member, no matter how large or small its economic weight, has one vote.[328] Voting takes place by ballot.[329] In principle, a simple majority suffices, it being understood as the majority of the votes cast. The quorum for voting to take place validly is a simple majority of Members that are entitled to vote.[330] There are however a few exceptions, namely (i) the interpretation of the WTO Agreement or of the Multilateral Trade Agreements: three-fourths majority of Members (Art. IX.2); (ii) the granting of a waiver, *i.e.* the waiving of an obligation imposed on a Member by the WTO Agreement or a multilateral trade agreement: three-fourths majority of Members (Art. IX.3); (iii) amendments of the provisions of the WTO Agreement or of the multilateral trade agreements: several modules, from two-thirds over three-fourths majority, up to consensus (Article X); (iv) accession: two-thirds majority

---

[324] "Lamy to NGOs: Your Criticism is Based on Misunderstandings of Service Talks", 17 November 2005, available on http://www.wto.org/English/news_e/news05_e/dg_letter_nov05_e.htm.
[325] "Open Letter Response to WTO Director-General Pascal Lamy's Reply to NGOs", 30 November 2005, available on http://www.wto.org/English/news_e/news05_e/reply_ngo_17nov05_e.pdf.
[326] "Reply to Open Letter by NGOs on Services Negotiations", 9 December 2005, available on http://www.wto.org/English/news_e/news05_e/reply_dg_9dec05_e.pdf.
[327] The WTO Agreement does not give any indication on the time period within which Members should seek consensus before resorting to voting. See P. VAN DEN BOSSCHE, *supra* note 30, p. 415.
[328] Even though WTO Members pay their contributions to the WTO budget based on their share in the volume of foreign trade, those contributions were never linked to an apportionment of votes in the GATT Council. There is thus no weighted voting, as is the case in the IMF or World Bank.
[329] It is however possible to vote by roll call or by raising of cards, on the request of a Member or the Chairman. In cases where a qualified majority is required, the Ministerial Conference may allow voting by airmail ballots or ballots transferred by telefax or telegraph. See Rules of Procedure for Sessions of the Ministerial Conference, *supra* note 310, rule 29 and Annex 1.
[330] Rules of Procedure for Meeting of Ministerial Conference and the General Council, *supra* note 310, rule 16.

(Article XII.2). In fact, voting has occurred once, when the accession of Ecuador was approved in 1995.[331]

There are several ways to conduct economic policymaking in the WTO.

1. Ministerial Decisions

245. The quickest and most common way to do so is by ministerial decisions. Ministerial decisions can relate to various issues. They range from decisions approving a cooperation agreement with another international organization to decisions on measures in favour of Least-Developed Countries. Ministerial decisions are made by normal majority, if consensus cannot be achieved.

Some specific decisions go further and in one way or another modify existing trade rules and require a specific procedure to be followed. These concern interpretations, amendments and waivers.

2. Interpretations

246. A rather subtle way of economic policymaking is the adoption of interpretations of the WTO Agreement and the Multilateral Agreements (annex 1 to the WTO Agreement). The Ministerial Conference and the General Council have the exclusive authority to adopt interpretations.[332] Interpretations must be supported by three-fourths of Members. It should be reiterated that voting only takes place if consensus cannot be reached. It should also be noted that a three-fourths majority of the overall membership is required. This is a significantly higher standard to meet than a majority of Members that are present. For interpretations of one of the Multilateral Trade Agreements, a preliminary recommendation by the Council overseeing the relevant Agreement is required.[333] The procedure for interpretation cannot be used to circumvent a more drastic modification of the trade rules, namely the amendment procedure.

3. Amendments

247. The amendment procedure is a complex one and is designed to avoid separate agreements on issues where some countries are willing to go further than others. In the GATT 1947 era, this led to the adoption of several 'codes'. The

---

[331] See L. BARTELS, 'The Separation of Powers in the WTO: How to Avoid Judicial Activism', *International Comparative Law* Quarterly (2004), pp. 864–865. Also under the WTO's predecessor, the GATT, voting was exceptional.
[332] Art. IX.2 WTO Agreement.
[333] *Ibid.*

right of initiative for amendment lies with each Member, the General Council, the Council for Trade in Goods, the Council for Trade in Services and the Council for Trade-Related Aspects of Intellectual Property Rights.[334] A proposal must be submitted to the Ministerial Conference. The Conference will then accept the proposal for amendment and submit it to Members. This decision is made by consensus. When this decision is not made within 90 days[335], it is still possible to submit the proposal if two thirds of the overall Membership still agrees to do so.

248. An amendment will eventually be submitted to the membership and must be approved (after having passed through the national ratification process)[336] by two thirds of all Members before it can take effect. An amendment takes effect at the point that two thirds of Members approve. If Members approve later, the amendment only takes effect on that moment.[337] In case of substantive amendments (*i.e.* amendments that 'alter the rights and obligations of Members') and amendments to certain GATS provisions in Parts I, II and III GATS, the Ministerial Conference may decide, by three-fourths majority, that Members that do not accept an amendment can only stay in the organization if the Conference consents to this. In fact, this puts serious pressure on Members to approve an amendment, unless they manage to get a 'permanent waiver'[338] for this amendment.

249. Nevertheless, in case of non-substantive amendments to the WTO Agreement or one of the multilateral agreements on trade in goods (Annex 1A) or TRIPS Annex 1C, or amendments to Parts IV, V and VI of GATS, an amendment will take effect for all Members (also the ones that have not expressed their consent to be bound) upon acceptance by two thirds of the overall Membership. This implies that all Members are bound on the international level, even if they did not consent to this amendment.

250. On the other hand, some amendments (still taken by two-thirds majority) do not need to be submitted to Members and can be accepted by the Ministerial Conference alone. This is the case for the Annex on Dispute Settlement

---

[334] Each for the Multilateral Trade Agreements they monitor. This means that Annex 2 (DSU) and 3 (TPRM) to the WTO Agreement can only be modified on the initiative of one of Members. Art. X.1 WTO Agreement.
[335] The Ministerial Conference can decide upon a longer period.
[336] This is done by depositing an instrument of acceptance with the WTO Director-General. Art. X.7 WTO Agreement.
[337] Art. X.3-4 WTO Agreement.
[338] *I.e.* the Ministerial Conference consents to the fact that a Member may remain in the Organization, even though it does not accept the amendment and thus faces different obligations than the other Members. In contrast to 'real' waivers (*infra* para. 253), this consent is permanent.

(amendment by consensus in the Ministerial Conference)[339], for the Annex on the Trade Policy Review Mechanism and for amendments of TRIPS in order to adjust to higher levels of intellectual property protection in other agreements (this also requires consensus in the Ministerial Conference).[340]

251. Some amendments require unanimity instead of a qualified majority. It concerns modifications of the decision-making procedure[341] and of the principle of MFN as laid down in Articles I and II GATT, Article II.1 GATS and Article 4 TRIPS, as well as of Article II GATT concerning tariff schedules.[342]

252. In every case, except for amendments on the Dispute Settlement Understanding, there is a requirement that Members transform amendments into domestic law in accordance with their national laws and regulations.[343]

4. Waivers

253. Waivers are temporary exceptions to the obligations stemming from the WTO Agreement and the Multilateral Trade Agreements (annex 1). They can be granted in exceptional circumstances and are only granted if three fourths of the overall membership approves this.[344] A distinction is to be made between on the one hand waivers from obligations in the WTO Agreement and the other hand from obligations in the Multilateral Trade Agreements. Requests for waivers from the WTO Agreement have to be submitted to the Ministerial Conference according to the procedure of submission and approval for amendments, as has been described above. If consensus is not reached within a maximum period of 90 days, a waiver requires a three-fourths majority of all Members to be approved.[345] Waivers from obligations in the Annex 1A (MATG), Annex 1B (GATS), Annex 1C (TRIPS) and their annexes, must be requested to respectively the Council for Trade in Goods, the Council for Trade in Services and the Council for Trade-Related Aspects of Intellectual Property Rights.[346] During a period of maximum 90 days, the relevant Council will draft a report and submit it to the Ministerial Conference, which can approve the waiver by a three-fourths majority of all Members. The decision by the Ministerial Conference will indicate the exceptional circumstances justifying the waiver. If the waiver is granted for more than one

---

[339] Art. X.8 WTO Agreement.
[340] *Ibid.* art. X.6 *juncto* art. 71.2 TRIPS.
[341] *Ibid.* art. IX.
[342] *Ibid.* art. X.2.
[343] *Ibid.* art. XVI.4.
[344] *Ibid.* art. IX.3.
[345] *Ibid.* art. IX.3 (a).
[346] *Ibid.* art. IX.3 (b).

year, the Ministerial Conference will review within a year and thereafter annually whether these exceptional circumstances still occur. Waivers from obligations subject to a transition period or a period of staged implementation where the requesting Member has not performed by the end of the stated period are granted by consensus.[347] Finally, it should be mentioned that a waiver is not general, but allows non-compliance by a particular Member.[348] It is clear that this procedure is not meant as an 'easy track' substitute for amendments.[349] Such a waiver has been granted among others for the Lomé Convention[350] and, more recently, the Cotonou Agreement[351] between the ACP countries, the EC and EU Member States.

5.   *Negotiating New Agreements*

254. The most far-reaching rule-making for global trade is nonetheless done by negotiating new agreements within the WTO. As has been explained, one of the main functions of the WTO is to provide a forum for further trade negotiations.[352] These negotiations should be aimed at further liberalizing trade in both areas of goods and services and at improving existing rules or adopting rules in new subject areas.[353]

B.   MINISTERIAL CONFERENCE

255. The highest authority in the WTO is the Ministerial Conference. It is composed of representatives of Members, in principle the foreign trade ministers.[354] Since the organization is member-driven, the Conference is composed of representatives of all Members and must meet at least once every two years.[355] In contrast, GATT 1947 ministerial meetings were irregular. The

---

[347]   See footnote to art. IX.3 WTO Agreement.
[348]   See the text of art. IX.3 WTO Agreement, stating that the decision waives 'an obligation imposed on *a* Member' [emphasis added].
[349]   J. JACKSON, *The World Trade Organization. Constitution and Jurisprudence, supra* note 29, p. 44.
[350]   See Fourth ACP-EEC Convention, signed in Lomé on 15 December 1989,O.J., 1991, L229/3.
[351]   Partnership Agreement between the members of the African, Caribbean and Pacific Group of States (ACP) of the one part, and the European Community and its Member States, of the other part, signed in Cotonou on 23 June 2000, O.J., 2000, L317.
[352]   Art. III.2 WTO Agreement.
[353]   INTERNATIONAL TRADE CENTER/COMMONWEALTH SECRETARIAT, *Business Guide to the World Trading System, supra* note 2, p. 40.
[354]   The Ministerial Conference is the successor to the Contracting Parties of the GATT 1947. P. VAN DEN BOSSCHE, *supra* note 30, p. 407.
[355]   Art. IV.1 WTO Agreement. The date of this Ministerial Conference will be fixed by the Ministerial Conference at the previous session. See Rules of Procedure for Sessions of the Ministerial Conference and the General Council, *supra* note 310, rule 1.

regular meetings are meant to strengthen the political guidance of the WTO and enhance the prominence and credibility of its rules in domestic political arenas.[356] It is possible that 'special sessions' will be held on the initiative of the Chairman of the Conference, at the request of a Member supported by a majority of the membership, or by decision of the General Council.[357]

256. The Ministerial Conference carries out the functions of the WTO. To this end, it takes all necessary actions. Each Member may request the Ministerial Conference to make decisions on all matters under any Multilateral Trade Agreement. Decision-making is governed by the rules laid down in the WTO Agreement and in the relevant multilateral agreement.[358] Specific tasks conferred upon the Ministerial Conference are providing authoritative interpretations,[359] waiving obligations in the Agreements[360], approving the accession of a new Member[361] and agreeing upon amendments of any of the Agreements.[362]

257. There have been six WTO Ministerial Conferences so far. The first Ministerial Conference took place in December 1996 in Singapore. This Conference resulted in a general Ministerial Declaration with a remarkable reference to core labour standards. [363] This was accompanied by decisions to establish working groups to examine three so-called 'Singapore-issues': the relationship between trade and investment; the interaction between trade and competition policy and transparency in government procurement. Further work was also intended on a fourth issue: simplification of trade procedures ('trade facilitation'). The second Conference was held in Geneva in December 1998[364] at the 50th anniversary of the World Trading System. This Conference did not produce many substantial results. Its main contribution was to raise the profile of the WTO, thanks to a number of speeches by several world leaders. The third Conference took place in Seattle from 30 November to 3 December 1999. The Conference finished in disarray because of the disputes between developed and developing countries, in a sphere of protests from various movements. The objective to launch the 'Millennium Round' of trade negotiations proved illusory. The next Conference

---

[356] B. HOEKMAN and M. KOSTECKI, *supra* note 9, p. 50.
[357] Rules of Procedure for Sessions of the Ministerial Conference and the General Council, *supra* note 310, rule 2.
[358] Art. IV.1 WTO Agreement.
[359] *Ibid.* art. IX.2.
[360] *Ibid.* art. IX.3.
[361] *Ibid.* art. XII.2.
[362] *Ibid.* art. X.1.
[363] Ministerial Declaration of Singapore, *supra* note 150.
[364] Ministerial Declaration of Geneva, done on 20 May 1998, WT/MIN(98)/DEC, available on http://www.wto.org/english/thewto_e/minist_e/min98_e/mindec_e.htm.

in Doha in November 2001[365] took place in the aftermath of the terrorist attacks of 9/11. The atmosphere was one of unity and the Conference managed to launch the 'Doha Development Agenda' (DDA), a new negotiation round which should lead to full integration of developing countries in the global trading system. The fifth Conference in Cancún in September 2003[366] broke down because of re-emerging disputes between developing and developed countries. The developing countries, united in the G20[367], refused to proceed in the negotiations unless an agreement was reached on agriculture. On the other hand, developed countries, especially the EU Member States held on to the 'Singapore issues', more precisely further negotiations on foreign investment, competition policy, transparency in government procurement and trade facilitation. A final move by the European Community to drop competition policy and foreign investment could not save the Conference. In July 2004, a General Council meeting in Geneva managed to put the negotiations back on track by adopting a decision further specifying points of negotiation.[368] The main issues of the decision are the agriculture negotiations, the framework for non-agricultural market access and the further negotiations on liberalization of services. Three of the 'Singapore issues', namely trade and investment, competition policy and transparency in government procurement, are deleted from the Doha Work Programme of trade negotiations. Trade facilitation is the only 'Singapore issue' that is still included.[369] This agreement was seen as a 'historic breakthrough'. Yet, the agreement included only few exact dates and levels of reduction of support. The sixth Ministerial Conference took place in Hong Kong in December 2005.[370] Even though this Conference was not seen as a failure, it cannot be called a success, either. Indeed, it appears that a great deal still needs to be done if the real 'development' elements of the Doha Round are to emerge and, indeed, if the Doha Round itself is to be successfully concluded.[371]

C. GENERAL COUNCIL

258. The General Council of the WTO is composed of representatives of all Members. In practice, these are ambassadors and heads of delegations in Geneva. The General Council is the real engine of the WTO. In addition to fulfilling the

---

[365] Ministerial Declaration of Doha, *supra* note 40.
[366] Cancún Ministerial Statement, adopted on 14 September 2003, WT/MIN(03)/20, available on http://www.wto.org/english/thewto_e/minist_e/min03_e/min03_20_e.doc.
[367] See *supra* para. 218.
[368] General Council Decision of 31 July 2004, WT/GC/W/535.
[369] *Ibid.* para. g.
[370] Ministerial Declaration of Hong Kong, *supra* note 19.
[371] See also *supra* para. 24.

tasks of the Ministerial Conference when it is not in session (1), the General Council also acts in two other capacities, namely as the Dispute Settlement Body (2) and as the Trade Policy Review Body (3).[372]

1. Acting on Behalf of the Ministerial Conference

259. In the intervals between the meetings of the Ministerial Conference, the General Council performs the day-to-day work of the WTO. The General Council meets about 12 times a year.[373] Decision-making takes place according to the same rules as for the Ministerial Conference.[374] Three specific councils work under supervision of the General Council: the Council for Trade in Goods, the Council for Trade in Services and the Council for Trade-Related Aspects of Intellectual Property Rights (TRIPS Council). These councils monitor the functioning of GATT, GATS, TRIPS, respectively and the related agreements. Like the Ministerial Conference, the General Council may provide authoritative interpretations of the Multilateral Trade Agreements based on the recommendation of the relevant Council.[375] The General Council also has the task of adopting the annual budget estimate of the WTO and the WTO financial regulations.[376] Such decision requires a special two-thirds majority comprising more than half of Members of the WTO.[377] A waiver of an obligation cannot be granted by the Ministerial Conference until after a report is submitted by the Council overseeing the agreement at issue.[378] The Councils can also propose amendments to the Ministerial Conference with regard to the respective agreements.[379]

260. Several subsidiary bodies (Committees and Working Groups) function under the Councils. *Committees* can be established in four different ways. First, it is possible that a Multilateral Trade Agreement establishes a Committee.[380] Second, each of the Trade Councils may establish a Committee to overview an area of trade that is the subject of its own agreement.[381] Third, also the Ministerial Conference can establish a Committee[382] and is even required to do so for certain

---

[372] Art. IV.3–4 WTO Agreement.
[373] In fact, there is no fixed rule. The Rules of Procedure for Sessions of the General Council provide that "[t]he General Council shall meet as appropriate". See Rules of Procedure for Sessions of the General Council, *supra* note 310, rule 1.
[374] See *supra* para. 244 and 256.
[375] Art. IX.2 WTO Agreement.
[376] See *supra* paras. 235–236.
[377] Art. VII.3 WTO Agreement.
[378] *Ibid.* art. IX.3 (a).
[379] *Ibid.* art. X.1.
[380] E.g. the Committee on Agriculture. See art. 18 Agreement on Agriculture.
[381] Art. IV.6 WTO Agreement. E.g. the Committee on Market Access. See Decision by the General Council on the Establishment of the Committee on Market Access, WT/L/47, 31 January 1995.
[382] Art. IV.7 WTO Agreement.

issues, as laid down in the WTO Agreement.[383] Finally, the Plurilateral Trade Agreements may provide for certain trade bodies.[384] These Committees consist of representatives of all Members and report to their supervising Trade Council[385] or to the General Council.[386] There is unequal information available on the diverse Committees. Sometimes a multilateral agreement clearly defines the functions and working of a Committee[387], but more often there is only a general description of the Committee.[388] This obviously does not promote the transparency of the WTO.[389]

261. The Ministerial Conference has established several committees to assist the Ministerial Conference and the General Council.[390] The WTO Agreement itself required the establishment of a number of Committees, and the Ministerial Conference is allowed to establish additional Committees "with such functions as it deems appropriate". The Conference has done so and currently 11 Committees figure under the Council for Trade in Goods, two under the Council for Trade in Services. There is also one plurilateral Committee coming under the Council for Trade in Goods (the Information Technology Agreement Committee). The Committees that function under the specific Council will be discussed below. In addition, six Committees act under the General Council, addressing matters that touch issues at the same time monitored by the Council for Trade in Goods, the TRIPS Council and the Council for Trade in Services. There are also two plurilateral Committees reporting to the General Council (the Committee on Trade in Civil Aircraft and the Committee on Government Procurement).

262. There are also a number of *Working Parties and Working Groups*. These bodies have an *ad hoc* nature, in the sense that they have a specific task to fulfil and once this is fulfilled, they cease to exist. A Working Party is set up each time a candidate Member prepares for accession to the WTO. This Working Party assesses a candidate's trade regime and prepares and presents a report to the General Council.[391] Working Groups and Working Parties are established at a

---

[383] See *infra* para. 261.
[384] Art. IV.8 WTO Agreement.
[385] This is the case for Committees that are established by one of the Trade Councils or under one of the Multilateral Trade Agreements.
[386] This is the case for Committees that are established by the Ministerial Conference or under one of the Plurilateral Trade Agreements. See Art. IV.7-8 WTO Agreement.
[387] E.g. for the Textile Monitoring Body: art. 8 Agreement on Textiles and Clothing, art. 4 Agreement on Rules of Origin.
[388] See e.g. art. 17 Agreement on Agriculture, art. 7 TRIMS.
[389] K. ADAMANTOPOULOS, *An Anatomy of the World Trade Organization*, (London, Kluwer Law International, 1997), p. 38.
[390] Art. IV.7 WTO Agreement.
[391] On the accession process, see *supra* paras. 204-211.

Chapter IV

meeting of the Ministerial Conference, which also decides on their termination and winding up. The decisions setting up these Working Groups and Working Parties define their mandate. The Working Parties on accession and all Working Groups are 'horizontal' and report to the General Council. Yet the Working Party on State-Trading Enterprises reports to the Council for Trade in Goods and the Working Parties on Domestic Regulation and on GATS rules report to the Council for Trade in Services.

Figure 2. Organization Chart of the WTO

WTO structure
All WTO members may participate in all councils, committees, etc, except Appellate Body, Dispute Settlement panels, and plurilateral committees.

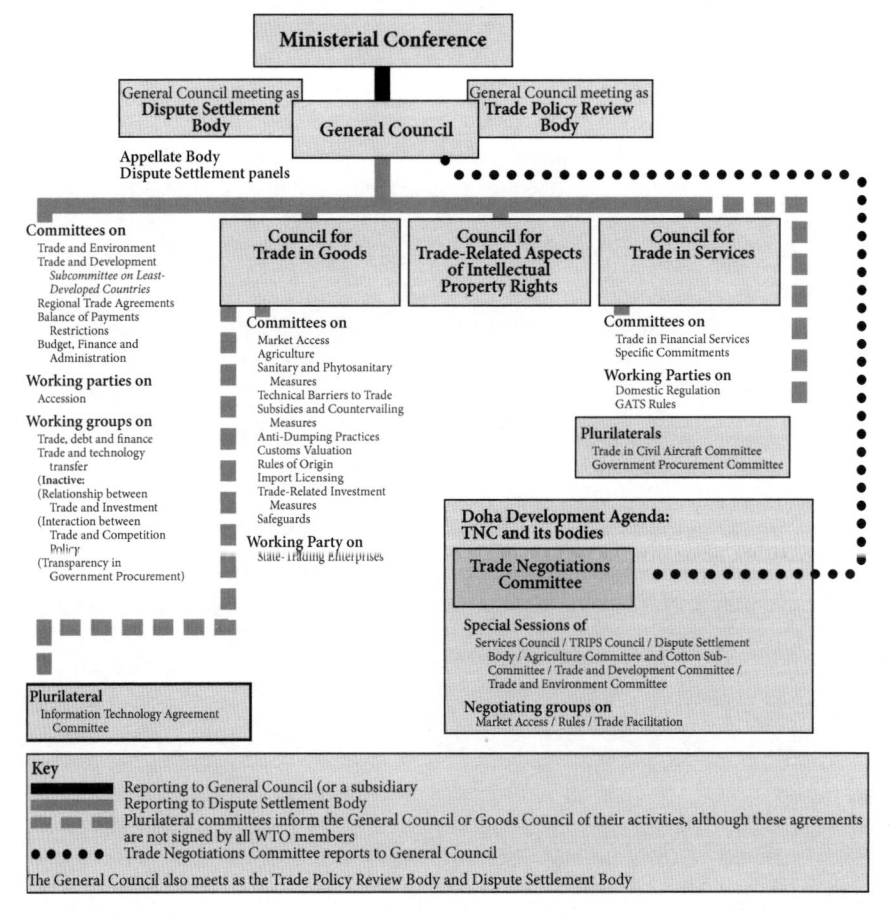

```
                         Ministerial Conference
         ┌───────────────────────┼───────────────────────┐
General Council meeting as                       General Council meeting as
   Dispute Settlement           General Council      Trade Policy Review
        Body                                              Body
   Appellate Body
   Dispute Settlement panels
```

Committees on
  Trade and Environment
  Trade and Development
    Subcommittee on Least-
    Developed Countries
  Regional Trade Agreements
  Balance of Payments
    Restrictions
  Budget, Finance and
    Administration

Working parties on
  Accession

Working groups on
  Trade, debt and finance
  Trade and technology
    transfer
  (Inactive:
  (Relationship between
   Trade and Investment
  (Interaction between
   Trade and Competition
   Policy
  (Transparency in
   Government Procurement)

Council for Trade in Goods

Committees on
  Market Access
  Agriculture
  Sanitary and Phytosanitary
    Measures
  Technical Barriers to Trade
  Subsidies and Countervailing
    Measures
  Anti-Dumping Practices
  Customs Valuation
  Rules of Origin
  Import Licensing
  Trade-Related Investment
    Measures
  Safeguards

Working Party on
  State-Trading Enterprises

Council for Trade-Related Aspects of Intellectual Property Rights

Council for Trade in Services

Committees on
  Trade in Financial Services
  Specific Commitments

Working Parties on
  Domestic Regulation
  GATS Rules

Plurilaterals
  Trade in Civil Aircraft Committee
  Government Procurement Committee

Doha Development Agenda: TNC and its bodies

Trade Negotiations Committee

Special Sessions of
  Services Council / TRIPS Council / Dispute Settlement Body / Agriculture Committee and Cotton Sub-Committee / Trade and Development Committee / Trade and Environment Committee

Negotiating groups on
  Market Access / Rules / Trade Facilitation

Plurilateral
  Information Technology Agreement Committee

Key
  ▬▬▬ Reporting to General Council (or a subsidiary)
  ▬▬▬ Reporting to Dispute Settlement Body
  ▬ ▬ ▬ Plurilateral committees inform the General Council or Goods Council of their activities, although these agreements are not signed by all WTO members
  • • • • Trade Negotiations Committee reports to General Council
The General Council also meets as the Trade Policy Review Body and Dispute Settlement Body

Source: WTO website.

263. The 'general' or 'horizontal'[392] Committees and Working Parties will be discussed first. The specific Committees and Working Group coming under the respective Councils will be addressed within the subsequent sections relating to each Council.

a. 'General' Committees

264. First, the *Committee on Trade and Development* serves as a focal point for consideration and coordination of work on development in the WTO and the initiatives in other multilateral agencies. It also reviews the developing country participation in the multilateral trading system. Further, it reviews periodically the provisions on special and differential treatment of the developing country Members and may report to the General Council for appropriate action. Finally, it provides guidelines and reviews periodically the technical cooperation activities of the WTO.[393] A *Subcommittee on Least-Developed Countries* comes under the Committee on Trade and Development.[394]

265. The second 'horizontal' Committee is the *Committee on Balance-of-Payments Restrictions*. This Committee carries out regular consultations with WTO Members that have imposed restrictive import measures for balance-of-payments purposes, as provided for in Articles XII and XVIII.B GATT. In fact, the Committee will assess in a report, based on the consultations, whether the condition of Articles XII and XVIII.B are fulfilled. The Committee reports to the General Council on these issues, which then has to approve the report. If the report provides for a planned phase-out of the balance-of-payments restrictions, the General Council may recommend that the Member be deemed to be in compliance with the provisions in Articles XII and XVIII.B as long as it adheres to this phase-out.[395] It should be noted that a Panel and the Appellate Body have declared themselves also competent to decide whether the conditions of these articles are fulfilled if such balance-of-payments restrictions are the subject of a dispute before them.[396]

---

[392] See M. FOOTER, *supra* note 309, p. 62.
[393] See Decision by the General Council on the establishment of the WTO Committee on Trade and Development, WT/L/46, 23 February 1995.
[394] See Decision by the Committee on Trade and Development on the establishment of the WTO Sub-Committee on Least Developed Countries, WT/COMTD/2, 18 July 1995.
[395] See Understanding on the Balance-of-Payments Provisions of GATT 1994, para. 13.
[396] See Panel Report: India – Quantitative Restrictions on Imports of Agricultural, Textiles and Industrial Products, WT/DS90/R (6 April 1999), para. 5.114, confirmed by the Appellate Body in its Appellate Body Report: India – Quantitative Restrictions on Imports of Agricultural, Textiles and Industrial Products, WT/DS90/AB/R (23 August 1999), paras. 80–109.

266. The third Committee, the *Committee on Budget, Finance and Administration* deals with the general budgetary and financial issues and the personnel matters of the WTO. The budget of the WTO was discussed above (see *supra* paras. 235-236).

267. The fourth 'horizontal' Committee is the *Committee on Trade and Environment*. This Committee was set up by a Ministerial Declaration made at Marrakesh in 1994. The Committee meets in 'regular' sessions and in 'special' sessions.

The *'regular' Committee* has two responsibilities: (i) identifying the relationship between trade measures and environmental measures, in order to promote sustainable development and (ii) making appropriate recommendations on whether any modifications of the provisions of the multilateral trade agreements would be required. A Ministerial Decision on Trade and Environment, taken in Marrakesh, sets out the agenda items of the Committee.[397] At the fourth Ministerial Conference in Doha, it was decided that the Committee on Trade and Environment and the Committee on Trade and Development needed to function as fora to identify and debate environmental and developmental aspects of upcoming WTO negotiations, in order to contribute to achieving the objective of sustainable development.[398] The Doha Declaration also called upon the Committee on Trade and Environment to focus on three items in its work programme. First, it had to focus on the impact that environmental requirements have on market access, especially for developing countries and least-developed countries.[399] It was recognized that environmental requirements pursue legitimate objectives, but that they may at the same time have the effect of trade barriers. Therefore, a

---

[397] It concerns (i) the relationship between trade provisions of the multilateral trading system and trade measures for environmental purposes, including those pursuant to multilateral environmental agreements; (ii) the relationship between environmental policies that are relevant to trade and environmental measures and that have significant trade effects, and the provisions of the multilateral trading system; (iii) the relationship between the provisions of the multilateral trading system and (a) charges and taxes for environmental purposes and (b) requirements for environmental purposes relating to products, including standards and technical regulations, packaging, labelling and recycling; (iv) the provisions of the multilateral trading system with respect to the transparency of trade measures used for environmental purposes and requirements that have significant trade effects; (v) the relationship between the dispute settlement mechanisms in the multilateral trading system and those found in multilateral environmental agreements; (vi) the effect of environmental measures on market access, especially in relation to developing countries, in particular to the least developed among them, and the environmental benefits of removing trade restrictions and distortions; (vii) the issue of the exports of domestically prohibited goods; (viii) the consideration of the work programme envisaged in the Decision on Trade in Services and the Environment and the relevant provisions of TRIPS. See Ministerial Decision on Trade and Environment, Part of the Final Act Embodying the Results of the Uruguay Round Agreements.
[398] Ministerial Declaration of Doha, *supra* note 40, para. 51.
[399] *Ibid.* para. 32 (i).

balance is needed between safeguarding the environment and ensuring market access. Environmental measures should be consistent with the WTO rules, take into account the capabilities of developing countries and meet the legitimate objectives of the importing country. The discussion in the Committee on Trade and Environment has highlighted a list of issues: transparency, notification, early warning, consultation, impact assessment, taking into account comments while a measure is being prepared, technical assistance and capacity building to assist the implementation of environmental requirements, and coordination within exporting countries. The Committee on Trade and Environment has made a compilation of the work on environmental standards undertaken in other WTO bodies and in other international organizations[400] and has considered the relevant work in the Committee on Technical Barriers to Trade and the Committee on Sanitary and Phytosanitary Measures. A second specific focus mandated in the Doha Declaration was the role of the TRIPS Agreement for the environment. The Committee has considered the relationship between TRIPS and the Convention on Biological Diversity.[401] A number of developing countries argue that the TRIPS provision on patentability[402] should be amended to include a requirement to disclose the source of biological materials. They are afraid that inventions would be patented that in fact are not new, but have been developed already in these countries (often being part of traditional knowledge). They also want to avoid local biological resources being exploited by foreigners without complying with domestic regulations and without giving adequate remuneration to the owners of these resources. Other countries are not convinced that such amendment is appropriate or necessary. A compromise that has been suggested is to develop a limited patent disclosure requirement at the international level. Disclosure would be limited to the origin or source of genetic material and related traditional knowledge and would have no substantive implications for patentability. A third specific focus concerns labelling requirements for environmental purposes.[403] It was thought necessary to consider how labelling to inform consumers about environmental protection could be done without jeopardizing the developing countries' abilities to export. These 'eco-labels', required in national legislation, may indeed be very complex and difficult for importers to provide. Some WTO Members have argued that this issue should better be dealt with in the Committee on Technical Barriers to Trade. Others see the debate in the Committee on Trade and Environment as an input to the discussions in the Committee on Technical Barriers to Trade.

---

[400] See Committee on Trade and Environment Note, Environmental Requirements and Market Access. Recent Work in OECD and UNCTAD, WT/CTE/W/244, 8 December 2006.
[401] Ministerial Declaration of Doha, *supra* note 40, para. 32 (ii).
[402] Art. 27 (3) (b) TRIPS.
[403] Ministerial Declaration of Doha, *supra* note 40, para. 33 (iii).

The Committee on Trade and Environment also meets in *'Special Sessions'*. In the Doha Declaration, WTO Members agreed to start further negotiations with regard to (i) the link between the WTO rules and specific trade obligations in multilateral environmental agreements;[404] (ii) the procedures for regular information exchange between the WTO Committees and secretariats linked to multilateral environmental agreements and criteria for observer status[405] and (iii) reduction or elimination of tariffs on environmental goods and services.[406] With regard to the first issue, a WTO Member has proposed within the Committee that a Ministerial Decision be adopted establishing core principles to govern the relationship between multilateral environmental agreements and WTO rules, and also setting out procedures to guide WTO bodies and dispute settlement Panels in their consideration of environmental issues. Yet, other Members thought that the relation between multilateral environmental agreements and the WTO rules was working well. Still others thought that such a Decision would not be within the mandate set out in the Doha Declaration.[407] After a period of standstill, this debate is now being revitalized. With regard to the second issue, discussions are on-going on complementing existing cooperation mechanisms and on supplementing existing criteria on observer status with specific criteria for environmental organizations.[408] Technical discussions are on-going on the third issue, highlighting the fact that many environmental products have a dual use, which is of importance when one situates these goods in the tariff classification lists. Two Members have suggested revised lists of environmental goods and others are reviewing their lists.[409]

268. A fifth 'horizontal' Committee is the *Committee on Regional Trade Agreements*.[410] This Committee has the task of examining trade agreements that have been notified to the Council for Trade in Goods (when trade in goods is covered) and/or the Council for Trade in Services (when trade in services is covered) or the Committee on Trade and Development (if an agreement is concluded pursuant to the Enabling Clause). The respective Councils or Committee will determine the procedures and terms of reference for assessing the notified regional trade agreement. The Committee will then assess the regional trade agreement in the light of the relevant provisions (Article XXIV GATT, Article V

---

[404] *Ibid.* para. 31 (i).
[405] *Ibid.* para. 31 (ii).
[406] *Ibid.* para. 31 (iii).
[407] Committee on Trade and Environment, Special Session, Report by the Chairman on the Special Session of the Committee on Trade and Environment to the Trade Negotiations Committee, WT/TE/16, 26 July 2006, paras. 2–4.
[408] *Ibid.* paras. 6–8.
[409] *Ibid.* paras. 10–11.
[410] See the terms of reference in the Decision of the General Council on the Committee on Regional Trade Agreements, WT/L/127, 7 February 1996.

GATS and Enabling Clause) and draft a Report for consideration by the relevant Council or Committee, which could then make the necessary recommendations.[411] A process for reviewing economic integration agreements already existed under the GATT 1947. If a trade agreement was notified, a GATT Working Party was set up. Yet, this system of *ad hoc* Working Parties was not very effective: almost no agreement resulted in an adopted Report.[412] When the WTO was established, it was hoped that the Committee would be more effective in reviewing regional trade agreements. Nevertheless, differences between Members on how to interpret the criteria for assessing the consistency of economic integration agreements with WTO rules have created a lengthening backlog of uncompleted reports in the Committee. Moreover, the institutional aspects for examining such agreements were not much different from those of the Working Parties of the GATT 1947. In order to address some of these problems, in 2006 a decision providing for a new Transparency Mechanism for Regional Trade Agreements was adopted.[413] This transparency mechanism will at least address the concerns with WTO Members that a 'spaghetti bowl' of trade agreements is emerging. There was indeed concern that it was becoming increasingly difficult to have an overview of all existing trade agreements. Therefore, as soon as negotiations on a regional trade agreement start, involved WTO Members should endeavour to inform the WTO of this fact.[414] As soon as information on a newly signed trade agreement is publicly available, the involved Members should send this information to the WTO.[415] The WTO will then make this information available on its website.[416] Prompt notification of Regional Trade Agreements is required. This notification should take place as soon as possible and no later than after the ratification by the parties. The notification must happen before the application of the trade agreement.[417] The examination by the Committee on Regional Trade Agreements (or the Committee on Trade and Development) will take place as soon as possible and will take no longer than one year after notification of the agreement.[418] It is also required that the notification provides sufficient detailed information.[419] This new mechanism may indeed play a role in making the 'spaghetti bowl' of trade

---

[411] For the conditions for regional trade agreements, see *supra* paras. 78–83 (GATT), 148 (GATS) and 88–92 (Enabling Clause).
[412] W. DAVEY, "Institutional Framework", *in* P. MACRORY, A. APPLETON and M. PLUMMER (eds.), *The World Trade Organization: Legal, Economic and Political Analyses*, (New York, Springer 2005), Volume I, p. 67.
[413] Negotiation Group on Rules, Transparency Mechanism for Regional Trade Agreements (Draft Decision), JOB(06)/59/Rev.5, 29 June 2006.
[414] *Ibid.* para. 1 (a).
[415] *Ibid.* para. 1 (b).
[416] *Ibid.* para. 2.
[417] *Ibid.* para. 3.
[418] *Ibid.* para. 6.
[419] *Ibid.* Annex.

agreements more transparent, but it remains to be seen whether and how the reviewing process will be enhanced.[420]

269. A sixth, and final, Committee reporting to the General Council is the *Trade Negotiations Committee*. This Committee has a broad task. It was set up by the Doha Ministerial Conference to supervise the overall conduct and progress of the new trade negotiations that started at this Conference.[421] Its mandate thus covers all aspects of the Doha Declaration. Under the supervision of the Trade Negotiations Committee, special sessions of the Services Council, TRIPS Council, Dispute Settlement Body (the General Council in a different role, see *infra* paras. 302-304), Agriculture Committee and Cotton Sub-Committee, Trade and Development Committee and Trade and Environment Committee are held. The Trade Negotiations Committee has also set up a number of Negotiation Groups. The *Negotiation Group on Market Access* conducts discussions on improved market access of non-agricultural goods (Non-Agricultural Market Access (NAMA)).[422] These negotiations should lead to further tariff reduction on the basis of a 'formula approach'. This means that tariff reductions are not negotiated product by product, but rather across the board. The total tariff reduction of a Member is calculated by use of a formula and thus allows comparisons between Members' tariff reductions. It leads to a more efficient negotiation process, is said to be more transparent and predictable, and would be more equitable and rules-based, since it restricts the use of bargaining power. Yet, a Report by the Chairman of this Committee noted that Members still have different interpretations of the formula and that important new steps are still required.[423] The Hong Kong Ministerial Conference took note of this Report and called for further negotiations while especially taking account of products that are of interest for the exports by developing countries and while noting that for developing countries, less than full reciprocity in reduction commitments is desirable.[424] A second Negotiation Group is the *Negotiation Group on Rules*. This Negotiation Group conducts specific discussions on the rules on Antidumping, Subsidies (especially fisheries subsidies) and provisions relating to Regional Trade Agreements. The aim is to clarify and improve disciplines while preserving the basic concepts and principles of these agreements, and taking into account the needs of developing and least-

---

[420] For a proposal for reforming the provisions on regional trade agreements: see C. PICKER, "Regional Trade Agreements v. the WTO: A Proposal for Reform of art. XXIV to Counter this Institutional Threat", *University of Pennsylvania Journal of International Economic Law* (2005), pp. 267–319.
[421] Ministerial Declaration of Doha, *supra* note 40, para. 46.
[422] *Ibid.* paras. 16, 31 (iii) and 50.
[423] Report of the Chairman of the Negotiation Group on Market Access to the Trade Negotiations Committee, Market Access for Non-Agricultural Goods, TN/MA/16, 24 November 2005.
[424] Ministerial Declaration of Hong Kong, *supra* note 19, para. 14.

developed countries. Discussion already resulted in a new WTO mechanism for transparency in regional trade agreements.[425] A final Negotiation Group is the *Negotiation Group on Trade Facilitation*. The issue of trade facilitation was mentioned for the first time at the Singapore Ministerial Conference (see *supra* para. 257). It was again mentioned in the Doha Declaration, and negotiations were finally started in July 2004.[426] Removing formal trade barriers does not necessarily mean that trade flows will improve immediately. Companies need to be able to acquire information on other countries' importing and exporting regulations and how customs procedures are handled. The negotiations are directed to clarify and improve GATT Article V (Freedom of Transit), Article VIII (Fees and Formalities connected with Importation and Exportation), and Article X (Publication and Administration of Trade Regulations).[427]

270. There are, however, also two *plurilateral* Committees reporting to the General Council. These Committees do not involve all WTO Members, but only Members of the plurilateral agreement concerned. It concerns, first, the *Committee on Trade in Civil Aircraft*. The WTO Agreement on Civil Aircraft is a pre-WTO agreement and dates from 1 January 1980 (see *supra* paras. 154–155). It has 30 signatories and eliminates import duties on all aircraft, other than military aircraft, as well as on all other products covered by the agreement – civil aircraft engines and their parts and components, all components and sub-assemblies of civil aircraft, and flight simulators and their parts and components. This Agreement established the Committee on Trade in Civil Aircraft, which reviews annually the implementation and operation of this plurilateral agreement. In this framework also, further negotiations had to take place with a view to broadening and improving the application of the agreement. The Committee may also provide a forum for consultation when a Party to the plurilateral agreement would introduce subsidies for civil aircraft[428] and will act as a reviewing body when a Party feels its interests under the agreement are adversely affected by another Party.[429] Nevertheless, the possibility for dispute settlement under the GATT (now WTO) remains unaffected as far as provisions of the multilateral trade agreements are affected.[430] The Committee has set up a Sub-Committee to consider technical issues.

---

[425] See *supra* para. 83.
[426] Decision Adopted by the General Council of the WTO on 1 August 2004 ('July Decision'), WT/L/579, Annex D.
[427] The Trade Negotiations Committee has made an extensive compilation of Members' proposals: see Negotiating Group on Trade Facilitation – WTO Negotiations on Trade Facilitation – Compilation of Members' Proposals – Revision, TN/TF/W/43/Rev. 10, 11 August 2006.
[428] Agreement on Trade in Civil Aircraft, done at Geneva on 12 April 1979, 26S/162, para. 8.6.
[429] *Ibid.* para. 8.7.
[430] *Ibid.* para. 8.8.

271. The *Committee on Government Procurement* is the second plurilateral Committee reporting to the General Council. It oversees the work undertaken within the framework of the Agreement on Government Procurement (see *supra* paras. 156–158). Negotiations on the revision of the text have proceeded to a relatively advanced stage, be it that discussions are still in progress with regard to the coverage of the agreement.[431]

b.   'General' Working Parties and Groups

272.   Only the Working Parties on accession of new Members are 'horizontal' bodies. All other Working Parties are specific and come under either the Council for Trade in Goods or the Council for Trade in Services.

To examine what progress can be made in the fields of investment, competition policy, transparency in government procurement and trade facilitation, the Ministerial Conference in Singapore established Working Groups in 1996. The Ministerial Conference in Doha established two further Working Groups.

273.   A first Working Group established by the Ministerial Conference in Singapore is the *Working Group on the Relation between Trade and Competition Policy*.[432] The Doha Ministerial Declaration specified the focus of the Working Group as performing work on (i) core principles for competition policy, including transparency, non-discrimination and procedural fairness; (ii) provisions on hard-core cartels; (iii) modalities for voluntary cooperation; and (iv) support for progressive reinforcement of competition institutions in developing countries through capacity building.[433] A synthesis paper on the relationship of trade and competition policy to development and economic growth was drafted.[434] This paper noted broad agreement among WTO Members on the importance and relevance of competition policy as a building block of economic development, yet such competition policy would not necessarily include comprehensive competition law. Most WTO Members emphasized the broad complementarity of competition policy and trade liberalization in creating incentives for innovation and productivity improvement and otherwise supporting efficient development patterns. Specifically with regard to developing countries, it was suggested that these countries do not necessarily need to implement all aspects of a competition policy from the beginning of the process. Rather, initial focus should be on

---

[431]   See Report of the Committee on Government Procurement, GPA/89, 11 December 2006.
[432]   Ministerial Declaration of Singapore, *supra* note 150, para. 20.
[433]   Ministerial Declaration of Doha, *supra* note 40, para. 25.
[434]   Working Group on the Interaction between Trade and Competition Policy, Synthesis Paper on the Relationship between Trade and Competition Policy to Development and Economic Growth, WT/WGTCP/W/80, 18 September 1998.

deterring hard-core cartels and on competition advocacy. Background notes were prepared on the relevance of WTO provisions on MFN, National Treatment and transparency for competition policy;[435] on the fundamental principles of competition policy;[436] on support for progressive reinforcement of competition institutions in developing countries through capacity building;[437] on provisions on hard-core cartels;[438] on means of voluntary cooperation;[439] on core principles, including transparency, non-discrimination and procedural fairness;[440] and on provisions on procedural fairness in existing WTO agreements.[441] However, this Working Group is currently inactive, since it was decided in the 'July Decision' to discontinue negotiations on trade and competition policy.[442]

274. A second Working Group established by the Singapore Ministerial Conference is the *Working Group on the Relation between Trade and Investment*.[443] This Working Group examines the implications of the relationship between trade and investment for development and economic growth and will perform an analysis of the existing international instruments and activities regarding trade and investment. On the basis of this work, common features and differences (e.g. overlaps and possible conflicts), as well as possible gaps in existing international instruments will be determined; the advantages and disadvantages of entering into bilateral, regional and multilateral rules on investment will be identified; the rights and obligations of home and host countries and of investors in host countries will be mapped out; and the relationship between existing and possible future international cooperation on investment policy and existing and possible

---

[435] Working Group on the Interaction between Trade and Competition Policy, Background Note on the Fundamental Principles of National Treatment, Most-Favoured-Nation Treatment and Transparency, WT/WGTCP/W/114, 14 April 1999.

[436] Working Group on the Interaction between Trade and Competition Policy, Background Note on the Fundamental Principles of Competition Policy, WT/WGTCP/W/127, 7 June 1999.

[437] Working Group on the Interaction between Trade and Competition Policy, Background Note on Support for Progressive Reinforcement of Competition Institutions in Developing Countries through Capacity Building, WT/WGTCP/W/182, 17 April 2002.

[438] Working Group on the Interaction between Trade and Competition Policy, Background Note on Provisions on Hardcore Cartels, WT/WGTCP/W/191, 20 June 2002.

[439] Working Group on the Interaction between Trade and Competition Policy, Background Note on Modalities for Voluntary Cooperation, WT/WGTCP/W/192, 28 June 2002.

[440] Working Group on the Interaction between Trade and Competition Policy, Background Note on core principles, including transparency, non-discrimination and procedural fairness, WT/WGTCP/W/209, 19 September 2002.

[441] Working Group on the Interaction between Trade and Competition Policy, Background Note on Provisions on Procedural Fairness in Existing WTO Agreements, WT/WGTCP/W/231, 22 May 2003.

[442] Decision Adopted by the General Council of the WTO on 1 August 2004, WT/L/579, para. 1 (g).

[443] Ministerial Declaration of Doha, *supra* note 40, para. 20.

future international cooperation on competition policy will be examined.[444] The Doha Ministerial Declaration specified further work of the Committee. The Declaration stated that the Committee should focus on the clarification of: scope and definition; transparency; non-discrimination; ways of pre-establishing commitments based on a GATS-type, positive list approach; development provisions; exceptions and balance-of-payments safeguards; consultation and the settlement of disputes between Members.[445] Like the Committee on the Relationship between Trade and Competition Policy, this Committee is currently inactive, since it was decided in the 'July Decision' to discontinue work on this issue.[446]

275. The Ministerial Declaration of Singapore set up a third Working Group: the *Working Group on Transparency in Government Procurement*.[447] There is already within the WTO framework an Agreement on Government Procurement (see *supra* paras. 156–158). Nevertheless, this agreement is a plurilateral agreement. At the Ministerial Conference of Singapore, it was decided to set up a multilateral Working Group to study the issue. The Doha Declaration also addressed the work of this Working Group and noted that the negotiations had to be limited to the transparency aspects and therefore would not restrict the scope for countries to give preferences to domestic supplies and suppliers. The Members committed themselves to ensuring adequate technical assistance and support for capacity building both during the negotiations and after their conclusion.[448] It was hoped that in a second phase, a multilateral agreement on transparency in government procurement would be concluded.[449] Nevertheless, also for this 'Singapore issue', the 'July Decision' halted the work.[450]

276. Two further Working Groups were set up by the Doha Ministerial Conference. The *Working Group on Trade, Debt and Finance* examines how trade-related measures can contribute to solving the external debt problems and financial crises from which developing countries have suffered. The Working Group also has to address how to strengthen the coherence of international trade and financial policies, with a view to safeguarding the multilateral trading system from the effects of financial and monetary instability.[451] The Working Group held discussions

---

[444] Report (1998) of the Committee on the Relationship between Trade and Investment to the General Council, WT/WGTI/2, 8 December 1998, Annex.
[445] Ministerial Declaration of Doha, *supra* note 40, para. 22.
[446] Decision Adopted by the General Council of the WTO on 1 August 2004, WT/L/579, para. 1 (g).
[447] Ministerial Declaration of Singapore, *supra* note 150, para. 21.
[448] Ministerial Declaration of Doha, *supra* note 40, para. 26.
[449] See Report (2003) of the Working Group on Transparency in Government Procurement to the General Council, WT/WGTGP/9, 15 July 2003, paras. 15–18.
[450] Decision Adopted by the General Council of the WTO on 1 August 2004, WT/L/579, para. 1 (g).
[451] Ministerial Declaration of Doha, *supra* note 40, para. 36.

on trade financing (financing of exports by traders in developing countries); on trade and financial markets (especially on the impact of trade on international financial stability and on the impact of exchange rate volatility on trade flows); on coherence between trade and finance (since the level of exchange rates influences trade flows, the international financial policies need to be coherent with trade policies); on the way trade liberalization could trigger internal economic reforms; on how trade liberalization is a source of growth; on market access and removal of other trade barriers and on the importance of commodities exports for developing countries.[452] The Hong Kong Ministerial Conference took note of this work.[453]

277. The second Working Group set up by the Doha Ministerial Conference is the *Working Group on Trade and Technology Transfer*.[454] The Working Group examines the relationship between trade and transfer of technology, and possible steps that might be taken within the mandate of the WTO to increase flows of technology to developing countries. To consider the relationship, the Working Group held several discussions with UNCTAD, since UNCTAD has performed a number of studies on this issue. The Working Group also examined different provisions contained in various WTO agreements relating to technology transfer and specific provisions contained in various WTO agreements which may have the effect of hindering the transfer of technology to developing countries.[455] The Hong Kong Ministerial Conference decided that this work should be continued.[456]

c.   Council for Trade in Goods

278. The Council for Trade in Goods monitors the functioning of the Multilateral Trade Agreements.[457] The Council for Trade in Goods has the responsibility of overseeing the functioning of all Multilateral Trade Agreements affecting trade in goods.

279. Eleven Committees figure under the Council for Trade in Goods. These Committees are open to all Members of the WTO. Their chairman changes every

---

[452] Report (2005) of the Working Group on Trade, Debt and Finance to the General Council, WT/WGTDF/4, 10 October 2005.
[453] Ministerial Declaration of Hong Kong, *supra* note 19, para. 42.
[454] Ministerial Declaration of Doha, *supra* note 40, para. 37.
[455] See Report (2005) of the Working Group on the Relation between Trade and Transfer of Technology to the General Council, WT/WGTTT/7, 14 November 2005. See also Report (2006) of the Working Group on the Relation between Trade and Transfer of Technology to the General Council, WT/WGTTT/8, 15 November 2006.
[456] Ministerial Declaration of Hong Kong, *supra* note 19, para. 43.
[457] Observers in the Council for Trade in Goods are FAO, the IMF, the World Bank, the International Textiles and Clothing Bureau, the OECD, the UN, UNCTAD and the World Customs Organization.

year. There is, however, also one plurilateral Committee functioning under the Council for Trade in Goods. The main task of the Committees is to review the functioning of the Agreement they are responsible for. In fact, it is in these Committees that the real day-to-day negotiation work of the WTO is performed.

280. The *Committee on Market Access* supervises the implementation of concessions relating to tariffs and non-tariff measures.[458] The Committee also provides a forum for consultation on these matters. Nevertheless, it cannot address market access issues that are already covered by another WTO body.[459] The Committee oversees the procedures of withdrawal of concessions, ensures that GATT Schedules are up to date and that modifications in these schedules are reflected.[460] It also addresses the documentation on quantitative restrictions and non-tariff barriers.[461] Finally, it oversees the 'Integrated Data Base'.[462] This Data Base[463] collects yearly information on Members' import statistics, customs tariff duties and quantitative restrictions. In the framework of the Agreement on Agriculture, tariffs are being reduced and non-tariff measures should be converted into tariffs. This is an area where the Committee on Market Access has an important role to play.[464]

281. A second Committee coming under the Council for Trade in Goods is the *Committee on Agriculture*. This committee is established by the Agreement on Agriculture[465] and oversees the implementation of this Agreement.[466] Moreover, this review process provides a forum for discussion and consultation on the agricultural measures of Members.[467] Members are required to notify their progress on these issues[468] and the Committee may also request Members to

---

[458] The ACP Group, FAO, the Inter-American Development Bank, the IMF, the International Textiles and Clothing Bureau, UNCTAD, the World Bank and the International Customs Organization have observer status in the Committee.
[459] Decision by the General Council on the Establishment of the Committee on Market Access, WT/l/47, 31 January 1995, (a).
[460] *Ibid.* (b) and (c).
[461] *Ibid.* (d).
[462] *Ibid.* (e).
[463] See GATT Council Decision of November 1987, BISD 34S/66.
[464] K. ADAMANTOPOULOS, *supra* note 389, p. 47.
[465] Art. 17 Agreement on Agriculture.
[466] Decision by the General Council on 31 January 1995, WT/L/43.
[467] To complement these discussions, some international organizations have observer status in the Committee on Agriculture. This is the case for the IMF, World Bank, FAO, World Food Programme, International Grains Council, UNCTAD, International Grains Council and the OECD. See D. LUFF, *supra* note 47, p. 245. Report of the Committee on Agriculture, G/L/417, 20 November 2000, para. 9 and art. 12.3 SPS.
[468] Moreover, Members may point to issues that ought to have been notified by other Members. Art. 18.7 Agreement on Agriculture.

provide information to facilitate the review process.[469] In addition, Members will consult annually in the Committee to discuss the growth in world trade in agricultural products.[470]

282. Pursuant to Article 12 SPS, the *Committee on Sanitary and Phytosanitary Measures* has been established. This Committee monitors and promotes the implementation of the SPS Agreement.[471] The Committee has developed, in cooperation with Members, several guidelines and procedures to help the latter implement their obligations under SPS.[472] Moreover, the Committee has the authority to grant a developing-country Member-specific, time-limited exceptions from the whole or part of the SPS Agreement if this Member is unable to implement these provisions.[473] It also promotes consultation between Members on SPS issues.[474] In this respect, the Committee pays particular importance to the harmonization of Members' SPS measures[475] and to the use of international standards, guidelines and recommendations. A list of such standards, guidelines and recommendations that are applied by Members is managed by the Committee.[476] Recent debates now also focus on the use of standards that are developed by private organizations (e.g. supermarkets) and that are often more rigid than those developed by international standard-setting bodies. Article 12.7 SPS required the Committee to perform a review three years after the entry into force of the SPS Agreement. In general, the Committee agreed that the SPS Agreement had provided a useful set of rules for trade-related SPS measures, although there were some implementation problems.[477] At the Doha Ministerial

---

[469] *Ibid.* art. 18.2.
[470] *Ibid.* art. 18.5.
[471] Art. 12.1 and 12.7 SPS.
[472] *Ibid.* art. 5.5. These include: the Recommended Procedures for Implementing the Transparency Obligations in the SPS Agreement, G/SPS/7/Rev.2, 2 April 2002 and the Guidelines to Further the Practical Implementation of art. 5.5 SPS, G/SPS/15, 22 June 2000.
[473] Art. 10.3 SPS.
[474] *Ibid.* art. 12.2. Also in this Committee, certain international governmental organizations have observer status, namely, Food and Agriculture Organization, FAO International Plant Protection Convention, Codex Alimentarius Commission, IMF, World Bank, International Organization for Standardization, International Trade Center, Office Internationale des Epizooties, UNCTAD and World Health Organization. Some other organizations have an *ad hoc* observer status: African Caribbean and Pacific (ACP) Group of States, European Free Trade Association, Inter-American Institute for Agricultural Cooperation, Organization for Economic Co-operation and Development, Regional International Organization for Plant Protection and Animal Health, Latin American Economic System.
[475] Art. 3.5 SPS requires the Committee on Sanitary and Phytosanitary Measures to develop a procedure to monitor international harmonization. See the Procedure to Monitor the Process of International Standardization, G/SPS/11, 16 October 1997.
[476] Art. 12.4 SPS.
[477] Review of the Operation and Implementation of the Agreement on the Application of Sanitary and Phytosanitary Measures, G/SPS/12, 11 March 1999.

Conference, Members decided to review the operation and implementation of the SPS Agreement at least once every four years.[478] A second review was completed in June 2005 and the Committee made 40 recommendations.[479] On this basis, the Committee has agreed to a programme that includes continued work on especially equivalence (Article 4 SPS requires governments to recognize other countries' measures even if they are different, so long as an equivalent level of protection is provided), transparency of the measures that are being adopted, monitoring international standards (with now an increased attention to standards by private companies), technical assistance (with a focus on the effectiveness of the assistance), special and differential treatment, regionalization (guidelines need to be developed for the recognition that an exporting region is disease-free or pest-free (or has a lower incidence)) and specific trade concerns (e.g. GMOs).

283. The *Committee on Technical Barriers to Trade* oversees the implementation of the Agreement on Technical Barriers to Trade. Its tasks are quite similar to those of the Committee on SPS. The Committee reviews annually the implementation of the TBT Agreement in the light of its objectives.[480] To this end, Members have to inform the Committee of all measures that relate to the implementation.[481] In addition, it performs a three-yearly review on the implementation and operation of the TBT Agreement.[482] This latter review helps the Committee to recommend possible adjustments of the rights and obligations of the Agreement. The Committee may even propose appropriate amendments to the TBT.[483] The Committee has recommended starting a process of sharing Members' experiences on good regulatory practice, to further improve the transparency in the national technical standards and in the provision of technical assistance and to coordinate this matter at the national, regional and international level. It has also set up a work programme to improve the understanding of conformity assessment procedures. Besides reviewing the TBT Agreement, the Committee also serves, in the same way as the SPS Committee, as a forum for consultation between Members.[484] The TBT Committee is enabled to grant

---

[478] Decision on Implementation-Related Issues and Concerns, done at Doha on 14 November 2001, WT/MIN(01)/17, para. 3.4.
[479] Review of the Operation and Implementation of the Agreement on the Application of Sanitary and Phytosanitary Measures, G/SPS/36, 11 July 2005.
[480] Art. 15.3 TBT. For the most recent review see Eleventh Annual Review of the Implementation and Operation of the TBT Agreement, G/TBT/18, 17 February 2006.
[481] Art. 15.2 TBT.
[482] Third Triennial Review of the Operation and Implementation of the Agreement on Technical Barriers to Trade, G/TBT/13, 11 November 2003.
[483] Art. 15.4 TBT.
[484] *Ibid.* art. 13.1. Numerous organizations attend the TBT Committee as observers: ACP, ALADI, EFTA, FAO, IEC, IMF, ISO, ITC, OECD, OIE, OIML, UNCTAD, UN/ECE, UNIDO, WHO, WHO/FAO Codex Alimentarius Commission and the World Bank. See Report (2003) of the Committee on Technical Barriers to Trade, G/L/657, 11 November 2003, p. 1, para. 7.

developing country Members time-limited exceptions – wholly or partially – from obligations under TBT.[485] This should help developing countries to comply with their obligations under TBT. The Committee must pay particular attention to the special position of the least-developed countries.[486]

284. Article 24 of the Agreement on Subsidies and Countervailing Measures establishes the *Committee on Subsidies and Countervailing Measures* (hereinafter also 'Committee on SCM').[487] This Committee has a prominent role to play in the Agreement on Subsidies and Countervailing Measures. First of all, it oversees the implementation of this Agreement. The Committee conducts an annual review of the implementation and operation of the SCM Agreement.[488] This task can be performed thanks to several notification obligations. Members are obliged to notify to the Committee on SCM any subsidy[489] that is granted within their territories.[490] The Members may even bring to the attention of the Committee the fact that another Member has not notified a certain subsidy.[491] Also all subsidy programmes existing before the signing of the WTO Agreement by a certain Member have to be notified if they are inconsistent with the provisions of the SCM Agreement.[492] This notification has to be done no later than 90 days after the entry into force of the WTO Agreement for such Member.[493] Members are not solely obliged to notify their subsidies, but also have to report their countervailing duty measures to the Committee.[494] Members have to report on this matter every six months. They also have to inform the Committee on the competent national authorities that may initiate countervailing duty investigations and the procedures that apply for such investigations.[495] The Committee on SCM has an important task with regard to developing countries. The Committee can decide upon the extension of the eight-year period during which developing countries may maintain – exceptionally – their export subsidies (see also *supra* para. 107). The

---

[485] Art. 12.8 TBT.
[486] *Ibid. in fine.*
[487] Intergovernmental organizations having observer status are FAO, IMF, UNCTAD and World Bank. The ACP Group and the OECD have *ad hoc* observer status.
[488] The Committee on SCM informs the Council for Trade in Goods of possible developments. See Art. 32.7 SCM Agreement. See for the most recent review: Report (2006) of the Committee on Subsidies and Countervailing Measures, G/L/798, 8 November 2006.
[489] As defined in art. 1 SCM Agreement.
[490] Art. XVI.1 GATT and art. 25 SCM Agreement.
[491] The Member first has to bring this fact to the attention of the Member concerned. Art. 25.10 SCM Agreement.
[492] *Ibid.* art. 28.1 (a).
[493] They have to be brought into conformity within three years after the date of entry into force of the WTO Agreement. See art. 28.1 (b) SCM Agreement.
[494] *Ibid.* art. 25.11.
[495] *Ibid.* art. 25.12.

Committee consults annually on the maintenance of the extension.[496] What is more, certain subsidy programmes[497] within developing countries may be immune from challenge under Part III of the SCM Agreement if these programmes are notified to the Committee and the exceptions only apply for a limited period.[498] It should finally be noted that the Committee used to have an important role to play in disputes on 'non-actionable subsidies'[499], a category of subsidies which was abolished in March 2000.[500] The Committee has nevertheless established a Permanent Group of Experts (PGE) in order to assist, as requested, dispute settlement Panels and to provide advisory opinions to the Committee. PGE members are elected by the Committee and one of them is to be replaced every year.[501]

285. A sixth Committee coming under the Council for Trade in Goods is the *Committee on Antidumping Practices*.[502] Again, this Committee oversees the implementation of the Antidumping Agreement[503] and acts as a forum for consultation between Members on matters relating to the Antidumping Agreement.[504] The Committee meets at least twice a year.[505] Members have the obligation to notify their laws and regulations on antidumping[506], as well as the procedures that apply to antidumping investigations and the national authorities that perform such procedures.[507] Finally, Members have to report all their antidumping actions to the Committee.[508] Another task conferred upon this Committee is the development of rules on the anti-circumvention of antidumping

---

[496] *Ibid*. art. 27.4.
[497] It concerns programmes that specifically serve the development of the country: debt forgiveness, subsidies to cover social costs, subsidies (relinquishments of government revenue and other transfers of liabilities) in the framework of privatization programmes.
[498] Art. 27.13 SCM Agreement.
[499] See *supra* para. 105.
[500] See Art. 31 SCM Agreement. The discussions on the extension of the provisions on non-actionable subsidies led nowhere. As a result, the procedures for non-actionable subsidies have been *de facto* deleted from the SCM Agreement. See also D. LUFF, *supra* note 47, p. 494.
[501] Art. 24.3 SCM Agreement.
[502] Art. 16 Antidumping Agreement.
[503] Every year, the Committee on Antidumping has to review the implementation and operation of the Agreement. (Art. 18.6 Antidumping Agreement.) See for the most recent report: Report (2006) of the Committee on Antidumping Practices, G/L/791, 27 October 2006.
[504] Art. 16.1 Antidumping Agreement. In carrying out its functions, the Committee may consult with and seek information form any source within the jurisdiction of a Member. (*Ibid*. art. 16.3) The IMF, UNCTAD and the World Bank have regular observer status in the Committee. OECD and the ACP Group have *ad hoc* observer status.
[505] *Ibid*.
[506] *Ibid*. art. 18.5.
[507] *Ibid*. art. 16.5.
[508] *Ibid*. art. 16.4. See also Minimum Information to be Provided under Article 16.4 of the Agreement in the Reports on All Preliminary or Final Antidumping Actions, Adopted by the Committee on Antidumping Actions on 30 October 1995, G/ADP/2, 21 November 1995.

measures.[509] This task has not been finished yet. The Committee has created a separate body, the Working Group on Implementation[510], which is open to all Members of the WTO, and which is expected to focus on technical issues of implementation, that is, the "how to" questions that frequently arise in the administration of antidumping laws.

286. Article 18 Agreement on Customs Valuation established the *Committee on Customs Valuation* to provide Members the opportunity of consulting on matters relating to the administration of customs valuation systems by any Member.[511] Again, the Committee reviews the implementation of the Agreement and therefore submits annually a report to Council for Trade in Goods.[512] The Committee has been given the additional task of monitoring the Agreement on Preshipment Inspection.[513] Next to the Committee on Customs Valuation, the Agreement established a *Technical Committee on Customs Valuation*. The Technical Committee has to take direct actions to ensure proper implementation of the Agreement. The tasks of the Technical Committee are elaborated in Annex II to the Agreement on Customs Valuation. The Committee gives advice on problems arising from the day-to-day administration of Members' customs valuation system and studies these systems as requested. Moreover, Members may request the Committee to provide information and advice on customs valuation. The Committee reports annually on the technical aspects of the operation of the Agreement and tries to further international acceptance of this Agreement through the provision of technical assistance. Finally, the Committee may provide the dispute settlement panels with technical advice on customs valuation.[514]

---

[509] An informal Group on Anti-Circumvention has been set up. Decision on Anti-Circumvention, LT/UR/D-3/1, 15 December 1993.
[510] Decision of the Committee on Antidumping Practices, G/ADP/M/7, 2 October 1996, section E.
[511] Art. 18.1 Agreement on Customs Valuation. The following intergovernmental organizations have observer status in the Committee: the World Bank, IMF, ACP Group, UNCTAD, Inter-American Development Bank and World Customs Organization. In April 1997 the Committee granted regular observer status to those organizations that had observer status on an ad hoc basis. See Committee on Customs Valuation Meeting of 25 April 1997, G/VAL/M/5, section 1. The World Bank and the IMF have observer status on the basis of an agreement between those organizations and the WTO.
[512] For the most recent report, see Report (2006) of the Committee on Customs Valuation to the Council for Trade in Goods, G/L/799 Corr.1, 10 November 2006.
[513] This was recommended by the Working Party on Preshipment Inspection (Report of the Working Party on Preshipment Inspection, G/L/300, 18 March 1999, para. 23) and was approved by the General Council on 15 June 1999 (General Council Meeting of 15 June 1999, WT/GC/M/40/Add.3, section 5).
[514] Agreement on Customs Valuation, Annex II.2 (a)–(f).

287. The *Committee on Rules of Origin* oversees the Agreement on Rules of Origin.[515] The Committee meets at least once a year to allow Members to consult on matters relating to the operation of the Agreement.[516] The Committee reviews annually the Agreement and reports to the Council for Trade in Goods.[517] Similar to the Agreement on Customs Valuation, the Agreement on Rules of Origin establishes a *Technical Committee on Rules of Origin*.[518] Its tasks are similar to those performed by the Technical Committee on Customs Valuation.[519] The Technical Committee works under the auspices of the World Customs Organization.[520] The Committee on Rules of Origin and the Technical Committee have the important task of managing the work programme to harmonize the rules of origin.[521] WTO Members have accepted that harmonization of rules of origin (the definition of rules of origin that will be applied by all countries and that will be the same whatever the purpose for which they are applied) would highly facilitate the flow of international trade. The Committee is responsible for the harmonization, whereas the Technical Committee provides support, technical research, analyses and reports to achieve this harmonization.[522] The Committee may advise, in cooperation with the Technical Committee of modifying the harmonized work programme. This may for instance be necessary to take into account new production processes as affected by technological change.[523]

288. The *Committee on Import Licensing*, as all previously described committees, provides a forum for consultation between Members on the Agreement it oversees (Agreement on Import Licensing).[524] Members have to notify to the Committee their rules and procedures on import licensing and have to indicate the national bodies that administer them. Also the lists of products that are subject to licensing requirements have to be published.[525] In addition, they have to inform the

---

[515] Art. 4.1 Agreement on Rules of Origin.
[516] Nine intergovernmental organizations have observer status in the Committee: the ACP Group, World Bank, IMF, EFTA, Inter-American Development Bank, International Textiles and Clothing Body, OECD, UNCTAD, World Customs Organization. Tenth Annual Review of the Implementation and Operation of the Agreement on Rules of Origin, G/RO/59, 10 December 2004.
[517] Art. 6.1 Agreement on Rules of Origin. See the most recent report: Report (2003) of the Committee on Rules of Origin to the Council for Trade in Goods, G/L/747, 4 October 2005.
[518] Art. 4.2 Agreement on Rules of Origin.
[519] *Ibid.* Annex I.
[520] The Agreement on Rules of Origin still mentions the name Customs Co-operation Council (CCC). The CCC changed its name in 1994 to World Customs Organization.
[521] Art. 9.2 (b) Agreement on Rules of Origin.
[522] See *ibid.* art. 9.3 (a) and Annex I.1.
[523] *Ibid.* art. 6.3.
[524] Art. 4 Agreement on Import Licensing. The IMF, World Bank and UNCTAD have regular observer status in the Committee.
[525] *Ibid.* art. 1.4 (a). The Members must inform the Committee on the publications in which this information will be published. (*Ibid.* art. 5.4).

Committee on any changes in these laws and regulations.[526] Nonetheless, the Committee has expressed its concern that the notification by Members has been very limited.[527] It is, however, also possible that Members notify licensing measures maintained by other Members ('counter-notification'). The Committee has to review at least once every two years the implementation and operation of the Agreement[528] and informs the Council for Trade in Goods on any recent developments.[529]

289. A tenth Committee overseeing a particular WTO agreement and reporting to the Council for Trade in Goods is the *Committee on Trade-Related Investment Measures*.[530] This committee monitors the application and implementation of the Agreement on Trade-Related Investment Measures (TRIMS). It also reports annually on this matter to the Council for Trade in Goods.[531] In addition, this Committee serves as a forum for consultation between Members.[532] Besides these 'general' tasks, this Committee has very few independent powers. It is the Council for Trade in Goods that receives notifications on measures relating to TRIPS,[533] which may grant a longer transition period to developing country Members[534] and who will perform a five-yearly review of TRIMS.[535] It should be noted that there also exists a *Working Group on the Relation Between Trade and Investment*[536] and that the work of the Council for Trade in Services may also involve investment issues.[537]

290. An eleventh, and final, committee coming under the Council for Trade in Goods is the *Committee on Safeguards*. This Committee oversees the implementation of the Agreement on Safeguards and acts as a forum for consultations.[538] Article 12 Agreement on Safeguards sets out a large number of

---

[526] *Ibid.* art. 8.2 (b).
[527] See Sixth Biannual Review of the Implementation and Operation of the Agreement on Import Licensing Procedures, G/LIC/16, 13 November 2006, para. 6.
[528] See for the most recent review: Sixth Biannual Review of the Implementation and Operation of the Agreement on Import Licensing Procedures, *supra* previous note.
[529] The Secretariat will prepare a factual report that will serve as a basis for this review. Art. 7 Agreement on Import Licensing.
[530] Five intergovernmental organizations have regular observer status. It concerns the IMF, the OECD, the UN, UNCTAD and the World Bank.
[531] Art. 7.3 TRIMS. For the most recent report, see Report (2006) of the Committee on Trade-Related Investment Measures, G/L/793, 27 October 2006.
[532] Art. 7.2 TRIMS.
[533] *Ibid.* art. 5.1.
[534] *Ibid.* art. 5.3.
[535] *Ibid.* art. 9.
[536] See *supra* para. 274.
[537] See *infra* para. 293.
[538] Intergovernmental organizations having observer status in this Committee are IMF, UNCTAD and World Bank. *Ad hoc* observer status is granted to the OECD and the ACP Group.

notification requirements. Members have to notify this Committee of the procedures they initiate in order to take safeguard measures and on the application of such safeguard measures, as well as on the outcomes of the required consultations prior to the application of a safeguard measure.[539] The Members have to notify the Committee before taking a provisional safeguard measure.[540] The Committee has to be informed on exceptional safeguard measures applied against Developing Country Members.[541] Finally, also Members' laws, regulations and administrative procedures relating to safeguard measures[542] and the existing measures[543] have to be notified.[544] Members may counter-notify other Members' laws, regulations and measures. The Committee will review Members' notifications,[545] and publish findings as to Members' compliance with respect to the procedural provisions of the Agreement for the application of safeguard measures,[546] assist with consultations,[547] and review proposed retaliation.[548] It reports to the Council for Trade in Goods on the general implementation of the Agreement.[549]

291. Finally, also the *Working Party on State-Trading Enterprises* comes under the Council for Trade in Goods. Article XVII GATT is the main provision dealing with State-Trading Enterprises. The Understanding on the Interpretation of Article XVII GATT set up this Working Party.[550] It has to examine the activities of state-trading enterprises that are notified by Members to the Council for Trade in Goods. This would increase transparency in their activities. The Working Party developed an Illustrative List of relationships between governments and state-trading enterprises.[551] The Council for Trade in Goods adopted this list, showing the kinds of relationships between governments and enterprises, and the kinds of activities, engaged in by these enterprises, which may be relevant for the purposes

---

[539] Art. 12.1 and 12.5 Agreement on Safeguards.
[540] *Ibid.* art. 12.4.
[541] *Ibid.* art. 9.1 *juncto* note 2.
[542] *Ibid.* art. 12.6.
[543] *Ibid.* art. 12.7.
[544] The Members even have the right to notify laws, regulations, administrative procedures and existing measures of another Member which have not been notified by the Member. This is the so-called 'counter-notification'. (art. 12.8 Agreement on Safeguards).
[545] Art. 13.1 (f) Agreement on Safeguards.
[546] *Ibid.* art. 13.1 (b).
[547] *Ibid.* art. 13.1 (c).
[548] *Ibid.* art. 13.1 (e).
[549] *Ibid.* art. 13.1 (a). See for the most recent report: Report (2006) of the Committee on Safeguards to the Council for Trade in Goods, G/L/795, 3 November 2006.
[550] Understanding on the Interpretation of Article XVII of the General Agreement on Trade in Goods, para. 5.
[551] Working Party on State Trading Enterprises, Illustrative List of Relationships Between Governments and State Trading Enterprises and the Kinds of Activities Engaged in by these Enterprises, G/STR/4, 30 July 1999.

of Article XVII.[552] On the basis of Guidelines set up by the Working Party,[553] the WTO Secretariat prepared a background paper titled "Operations of State Trading Enterprises as they Relate to International Trade".[554]

292. It should finally be mentioned that also a *plurilateral Committee* reports to the Council for Trade in Goods. At the Ministerial Conference in Singapore, a Ministerial Declaration on Trade in Information Technology Products was adopted.[555] The *Committee of Participants on the Expansion of Trade in Information Technology Products* was set up by a decision of the Council for Trade in Goods.[556] The Committee conducts negotiations on the broadening of the product coverage of the Declaration on Trade in Information Technology Products. But, to date, this has not been a success. It has also worked on a number of other issues since its inception. These include the examination of classification divergences, consultations on non-tariff barriers, invoking new participants, and discussing implementation matters.

d. Council for Trade in Services

293. The Council for Trade in Services oversees the General Agreement on Trade in Services.[557] The Council reviews the MFN exceptions of the GATS, the Annex on Air Transport Services and the Understanding on Accounting Rates. The Council for Trade in Services has four subsidiary bodies: the Committee on Trade in Financial Services, the Committee on Specific Commitments, the Working Party on Domestic Regulation and the Working Party on GATS Rules.

294. The *Committee on Trade in Financial Services* comes under the Council for Trade in Services.[558] This Committee carries out discussions on matters relating to trade in financial services and may formulate proposals for consideration by the Council. It also monitors compliance with the GATS in the field of Financial

---

[552] Council for Trade in Goods, Minutes of the Meeting of 15 October 1999, G/C/M/41, 22 November 1999, para. 3.1.
[553] Working Party on State Trade Enterprises, Minutes of the Meeting of 6 April 1995, 8 June 1995.
[554] Operations of State Trading Enterprises as they relate to International Trade, G/STR/2, 26 October 1995.
[555] Ministerial Declaration on Trade in Information Technology Products, done at Singapore on 13 December 1996, WT/MIN/96/16.
[556] Council for Trade in Goods, Implementation of the Ministerial Declaration on Trade in Information Technology Products, G/L/160, 2 April 1997.
[557] Observers in the Council for Trade in Services are the IMF, ITU, ITC, UN, UNCTAD and the World Bank. Some intergovernmental organizations have *ad hoc* observer status: International Civil Aviation Organization, World Health Organization and World Tourism Organization.
[558] The ACP Group, the IMF, the World Bank, the OECD, the UN and UNCTAD have observer status in the Committee.

Services.[559] Current work of the Committee concerns mainly the follow-up of the acceptance of the Fifth Protocol to the GATS[560], technical issues such as the distinction between mode 1 and 2 of services supply (in case of cross-border financial services transactions through electronic means)[561] and the gradual opening up of the Chinese financial services market.[562]

295. The *Committee on Specific Commitments* guides the specific commitments that Members make under the GATS.[563] As explained above,[564] the principles of Market Access and National Treatment in the GATS only apply as far as Members have made specific commitments. One of the realizations of the Committee is the *Guidelines for the Scheduling of Specific Commitments under the General Agreement on Trade in Services*.[565] This Committee has also established procedures to be followed when Members want to modify their schedules of specific commitments.[566] The Committee finally also works on the classification of service sectors. The classification of the services sectors is indeed a contentious issue since the services sector is subject to constant change because of technological developments.

296. The *Working Party on Domestic Regulation* drafts disciplines relating to technical standards, licensing and qualification requirements for all services sectors. Until 26 April 1999, this Working Party was known as the Working Party on Professional Services and had a narrower focus. In the field of services, an optimal balance has to be found between liberalization and regulation. The Working Party aims to contribute to this process of regulatory adjustment to avoid that these regulations constituting unnecessary barriers to trade. A major discussion is whether disciplines should be developed per sector or rather 'horizontally', covering all sectors. Until now, the main result of the work in the Working Party on Domestic regulation has been the Disciplines on Domestic Regulation for the Accountancy Sector, adopted by the Services Council on 14 December 1998.[567] The Hong Kong Ministerial Declaration required Members

---

[559] Decision on Financial Services, L/UR-D5/2, 15 April 1994, para. 2.
[560] The Fifth Protocol to the GATS establishes the Financial Services Agreement, which forms the basis for financial services liberalization. In 2007, three Members still had not accepted the Fifth Protocol: Brazil, the Philippines and Jamaica.
[561] See Communication of Brazil on Financial Services and Electronic Commerce, Job(05)/103.
[562] See the discussion in: Committee on Financial Services, Report of the Meeting Held on 19 September 2005, S/FIN/M/50, 23 September 2005.
[563] See *supra* para. 137.
[564] See *supra* paras. 143–145.
[565] Guidelines for the Scheduling of Specific Commitments under the General Agreement on Trade in Services, S/L/92, 23 March 2001.
[566] Procedures for the Certification of Rectifications or Improvements to Schedules of Specific Commitments, S/L/84, 14 April 2000.
[567] Council for Trade in Services, Disciplines on Domestic Regulation for the Accountancy Sector, S/L/63, 17 December 1998.

to develop disciplines on Domestic Regulation before the end of the Doha Round.[568] Members have put forward some proposals, but negotiations have not resulted in any further agreements yet.[569]

297. The GATS is 'work in progress' since many parts of the Agreement need further elaboration through negotiations. This is especially the case for the GATS provisions on safeguards,[570] government procurement[571] and subsidies.[572] A time limit was set for the development of rules on safeguards (no later than three years from the date of entry into force of the WTO Agreement) and government procurement (no later than two years).[573] To this end, the Council for Trade in Services established a *Working Party on GATS Rules.* However, deadlines have been regularly extended and until now, no further rules on safeguards, government procurement or subsidies have been agreed within GATS. The Ministerial Declaration of Hong Kong called upon WTO Members to "intensify their efforts to conclude the negotiations on rule-making under GATS Articles X, XIII, and XV in accordance with their respective mandates and timelines".[574] However, negotiations are still in progress. With regard to safeguard measures, the WTO Secretariat has prepared a Note summarizing the main views of Members.[575] Concerning subsidies, discussions are going on to agree upon a working definition of subsidy.[576] With regard to government procurement, the European Communities has proposed a legal text for an Annex to the GATS on government procurement, which appears to form a basis for further discussions.[577]

---

[568] Ministerial Declaration of Hong Kong, *supra* note 19, Annex C.5.
[569] See Working Party on Domestic Regulation, Report of the Meeting Held on 19 and 20 June 2006, S/WPDR/M/35, 14 August 2006.
[570] See Art. X.1 GATS.
[571] *Ibid.* art. XIII.2.
[572] *Ibid.* art. XV.1. Members only recognized that subsidies may, in certain circumstances, have distortive effects on trade in services.
[573] With regard to subsidies, it was only indicated in the GATS that a future work programme should determine how, and in what time frame, the negotiations on such disciplines will be conducted.
[574] Ministerial Declaration of Hong Kong, *supra* note 19, Annex C.4.
[575] See Working Party on GATS Rules, Report of the Meeting of 26 June 2006, S/WPGR/M/56, 4 July 2006.
[576] *Ibid.*
[577] For the proposed text, see Working Party on GATS Rules, Communication from the European Communities. Government Procurement Services, S/WPGR/W/54, 20 June 2006.

e. Council for Trade-Related Aspects of Intellectual Property Rights

298. The TRIPS Council is responsible for administering the TRIPS Agreement.[578] Members have to notify the TRIPS Council of their relevant laws and regulations.[579] This improves the transparency of the regulations on intellectual property. Members also have to notify exceptions to MFN following from international agreements that existed prior to the entry into force of the TRIPS[580] and have to notify the existence of contact points to exchange information on the sale of goods which infringe rules on intellectual property.[581] To implement these notification obligations, the TRIPS Council has adopted guidelines.[582]

299. In accordance with Article 27.3.b TRIPS, the TRIPS Council reviews the possibility of Members of excluding certain plants, animals and biological processes from patentability. The Council also reviews the relationship between TRIPS and the Convention on Biological Diversity[583] as well as the protection of traditional knowledge and folklore.[584]

300. A final important issue that is discussed in the TRIPS Council is the role of TRIPS in public health. In a follow-up on a separate declaration during the Doha Ministerial Conference (claiming that TRIPS does not and should not prevent Members from taking measures to protect public health[585]) negotiations in the TRIPS Council led to the Decision by the General Council on the

---

[578] Under Art. 71, it reviews the implementation of the Agreement. Intergovernmental Organizations that have observer status in the TRIPS Council are the IMF, FAO, International Union for the Protection of New Varieties of Plants (UPOV), OECD, UN, UNCTAD, World Bank, World Customs Organization (WCO), World Intellectual Property Organization (WIPO). The WHO has *ad hoc* observer status. When discussions concern TRIPS and Public Health, also UNAIDS has observer status.
[579] Art. 63.2 TRIPS.
[580] *Ibid.* art. 4 (d).
[581] *Ibid.* art. 69. The use of certain possibilities of the Paris Convention, Berne Convention or Rome Convention also have to be notified. See art. 2, art. 1.3 and art. 3.1 TRIPS.
[582] Technical Cooperation Handbook on Notification Requirements, WT/TC/NOTIF/TRIPS/1, 15 October 1996.
[583] Convention on Biological Diversity, done at Rio de Janeiro on 5 June 1992, *UNTS* No. 30619.
[584] There is a fear that traditional knowledge or folklore will be appropriated by companies when they claim a patent on it. Local and indigenous communities would then not be able to enjoy the benefits of their knowledge. The Doha Ministerial Conference has put these issues on the Agenda of the WTO. See Ministerial Declaration of Doha, *supra* note 40, para. 19. For recent discussions in the TRIPS Council, see Council for Trade-Related Aspects of Intellectual Property Rights, Minutes of the Meeting held in Centre William Rappard on 14–15 March 2006, IP/C/M/50, 16 May 2006, paras. 10–86.
[585] Ministerial Declaration on the TRIPS Agreement and Public Health, adopted in Doha on 14 November 2002, WT/MIN(01)/DEC/2, 20 November 2001, *supra* note 510, para. 4.

Implementation of paragraph 6 of the Doha Declaration on the TRIPS Agreement and Public Health.[586] This decision clarifies the conditions for compulsory licences and makes the import of cheap drugs, made under compulsory licence, in poorer countries possible. This decision will be made permanent when two thirds of Members have formally accepted it. It is hoped that this will be achieved by 1 December 2007.[587]

301. The TRIPS Council also meets in "special sessions". These involve negotiations on a multilateral system for notifying and registering geographic indications for wines and spirits, under the Doha Development Agenda.

2. *Dispute Settlement Body*

302. The General Council acting as Dispute Settlement Body deals with all disputes between Members with regard to one or more of the WTO Agreements.[588] The Dispute Settlement Body (hereinafter also 'DSB') has the authority to establish Panels, adopt Panel reports, scrutinize implementation of recommendations and authorize retaliatory measures if the losing party to a dispute does not abide by the Panel's recommendations.[589] Decisions in the DSB are made by consensus.[590] The DSB has two subsidiaries: the Panels of experts, established for each arising dispute, and the Standing Appellate Body, a permanent body dealing with appeals against Panel reports.

303. The Panels are similar to a court of law, with the important difference that the members are chosen from a list[591] in consultation with the parties that are involved in the dispute. In the (rare) case that the parties do not agree, the WTO Director-General will appoint them.[592] The Secretariat maintains an indicative list of governmental and non-governmental individuals that qualify to sit on a Panel. WTO Members may from time to time propose new individuals for inclusion in the list. These persons will be included upon approval by the DSB. The specific areas of expertise of the individuals should be indicated.[593] Panel Members are to be selected with a view to ensuring their independence, a

---

[586] Implementation of paragraph 6 of the Doha Declaration on the TRIPS Agreement and Public Health, *supra* note 510.
[587] See also *supra* para. 152.
[588] Art. IV.3 WTO Agreement.
[589] Art. 2.1 DSU.
[590] *Ibid.* art. 2.4.
[591] The Secretariat maintains an indicative list of governmental and non-governmental individuals that qualify to sit on a Panel. WTO Members may from time to time add individuals to this list.
[592] Art. 8.7 DSU.
[593] *Ibid.* art. 8.4.

sufficiently diverse background and a wide spectrum of experience.[594] Additional guarantees are elaborated upon in the Rules of Conduct for the Understanding on Rules and Procedures Concerning the Settlement of Disputes (see *infra* para. 337).[595]

304. The Appellate Body consists of seven persons, who are appointed for a four-year term. They have to be persons with demonstrated expertise in law, international trade and the subject matter of the covered agreements generally. They cannot be affiliated to any government and shall not participate in the consideration of any disputes that would create a direct or indirect conflict of interest.[596] The Appellate Body hears appeals against Panel reports. It has a Secretariat at its disposal, which is separate and independent from the WTO Secretariat.[597]

See Chapter IV, § 3. Dispute Settlement.

3. *Trade Policy Review Body*

305. In order to facilitate international trade[598], the WTO provides to individuals and companies reviews of Members' trade policies. This mechanism is called the Trade Policy Review Mechanism (TPRM). The reviews are conducted by the Trade Policy Review Body. This Body is the third manifestation of the General Council. These reviews are aimed at increasing transparency and understanding of the trade policies of Members.[599] They are also intended to improve the quality of public and intergovernmental debate on trade issues and to enable a multilateral assessment of the impact of these policies on global trade.[600] They are not meant

---

[594] *Ibid.* art. 8.2.
[595] Rules of Conduct for the Understanding on Rules and Procedures Concerning the Settlement of Disputes, adopted by the WTO in December 1996.
[596] Art. 17.3 DSU.
[597] Document on the Establishment of the Appellate Body, WT/DSB/1, 19 June 1995, para. 17.
[598] According to section A.i Trade Policy Review Mechanism, the mechanism wants to contribute "to the smoother functioning of the multilateral trading system, by achieving greater transparency in and understanding of the trade policies and practices of Members".
[599] Observers in the TPRB are the European Bank for Reconstruction and Development, the European Free Trade Association, the FAO, the IMF, the World Bank, the OECD and UNCTAD.
[600] P. Van den Bossche, *supra* note 30, p. 423. The trade policy reviews already started at the beginning of the Uruguay Round. The Participants in this Round agreed already at the Ministerial meeting in December 1988 to set up the reviews. See World Trade Organization, *Understanding the WTO*, *supra* note 178, p. 53. In fact, the mechanism is based on the 1979 Understanding on Notification, Consultation, Dispute Settlement and Surveillance, adopted at Tokyo on 28 November 1979, L/4907, under which Contracting Parties agreed to conduct a regular and systematic review of developments in the trading system. See B. Hoekman and M. Kostecki, *supra* note 9, p. 63. See also J. Francois, 'Trade Policy Transparency and Investor Confidence – The Implications of an Effective Trade Policy Review Mechanism',

to serve as an enforcement mechanism of specific obligations under the multilateral WTO Agreements or for dispute settlement procedures, or to impose new policy commitments on Members.[601] Nevertheless, the 'naming and shaming' of non-complying Members may have a certain impact on Members. The frequency of the reviews depends on the share of a Member in world trade. The four Members with the largest share are subject to a two-yearly review. The next 16 largest traders are reviewed every four years and all other Members every six years.[602] It may be agreed that developing countries will be reviewed at longer intervals. Members have to prepare a report for the review which will be considered by the Trade Policy Review Body, together with a report prepared by the WTO Trade Policies Review Division of the WTO Secretariat.[603] During the meeting of the Trade Policy Review Body, two Members lead the discussion and the Trade Policy Review Body chairman summarizes it.[604] Between reviews, Members have to provide annual updates of their statistical trade information and provide details of possible major policy changes.[605]

306. It has been stated that the TPRM helps shift the balance of power in favour of the developing countries. Larger traders are indeed submitted more frequently to reviews.[606] Moreover, interest groups are provided with information on the pros and the cons of the trade policies of certain countries. Unfortunately, TPRM reports have in the past not been published on a regular basis, which limited their availability.[607] In addition, even if available, the reports are often difficult to understand and to draw conclusions from. They often fail to determine the economic effects of the trade policy at issue.[608]

Review of International Economics (2001), pp. 303–316 and B. HOEKMAN and P. C. MAVROIDIS, 'WTO Dispute Settlement, Transparency and Surveillance', http://www1.worldbank.org/wbiep/trade/papers_2000/dispute_settlement.pdf.

[601] Section A.i Trade Policy Review Mechanism.
[602] Trade Policy Review Mechanism, C.ii.
[603] B. HOEKMAN and M. KOSTECKI, *supra* note 9, p. 63.
[604] See W. DAVEY, *supra* note 412, p. 59.
[605] Trade Policy Review Mechanism, D. See K. ADAMANTOPOULOS, *supra* note 389, p. 71.
[606] J. FRANCOIS, 'Maximizing the Benefits of the Trade Policy Review Mechanism for Developing Countries', *Mimeo* (1999), www.worldbank.org/trade.
[607] Appraisal of the Operation of the Trade Policy Review Mechanism, WT/MIN(99)/2, 9 October 1999, para. 12.
[608] B. HOEKMAN and M. KOSTECKI, *supra* note 9, p. 64 and P. VAN DEN BOSSCHE, *supra* note 30, p. 423.

D. WTO SECRETARIAT

1. Secretariat

307. The WTO only possesses a Secretariat in Geneva[609], consisting of 637 civil servants in 2007.[610] The Secretariat is headed by the Director-General.[611] As has been indicated, the Secretariat has no formal decision-making power. The WTO is Member-driven: thus it is Members who decide how the organization will proceed. Nevertheless, the Secretariat is of great importance. It offers technical assistance to developing countries, conducts studies, keeps the public and the media informed on the WTO and performs a not-to-be-underestimated role as clerk (and writer) for the Panels within the framework of the Dispute Settlement Mechanism.

308. One of the few fields where the Secretariat can take action on its own responsibility is in the undertaking of periodical reviews of Members' trade policies.[612] The members of the Secretariat have important technical skills and are familiar with all kinds of trade issues. This makes them invaluable for assistance in Panel procedures. The Secretariat also has an important role to play in the numerous informal and formal interactions with not only governments but also other intergovernmental and non-governmental organizations.

2. Director-General

309. The present Director-General of the WTO is Pascal Lamy (the former EU Commissioner for Trade). The Director-General has no power of initiative. He or she cannot initiate dispute settlement proceedings against a Member, cannot pass judgments on the conformity of a certain Member's trade policy with the WTO rules and cannot provide authoritative interpretations of WTO law. The Director-General has no real agenda-setting power either. He or she may nonetheless convene General Council meetings.[613]

310. The Director-General is seen as "the guardian of the collective interest of Member States".[614] He or she will try to facilitate negotiations and act as a go-between when negotiations reach deadlock. The Director-General tries to remind and encourage Members to choose the road of multilateral trade liberalization. The Director-General has no right of initiative in the decision-

---

[609] Art. VI WTO Agreement.
[610] This number seems very small for such an important international organization. Nonetheless, it gives a somewhat inaccurate picture, since WTO cooperates with a large number of civil servants in the different capitals of its Members.
[611] See *infra* paras. 309–310.
[612] See Annex 3 to the WTO Agreement.
[613] See rule 2 of the rules of procedure for sessions of General Council.
[614] B. HOEKMAN and M. KOSTECKI, *supra* note 9, p. 54.

making. It is, however, always possible that the Director-General or the Secretariat make proposals. Such happens indeed on an informal basis.[615]

E. LEGITIMACY, DEMOCRACY AND EFFICIENCY IN THE WTO

311. The recurring protests that can be seen each time the Ministerial Conference of the WTO meets show clearly the growing dissatisfaction with the way the WTO is functioning today. The international trade rules that are being developed and applied in the organization are seen as having an important impact on the daily lives of ordinary people. Still, the rules seem to fail to deliver the goals proclaimed in the preamble of the WTO Agreement ("raising standards of living, ensuring full employment and a large and steadily growing volume of real income and effective demand, and expanding the production of and trade in goods"). This is felt mainly in developing countries, for which the WTO does not appear to live up to the expectations. Yet, also citizens in industrialized countries experience the negative effects of trade liberalization: jobs moving abroad to low-wage countries, environmental protection measures being rejected by the Dispute Settlement Body of the WTO, human health protection measures being found WTO-inconsistent etc. It is claimed that the WTO develops and advances rules that are supported only by a minority of rich WTO Members (lack of horizontal democratic participation) and that it insufficiently takes into account the considerations of the populations in its Member States (lack of vertical democratic participation). It should be noted, however, that increased democratic participation may to some extent decrease efficiency in the policymaking system within the WTO, which is already fraught with delays and stalemates.

312. *Horizontal* democratic participation would be insufficient, since only a few countries would dominate the political branch (especially the 'Quad' (see *supra* para. 217)). As explained, in principle, decisions are reached within the WTO when every Member agrees to the new agreement. In practice, however, the decision-making process works by consensus. This supposes that there will only be a vote when consensus cannot be reached. If this occurs, every Member government has one vote and thus can potentially veto decisions with which it does not agree.[616] The Member will thus have to be persuaded to accept the proposed agreement. This immediately suggests that the GATT/WTO negotiation rounds are extremely sensitive to power talk and intimidation. The relevant power not only includes economic power (e.g. the size of a country's market), but also power in other spheres. Through *intra*-WTO linkages (*i.e.* the linkages in the

---

[615] M. FOOTER, *supra* note 309, p. 134.
[616] WTO, *WTO Policy Issues for Parliamentarians* (Geneva, WTO Publications 2001), p. 14.

'package' of negotiations such as e.g. trading market access for textiles in exchange for pharmaceutical patent recognition) and more subtle exertions of influence, bargains are struck.[617] Moreover, the richer the country, the more resources it has to defend and support its proposals and positions. Often, developing countries do not have enough civil servants to attend all WTO meetings, let alone to prepare them sufficiently.[618] Since, in the case of decision-making by consensus, a decision is agreed upon as soon as no Member present in the meeting opposes, this does not guarantee the rights of Members that are absent.[619] The fact that there are no objections by Members present does not necessarily mean that a majority of countries agree. On the other hand, a system where each Member, no matter how important in world trade, has a veto right may also seriously hamper effective decision-making in the WTO. The veto by one Member may block further progress in the trade negotiations for reasons that may have nothing to do with the specific negotiations in question. It thereby is an important obstacle to increased efficiency in WTO policymaking.

313. Several proposals for reform have been made to improve effective decision-making in the WTO. At the same time, attempts are made to take into account the requirements of horizontal democratic participation. It has for instance been suggested that a high-level executive committee should be created composed of the major trading nations and representatives of groupings of countries.[620] Such system is currently applicable in the World Bank and the IMF. Because of the lack of a formalized system that would divide the decision-makers in specific groups, informal groupings take the lead in negotiations, often to the detriment of voices of smaller (mostly developing) countries. It is also sometimes suggested that a system of weighted voting should be introduced, based on the trading power of each WTO Member.[621] However, such a system would hardly increase the horizontal democratic participation in the WTO. The perceived lack of efficient and democratic policymaking in the WTO was one of the issues addressed in the *Report on the Future of the WTO*, drafted by the Consultative Board to the Director-General of the WTO on the eve of the tenth anniversary of the WTO.[622]

---

[617] J. ATIK, 'Democratizing the WTO', *George Washington International Law Review* (2001), p. 469.
[618] P. SUTHERLAND and J. SEWELL, 'Challenges facing the WTO and policies to address global governance', in G.P. SAMPSON (ed.), *The Role of the World Trade Organization in Global Governance* (Tokyo, United Nations University Press 2001), p. 88.
[619] B. HOEKMAN and M. KOSTECKI, *supra* note 9, p. 57.
[620] See A. NARLIKAR, 'The Politics of Participation: Decision-Making Processes and Developing Countries in the World Trade Organization', *The Round Table* (2002), p. 177.
[621] See T. COTTIER and S. TAKENOSHITA, 'The Balance of Power in WTO Decision-Making: Towards Weighted Voting in Legislative Response', *Aussenwirtschaft* (2003), pp. 184–186.
[622] See *The Future of the WTO. Addressing Institutional Challenges in the New Millennium*. Report by the Consultative Board to the Director-General Supachai Panitchpakdi, (Geneva, World Trade Organization 2004), 83 p.

The Report noted that the consensus decision-making approach has many strengths (e.g. each Member has a veto and it entails a larger sense of legitimacy).[623] Even though there are also disadvantages with the consensus system (*inter alia* rigidity), the Consultative Board did not find it wise to reform the consensus system. It only made two recommendations. First, WTO Members should examine whether there are a number of (e.g. procedural) decisions that are less contentious and therefore can easily be adopted by voting.[624] The second recommendation was to install a system that would require Members to declare in writing the reasons why they used their veto powers against a decision which otherwise has very broad consensus support.[625] It would also be useful, according to the Consultative Board, to re-examine the plurilateral approach to WTO negotiations, where some Members would be allowed to proceed when others refuse to do so ('variable geometry').[626] One could even go so far as using a system like the 'Scheduling' in the GATS: each Member can individually take commitments on how far its liberalization commitments would go.[627]

314. Criticism is also often levelled at the lack of *vertical* democratic participation in the WTO. Citizens in the States that are Members of the WTO have the feeling that by agreeing – through their parliaments – to become Members of the WTO, they have given away some autonomous policymaking. Although this is not uncommon in international relations (agreeing to a treaty necessarily means that a country is no longer pursuing certain policy objectives in a unilateral manner, but is taking into account the interests of other parties to the treaty), in the case of the WTO, the transfer of domestic powers is particularly sensitive. The matters that the WTO deals with appear to most people as highly abstract. Nevertheless, decisions made within the WTO have clear and tangible effects on people's lives. Citizens feel that decisions are being made in which the subjects themselves no longer have sufficient democratic impact through their representatives in parliament. Therefore, there is an increasingly widespread perception that the WTO lacks adequate democratic legitimacy. The WTO may have a '*democratic deficit*', much in the same way as is debated in case of the European Union.[628]

315. It is sometimes argued that the existence of a democratic deficit within the WTO should not be feared. The agreements that are reached are monitored and

---

[623] *Ibid.* paras. 281–282.
[624] *Ibid.* para. 288.
[625] *Ibid.* para. 289.
[626] *Ibid.* para. 300.
[627] *Ibid.* para. 304.
[628] See R. Howse, 'How to Begin to Think About the "Democratic Deficit" at the WTO', in S. Griller, (ed.), *International Economic Governance and Non-Economic Concerns: New Challenges for the International Legal Order*, (Vienna, Springer 2003), pp. 79–101.

approved by national parliaments in many Member States.[629] Diplomats who negotiate the agreements are in principle responsible to a democratically elected minister. However, this formal legitimacy is mostly insufficient to guarantee effective democratic participation by the people in decision-making that directly affects them. The fact that national parliaments have the power to approve or reject an agreement that is the outcome of WTO negotiations is often not an appropriate and effective safeguard.[630]

316. It is first important to note that being a democratic State is not a condition for WTO membership (see *supra* para. 204-211) on the accession of new Members. It has been suggested that requiring a minimal level of democratic practice from WTO Members could possibly help further democratize the WTO.[631] Even if such amendment of the WTO Agreement were to be possible, it remains questionable whether a WTO Member should be sanctioned when it violates democratic standards.[632]

317. But even if all WTO Members had vigilant parliaments, their control would always be quite limited. Parliaments do not really have the option of amending the agreement resulting from WTO negotiations. Since negotiation is done through 'packages', the rejection of the package because of one contentious issue will immediately mean a rejection of all other components, which might be very advantageous for the country. This undoubtedly puts pressure on the parliaments to approve. Since the negotiating agents have considerable agenda-setting ability, they are able to combine components in such a way that the parliament has no other choice than to approve the package. The fear of forgoing the advantageous aspects induces parliament to approve. Although this certainly helps achieve agreements with something advantageous for everyone and to reach a compromise on contentious issues, the impression remains that it also allows negotiation agents to manipulate the approval by parliament.

318. Some proposals to enhance parliamentary control of the WTO have been made. In its resolution on the preparation of the Seattle conference, the European

---

[629] See J. BACCHUS, 'A Few Thoughts on Legitimacy, Democracy, and the WTO', *Journal of International Economic Law* (2004), pp. 667–677 and M. MOORE, 'After Seattle – The WTO and Developing Countries, Formal Evidence to the International Development Committee of the House of Commons and Remarks to the All Party Parliamentary Group on Overseas Development of the House of Commons', 7 March 2000, available on http://www.wto.org/english/news_e/spmm_e/spmm26_e.htm.

[630] See E.-U., PETERSMANN, 'European and International Constitutional Law: Time for Promoting 'Cosmopolitan Democracy' in the WTO' in G. DE BURCA and J. SCOTT (eds.), *The EU and the WTO: Legal and Constitutional Issues* (Oxford, Oxford University Press 2001), p. 98.

[631] G. Fox, 'Strengthening the State', *Indiana Journal of Global Legal Studies* (1999), p. 63.

[632] See J. ATIK, 'Democratizing the WTO', *George Washington International Law Review* (2001), p. 466.

Parliament referred to the need for a permanent body to provide for parliamentary scrutiny.[633] The idea of a 'consultative parliamentary assembly at the WTO' was advanced by Pascal LAMY, when he was EU Commissioner for Trade.[634] Moreover, former Director-General of the WTO Mike MOORE admitted that parliamentarians have an essential role to play with regard to the ratification of the results of negotiations concluded in the WTO.[635] Such a parliamentary assembly was apparently created at Seattle but was never composed. Nevertheless, there have been a number of Parliamentary Conferences on the WTO, as a joint undertaking of the Inter-Parliamentary Union and the European Parliament. The first ever global parliamentary meeting on international trade was organized by the Inter-Parliamentary Union and took place in the Geneva International Conference Centre on 8 and 9 June 2001.[636]

There have been organized parliamentary meetings parallel to the Ministerial Conferences in Doha (11 November 2001[637]), in Cancún (9 and 12 September 2003[638]) and in Hong Kong (12 and 15 December 2005[639]). Although the WTO seems to recognize the importance of these meetings and encourages them, they still happen *outside* its institutional framework. There was no reference to a consultative parliamentary assembly in the Ministerial Declaration at Doha or in the Concluding Ministerial Declaration of Cancún. In its resolution on the ministerial conference of Cancún the European Parliament called for "enhanced democratic accountability and openness of the WTO and for the creation of a WTO Parliamentary Assembly".[640] It is very unlikely that such WTO Parliamentary Assembly will be created soon.

---

[633] European Parliament Resolution on the communication from the Commission to the Council and the European Parliament on the EU approach to the WTO Millennium Round, COM(1999), 18 November 1999, O.J. 2000, C189/213, para 74; European Parliament Resolution on the Third Ministerial Conference of the World Trade Organization in Seattle, 15 December 1999, O.J. 2000, C296/121.

[634] P. LAMY, 'What are the Options After Seattle?', Speech to European Parliament, 25 January 2000, http://europa.eu.int/comm/commissioners/lamy/speeches_articles/spla09_en.htm.

[635] See 'The WTO: The Role of Parliamentarians', *Public Symposium: The Doha Development Agenda and Beyond, Summary Report*, 6 May 2002, http://www.revistainterforum.com/english/articles/050602artprin_en3.html.

[636] See Final Declaration of the Parliamentary Meeting on International Trade, Geneva, 8–9 June 2001, available on http://www.ipu.org/splz-e/trade01dclr.htm.

[637] See Parliamentary Meeting on the Occasion of the fourth WTO Ministerial Conference in Doha, http://www.ipu.org/splz-e/doha.htm.

[638] See Cancún Session of the Parliamentary Conference on the WTO, http://www.ipu.org/splz-e/cancun.htm#post-doha.

[639] See Hong Kong Session of the Parliamentary Conference on the WTO, http://www.ipu.org/splz-e/hk05/advance.pdf.

[640] European Parliament Resolution on the Fifth Ministerial Conference of the WTO in Cancún, 25 September 2003, para. 20, available on http://europa.eu.int/comm/trade/issues/newround/doha_da/epr250903_en.htm.

Chapter IV

319. It is not only the lack of parliamentary involvement within the WTO that is being criticized. There is also a widespread call for NGO involvement in the WTO.[641] The WTO is now coming to the realization that involvement of NGOs can be an added value. On the practical arrangements for NGO involvement, see *supra* para. 202).

320. Because of the ineffective decision-making in the legislative branch of the WTO, it appears to many that the main source of WTO law-making is now dispute settlement by Panels and the Appellate Body.[642] Therefore, there is an often-heard call for putting a halt to the 'judicial activism' by Panels and the Appellate Body.[643] Nevertheless, much of the criticism on the outcome of certain dispute settlement decisions in fact should be directed at the inadequacy and poor drafting of the WTO Agreements themselves.[644]

§ 3. DISPUTE SETTLEMENT MECHANISM

321. The WTO's Dispute Settlement Mechanism is without a doubt the cream of the crop of the WTO law.[645] The mechanism's efficient functioning explains to a

---

[641] According to Daniel ESTY "NGOs offer the promise of serving as a 'connective tissue' that will help bridge the gap between WTO decision-makers and the distant constituencies which they are meant to serve, thereby ensuring that the WTO's actions are perceived as responsive and fair." See D. ESTY, 'Non-Governmental Organizations at the World Trade Organization: Cooperation, Competition or Exclusion', *Journal of International Economic Law* (1998), pp. 125–126.

[642] See P. STEPHAN, 'The New International Law – Legitimacy, Accountability, Authority and Freedom in the New Global Order', *University of Colorado Law Review* (1999), pp. 1559–1560.

[643] See C. BARFIELD, *Free Trade, Sovereignty, Democracy: The Future of the World Trade Organization*, (Washington, AEI Press 2001), ix+251 p.

[644] See L. BARTELS, 'The Separation of Powers in the WTO: How to Avoid Judicial Activism', *I.C.L.Q.* (2004), p. 868. BARTELS notes that there would only be danger of judicial activism when the Panel or Appellate Body (i) is deciding a case where the law is genuinely indeterminate and (ii) where a decision by the quasi-judicial organs interferes with the powers of political organs. *Ibid.* p. 849.

[645] The former Director-General R. RUGGIERO called the Dispute Settlement Mechanism *"the WTO's most individual contribution to the stability of the global economy"*. For general books on this issue see *inter alia* J. CAMERON and K. CAMPBELL (eds.), *Dispute Resolution in the World Trade Organization*, (London, Cameron May 1998), 421 p.; P. GALLENGHER, *Guide to the Dispute Settlement*, (The Hague, Kluwer 2002), 148 p.; J.M. MATHIS, 'GATT Dispute Settlement Procedures', in *The Trade Policy of the European Community*, (Maastricht, European Institute for Public Administration 1993), pp. 19–23; F. ORTINO and E.-U. PETERSMANN (eds.), *The WTO Dispute Settlement System 1995–2003*, (The Hague, Kluwer Law International 2003), 640 p.; D. PALMETER and P.C. MAVROIDIS, *Dispute Settlement in the World Trade Organization. Practice and Procedure*, (The Hague, Kluwer Law International 1999), xvi + 313 p.; P. PESCATORE, *Handbook of GATT dispute settlement*, (Ardsley on Hudson, Transnational, Deventer, Kluwer, 1991–1995, 2 vol.); E.U. PETERSMANN, *The GATT/WTO Dispute Settlement System: International Law, International Organizations and Dispute Settlement*, (London, Kluwer 1997), xvii + 344 p.; E.U. PETERSMANN (ed.), *International Trade Law and the GATT/WTO Dispute Settlement System*,

Institutional Framework

large extent the WTO's success. Although during the GATT era (1947–1994) there was no fixed terms for the settlement of disputes and decisions could easily be blocked, since the Marrakech Agreement dispute settlement is the showpiece of the WTO. The dispute settlement system is central to providing "security and predictability to the multilateral trading system".[646] Knowing that the rules that Members have agreed to regulate the conduct of international trade will be respected, and if not, enforced, is essential for traders. During the GATT era, dispute settlement was characterized by its exclusively diplomatic character. In the WTO it concerns a quasi-judicial system, which nevertheless still shows some diplomatic elements. There is still a preference for consultations and mutual informal settlement of a dispute among the concerned Members.

322. The original principles for the management of disputes are laid down in Articles XXII and XXIII of the GATT.[647] More elaborated rules governing dispute settlement are attached as Annex 2 to the WTO Agreement. The *Understanding on Rules and Procedures Governing the Settlement of Disputes* (DSU) applies to consultations and the settlement of disputes between Members concerning the rights and obligations included in the Agreements in Annex 1 to the WTO Agreement, the WTO Agreement itself[648] and all understandings taken in isolation or in combination with any other covered agreement,[649] as well as the Plurilateral Trade Agreements.[650] It should be noted that some of the annexed

---

(London, Kluwer Law International 1997), xviii + 704 p.; E.U. PETERSMANN, 'The Dispute Settlement System of the World Trade Organization and the Evolution of the GATT Dispute Settlement System since 1948', *Common Market Law Review* (1994), pp. 1157–1244; P.T. STOLL, 'World Trade, Dispute Settlement', *in* R. BERNHARDT (ed.), *Encyclopedia of Public International Law*, (Amsterdam, North Holland, IV), pp. 1520–1529; E.-U. PETERSMANN, *The GATT/WTO Dispute Settlement System: International Law, International Organizations and Dispute Settlement*, (London, Kluwer 1997), xvii + 344 p.; T.P. STEWART and A.S. DWYER, *Handbook on WTO Trade Remedy Disputes. The First Six Years (1995–2000)*, (Ardsley, Transnational Publishers 2001), xvii + 560 p. and G. VERHOOSEL, *National Treatment and WTO Dispute Settlement: Adjudicating the Boundaries of Regulatory Autonomy*, (Oxford, Hart 2002), xi + 124 p.

[646] Art. 3.2 DSU.
[647] *Ibid.* art. 3.1. These basic rules, which date from the pre-WTO era, were obviously not sufficient to guide the dispute settlement procedures. The GATT 1947 provisions were to be complemented with an elaborated dispute settlement system in the framework of the ITO. As explained, the ITO never came into being. See J. JACKSON, *The World Trade Organization. Constitution and Jurisprudence*, *supra* note 29, p. 65.
[648] Art. XVI.4 is a frequent basis for complaints.
[649] Thus also a violation of the DSU can be challenged.
[650] Art. 1.1 DSU. Note again that the applicability of the dispute settlement to the plurilateral agreements is subject to the adoption of a decision by the parties to such agreement setting out the terms for the application of the DSU to the individual agreement. This decision may specify any special or additional rules or procedures. See Appendix 1 to the DSU. The Committee on Government Procurement has adopted such decision, but not the Committee on Trade in Civil Aircraft.

trade agreements contain special dispute settlement provisions.[651] In case of conflict with the general dispute settlement rules, the specific rules apply.[652]

A. ACCESSIBILITY OF THE WTO DISPUTE SETTLEMENT SYSTEM AND *LOCUS STANDI*

323. It is first of all important to consider who may participate in WTO dispute settlement. The dispute settlement system of the WTO is only available to Members who can participate as parties or third parties. Intergovernmental organizations, regional or local authorities or private companies, non-governmental organizations or individuals cannot pursue claims before this mechanism. Yet, it should be recognized that these actors can still try to persuade their government to bring a case before the WTO. Many countries have adopted regulations setting out procedures to make this possible.[653]

324. A further question is whether a Member needs to have a legal interest in order to initiate a dispute settlement procedure. This concerns the issue of *standing*. It is a general principle of international law that a Member needs to have a legal interest in order to participate in a claim.[654] Nonetheless, the Appellate Body noted that there is no DSU provision requiring such 'legal interest'.[655] Indeed, Members have broad discretion whether or not to bring a case.[656] Being a producer and having a potential export interest in the product in question would be sufficient. Moreover, due to increased interdependence between Members, they have a "greater stake in enforcing WTO rules than in the past".[657] Yet, the Appellate Body warned that these findings should not be seen as a general principle applied to all disputes.[658]

---

[651] Enumerated in Appendix 2 to the DSU.
[652] Art. 1.2 DSU.
[653] See for the European Community: Council Regulation (EC) No. 3286/94 of 22 December 1994 laying down Community procedures in the field of the common commercial policy in order to ensure the exercise of the Community's rights under international trade rules, in particular those established under the auspices of the World Trade Organization, O.J., 1994, L349/71 and for the United States: Section 301 *et seq.* of the United States Trade Act of 1974, 19 USC. §2411.
[654] See I. BROWNLIE, *Principles of Public International Law*, (Oxford, Claredon Press 1990), p. 446.
[655] Appellate Body in the Appellate Body Report: European Communities – Regime for the Importation, Sale and Distribution of Bananas, WT/DS27/AB/R, (25 September 1997), para. 132.
[656] *Ibid.* para. 135.
[657] *Ibid.* para. 136.
[658] *Ibid.* para. 138.

B. LEGAL BASIS FOR INITIATING A WTO DISPUTE SETTLEMENT CASE

325. Each of the WTO Agreements contains one or more provisions on consultation and dispute settlement. These provisions set out when a Member can have recourse to the WTO Dispute Settlement System.[659] The basic provisions that set out the courses of action are Article XXII and XXIII.1 GATT and Article XXIII GATS. Provisions relating to dispute settlement in most other WTO Agreements refer to these provisions. Article XXII GATT on consultations will be discussed in the next paragraph. Some preliminary attention should be paid to Article XXIII.1 GATT, which is a central provision for WTO dispute settlement.

326. As explained, the WTO Agreements should ensure the efficient conduct of international trade, without barriers and discriminatory treatment. If WTO Members experience that trade practices by other Members nevertheless impede trade, they should be able to assess this problem through the relevant WTO bodies. Article XXIII.1 provides such possibility in case any benefit accruing directly or indirectly to Member under any WTO Agreement[660] is "nullified or impaired". 'Nullification' means that the attainment of the objectives in the WTO Agreements is wholly or partially denied. 'Impairment' means that the attainment of these objectives is impeded. This nullification or impairment must be the result of one of the scenarios specified in subparagraphs (a), (b) and (c) of Article XXIII.1 GATT. These scenarios involve (a) violation complaints, (b) non-violation complaints and (c) situation complaints.[661]

327. A Member can introduce a *violation complaint* if it proves that two separate conditions are fulfilled.[662] First, there must be a violation of the terms of the GATT or any covered agreement. Second, this violation must amount to a nullification or impairment.[663] Nevertheless, GATT practice showed that once a

---

[659] UNCTAD, *Course on Dispute Settlement. WTO Module 3.1 Overview*, (New York/Geneva, United Nations 2003), available on http://www.unctad.org/en/docs//edmmisc232add11_en.pdf, 44–45.
[660] Art. XXIII.1 (a) only refers to "this Agreement", which means the GATT. However, as explained, other WTO Agreements refer to art. XXIII and thus the same conditions for addressing impediments to international trade under the WTO bodies apply.
[661] Note that situation complaints are not provided for under the GATS. Furthermore, art. 64.2 TRIPS excluded non-violation and situation complaints for the first five years from the entry into force of the WTO Agreement. The TRIPS Council had to examine the scope and modalities of for such complaints during the period of five years. Despite the passing of this period, the TRIPS Council has not submitted any recommendations. There is disagreement among WTO Members whether this means that now also non-violation and situation complaints can be brought. Still, until now, no such complaints were brought under the TRIPS.
[662] Art. XXIII.1 (a) GATT.
[663] It should be noted that the GATS abandoned the 'nullification or impairment' requirement for violation complaints. Art. XXIII.1 GATS merely states that "[i]f any Member should consider

Member could prove the violation of provisions of the GATT, there was a presumption that this violation would amount to a *prima facie* nullification or impairment.[664] There is no need for the complaining party to demonstrate actual harm.[665] It would then be up to the defending Party to rebut the charge. On the establishment of the WTO, this presumption was included in Article 3.8 DSU. It should be noted that this presumption in fact serves as an irrefutable one.[666] In practice, if the defendant still tries to rebut the presumption, the Panel only dedicates a brief paragraph at the end of the Report to the issue of nullification and impairment. It is nevertheless important that the presumption of nullification and impairment, as set out in Article 3.8 DSU, and the question whether there is a violation of WTO provisions are not confused and are considered separately.[667] They form two distinct conditions. If the measure is indeed found to violate provisions of any of the covered agreements and (thus) cause nullification and impairment, the measure will have to be withdrawn.

328. The second type of possible complaint within the WTO concerns *non-violation complaints*. It may at first sight seem remarkable that even though a certain measure by a Member does not violate any provision,[668] the measure can still be challenged before the WTO dispute settlement system. Nonetheless, the GATT 1947 negotiators believed it useful to include a provision providing for relief from unforeseen events that could not yet be anticipated. Indeed, "you never can tell what might happen".[669] Certain policy measures by WTO Members,

---

that any other Member fails to carry out its obligations or specific commitments under this Agreement, it may with a view to reaching a mutually satisfactory resolution of the matter have recourse to the DSU". No mention of 'nullification or impairment' is made.

[664] GATT Panel Report: Uruguayan Recourse to Article XXIII, (16 November 1962), BISD 11S/95, para. 15. See also Agreed Description of the Customary Practice of the GATT, Adopted at the Tokyo Round, 1979, BISD, 26S/210, p. 216, annex para. 5.

[665] P. GALLAGHER, *Guide to Dispute Settlement*, The Hague, Kluwer Law International, 2002, p. 19.

[666] See *inter alia* GATT Panel Report: United States – Taxes on Petroleum and Certain Imported Substances, (17 June 1987), BISD 34S/136, para. 5.1.6. The Panel stated that "there was no case in the history of the GATT in which a contracting party had successfully rebutted the presumption that a measure infringing obligations causes nullification and impairment". See also GATT Panel Report: Italy – Italian Discrimination against Imported Agricultural Machinery, (23 October 1958), BISD 7S/60, para. 21–22, GATT Panel Report: Canada – Administration of the Foreign Investment Review Act, (7 February 1984), BISD 30S/140, para. 6.76 and GATT Panel Report: Panel on Japanese Measures on Imports of Leather, (15 May 1984), BISD 31S/94, para. 46–47 and 54–56. The *de facto* irrefutability of the presumption has been endorsed by the Appellate Body in the Appellate Body Report: European Communities – Regime for the Importation, Sale and Distribution of Bananas, *supra* note 655, paras. 252–256.

[667] Appellate Body Report: United States – Measures Affecting Imports of Woven Wool Shirts and Blouses from India, WT/DS33/AB/R, (15 April 1997), p. 13–14.

[668] The relevant provision reads: "the application by another contracting party of any measure, whether or not it conflicts with the provisions of this Agreement". Art. XXIII.1 (b) GATT.

[669] A.F. LOWENFELD, *International Economic Law*, (Oxford, Oxford University Press 2003), p. 177. There were for instance few provisions in the GATT 1947 addressing protection through non-

which are perhaps consistent with the WTO provisions, may nevertheless cause nullification or impairment of another Member's trade benefits in a way that could not reasonably be anticipated by the injured Member. A Member bringing a non-violation complaint should first of all identify a benefit that is nullified or impaired. Thus, contrary to what is the case for violation complaints,[670] in order to prove nullification or impairment, the complainant has to prove the existence of harm. Moreover, nullification and impairment will only be acknowledged if this harm could not reasonably be anticipated. The Member must show that it relied on the non-occurrence of the other Member's measure, which is now causing the harm.[671] The latter condition of 'reasonable expectations' has been introduced by GATT jurisprudence as an additional condition for having nullification or impairment, even if this condition cannot be found in Article XXIII GATT or Article 26 DSU.[672] Second, Member has to define the measure by another Member that is responsible for this nullification or impairment. Third, there must be a causal link between this measure and the nullification or impairment of the trade benefit.[673] When the non-violation complaint is accepted and found proven, the measure may stay in place, but the nullification or impairment of benefits should be redressed by other measures.[674]

329. A third possible complaint is the *situation complaint*. Members can challenge nullification or impairment of any of their trade benefits caused by the "existence of any other situation [than the two scenarios described above]".[675] Situation complaints have until now never been addressed by a Panel. This kind

---

tariff barriers. The non-violation complaint would be a useful tool to challenge such protection. See P. GALLAGHER, *supra* note 665, p. 18. The complaint could also be used to address negligence by the another Member's competition authorities with regard to anticompetitive practices in this country, harming the trade of another country. There is indeed no 'competition agreement' within the WTO, which implies that one cannot point to an outright violation of any WTO provision. See Panel Report: Japan – Measures Affecting Consumer Photographic Film and Paper, WT/DS44/R, (31 March 1998).

[670] A violation of a provision of one of the covered agreements would involve a refutable (*de facto* irrefutable) presumption of nullification and impairment.
[671] A.F. LOWENFELD, *supra* note 669, p. 179.
[672] GATT Working Party Report: The Australian Subsidy on Ammonium Sulphate, (3 April 1950), BISD II/188, para. 12 and GATT Panel Report: European Communities – Payments and Subsidies Paid to Processors and Producers of Oilseeds and related Animal-Feed Proteins, (25 January 1990), BISD 37S/86, para. 150.
[673] Art. 26 DSU. See also M. MATSUSHITA, T.J. SCHOENBAUM and P.C. MAVROIDIS, *The World Trade Organization. Law, Practice and Policy*, (Oxford, Oxford University Press 2006), p. 121, with references.
[674] Art. 26.1 (b) DSU.
[675] Art. XXIII.1 (c) GATT and art. 26.2 DSU. It should be noted that for the GATS, no situation complaints exist.

Chapter IV

of complaint seems to be introduced to address situations where a State is confronted with massive unemployment or depression.[676]

Once a complaint is made, several steps in the dispute settlement procedure will be taken: consultations, panel proceedings, possibly appellate proceedings, implementation and possibly retaliation.

Figure 3. Schematic Overview of Dispute Settlement Procedure

Timing	Stage	Parallel track
60 days	Consultations (Art. 4)	During all stages good offices, conciliation, or mediation (Art. 5)
by 2nd DSB meeting	Panel established by Dispute Settlement Body (DSB) (Art. 6)	
0–20 days	Terms of reference (Art. 7) Composition (Art. 8)	Note: a panel can be 'composed' (i.e. panellists chosen) up to about 30 days after its 'establishment' (i.e. after DSB's decision to have a panel)
20 days (+ 10 if Director-General asked to pick panel)	Panel examination Normally 2 meetings with parties (Art. 12), 1 meeting with third parties (Art. 10)	Expert review group (Art. 13; Appendix 4)
	Interim review stage Descriptive part of report sent to parties for comment (Art. 15.1) Interim report sent to parties for comment (Art. 15.2)	Review meeting with panel upon request (Art. 15.2)
6 months from panel's composition, 3 months if urgent	Panel report issued to parties (Art. 12.8; Appendix 3 par 12(j))	
up to 9 months from panel's establishment	Panel report issued to DSB (Art. 12.9; Appendix 3 par 12(k))	
60 days for panel report unless appealed ...	DSB adopts panel/appellate report(s) including any changes to panel report made by appellate report (Art. 16.1, 16.4 and 17.14)	Appellate review (Art. 16.4 and 17) — max 90 days ... 30 days for appellate report
'REASONABLE PERIOD OF TIME': determined by: member proposes, DSB agrees; or parties in dispute agree; or arbitrator (approx. 15 months if by arbitrator)	Implementation report by losing party of proposed implementation within 'reasonable period of time' (Art. 21.3)	TOTAL FOR REPORT ADOPTION: Usually up to 9 months (no appeal), or 12 months (with appeal) from establishment of panel to adoption of report (Art. 20)
	In cases of non-implementation parties negotiate compensation pending full implementation (Art. 22.2)	Dispute over Implementation: Proceedings possible, including referral to initial panel on implementation (Art. 21.5) — 90 days
30 days after 'reasonable period' expires	Retaliation If no agreement on compensation, DSB authorizes rataliation pending full implementation (Art. 22) Cross-retaliation same sector, other sectors, other agreements (Art. 22.3)	Possibility of arbitration on level of suspension procedures and principles of retaliation (Art. 22.6 and 22.7)

Source: WTO, *Understanding the WTO*, February 2007, p. 59.

---

[676] A.F. LOWENFELD, *supra* note 669, p. 176.

C. CONSULTATIONS

1. Procedure

330. Since the WTO dispute settlement still has a preference for a mutually acceptable solution of a dispute, the first phase of the dispute settlement procedure consists of consultations between the Parties to a dispute. The Member experiencing an obstacle to its trade should make a request for consultations with the allegedly impeding Member. The latter Member has to reply to this request within 10 days after the day of receipt.[677] Consultations have the objective to reach a mutually satisfactory solution and help the Parties to understand the factual situation. They shall be started within a period of maximum 30 days. When there is no reply within 10 days or Member refuses to enter in consultations within 30 days, the affected Member may directly request the establishment of a Panel. Consultations must be held for at least 60 days. During consultations the Parties may request the good offices, conciliation and mediation by the WTO Director-General.[678] The Director-General will offer its personal advice in conjunction with the advice of key advisors of the WTO Secretariat, including the head of the legal division. This advice is not binding and cannot be cited in the later Panel report.[679] If a mutually acceptable solution is reached, this has to be notified to the Dispute Settlement Body and the relevant Councils and Committees.[680]

331. If it proves impossible to reach a mutually acceptable solution within 60 days after the date of receipt of the request for consultations, the complaining Party may request the establishment of a Panel.[681] In two specific cases it is possible to request the establishment of a Panel *before* the period of 60 days has expired. It may first be possible that both Parties agree that the consultations have failed to settle the dispute, and that there is no chance of reaching a dispute, even though the period has not expired yet.[682] Second, in cases of urgency,[683] the failure to reach a solution within 20 days after the day of receipt of the request gives the complaining Party the right to request the establishment of a Panel.[684] In those urgent cases, the Parties also have to enter into consultations within a period of 10 days (instead of the normal 30 days).

---

[677] Art. 4.3 DSU.
[678] *Ibid.* art. 5.6.
[679] K. ADAMANTOPOULOS, *supra* note 389, p. 61.
[680] Art. 3.6 DSU.
[681] In practice, the complaining Party will not immediately upon the expiry of the period of sixty days request the establishment of a Panel. Most often, the Party will allow more time to settle the dispute by consultations.
[682] Art. 4.7 *in fine* DSU.
[683] For example when it concerns perishable goods.
[684] Art. 4.8 DSU.

2. Third Parties

332. Third Parties who claim to have a substantial trade interest in the dispute may notify the DSB and the Parties to the dispute and request to be invited to the consultations. Such request should be made within 10 days after the circulation of the request for consultations.[685] It should be noted that third parties *cannot* be allowed to participate in the consultations when these consultations have been initiated on the basis of Article XXIII GATT or the corresponding provisions in the other Agreements.[686] Third parties can only join if the request for consultations is made on the basis of Article XXII GATT, Article XXII.1 GATS or the corresponding provisions in other covered agreements. In that case, the decision whether the third Party can be included in the consultations is made by Member to whom the original request for consultations is made (respondent). In case of refusal by the latter Member, the third Party may still try to address the problems it experiences because of a trade measure under review by initiating a separate dispute settlement procedure.

D. PANEL

1. Request for a Panel

333. If the complaining Party wants a Panel to be established, it will have to make a written request to the DSB.[687] This request must "identify the specific measures at issue and provide a brief summary of the legal basis of the complaint sufficient to present the problem clearly".[688] The Appellate Body noted that all claims must be identified in the request for the establishment of the Panel. Not all arguments have to be included in the request.[689] Claims have to indicate at a minimum a list of references to the articles of the covered Agreements that are alleged to have been breached.[690] In some cases a "mere listing" of the Articles may not be enough to indicate what legal claims the complainant is making. In any case, the request should allow the other Parties to the dispute to know the legal basis of the request and adequately prepare their defence.[691]

---

[685] *Ibid.* art. 4.11.
[686] *Ibid.* and UNCTAD, *Course on Dispute Settlement. WTO Module 3.2 Panels*, available on http://www.unctad.org/en/docs//edmmisc232add12_en.pdf, 4.
[687] In accordance with the time frame set out above.
[688] Art. 6.2 DSU.
[689] Appellate Body Report: European Communities – Regime for the Importation, Sale and Distribution of Bananas, *supra* note 655, para. 143.
[690] *Ibid.* para. 141.
[691] Appellate Body Report: European Communities – Customs Classification of Certain Computer Equipment, WT/DS62/AB/R, WT/DS67/AB/R, WT/DS68/AB/R, (22 June 1998), para. 70 and

334. The request for the establishment of a Panel also defines the 'terms of reference' of the Panel.[692] The terms of reference give the Parties to the dispute and third Parties sufficient information on the claims and allow parties to respond adequately. In addition, these terms of reference delineate the jurisdiction of the Panel.[693] Claims that are not included in the Panel's terms of reference cannot be considered.[694]

335. It is possible that several Members together file a complaint against another Member and request the establishment of a Panel. In that case, as far as possible, one single Panel will examine all complaints together.[695] Each Party to the dispute may request the Panel to submit separate reports.[696]

2. Establishment and Composition of Panels

336. The Panel will be established no later than on the DSB meeting following the meeting at which the request for establishment is raised.[697] Contrary to what was the case in the GATT era, it has become almost impossible for the allegedly infringing Party to block the establishment of a Panel. Before the establishment of the WTO, Panels could only be established by consensus. However, since 1995, to avoid the establishment of a Panel, the DSB has to decide by consensus *not* to do so.[698] This implies that all WTO Members have to agree that it is *not* opportune to establish the Panel, which is almost unimaginable. The fact that there has to be a consensus to block the establishment of a Panel, firmly establishes the 'right to a Panel'.[699]

337. Panels are formed for each different dispute (*'ad hoc'*). They comprise persons with relevant trade policy, law or economics experience.[700] In principle,

---

Appellate Body Report: Korea – Definitive Safeguard Measures on Imports of Certain Diary Products, WT/DS98/AB/R, (12 January 2000), para. 120.

[692] Art. 7.1 DSU. It is possible that, within 20 days of the establishment of the Panel, the Chairman of the DSB defines special terms of reference together with the Parties to the dispute (Art. 7.3 DSU). This happens only rarely. See for an example, Appellate Body Report: Brazil – Measures Affecting Desiccated Coconut, *supra* note 186.

[693] As such, the terms of reference perform an important due process function. See Appellate Body Report: Brazil – Measures Affecting Desiccated Coconut, *supra* note 186, p. 20.

[694] Appellate Body Report: India – Patent Protection for Pharmaceutical and Agricultural Chemical Products, WT/DS50/AB/R, (16 January 1998), para. 93.

[695] Art. 9 DSU.

[696] This was for instance the case in EC – Conditions for the Granting of to Developing Countries, WT/DS246 (Appellate Body Report issued on 7 April 2004).

[697] Art. 6.1 DSU.

[698] *Ibid.*

[699] P. Van den Bossche, *supra* note 30, p. 419.

[700] Art. 8.1 DSU. It concerns "well-qualified governmental and/or non-governmental individuals including persons who have served on or presented a case to a panel, served as a representative

there are three panellists. If the Parties so agree, the Panel may be composed of five members.[701] The procedure of Panel composition is clearly inspired by international arbitration, where in fact the parties are free to compose their own tribunal or to indicate the person who will appoint the members.[702] This indicates again that, even though the dispute settlement of the WTO is increasingly judicial, some more 'diplomacy' elements are still present. It should nevertheless be noted that freedom here is rather limited: the nominations should be drawn from a roster of names and qualifications, maintained by the Secretariat.[703] It is the WTO Secretariat who shall propose the nominations. The Parties can only oppose nominations for "compelling reasons".[704] In the case where the parties do not agree on who will serve in the Panel[705], the WTO Director-General will appoint the panellists.[706] Clearly, the focus is on avoiding delaying the resolution of a dispute through objections to panellists.[707] The selection of the Panel members should be guided by the need for independence, diversity in background and experience.[708] Especially the first condition may raise some problems in practice. Even though Article 8.3 requires that citizens of Parties involved in the dispute at hand cannot serve in the Panel, the article still provides the loophole of an agreement between the Parties to the dispute to appoint citizens. To be sure, this might indeed be useful if a particular case requires a thorough understanding of the complex legislation of one of the Parties. On the other hand, the DSU requires absolute independence, also from officials of one of the Parties. Additional safeguards to ensure independence and impartiality have been laid down in the *Rules of Conduct for the Understanding on Rules and Procedures Concerning the Settlement of Disputes*.[709] The persons covered[710] by the Rules of Conduct "shall

---

of a Member or of a contracting party to GATT 1947 or as a representative to the Council or Committee of any covered agreement or its predecessor agreement, or in the Secretariat, taught or published on international trade law or policy, or served as a senior trade policy official".

[701] Art. 8.5 DSU.
[702] A. REDFERN and M. HUNTER, *Law and Practice of International Commercial Arbitration*, (London, Sweet & Maxwell 1999), p. 8.
[703] Art. 8.4 DSU.
[704] *Ibid.* art. 8.6.
[705] The Parties must agree within 20 days after the date of the DSB decision to establish a Panel.
[706] Art. 8.7 DSU. LOWENFELD states that "contrary to the design of the DSU, the Director-General was obliged to appoint the panel in close to half the cases". See A.F. LOWENFELD, *supra* note 669, p. 164.
[707] A.F. LOWENFELD, *supra* note 669, p. 161.
[708] Art. 8.2 DSU.
[709] Rules of Conduct for the Understanding on Rules and Procedures Concerning the Settlement of Disputes, WT/DSB/RC/1, 11 December 1996 (hereinafter 'DSU Rules of Conduct'). On these Rules of Conduct, see J. WIERS, 'The WTO's Rules of Conduct for Dispute Settlement', *Leiden Journal of International Law* (1998), pp. 265-274.
[710] These 'covered persons' are panellists and members of the Appellate Body, arbitrators and experts acting pursuant the various provision of the DSU and other WTO Agreements,

be independent and impartial, shall avoid direct or indirect conflicts of interest and shall respect the confidentiality of proceedings of bodies pursuant to the dispute settlement mechanism, so that through the observance of such standards of conduct the integrity and impartiality of that mechanism are preserved".[711] Moreover, these persons have the obligation to disclose information that may raise doubts about their impartiality or independence.[712] Panellists cannot receive instructions from or be influenced by any Member[713] (and certainly not the own). What is more, there is always a second review possible by the standing Appellate Body. Appellate Body Members must be unaffiliated with any government.[714] There are thus several provisions that deal with the partiality or the appearance of partiality of Panel Members that are also government officials. Despite the fact that, from the perspective of the protagonists of a complete judicial procedure, this loophole should be closed, it can be acknowledged that the DSU tries to find the balance between pragmatism and legalism.[715]

The WTO Secretariat provides legal and administrative support to Panels. Usually, a Panel is assisted by at least two members of the staff of the Secretariat, one secretary and one legal officer. Most often, one of them comes from the division in the Secretariat that is responsible for the covered agreement and the other one of the Legal Affairs Division. In case of disputes relating to antidumping or subsidies, the staff of the Rules Division assists the Panels.[716]

3.   *Procedure before the Panel*

338.   It should first be noted that during the whole panel procedure Panels should encourage the Parties to the dispute to settle the matter voluntarily. Indeed, the WTO has a preference for a "mutually agreed solution".[717] The Complainant State will make a written submission to which the respondent State

---

members of the WTO Secretariat assisting in the panel or arbitration proceedings, Appellate Body support staff and the Chairman and Secretariat members of the Textiles Monitoring Body. See art. IV and V DSU Rules of Conduct.
[711] Art. II DSU Rules of Conduct.
[712] Art. III and art. VI.2 DSU Rules of Conduct.
[713] Art. 8.9 DSU.
[714] *Ibid.* art. 17.3.
[715] T.J. DILLON, *supra* note 240, pp. 383-384. DILLON states that the text of the DSU at least formally tends to legalism.
[716] See WTO, *A Handbook on the WTO Dispute Settlement System*, (Cambridge, Cambridge University Press 2004), p. 22.
[717] Examples of cases where a mutually agreed solution was agreed before the finalization of the Panel process are: European Communities – Trade Description of Scallops, Complaints by Canada, Peru and Chile, WT/DS7, WT/DS12 and WT/DS14 and European Communities – Measures affecting Butter Products, Complaint by New Zealand, WT/DS72.

will reply. The Panel determines a timetable for the procedure[718] and will set deadlines for written submissions.[719] The DSU requires the Panel to show some flexibility in its procedures in order to achieve reports of high quality, while at the same time avoiding undue delays.[720] The first step in the procedure is the introduction of written submissions by the Parties and by the Third Parties. Thereafter, a first substantive meeting will be held at which the complaining Party will have to present its case and the defending Party will present its point of view.[721] Third Parties may also present their views, but are not allowed to speak in the rest of the meeting. After this first meeting, further written rebuttals by the Parties will be submitted simultaneously[722] and eventually a second meeting will be held.[723] The Panels meet to hear and evaluate the arguments of both parties. They can ask questions and explanations to the Parties at any time during the meetings or in between in writing.[724] Members have an obligation to respond to the Panel's request for information.[725] If a Party refuses to provide certain information, the Panel may draw 'adverse inferences' from the refusal.[726]

In addition the Panels have the authority to request information and technical advice from different external sources.[727] Nevertheless, before it can seek information from an individual or body, the Panel must inform the authorities of Member under whose jurisdiction this individual or body operates.[728] If a particular dispute is of a technical nature, it is possible that the Panel requests the assistance of an Expert Review Group (ERG). The ERG is under the Panel's

---

[718] Art. 12.3 DSU. See the indicative timetable in Appendix 3.12 DSU.
[719] *Ibid.* art. 12.5.
[720] *Ibid.* art. 12.2. However, the freedom of the Panel to adopt working procedures does not give a right to modify DSU provisions. See Appellate Body Report: India – Patent Protection for Pharmaceutical and Agricultural Chemical Products, WT/DS79/R, (24 August 1998), para. 92.
[721] Appendix 3.5 DSU.
[722] *Ibid.* art. 12.6.
[723] *Ibid.* appendix 3.7.
[724] *Ibid.* appendix 3.8.
[725] See Appellate Body Report: Canada – Measures Affecting the Export of Civilian Aircraft, WT/DS70/AB/R (23 July 1999), para. 189.
[726] P. GALLAGHER, *supra* note 665, p. 29. See Appellate Body Report: Canada – Measures Affecting the Export of Civilian Aircraft, WT/DS70/AB/R, (2 August 1999), para. 203 and Appellate Body Report: United States – Definitive Safeguard Measures on Imports of Wheat Gluten from the European Communities, WT/DS166/AB/R, (22 December 2000), para. 172.
[727] Art. 13.1 DSU. The Panels should determine the need for information and advice in a specific case, to ascertain the acceptability and relevancy of information or advice received, and to decide what weight to ascribe to that information or advice […]. They have an "ample and extensive authority to undertake and to control the process by which it informs itself both of the relevant facts of the dispute and of the legal norms and principles applicable to such facts". See Appellate Body Report: United States – Import prohibition of certain shrimp and shrimp products, WT/DS58/AB/R (12 October 1998), paras. 104 and 106.
[728] Art. 13.1 DSU.

authority and its working procedures will be decided by the Panel.[729] The independence of the members of the ERG should be ensured. It is in principle[730] not open to citizens of the Parties to the dispute.[731] The ERG may also seek information and advice from appropriate sources.[732] This ERG will provide an advisory[733] report concerning any scientific or other technical matter raised by a Party to the dispute.[734] The report is to be submitted to the Parties for their comments before being submitted in final form to the Panel.[735] Until now, rather than establishing an ERG, Panels have consulted experts on an individual basis. The provisions on the right of the Panel to seek information play an important role in the discussion on whether Panels should accept unrequested submissions by non-State actors.[736]

339. Like the preceding consultations[737] and the subsequent Appellate Body procedure,[738] the proceedings before the Panel are confidential.[739] However, it is possible that the Parties to the dispute agree that they open up the proceedings to the public.[740] The Parties to a dispute only meet with the Panel if the Panel so desires. The Panel members will draft a report without the presence of the Parties to the dispute. The Secretariat officials often play an important assisting role in the drafting of the Panel report, "especially on the legal, historical and procedural aspects of the matters dealt with".[741] Panels can decide themselves upon the decision-making and drafting procedure among the members. Contrary to what was the case in the GATT era, dissenting opinions are rare.[742]

---

[729] Appendix 4.1 DSU.
[730] Unless when the Panel decides that no other specialized scientific experts can be found.
[731] Appendix 4.3 DSU.
[732] Appendix 4.4 DSU.
[733] Appendix 4.6 *in fine* DSU. Of course, it carries considerable weight in the procedure. See K. ADAMANTOPOULOS, *supra* note 389, p. 47.
[734] Art. 13.2 DSU.
[735] Appendix 4.6 DSU.
[736] See *infra* para. 363.
[737] Art. 4.6 DSU.
[738] *Ibid.* art. 17.10.
[739] *Ibid.* art. 14.1.
[740] This was agreed during the retaliation proceedings in the Hormones dispute (see Communication of the Chairman of the Panel, WT/DS321–322/8, 2 August 2005) as well as in the dispute before the WTO subsidies for large civil aircraft (Airbus and Boeing disputes) (DS316 and DS317).
[741] *Ibid.* art. 27.1.
[742] P. GALLAGHER, *supra* note 665, p. 33. See for a rare dissenting opinion, not mentioning the name of the Panelist concerned: Panel Report: United States – Import Measures on Certain Products from the European Communities, WT/DS165/R, (17 July 2000), paras. 6.60 and 6.61.

340. An important final stage in the Panel procedure is the 'interim review'.[743] After the written and oral procedures, the Panel distributes a draft report to the Parties. This report does not include a decision on the matter, but only outlines the facts of the dispute and the arguments of the Parties. This allows the Parties to comment and to make sure their arguments are explained correctly.[744] The Panel may hold additional meetings with the Parties. Thereafter, the Panel issues an interim report, taking into account the comments by the Parties. This report includes the findings of the Panel and at this point the Parties know who has won the case. The Parties still have the opportunity of issuing comments on the interim report before it becomes final. This stage is, like the rest of the Panel procedures, in principle confidential. In practice the general tendency of the report nevertheless will be leaked, mostly by the Party who is about to win. The final report will be submitted to the Parties and will be circulated to Members after three weeks and be published on the WTO website and in the official WTO Dispute Settlement Reports.

341. The whole Panel procedure should not take more than six months from the date of composition of the Panel until the date of the final report.[745] The fixed time frame stands in stark contrast with the GATT 1947 procedures and significantly improves the efficiency of the procedures. The period is shortened to three months in cases of urgency. Given the often complex set of facts in the disputes before the Panel, the six-month period is often not sufficient to decide. It is therefore possible that the period is extended with a maximum of three months.[746] In that case the Panel has to inform the DSB of the reasons of the delay.

342. The final Panel report is adopted by the DSB within 60 days;[747] unless one of the parties notifies its decision to appeal the decision or that there is a consensus within the DSB to reject the report (by so-called 'inverted consensus').[748] All WTO Members can make comments on the report.[749] During the GATT 1947

---

[743] Art. 15 DSU.
[744] Most often, Parties limit their comments to minor factual issues. They save their legal arguments for an appeal procedure. See UNCTAD, *Course on Dispute Settlement. WTO Module 3.2 Panels*, supra note 686, p. 36.
[745] Art. 12.8 DSU. The Complaining Party may request the suspension of the Panel's work for a maximum of 12 months. If the Panel is not allowed to take up its work again within 12 months, its authority lapses. (art. 12.12 DSU).
[746] Art. 12.9 DSU.
[747] Nevertheless, the report will not be considered by the DSB until 20 days after the date of circulation to Members. This may provide Members sufficient time to examine the report. (Art. 16.1 DSU).
[748] See art. 16.4 DSU.
[749] Written reasons to explain these objections have to be circulated at least 10 days prior to the DSB meeting. (art. 16.2–3 DSU).

era, Panel reports had to be adopted by the General Council by unanimity. The result of this was that the losing party could easily block the adoption of the report, something that happened regularly. The rule of 'inverted consensus' turns this all around and makes it almost impossible to block the adoption of a report.

4. Third Parties

343. The Panel has the obligation to take fully into account the interests of all Members under a covered agreement.[750] Third Parties that have a substantial interest in the dispute will have the opportunity to be heard by the Panel and make written submissions, after having notified its interest to the DSB. The Parties to the dispute will be informed of these submissions. They receive these submissions and are present at the first substantive meeting when Third Parties can present their view. The Panel and the Parties, through the Panel, can question the Third Parties. However, the Third Parties are not allowed to question the Parties. The final Panel report has to address the issues raised in the third Party submissions.[751]

5. Standard of Review and Treaty Interpretation

344. A Panel has the task of investigating objectively the facts of the dispute, in the light of the particular agreement alleged to be breached.[752] It does not need to consider every matter in a case. It is sufficient to address the issues that it considers necessary to resolve the dispute.[753] On the other hand, the Panel is constrained by its 'terms of reference'.[754] Panels shall make an "objective assessment of the matter before it, including an objective assessment of the facts of the case and the applicability of and conformity with the relevant covered agreements". This phrasing is rather vague and provides "little [...] substantive guidance on the nature and intensity of the review which panels should apply to national measures".[755] Rather, to determine the degree of deference the Panel has to apply, one should look at a more substantial standard of review. This determination is of particular importance since it affects the delicate balance between the autonomy Members have in making their decisions and the monitoring task the dispute

---

[750] Art. 10.1 DSU.
[751] *Ibid.* 10.2.
[752] *Ibid.* 11.
[753] P. GALLAGHER, *supra* note 665, p. 28. This is inspired by the need for 'judicial economy'.
[754] See *supra* para. 334. If the Panel acts outside its terms of reference, it acts contrary to art. 11 DSU. Appellate Body Report: Chile – Price Band System and Safeguard Measures Relating to Certain Agricultural Products, WT/DS207/AB/R, (9 September 2002), para. 173.
[755] C.-D. EHLERMANN and N. LOCKHART, 'Standard of Review in WTO Law', *Journal of International Economic Law* (2004), p. 495.

settlement system has in order to guarantee a consistent application of the WTO rules to all Members.[756] This standard varies depending on whether the Panel assesses legal or factual issues.[757]

345. Article 3.2 DSU indicates that legal interpretations should be made in accordance with customary rules of interpretation of public international law. The Appellate Body has stressed that such interpretations should be based on the Articles 31 and 32 of the Vienna Convention on the Law of Treaties (VCLT).[758] Article 31 VCLT states that provisions in international agreements should be interpreted "in good faith in accordance with the ordinary meaning to be given to the terms of the treaty in their context and in the light of its object and purpose". The Panel should consider first the ordinary meaning of a treaty provision, even if the national authorities' decision is based on an alternative reasonable reading of the text.[759] The ordinary meaning of term is often determined by reference to dictionary definitions.

346. The context for the purpose of the interpretation of a treaty includes, in addition to the text (including its preamble and annexes), any agreement relating to the treaty which was made between all the parties in connection with the conclusion of the treaty. Moreover, also subsequent agreements and practices relating to the interpretation of the treaty and any relevant rules of international law applicable in the relations between the parties must be taken into account, together with the context.[760] It might thus be possible that a WTO Panel or the Appellate Body considers non-WTO agreements to interpret provisions in the WTO Agreements. Nevertheless, it is required that these agreements are at least implicitly[761] approved by *all* WTO Members (and not solely by the Parties to a

---

[756] See S.P. CROLEY and J.H. JACKSON, 'WTO Dispute Procedures, Standard of Review, and Deference to National Governments', *American Journal of International Law* (1996), p. 194.

[757] See Appellate Body Report: European Communities – Measures Concerning Meat and Meat Products (Hormones), WT/DS26 and 48/AB/R, (13 February 1998), para. 116.

[758] Vienna Convention on the Law of Treaties, done at Vienna on 23 May 1969, *UNTS* no. 18232. See the references in the Appellate Body Report: United States – Standards for Reformulated and Conventional Gasoline, WT/DS2/AB/R, (20 May 1996), p. 15 and in Appellate Body Report, Japan – Taxes on Alcoholic Beverages, WT/DS8/AB/R, WT/DS10/AB/R, WT/DS11/AB/R, (1 November 1996), pp. 9–10.

[759] C.-D. EHLERMANN and N. LOCKHART, *supra* note 755, p. 498.

[760] Art. 31 VCLT. The International Court of Justice has recognized repeatedly that Article 31 VCLT reflects customary international law. See *Case Concerning the Territorial Dispute (Libyan Arab Jamahiriya/Chad), Judgment*, ICJ Reports (1994), 21, para. 41; *Case Concerning Oil Platforms (Islamic Republic of Iran/United States of America), Preliminary Objections, Judgment*, ICJ Reports (1996) (II), 812, para. 23 and, specifically on art. 31.3, *Case Concerning Kasikili/Sedudu Island, Judgment*, ICJ Reports (1994), para. 48.

[761] The fact that the International Law Commission decided to change the phrase "subsequent practice… of *all* the parties" into "subsequent practice of … the parties" does not mean that it is not necessary that all Parties should have accepted the practice. It was only meant to indicate

dispute).⁷⁶² It is sometimes argued that, in certain cases, a non-WTO rule can be relevant, even if it is not binding on all WTO Members. This would be the case when the rule at hand expresses the 'contemporary concerns of the community of nations'.⁷⁶³ Nevertheless, in our view, leaving aside norms of *jus cogens*, this would not respect sufficiently the autonomy of WTO Members that are involved in a dispute. They could be faced with a situation where norms are being used for interpreting the WTO Agreements without their ever having approved, explicitly or implicitly, these norms.

347. A more moderate position can be found in the Report by a Study Group set up by the International Law Commission (ILC) to examine the fragmentation of international law. This Report suggested that non-WTO rules should possibly be relied on as part of the context for interpretation if all parties in dispute are bound by this non-WTO rule (e.g. a treaty). It would thus not be necessary that it is binding for all WTO Members. According to the study, "although this creates the possibility of eventually divergent interpretations (depending on which States are also parties to the dispute), that would simply reflect the need to respect (inherently divergent) party will as elucidated by reference to those other treaties as well as the bilateralist character of most treaties underpinned by the practices regarding reservations, inter se modification and successive treaties".⁷⁶⁴ It should be noted, however, that this is a study commissioned by the ILC and not an ILC statement itself. One should thus not attach more value to this than to the works of learned writers.

348. Nevertheless, recent WTO case-law may still leave open the use of international treaties as a tool for interpretation of WTO law, even if not all WTO

---

that it was sufficient that the States had accepted the principles and that it is not essential that each and every State has explicitly followed the principles in practice. The adherence of the State to the principles that are laid down in a certain international instrument can be presumed by the absence of a reaction by this State. Compare M.K. YASSEEN, 'L'interprétation des traités d'après la Convention de Vienne sur le droit des traités', *Rec. Cours* (1976), III, p. 49. Thus, only if a WTO Member has explicitly stated that it does not agree with the principles laid down in the Convention would it be unacceptable to use the Convention as a tool for interpreting WTO provisions.

⁷⁶² See GATT Panel Report: United States – Prohibition of Imports of Tuna and Tuna Products from Canada, 22 February 1982, BISD 29S/91 and Panel Report: Canada – Patent Protection of Pharmaceutical Products, WT/DS114/R (17 March 2000), para. 4.31. This was confirmed in Panel Report: European Communities – Measures Affecting the Approval and Marketing of Biotech Products, WT/DS291, 292, 293/R (29 September 2006), para. 7.70–7.72.

⁷⁶³ See J. PAUWELYN, *Conflict of Norms in Public International Law*, (Cambridge, Cambridge University Press 2003), p. 576.

⁷⁶⁴ See Fragmentation of International Law: Difficulties arising from the Diversification and Expansion of International Law. Report of the Work of the Study Group of the International Law Commission, Finalized by Martti Koskenniemi, A/CN.4/L.682, 18 July 2006, para. 472.

Members are parties to the treaty. Yet, the use of this treaty would only be very limited. In a recent dispute, the Panel, when applying Article 31.3 (c) VCLT, confirmed that it could only take into account other rules of international law if these rules were applicable in the relations between *all* WTO Members.[765] It would thus not be sufficient that all parties to a dispute were also parties to another rule of international law that is used as a tool for interpretation. However, the Panel did not leave it there. Rules of international law which were *not* applicable in the relations between all WTO Members could still be used for interpreting the terms of the WTO Agreements to define their 'ordinary meaning'. These treaties would then not be considered as legal rules, but would provide evidence of the ordinary meaning of terms (see Article 31.1 VCLT) of the WTO Agreements in the same way that dictionaries do, and be considered because of their 'informative character'.[766] Yet, in the end, the Panel did not rely on such international treaties to define the ordinary meaning. It found it not necessary or appropriate to do so in that case because it could derive the ordinary meaning from other elements.[767]

349. Article 32 VCLT provides for supplementary means of interpretation, such as the preparatory works. Such supplementary means can help confirm, clarify or correct the outcome of the interpretation process according to Article 31. Panels will therefore have to redo the legal reasoning the national authority has developed. This amounts to a *de novo* review of the legal reasoning. Ensuring that the legal rules of international trade are interpreted and applied uniformly is the only way to provide "security and predictability to the multilateral trading system".[768] It should be noted, however, that the Panels and Appellate Body mostly rely on the ordinary meaning and context rather than on the object and purpose of the provisions that are being interpreted.[769]

---

[765] Panel Report: European Communities – Measures Affecting the Approval and Marketing of Biotech Products, *supra* note 762, para. 7.68.
[766] *Ibid.* para. 7.92.
[767] *Ibid.* para. 7.95.
[768] Art. 3.2 DSU. It should be noted that the Agreement on Antidumping provides a specific, different standard of review. Art. 17.6 (ii) Antidumping Agreement states that when different permissible interpretations are available, "the panel shall find the authorities' measure to be in conformity with the Agreement if it rests upon one of those permissible interpretations". See on this matter: L.D. HAMILTON, 'US Antidumping Decisions and the WTO Standard of Review: Deference or Disregard?', *Chicago Journal of International Law* (2003), p. 265 and S.P. CROLEY and J.H. JACKSON, *supra* note 756, p. 198.
[769] See WTO, *A Handbook on the WTO Dispute Settlement System*, (Cambridge, Cambridge University Press 2004), p. 5. Nevertheless, in the *US-Gambling* dispute the determination of the Appellate Body mainly relied on the supplementary means of interpretation. See for a critique: F. ORTINO, 'Treaty Interpretation and the WTO Appellate Body Report in *US-Gambling*: A Critique', *Journal of International Economic Law* (2006), pp. 117–148.

350. When the Panel addresses factual issues, it should neither conduct a *de novo* review of the facts nor apply total deference.[770] Instead, the Panel's review will depend on the WTO agreement and the provisions of that particular agreement at issue.[771] First, when the authorities of a Member have performed a national investigation before adopting a measure, as required by a WTO Agreement,[772] the Panel will only review the investigation and determination that has been carried out at the national level, based upon the facts available at the time of the national investigation.[773] Indeed, the factual determinations will already be made by the national authorities and the Panel should not seek to "displace the national authority by doing its own factual investigation".[774] In case of the Antidumping Agreement, Members have an even greater margin of appreciation. In such a dispute, the Panel can only determine whether the establishment of the facts by the antidumping authorities was proper and whether the evaluation of the facts was unbiased and objective. If so, the Panel must accept the determination on antidumping, even if it may have reached a different conclusion about these facts.[775] On the other hand, when there is no national factual investigation required by the relevant WTO Agreement before the measure in question can be adopted,[776] the Panel can perform its own factual investigation. The reason for deference (the primary position the WTO Agreement has given to the factual determinations made by the national authorities) is in that case not relevant.[777] There are finally some agreements that require no elaborate factual determination, but still call for some scientific or technological basis for an adopted measure.[778] Also in this case, the Panel can reassess and recollect the

---

[770] Appellate Body Report: European Communities – Measures Concerning Meat and Meat Products (Hormones), WT/DS26 and 48/AB/R, (13 February 1998), para. 118.
[771] C.-D. EHLERMANN and N. LOCKHART, *supra* note 755, p. 520.
[772] See for instance art. 3 and 17.6 Antidumping Agreement, art. 7 Agreement on Safeguards and art. 21 Agreement on Subsidies and Countervailing Measures.
[773] See Panel Report: Guatemala – Definitive Antidumping Measures on Grey Portland Cement from Mexico, WT/DS156/R, (17 November 2000), para. 8.19. See also Appellate Body Report: United States – Transnational Safeguard Measures on Combed Cotton Yarn from Pakistan, WT/DS192/AB/R, (5 November 2001), para. 78. It is not clear whether the Panel can consider new arguments related to and new analysis of the available data. See C.-D. EHLERMANN and N. LOCKHART, *supra* note 755, p. 509, note 51.
[774] C.-D. EHLERMANN and N. LOCKHART, *supra* note 755, p. 502.
[775] See art. 17.6 Antidumping Agreement.
[776] See for instance art. III and art. XX GATT.
[777] EHLERMANN and LOCKHART argue that there is no reason to apply greater deference when the national authorities have instigated a formal factual investigation, even though this was not required by the agreement. This is because the agreement in question clearly did not give primary importance to the national determinations. See C.-D. EHLERMANN and N. LOCKHART, *supra* note 755, p. 514.
[778] This is the case for the TBT Agreement and the SPS Agreement. These agreements do *not* impose a minimum procedural requirement for preliminary assessment. See Appellate Body Report: European Communities – Measures Concerning Meat and Meat Products (Hormones), *supra* note 770, para. 193.

factual data, be it that the Panel will have to adopt some deference when it comes to the policy choices the national authorities have made based on their data.[779]

351. It is also essential that the dispute settlement procedures cannot "add to or diminish the rights and obligations provided in the covered agreements".[780] Thus, there is a warning in the DSU against 'judicial activism'.[781] Moreover, there is no principle of *stare decisis* in international trade law. Strictly legally, there is no binding force of precedent of dispute settlement reports. In practice, however, because of the poor drafting and vague formulation of many of the provisions of the WTO Agreements, the dispute settlement system has an important role to play in setting and modifying the rules of international trade.[782] What is more, a dispute settlement report becomes part of the practice under the WTO Agreements and is often referred to in later proceedings.[783] To be sure, the dispute settlement system of the WTO should clarify the provisions of the WTO Agreements.[784] It has been stated that "if the legislative fell short in legislating, the judiciary arm [has] the tendency to fill the gap".[785] Still, the role of dispute settlement should not be to produce judge-made law, but to give guidance on the basis of a case.

E. STANDING APPELLATE BODY

1. Composition of the Appellate Body

352. Appeals against Panel reports are heard by the standing Appellate Body. This permanent body consists of seven members who are appointed for four years. They do not have to reside in Geneva, since the membership of the Appellate Body was not expected to be a full-time job.[786] In practice, the workload of the Appellate

---

[779] See on the freedom to determine the own individual level of protection Appellate Body Report: Australia – Measures Affecting Importation of Salmon, WT/DS18/AB/R, (6 November 1998), para. 199. In fact, this deference to policy choices is also required for other measures than under SPS or TBT. See Appellate Body Report: European Communities – Measures Affecting Asbestos and Asbestos-Containing Products, WT/DS135/AB/R. (12 March 2001), para. 168.
[780] Art. 3.2 *in fine* and art. 19.2 DSU.
[781] See UNCTAD, *Course on Dispute Settlement. WTO Module 3.2 Panels, supra* note 686, p. 15.
[782] See J. JACKSON, *The World Trade Organization. Constitution and Jurisprudence, supra* note 29, p. 45.
[783] The Appellate Body has stated that these reports create legitimate expectations among WTO Members and should therefore be taken into account where they are relevant to any dispute. See Appellate Body Report: Japan – Taxes on Alcoholic Beverages, WT/DS8, 10 and 11/AB/R (4 October 1996), p. 13.
[784] Art. 3.2 DSU.
[785] Statement by the representative of the European Communities, Minutes of the Meeting of the General Council on 22 November 2000, WTO Doc. WT/GC/M/60, 23 January 2001, para. 96.
[786] At the time of drafting of the DSU, it was unclear how many appeals could be expected.

body makes it a full-time job. This term is renewable only once. The Appellate body is composed of persons of recognized authority, "with demonstrated expertise in law, international trade, and the subject matter of the covered agreements generally".[787] They must be "broadly representative of Membership of the WTO".[788] Until now, either three or four Appellate Body members have always been citizens of a developing country Member.[789] In contrast with what is the case for Panel members, there is an absolute prohibition for Appellate Body Members to be affiliated with any government.[790] Each case will be considered by a division of three persons.[791] There are no specific chambers specialized in particular trade problems. The Appellate Body should ensure continuity and consistency in the interpretation of the various WTO Agreements.[792]

2. *Appeal Process*

353. Parties in the dispute (not third parties) can take the Panel report to appeal.[793] Appeal is only possible on issues of law, the legal interpretations developed by the Panel and the procedures under the DSU the Panel should have followed.[794] One cannot appeal on issues of fact.[795] Of course, the distinction is sometimes difficult to make.[796] Moreover, often disputes result in unsatisfactory

---

[787] The current members are G.M. Abi-Saab (Egypt), L. Olavo Baptista (Brazil), A.V. Ganesan (India), M.E. Janow (United States), G. Sacerdoti (Chairman – Italy), Y. Tanigushi (Japan) and D. Unterhalter (South Africa). The Chairman of the Appellate Body is elected at the beginning of each year. See Working Procedures for Appellate Review, WT/AB/WP/7, 1 May 2003, section 5.

[788] Art. 17.3 DSU.

[789] WTO, *A Handbook on the WTO Dispute Settlement System*, (Cambridge, Cambridge University Press 2004), p. 24.

[790] Nonetheless, there is no provision barring a member of the Appellate Body from hearing a case in which the country of which he is a national is involved. The qualifications required for the members (*inter alia* the requirement of independence of any government and the withdrawal in case of direct or indirect conflict of interest) should be a sufficient guarantee against any bias. See Letter from Chairman Lacarte-Muró of the Appellate Body to Celso Lafer, Chairman of he WTO Dispute Settlement Body, WTO Press Release, 7 February 1996. Also the Working Procedures for Appellate Review indicate that the selection of the three serving members for a case is made at random and should be "regardless of their national origin". See Working Procedures for Appellate Review, WT/AB/WP/3, 28 February 1997, para. 6.2.

[791] Art. 17.1 DSU.

[792] A.F. Lowenfeld, *supra* note 669, p. 167.

[793] Art. 17.4 DSU.

[794] *Ibid.* art. 17.6.

[795] Appellate Body Report: European Communities – Measures Concerning Meat and Meat Products (Hormones), *supra* note 770, para. 132.

[796] For some examples see Appellate Body Report: European Communities – Measures Concerning Meat and Meat Products (Hormones), *supra* note 770, para. 132 (Determination of whether or not a certain event occurred in time and space is typically a question of fact. On the other hand, the consistency or inconsistency of a given fact or set of facts with the requirements of a given treaty provision is [...] a legal characterization issue. It is a legal question. [...]); Appellate

outcomes because the Appellate Body has only limited factual information. Since it cannot address issues of fact, no additional factual information can be collected. Therefore, it is sometimes proposed to establish the possibility of 'remand' for the Appellate Body. Indeed, as explained, the Panel often limits itself to addressing one legal question if this is sufficient to solve a case and because of 'judicial economy'. If the Appellate Body afterwards reverses the Panel's finding on this matter, it has to complete the legal analysis.[797] This is only possible if there is sufficient factual information available. A possibility of 'remand' would thus be extremely useful. In that case the Appellate Body will be able to send the case again to the Panel to make appropriate factual findings or address the other legal questions. The appellant should make written submissions to the Appellate Body within ten days after the filing of the notice of appeal. The appellee then has fifteen days for its response.[798] An oral hearing will be held thirty days after the filing of the notice of appeal.[799] In principle there is no second round of submissions, even though the Appellate Body division may request additional submissions by any participant.[800]

354. The Appellate Body may uphold the legal findings and conclusions of the Panel, modify its reasoning but maintain the conclusion, or reverse these legal findings and conclusions.[801] The Appellate Body report needs to be adopted by the Dispute Settlement Body (again by 'reverse consensus') within 30 days after the circulation of the report.

Body Report: European Communities – Regime for the Importation, Sale and Distribution of Bananas, *supra* note 655, para. 239 (The Panel's findings regarding the nationality, ownership and control of certain companies, as well as their respective market shares, were findings of fact.) and Appellate Body Report: Korea – Taxes on Alcoholic Beverages, WT/DS75/AB/R and WT/DS84/AB/R, (17 February 1999), para. 161 (The Panel's examination and weighing of evidence is a matter of fact, be it that this examination should be in accordance with art. 11 DSU. (See also Appellate Body Report: United States – Definitive Safeguard Measures on Imports of Wheat Gluten from the European Communities, WT/DS166/AB/R (19 January 2001), para. 151 and Appellate Body Report: European Communities – Trade Description of Sardines, WT/DS231/AB/R (23 October 2002), para. 299)).

[797] See Appellate Body Report: Australia – Measures Affecting the Importation of Salmon, WT/DS18/AB/R, (6 November 1998), para. 117.
[798] Working Procedures for Appellate Review, para. 21 and 22.
[799] *Ibid.*, para. 27 and Annex I.
[800] A.F. Lowenfeld, *supra* note 669, p. 169. Lowenfeld refers to the US-Gasoline case, where such second submissions were requested. See Panel Report: United States – Standards for Reformulated and Conventional Gasoline, WT/DS2/R, 29 January 1996 and Appellate Body Report: United States – Standards for Reformulated and Conventional Gasoline, WT/DS2/AB/R, (29 April 1996).
[801] Art. 17.13 DSU.

3. Third Parties

355. Third Parties who have an acknowledged substantial trade interest in the Panel procedure[802] may make written submissions and may be heard by the Appellate Body.[803] However, these parties cannot appeal the Panel report. Third Parties that choose to participate by making written submissions are then called 'Third Participants'.[804]

F. IMPLEMENTATION AND ENFORCEMENT

356. Condemnations of Members have little weight if sanctions cannot be imposed to enforce them. Nonetheless, trade sanctions cannot be imposed just like that. At a DSB meeting held within 30 days after the date of adoption of the Panel or Appellate Body report, Member concerned must inform the DSB of its intentions regarding implementation of the recommendations and rulings of the DSB. If it is impossible to comply immediately with the recommendations, Member concerned receives a reasonable period of time in which to do so.[805] If a Member fails to deal with the matter *within a reasonable period of time*, it has to enter into negotiations with a view to developing mutually acceptable compensation.[806] If no satisfactory compensation has been agreed within 20 days after the date of expiry of a reasonable period of time, the complainant may request authorization from the DSB to apply limited trade sanctions ('retaliation') to Member concerned (suspend the application of concessions or other obligations under the covered agreements). The DSB has to grant this authorization within 30 days after expiry of the reasonable period of time, unless there is a consensus against the request.[807]

357. More often than not, there is disagreement on whether the measures taken to comply with a ruling exist or whether they are consistent with the covered WTO Agreement. In that situation, the original Panel that dealt with the case rules upon the disagreement. This Panel has to decide within 90 days after the case has been referred to this Panel.[808] Nevertheless, when the DSB has granted authorization to apply limited trade sanctions (under the form of suspension of

---

[802] See *supra* para. 343.
[803] Art. 17.4 DSU.
[804] UNCTAD, *Course on Dispute Settlement. WTO Module 3.3 Appellate Review*, http://www.unctad.org/en/docs/edmmisc232add17_en.pdf, 9.
[805] Art. 21.3 DSU.
[806] E.g. tariff reductions for products, which are of particular interest for the complainant(s).
[807] Art. 22.6 DSU.
[808] *Ibid.* art. 21.5.

trade concessions) and Member concerned "objects to the level of suspension proposed, or claims that the principles and procedures set forth in paragraph 3 have not been followed [...] the matter shall be referred to arbitration" by the original Panel.[809] This Panel has to decide within 60 days after the date of expiry of the reasonable period of time. There is a fair amount of discussion on the relationship between these two provisions (Art. 21.5 and 22.6 DSU). Indeed, it seems difficult to imagine that the Panel, on the one hand, has to decide within 60 days after the date of expiry of the reasonable period of time on the level and procedure to apply the trade sanctions, but, on the other hand, has nevertheless 90 days, after referral of the case, to decide whether sanctions were even necessary. Hence it is possible that a procedure is initiated under Article 21.5 when the expiry of the reasonable period of time draws near. The Panel has a period of 90 days to complete this procedure. However, the period for the procedure under Article 22.6 will clearly be irreconcilable. Indeed, this procedure already expires 60 days after the expiry of the reasonable period of time.[810] This is the so-called 'sequencing problem'. An Arbitration Panel has nevertheless decided that it is necessary to find a logical solution. The Panel argued that it could already decide whether the measures taken are consistent with the WTO Agreements during the procedure under Article 22.6 (concerning the level and procedure of suspension).[811]

358.   In principle, the sanctions have to be taken in the same sector as the one concerned in the dispute. If this proves ineffective, sanctions may be related to another sector or even another covered agreement (so-called 'cross-retaliation'). Thus, trade sanctions can only be the *ultimum remedium*.[812] Certainly, these

---

[809]   Ibid. art. 22.6.
[810]   See Arbitration Panel Report: European Communities – Regime for the importation, sale and distribution of bananas – Recourse to arbitration by the European Communities under article 22.6 of the DSU, WT/DS27/ARB (9 April 1999), para. 4.11, note 86.
[811]   Ibid. Paras 4.11–4.15.
[812]   It is to be noted that the European Community currently pays with respect to the *Hormones* case (a dispute that has already lasted for more than 18 years) a trade sanction of USD 116.8 million per year in the form of suspension of trade concessions by the US. The EC still refuses to open up its market for hormone-treated beef from the US and Canada. What is more, the WTO authorized (among others) the US to impose trade sanctions of up to 191 million USD. This *Bananas* dispute, which concerned the more favourable treatment by the EC of bananas originating in certain developing countries, was finally settled in 1999. On the other hand, the EC threatened in the *US-Steel Tariffs* case to impose on the US sanctions up to USD 2.2 billion of US imports if the US persisted in refusing to remove its tariffs of 30% on steel imports in the US. The US finally did so on 4 December 2003. Finally, the EC also maintains, in the *US-Foreign Sales Corporations* case up to USD 200 million of trade sanctions (a tariff of 5% on imports worth USD 4 billion. It should be noted that the WTO has granted the EC the right to impose tariffs of 100%!). This case concerned the tax benefit the US had granted to US firms that are mainly involved in exports, which came down to an export subsidy. This case has not been settled satisfactorily; later legislation by the US has also been found unacceptable by the WTO.

sanctions go directly against the WTO's objective (trade liberalization) and therefore against the economic interest of either party.[813] Moreover, these sanctions are of little use to poorer Members. When they win against a rich, industrialized country (e.g. because this country impedes the import from this poorer country) and impose trade sanctions, this will not hit the richer Member hard. The export of this richer State to the poorer, winning country will only represent a fraction of the total export of this rich country and therefore trade sanctions will be negligible.[814]

G. TRANSPARENCY OF THE DISPUTE SETTLEMENT PROCESS – *AMICUS CURIAE* BRIEFS

359. The broad and active role of the Dispute Settlement System is causing problems of transparency and accountability. The dispute settlement organs of the WTO had to decide in recent years on politically sensitive issues such as environmental protection, public health and development policy, where they often lack expertise. The fierce reactions to decisions such as the Shrimp [815] and Hormones cases[816] show the unease of many people with the current inaccessible dispute settlement system. Therefore, proposals have been made by the United States to open up the dispute settlement process for civil society and members not party to a dispute but with a legitimate interest in the case.[817] This may be done by accepting *amicus curiae* briefs. These briefs are submitted by persons or entities that are not parties to the dispute, but nevertheless feel that they can bring expertise or experience to the Panel or Appellate Body.[818] The African Group

---

[813] See Arbitration Panel in the Bananas dispute: "The suspension of concessions is not in the economic interest of either [party]". Arbitration Panel Report: European Communities – Regime for Importations, Sale and Distribution of Bananas – Recourse to Arbitration by the EC under art. 22.6 DSU, *supra* note 810, para. 2.13.
[814] J. PAUWELYN, 'Enforcement and Countermeasures in the WTO: Rules are Rules – Toward a More Collective Approach', *American Journal of International Law* (2000), p. 338.
[815] Appellate Body Report: United States – Import prohibition of certain shrimp and shrimp products, WT/DS58/AB/R, (12 October 1998).
[816] Appellate Body Report: European Communities – Measures concerning meat and meat products (Hormones), WT/DS26 and 48/AB/R, (13 February 1998).
[817] Contribution of the United States to the Improvement of the Dispute Settlement Understanding of the WTO Related to Transparency, TN/DS/W/13, 9 August 2000.
[818] Such *amicus curiae* briefs have also recently been accepted by an ICSID (International Centre for the Settlement of Investment Disputes) tribunal in the case Suez, Sociedad General de Aguas de Barcelona, S.A., and Vivendi Universal S.A. v. The Argentine Republic, ICSID Case No. ARB/03/19, Order in Response to a Petition by Five Non-Governmental Organizations for Permission to Make an Amicus Curiae Submission, 12 February 2007, available on http://ita.law.uvic.ca/documents/SuezVivendiamici.pdf.

submitted its own communication in September 2002.[819] The Group did not focus on transparency issues, but denounced the structural impediments for dispute settlement access for developing countries. As far as transparency is concerned, it confined itself to demanding technical and financial assistance for *amicus curiae* briefs. It rejected opening up the DSM to the public at this time.[820] India also filed a communication aimed at explicitly prohibiting Panels and the Appellate Body from accepting and considering unsolicited information and advice.[821]

360. The Appellate Body itself made a move towards more openness and accepted the right of Panels and the Appellate Body to accept *amicus curiae* briefs filed by non-parties in its Shrimp[822], Steel[823] and Asbestos[824] decisions. These decisions faced fierce objections by the majority of Members.[825] Mostly developing countries feared that well-equipped organizations from industrial countries would unduly interfere in the dispute settlement process, thereby sidelining the parties themselves.

361. Costa Rica noted that "such a measure represented a risk for developing countries as it would put them in a situation where they would be sort of possibilities of defence".[826] Other objections include the possibility of trials by the media and the risk of making the proceedings more burdensome. Nevertheless, the Panels and Appellate Body do not seem to be accepting large numbers of briefs because the briefs rarely meet the procedural requirements the Panels or Appellate Body set.

---

[819] Negotiations on the Dispute Settlement Understanding, Proposal by the African Group, TN/DS/W/15, 9 September 2002, available on http://www.law.georgetown.edu/iiel/research/projects/dsureview/documents/W15.doc

[820] *Ibid.*, para. 12.

[821] Proposal on DSU by India et. al., TN/DS/W/18, 7 October 2002, p. 2.

[822] Appellate Body Report: United States – Import prohibition of certain shrimp and shrimp products, WT/DS58/AB/R, (12 October 1998).

[823] Appellate Body Report: United States – Imposition Of Countervailing Duties On Certain Hot-Rolled Lead And Bismouth Carbon Steel Products Originating In The United Kingdom, WT/DS138/AB/R, (10 May 2000).

[824] Appellate Body Report: European Communities – Measures affecting asbestos and products containing asbestos WT/DS135AB/R, (12 March 2001). Document inviting briefs: WT/DS135/9, 8 November 2000.

[825] Some WTO members had serious concerns about the initiative of the Appellate Body and requested an extraordinary meeting of the WTO General Council. This meeting took place on 22 November 2000. However, the United States '*believed that the Appellate Body had acted appropriately*' (Minutes of the Meeting of the General Council on 22 November 2000, WT/GC/M/60, 23 January 2001, para 74), whereas the EC stated that there was a need for rule-making on this issue, and that '*if the legislative fell short in legislating, the judiciary arm had the tendency to fill the gap*' (Minutes of the Meeting, para 96).

[826] Minutes of the Meeting, para 70.

362. Surely, the Appellate Body in *EC-Asbestos* did *not* rule that there is a duty to accept and comment on the briefs.[827] The Panels and the Appellate Body can easily reject them and do so often with vague reasons.[828] Although it is undeniable that *amicus curiae* briefs can help the Dispute Settlement Bodies produce a well-elaborated decision, taking into account all interests, it should not be ignored that the NGOs and other interested parties that submit the briefs may represent only a narrow interest.[829]

363. There is an undeniable need for clearly elaborated criteria for *amicus curiae* brief-filing. These criteria can provide a certain filter for briefs being allowed. On the other hand, one should be aware that these criteria are not used arbitrarily to restrict access. Indeed the statements by the EC that there is a need for rule-making on this issue and that "if the legislative fell short in legislating, the judiciary arm [has] the tendency to fill the gap"[830] point to this danger. Unfortunately, none of the proposals regulating the filing of *amicus curiae* briefs[831] and none of the proposals to allow Panel meetings and Appellate Body hearings to be open to the public[832] have been retained in the "Chairman's Text" on the current Dispute Settlement Understanding Negotiations.[833] This "Chairman's Text" is the basis for further amendments to the Dispute Settlement Understanding.

---

[827] For a critical analysis, see P. MAVROIDIS, '*Amicus Curiae* Briefs Before the WTO: Much Ado About Nothing', *Jean Monnet Working Paper 2/01*, New York University School of Law, 2001, available on http://www.jeanmonnetprogram.org/papers/01/010201.html. See also P. ALA'I, 'Judicial Lobbying at the WTO: the debate over the Use of Amicus Curiae Briefs and the US Experience', *Fordham International Law Journal* (2000), pp. 62-94 and A. ANTONIADIS, 'Enhanced Third Party Rights in the WTO Dispute Settlement Understanding', *Legal Issues of Economic Integration* (2002), pp. 285-304.

[828] P. MAVROIDIS, *supra* note 827, pp. 10 and 12.

[829] According to MAVROIDIS, "many friends of the court are rather friends of themselves. They do not care about systemic issues, they do not care for the truth. They want to sell a message." *Ibid.*, p. 12.

[830] Minutes of the Meeting of the General Council on 22 November 2000, WTO Doc. WT/GC/M/60, 23 January 2001, para 96.

[831] See Contribution of the European Communities and its Member States to Improvement of the WTO Dispute Settlement, 13 March 2002, TN/DS/W/1, p. 7. See the remarks on the EC's proposal by India: Proposals Relative to the Improvement of the Dispute Settlement Understanding – Communication from India, 29 April 2002, TN/DS/W/5.

[832] See Contribution of the United States to the Improvement of the Dispute Settlement Understanding of the WTO Related to Transparency, 9 August 2000, TN/DS/W/13.

[833] See the annex to the Report by the Chairman, Ambassador Péter Balás, to the Trade Negotiations Committee, TN/DS/9, 6 June 2003.

H. POSITION OF DEVELOPING COUNTRIES IN THE DISPUTE SETTLEMENT SYSTEM

364. It has been argued that the dispute settlement system of the WTO does not deliver to the developing countries what had been promised. Instead of creating a system that would allow dispute settlement on the basis of the rule of law, rather than on the basis of economic power, the system would be costlier, more complex and more mechanical.[834] Developing Countries would lack the practical ability to participate in dispute settlement. They would have insufficient legal expertise and human resources available to assess whether a claim could be brought and to pursue the claim successfully until the end. Of course, developing countries could hire a private law firm to bring their claims. Nevertheless, this would not always be desirable because the pursuance of a legal claim should be in tune with the commercial policy of Member bringing the claim. Indeed, while a claim is being brought on a certain issue, positions that are consistent with this claim need to be defended by the government officials of this Member in the other WTO bodies.[835] Moreover, before a law firm is hired to bring the claim, the government officials of Member need to be able to assess whether a successful claim could be brought and thus whether the potential benefits of the procedure outweigh the costs. Furthermore, the fact that it is known that developing countries have difficulties in pursuing their claim effectively also disadvantages them in the pre-trial (consultation) phase. Since it is difficult for them to make it credible that they will pursue a claim at all cost, they are in a weak position to achieve a favourable deal during consultations.[836] Finally, as has already been mentioned in the previous section, the small portion of trade flowing into developing countries makes them often unable to retaliate effectively against larger Members that lose a dispute settlement case.

365. Nevertheless, the DSU has a number of provisions on differential treatment of developing countries in dispute settlement. Some of these provisions are operative obligations. Yet, some other provisions are phrased as 'best endeavours'. A first obligation in the DSU is Article 3.12. This article grants the right to developing countries to invoke the provisions of the so-called 'Decision of 1966'[837] if a complaint is brought against it. This Decision provides an accelerated

---

[834] See T. STOSTAD, 'Trappings of Legality: Judicialization of Dispute Settlement in the WTO, and its Impact on Developing Countries', *Cornell International Law Journal* (2006), p. 834.
[835] J. GABILONDO, 'Developing Countries in the WTO Dispute Settlement Procedures. Improving Their Participation', *Journal of World Trade* (2001), p. 485.
[836] See M. BUSCH and E. REINHARDT, 'Developing Countries and General Agreement on Tariffs and Trade/World Trade Organization Dispute Settlement', *Journal of World Trade* (2003), p. 732.
[837] Decision on Procedures under Article XXIII, 5 April 1966, BISD 14S/18.

procedure as an alternative to the normal procedures of the DSU. If the consultations between the developing country Member and the other Member are not satisfactorily, the developing country may refer the matter to the Director-General, which may then use his good offices. The Director-General will draft a report if there is no result within two months. The Dispute Settlement Body may then establish a Panel with the approval of both parties. The Panel has 60 days to draft a report in which it should give due account to the impact on trade and economic development of the developing country. The Decision of 1966 has only once been relied upon during the GATT 1947 era[838] and never since. This is mainly due to the fact that developing countries rather require extended time limits and not accelerated procedures. A second specific operative obligation in the DSU is Article 8.10. This provision requires that Panels shall include at least one member from a developing country when a dispute is in question in which a developing country is involved. The inclusion of the Panel member from a developing country occurs upon the request of the developing country. Third, according to Article 12.10, the Panel must, when examining a complaint against a developing country, accord sufficient time to this country to prepare and present its argumentation.[839] Nevertheless, this cannot influence the total time in which a Panel needs to complete a procedure. Fourth, Article 12.11 requires Panels to indicate the relevant provisions on differential treatment in the agreements that are raised in the dispute. Finally, Article 27.2 obliges the WTO Secretary to assist developing countries when they are involved in dispute settlement. To this end, the Secretariat is required to make available a qualified legal expert from the WTO technical cooperation services to any developing country member which so requests. It was difficult, however, to ensure the impartiality of the WTO Secretariat when it got involved in supporting the developing country Member. Therefore, an independent Advisory Centre on WTO Law was established (see *supra* paras. 195-201).

366. The first 'best endeavour' provision with regard to developing countries and dispute settlement is Article 4.10. This provision calls upon WTO Members to use their best endeavours to give special attention to the problems and interests of developing countries during consultations. Second, Article 21.2 requires the 'best endeavours' of WTO Members to pay special attention to matters affecting developing countries in surveillance of the implementation of Dispute Settlement Body recommendations. Third, the Dispute Settlement Body needs to consider

---

[838] See the (first) *Bananas* case: GATT Panel Report: EEC – Member States' Import Regimes for Bananas, (3 June 1993), DS32/R.
[839] Extended time to prepare was granted in a case against India. See Panel Report: India – Quantitative Restrictions on Imports of Agricultural, Textiles and Industrial Products, WT/DS90/R, (6 April 1999), para. 5.10.

further action appropriate in the circumstances when it considers the implementation of rulings in a case which is brought by a developing country Member (Article 21.7 and 21.8). Fourth, due restraint must be taken into account when a dispute involves a least developed country and when compensation is requested or authorization is sought to suspend obligations. In that case, if consultations are unsuccessful, the DSU also specifically provides good offices, conciliation and mediation by the Director-General of the WTO or the Chairman of the Dispute Settlement Body.

367. Despite these provisions on special and differential treatment, the discussions on how to enable developing countries to make better use of the WTO dispute settlement system are on-going. A major step in improving their capacity was the establishment of the Advisory Centre on WTO Law (see *supra* paras. 195-201). This Centre provides assistance in all stages of the proceedings, starting from the consideration on whether to bring a case. Proposals have also been made to improve the effectiveness of retaliation by developing countries. It has been suggested that 'collective retaliatory action' should be allowed by all WTO Members against the offending Member.[840] Yet, there is wide disagreement among WTO Members on this issue and therefore, it was not included in the text which forms the basis for further negotiations on DSU reform.[841] Some scholars also argue in favour of introducing a system of 'retroactive damages', where violating WTO Members are obliged to pay compensation also for past violations.[842] Also this proposal has not been taken up in further discussions.

The current text that forms the basis for reform negotiations includes a number of proposals to make the provisions in the DSU that grant special and differential treatment more specific and more operative.[843] It contains a proposal to allow the extension of any time period by mutual agreement of the parties to the dispute, giving special attention to developing countries.[844] With regard to least-developed countries, it is proposed to allow the consultation phase to take place in the capital of the least-developed country.[845] It is also proposed to allow developing countries to request a postponement of the establishment of a Panel until the next DSB

---

[840] See J. PAUWELYN, *supra* note 814, pp. 342–345 and T. STOSTAD, *supra* note 834, p. 842.
[841] See Report by the Chairman, Ambassador Péter Balás, to the Trade Negotiations Committee, TN/DS/9, 6 June 2003, para. 6.
[842] See P. MAVROIDIS, 'Remedies in the WTO Legal System: Between a Rock and a Hard Place', *European Journal of International Law* (2000), pp. 763–813.
[843] E.g. the 'should' in art. 4.10 and art. 21.2 would be replaced by 'shall'. See the Annex to the Report by the Chairman, Ambassador Péter Balás, to the Trade Negotiations Committee, *supra* note 841.
[844] See proposed art. 3.13.
[845] See proposed amendment to art. 4.10.

meeting, in dispute cases brought against the developing country Member.[846] Furthermore, in disputes between developing country Members and developed country Members, there would be an automatic inclusion of a panel member from a developing country, unless this country would agree otherwise. This applies also to disputes against least-developed countries. Yet, if no panellist could be found from a least-developed country, a panellist from a developed country can be included.[847] The application of provisions on special and differential treatment should not only be mentioned explicitly, but their application should be raised as soon as possible in the dispute, and developed country Members in the dispute should address such arguments explicitly.[848] Special attention should be paid to finding a suitable form of compensation when a developing or least-developed country was the complaining party.[849] To enable poorer countries to bring cases effectively without being deterred by the costs, it is proposed that some of the litigation costs could be rewarded by the Panel or Appellate Body.[850] It remains to be seen what proposals will finally be adopted.

---

[846] See proposed amendment to art. 6.1.
[847] See proposed art. 8.10.
[848] See proposed art. 12.11.
[849] See proposed art. 22.2 *bis*, (c).
[850] See proposed art. 28.

SELECT BIBLIOGRAPHY

1. GENERAL PUBLICATIONS ON THE WTO AND INTERNATIONAL ECONOMIC LAW

Arup, C., *The New World Trade Organization Agreements. Globalizing Law through Services and Intellectual Property* (Cambridge, Cambridge University Press, 2000), xiii + 340 p.

Barfield, C.G., *Free Trade, Sovereignty, Democracy: The Future of the World Trade Organization* (London, AEI Press, 2001), 247 p.

Bélanger, M., *Institutions économiques internationales* (Paris, Economica, 1992, 5th ed.), 188 p.

Bronckers, M.C.E.J., *A cross-section of WTO law* (London, Cameron May, 2000), 300 p.

Callagher, P., *Guide to the WTO and developing countries* (The Hague, Kluwer, 2000), xxii + 343 p.

Carreau D. and Juillard, P., *Droit international économique* (Paris, L.G.D.J., 1998, 4th ed.), xxxvi + 720 p.

Croome, J., *Guide to the Uruguay round agreements* (The Hague, Kluwer, 1999), xx + 285 p.

Fontanel, J., *Organisations économiques internationales* (Paris, Masson, 1995, 2nd ed.), 186 p.

Footer, M., *An Institutional and Normative Analysis of the World Trade Organization*, (Rotterdam, Erasmus Universiteit 2005), xxiii + 384 p.

Goyal, A., *WTO in the new millennium. Commentary, case law, legal texts* (MVIRDC World Trade Centre, 2000), xxxii + 881 p.

Herdegen, M., *Internationales Wirtschaftsrecht: ein Studienbuch* (München, Beck, 1995), 2nd ed., xiv + 251 p.

Hilf, M. and Oeter, S., *WTO-Recht. Rechtsordnung des Welthandels*, (Baden-Baden, Nomos 2005), xxxviii + 738 p.

Hoekman, B.M. and Kostecki, M.M., *The political economy of the World Trading System: the WTO and beyond* (Oxford, Oxford University Press, 2001, 2nd ed.), xxi + 547 p;

Hoekman, B.M. and Evenett, S.J., *Economic Development and Multilateral Trade Cooperation*, (London, Palgrave Macmillan 2006), xliv + 477 p.

Hoekman, B.M., and Mavroidis, P.C., *The World Trade Organization. Law, Economics and Politics*, (London, Routledge 2007), 143 p.

Hudec, R.E., *The GATT Legal System and World Trade Diplomacy* (Salem, Butterworth, 1990, 2nd ed.), xxi + 376 p.

Jackson, J.H., *The World Trading System. Law and Policy of International Economic Relations* (Cambridge, MIT Press, 1997, 2nd ed.), viii + 441 p.

Jackson, J.H., *The World Trade Organization. Constitution and Jurisprudence* (London, Royal Institute of International Affairs, 1998), xiv + 193 p.

Jackson, J.H., *The Jurisprudence of the GATT and the WTO: Insights on Treaty Law and Economic Relations* (New York, Cambridge University Press 2000), xiii + 497 p.

Jackson, J.H., Davey, W.J. and Sykes, A.O., *Legal Problems of International Economic Relations. Cases, Materials and Text* (St. Paul, West, 1995, 3rd ed.), lvi + 1248 p.

Lowenfeld, A., *International Economic Law* (Oxford, Clarendon Press, 2002), xliv + 776 p.

Luff, D., *Le droit de l'Organisation mondiale de commerce: analyse critique*, (Brussels, Bruylant 2004), xliv + 1277 p.

Macrory, P., Appleton, A. and Plummer, M. (eds.), *The World Trade Organization. Legal, Economic and Political Analysis*, (New York, Springer 2005), 3 vol.

Matsushita, M., Schoenbaum, T.J. and Mavroidis, P., *The World Trade Organization: law, practice, and policy*, (Oxford, Oxford University Press, 2006), cvii + 989 p.

Moore, M., *Doha and Beyond. The Future of the Multilateral Trading System*, (Cambridge, Cambridge University Press 2004), xx + 184 p.

Narlikar, A., *International Trade and Developing Countries: bargaining coalitions in the GATT & WTO*, (London, Routledge, 2003), xviii + 238 p.

Narlikar, A., *The World Trade Organization. A Very Short Introduction*, (Oxford, Oxford University Press 2005), 155 p.

Ortino, F., *Basic Legal Instruments for the Liberalization of Trade: a Comparative Analysis of EU and WTO Law*,(Oxford, Hart Publishing, 2004), xxii + 502 p.

Qureshi, A.H., *The World Trade Organization* (Manchester, Manchester University Press, 1996), xi + 260 p.

Qureshi, A.H. *International Economic Law* (London, Sweet & Maxwell, 1999), xxviii + 417 p.

Rao, M.B., *WTO and international trade* (New Delhi, Vikas Publ. House, 2001), xxviii + 479 p.

Rey, J.-J. and Dutry, J., *Institutions économiques internationales* (Brussels, Bruylant, 2001, 3rd ed.), 229 p.

Ruttley, P. (ed.), *The WTO and International Trade Regulation* (London, Cameron May, 1999), 270 p.

Sanviti, G. and Marcolungo, C., 'I principi fondamentali del WTO', *Revista Trimestriale di diritto pubblico* 2003, pp. 749–768.

Schachtschneider, K.A. and Emmerich-Fritsche, A., *Rechtsfragen der Weltwirtschaft* (Berlin, Duncker & Humblot, 2002), 514 p.

Schirm, S. (ed.), *New Rules for Global Markets. Public and Private Governance in the World Economy*, (New York, Palgrave Macmillan 2004), xix + 265 p.

Seidl-Hohenveldern, I., *International Economic Law* (Dordrecht, Nijhoff, 1992, 2nd ed.), xiii + 286 p.

Senti, R., *WTO: System und Funktionsweise der Welthandelsordnung* (Zürich, Schulthess, 2000), xxiv + 728 p.

Senti, R. and Conlan, P., *Regulation of World Trade after the Uruguay Round* (Zürich, Schulthess, 1998), 131 p.

Siegel, D., 'Legal Aspects of the IMF/WTO Relationship: The Fund's Articles of Agreement and the WTO', *American Journal of International Law* (2002), pp. 561–599.

Stoll, P.-T. and Schorkopf, F., *WTO. Welthandelsordnung und Welthandelsrecht* (Köln, Heymann, 2002), xvii + 294 p.

Trebilcock, M.J. and Howse, R., *The Regulation of International Trade* (London, Routledge, 2005, 3rd ed.), xiv + 759 p.

Trépant, I., *L'Organisation mondiale du commerce*, (Brussels, CRISP 2005), 102 p.

Van den Bossche, P., *The Law and Policy of the World Trade Organization. Text, Cases and Materials*, (Cambridge, Cambridge University Press 2005), xxxviii + 737 p.

Van Hamel, H.H.R., *The World Trade Organization: Selective Bibliography* (The Hague, Peace Palace Library, 2000, Upd. 2nd ed.), vi + 246 p.

Van Houtte, H., *The Law of International Trade* (London, Sweet & Maxwell, 2001, 2nd ed.), xli + 429 p.

Van Meerhaeghe, M.A.G., *International Economic Institutions* (Dordrecht, Kluwer Academic Publishers, 1992), 5th ed., 398 p.

Voitovich, S.A., *International Economic Organizations in the International Legal Process* (Dordrecht, Nijhoff, 1995), 199 p.

Warêgne, J.-M., *L'Organisation mondiale du commerce: règles de fonctionnement et enjeux économiques* (Brussels, CRISP, 2000), 381 p.

Weiler, J.H.H. (ed.), *The EU, the WTO, and the NAFTA: towards a common law of international trade?* (Oxford, Oxford University Press, 2001), xx + 238 p.

Weiβ, W., Herrmann, C.W. and Ohler, C., *Welthandelsrecht* (München, Beck, 2003), xxvii + 491 p.

Wilkinson, R., *Multilateralism and the World Trade Organization: The Architecture and Extension of International Trade Regulation* (London, Routledge, 2000), x + 166 p.

Wouters, J. and De Meester, B., 'Safeguarding Coherence in Global Policy-Making on Trade and Health: the EU-WHO-WTO Triangle', *International Organizations Law Review* (2005), p. 395–433.

Wouters, J. and Coppens, D., 'International Economic Policy-Making: Exploring the Legal Linkages between the World Trade Organization and the Bretton Woods Institutions', *International Organizations Law Review* (2006), p. 267–315.

WTO, *The Legal Texts, the Results of the Uruguay Round of Multilateral Trade Negotiations* (Cambridge, Cambridge University Press), 1999, 566 p.

WTO, *From GATT to the WTO: the Multilateral Trading System in the New Millennium* (The Hague, Kluwer, 2000), xiii + 183 p.

Yi-Chong, X. and Weller, P., *The Governance of World Trade. International Civil Servants and the GATT/WTO*, (Cheltenham, Elgar 2004), x + 311 p.

2. HISTORY OF WTO – GATT 1947

Croome, J., *Reshaping the World Trading System. A History of the Uruguay Round* (The Hague, Kluwer, 1998), 360 p.

Demaret, P., 'Les métamorphoses du GATT: de la chartre de La Havane à l'organisation mondiale du commerce', *Journal des Tribunaux Droit Européen* (1994), pp. 121–130.

Graz, J.-C., *Aux sources de l'OMC: la Charte de la Havane 1941-1950 / Precursor of the WTO: the stillborn Havana charter, 1941-1950* (Geneva, Droz, 1999), xxvii + 367 p.

Stewart, T.P., *The GATT Uruguay Round: a negotiating history, 1986-1992* (Deventer, Kluwer, 1993), 3 vol., ix + 2921; ix + 973 p.

Woolcock, S., 'Uruguay Round Negotiations', *The Trade Policy of the European Community* (1993), pp. 25-31.

3. DISPUTE SETTLEMENT IN THE WTO

Barrata, R., 'La legittimazione dell'amicus curiae dinanzi agli organi giudiziali della Organizzazione mondiale del commercio', *Rivista di diritto internazionale* (2002), p. 549-572.

Blackmore, D., 'Eradicating the Long-Standing Existence of a No-Precedent Rule in International Trade Law: Looking Towards Stare Decisis in WTO Dispute Settlement', *North Carolina Journal of International Law and Commercial Regulation* (2004), pp. 487-519.

Boisson de Chazournes, L., 'Transparency and Amicus Curiae Briefs', *The Journal of World Investment and Trade* (2004), pp. 333-336.

Bowsn, C. and Hoekman, B., 'WTO Dispute Settlement and the Missing Developing Country Cases. Engaging the Private Sector', *Journal of International Economic Law* (2005), pp. 861-890.

Bronkers, M. and Van den Broeck, N., 'Financial Compensation in the WTO: Improving Remedies in WTO Dispute Settlement', *Journal of International Economic Law* (2005), pp. 101-126.

Busch, M. and Reinhart, E., 'Three's a Crowd: Third Parties and WTO Dispute Settlement', *World Politics* (2007), pp. 446-477.

Canal-Fourgues, E., *Le règlement de différends à l'OMC*, (Brussels, Bruylant, 2003), 161 p.

Cottier, T. (ed.), *The Challenge for the WTO. Collected Essays*, (London, Cameron May 2007), 615 p.

Davey, W., 'WTO Dispute Settlement: The First Ten Years', *Journal of International Economic Law* (2005), pp. 17-50.

Davey, W., *Enforcing World Trade Rules. Essays on WTO Dispute Settlement and GATT Obligations*, (London, Cameron May 2006), 339 p.

Ehlermann, C.-D., 'Reflections on the Appellate Body of the WTO', *American Society of International Law Proceedings* (2003), pp. 77-86.

Emsch, A., 'The European Court of Justice and WTO Dispute Settlement Rulings: The End of the Flirt', *The Journal of World Investment and Trade* (2006), pp. 563-586.

Fukunaga, Y., 'Securing Compliance through the WTO Dispute Settlement Mechanism: Implementation of the DSB Recommendations', *Journal of International Economic Law* (2006), pp. 383-426.

Gallagher, P., *Guide to Dispute Settlement* (The Hague, Kluwer Law International, 2002), xi + 148 p.

Georgiev, D. and Van der Borght, K. (eds.), *Reform and Development of the WTO Dispute Settlement System*, (London, Cameron May 2006), 288 p.

Greisberger, A., 'Enhancing the Legitimacy of the WTO: Why the United States and the European Union Should Support the Advisory Centre on WTO Law', *Vanderbilt Journal of Transnational Law* (2004), pp. 827–860.

Josling, T. and Taylor, T., *Banana Wars. The Anatomy of a Trade Dispute*, (Wallingford, CABI 2003), x + 210 p.

Kouris, S., 'The WTO's Dispute Settlement Procedures: Are They Up to the Task after 10 Years?', *The Journal of World Investment and Trade* (2006), pp. 235–255.

Larouer, C., 'WTO Non-violation Complaints. A Misunderstood Remedy in the WTO Dispute Settlement System', *Netherlands International Law Review* (2006), pp. 97–126.

Layton, D. and Miranda, J., 'Advocacy before World Trade Organization Dispute Settlement Panels in Trade Remedy Cases', *Journal of World Trade* (2003), pp. 69–103.

Leitner, K. and Lester, S., 'WTO Dispute Settlement 1995–2003: a Statistical Analysis', *Journal of International Economic Law* (2004), pp. 169–181.

Leitner, K. and Lester, S., 'WTO Dispute Settlement from 1995–2005: a Statistical Analysis', *Journal of International Economic Law* (2006), pp. 219–231.

Lockhart, J. and Voon, T., 'Reviewing Appellate Review in the WTO Dispute Settlement System', *Melbourne Journal of International Law* (2005), pp. 474–484.

Marceau, G., 'The WTO Dispute Settlement and Human Rights', in F. Abott, C. Breining-Kaufmann and T. Cottier (eds.), *International Trade and Human Rights: Foundations and Conceptual Issues*, (Ann Arbor, University of Michigan Press 2006), pp. 181–258.

Mathis, J.H., 'GATT Dispute Settlement Procedures', *The trade policy of the European Community* (1993), pp. 19–23.

Matsushita, M., 'Transparency, Amicus Curiae Briefs and Third Party Rights', *Journal of World Investment and Trade* (2004), pp. 329–332.

Mavroidis, P. and Sykes, A.O. (eds.), *The WTO and International Trade Law/Dispute Settlement*, (Cheltenham, Elgar 2005), vii + 697 p.

McRae, D., 'What is the Future of WTO Dispute Settlement?', *Journal of International Economic Law* 2004, pp. 3–21.

Meagher, N., 'So Far So Good. But What Next? The Sutherland Report and Dispute Settlement', *World Trade Review* (2005), pp. 409–417.

de Mestral, A. and Auerbach-Ziogas, M., 'A Proposal to Introduce an Advocate-General's Opinion in WTO Dispute Settlement', in S. Charnovitz, D. Stieger and P. Van den Bossche (eds.), *Law in the Service of Human Dignity. Essays in Honour of Florentino Feliciano*, (Cambridge, Cambridge University Press 2005), pp. 159–180.

Mosoti, V., 'Africa in the First Decade of WTO Dispute Settlement', *African Yearbook of International Law* (2006), pp. 67–103.

Oesch, M., *Standards of Review in WTO Dispute Resolution*, (Oxford, Oxford University Press, 2003), 296 p.

Palma, L., 'The Participation of Developing Countries in WTO Dispute Settlement and the Role of the Advisory Centre on WTO Law', in S. Charnovitz, D. Stieger and P. Van den Bossche (eds.), *Law in the Service of Human Dignity. Essays in Honour of Florentino Feliciano*, (Cambridge, Cambridge University Press 2005), pp. 90–102.

Palmeter, D. and Mavroidis, P.C., *Dispute Settlement in the World Trade Organization. Practice and Procedure* (The Hague, Kluwer, 1999), xvi + 313 p.

Panizzon, M., 'Good Faith in the Jurisprudence of the WTO. The Protection of Legitimate Expectations, Good Faith Interpretation and Fair Dispute Settlement', in X. *Studies in International Law* (Oxford, Hart 2006), pp. 375–388.

Pauwelyn, J., 'How to Win a World Trade Organization Dispute Based on Non-World Trade Organization Law?', *Journal of World Trade* (2003), pp. 997–1030.

Perez-Aznar, F., *Countermeasures in the WTO Dispute Settlement System: An Analysis of their Characteristics and Procedure in the Light of General International Law*, (Geneva, Graduate Institute of International Studies 2006), 138 p.

Pescatore, P., *Handbook of GATT Dispute Settlement* (Ardsley on Hudson, Transnational, Deventer, Kluwer, 1991–1995), 2 vol.

Petersmann, E.-U., 'Improvements to the Functioning of the GATT System Including Dispute Settlement', *A new GATT for the Nineties and Europe'92* (Baden-Baden, Nomos Verlag, 1991), pp. 109–130.

Petersmann, E.-U., *The GATT/WTO Dispute Settlement System: International Law, International Organizations and Dispute Settlement* (London, Kluwer, 1997), xvii + 344 p.;

Petersmann, E.-U. (ed.), *International Trade Law and the GATT/WTO Dispute Settlement System* (London, Kluwer, 1997), xviii + 704 p.;

Petersmann, E.U., 'WTO Negotiators Meet Academics: the Negotiations on Improvements of the WTO Dispute Settlement System', *Journal of International Economic Law* (2003), pp. 237–250.

Sacerdoti, G., Yanovich, A. and Bohanes, J. (eds.), *The WTO at Ten. The Contribution of the Dispute Settlement System*, (Cambridge, Cambridge University Press 2006), xliv + 531 p.

Spamann, H., 'The Myth of "Rebalancing" Retaliation in WTO Dispute Settlement Practice', *Journal of International Economic Law* (2006), pp. 31–79.

Stewart, T.P. and Dwyer, A.S., *Handbook on WTO Trade Remedy Disputes. The First Six Years (1995-2000)* (Ardsley, Transnational Publishers, 2000), xvii + 560 p.

Tanigushi, Y. and Yanovich, A. (eds.), *The WTO in the Twenty-First Century. Dispute Settlement, Negotiations and Regionalism in Asia*, (Cambridge, Cambridge University Press 2007), lvii + 507 p.

Trachtman, J. and Moremen, P., 'Costs and Benefits of Private Participation in WTO Dispute Settlement: Whose Right is it Anyway?', in J. Trachtman (ed.), *The International Economic Law Revolution and the Right to Regulate*, (London, Cameron May 2006), pp. 479–513.

Van den Bossche, P., 'Reform of the WTO Dispute Settlement System. What to Expect from the Doha Development Round?', in S. Charnovitz, D. Stieger and P. Van den Bossche (eds.), *Law in the Service of Human Dignity. Essays in Honour of Florentino Feliciano*, (Cambridge, Cambridge University Press 2005), pp. 103–126.

Van der Borght, K., *The World Trade Court. An Analysis of the Legal Nature of the Dispute Settlement System of the World Trade Organization*, (Doctoral Thesis VUB, 2005), iii + 386 p.

Verhoosel, G., *National Treatment and WTO Dispute Settlement* (Oxford, Hart publishing, 2002), xi + 144 p.

Vranes, E., 'Jurisdiction and Applicable Law in WTO Dispute Settlement', *German Yearbook of International Law* (2005), pp. 265-289.

WTO, *A Handbook on the WTO Dispute Settlement System* (Cambridge, Cambridge University Press, 2004), xvii + 215 p.

Yang, G., Mercurio, B. and Li, Y., *WTO Dispute Settlement Understanding: A Detailed Interpretation*, (The Hague, Kluwer Law International 2005), xiii + 592p.

Yerxa, R., and Wilson, B. (eds.), *WTO Dispute Settlement. The First Ten Years*, (Cambridge, Cambridge University Press 2005), xxxviii + 289 p.

Zimmermann, T., *Negotiating the Review of the WTO Dispute Settlement Understanding*, (London, Cameron May 2006), 350 p.

4. MFN/NON-DISCRIMINATION AS FUNDAMENTAL PRINCIPLES OF THE WTO

Abu-Akeel, A., 'The MFN as it Applies to Services Trade: New Problems for an Old Concept, *Journal of World Trade* (1999), pp. 103-129.

Broesskamp, M., 'Meistbegünstigung und Gegenseitigkeit im GATT; Dissertation Münster Westf.', *Studien zum öffentlichen Wirtschaftsrecht BD. 13* (Köln, Heymann 1990), xiv +145 p.

Dordi, C., *La discriminazione commerciale nel diritto internazionale*, (Milano, Guiffré 2002), xii + 350 p.

Ehring, L., '*De Facto* Discrimination in World Trade Law: National and Most-Favoured-Nation Treatment – or Equal Treatment?', *Journal of World Trade* (2002), pp. 921-977.

Gerhart, P. and Baron, M., 'Understanding National Treatment. The Participatory Vision of the WTO', *Indiana International and Comparative Law Review* (2004), 505-552.

Horn, H. and Mavroidis, P., 'Still Hazy After All these Years: the Interpretation of National Treatment in GATT/WTO Case Law on to Tax Discrimination', *European Journal of International Law* (2004), pp. 39-69.

Hudec, R. 'GATT/WTO Constraints on National Regulation. Requiem for an "Aim and Effects" Test', *International Lawyer* (1998), pp. 619-649.

Melloni, M., *The Principle of National Treatment in the GATT: A Survey of the Jurisprudence, Practice and Policy*, (Brussels, Bruylant 2005), xxii + 253 p.

Schwartz, W. and Sykes, S., 'Towards a Positive Theory of the Most Favoured Nation Obligation and its Exceptions in the WTO/GATT system', *International Review of Law and Economics* (1996), pp. 27-51.

Trebilcock, M. and Giri, S., 'The National Treatment Principle in International Trade Law', in E. Kwan Choi and J. Hartigan (eds.), *Handbook on Trade Law*, (Malden, Blackwell 2005), Vol. 2, pp. 185-238.

Trebilcock, M. and Iacobucci, E., 'National Treatment and Extraterritoriality. Defining the Domains of Trade and Antitrust Policy', in R. Epstein and M. Greve (eds.), *Competition Laws in Conflict. Antitrust Jurisdiction in the Global Economy*, (Washington D.C., AEI Press 2004), pp. 152–176.

UNCTAD, *Most-Favoured-Nation Treatment*, (New York, United Nations 1999), viii + 54 p.

Verhoosel, G., *National Treatment and WTO Dispute Settlement* (Oxford, Hart publishing 2002), xi + 144 p.

5. SPS AND TBT

Appleton, A., 'The Agreement on Technical Barriers to Trade', in Macrory, P., Appleton, A. and Plummer, M. (eds.), *The World Trade Organization. Legal, Economic and Political Analysis*, (New York, Springer 2005), Vol. 1, pp. 371–409.

Bartenstein, K. and Lavallée, S., 'L'écolabel est-il un outil du protectionnisme "vert"?', *Les Cahiers de droit* (2003), pp. 361–393.

Bechmann, P. and Mansuy, V., *Le principe de précaution*, (Litec, 2002), xi + 238 p.

Bossis, G., 'Gestion des risques alimentaires et droit international: la prise en compte de facteurs non-scientifiques', *Revue Générale de Droit International Public* (2003), pp. 693–713.

Compton, M., 'Applying World Trade Organization Rules to the Labelling of Genetically Modified Foods', *Pace International Law Review* 2003, pp. 3059–409.

Gehring, M., 'The Precautionary Principle in Recent World Trade Organization (WTO) Practice', *Thesaurus Acroasium* 2002, pp. 583–599.

Heiskanen, V., 'The Regulatory Philosophy of International Trade Law', *Journal of World Trade* (2004), pp. 1–36.

Henson, S., 'How Developing Countries View the Impact of Sanitary and Phytosanitary Measures on Agricultural Products', in M. Ingco and A. Winters (eds.), *Agriculture and the New Trade Agenda. Creating a Global Trading Environment for Development*, (Cambridge, Cambridge University Press 2004), pp. 359–375.

Henson, S. and Wilson, J. (eds.), *The WTO and Technical Barriers to Trade*, (Cheltenham, Elgar 2006), xxv + 531 p.

Iynedjian, M., *L'accord de l'Organisation mondiale du commerce sur l'application des mesures sanitaires et phytosanitaires: une analyse juridique* (Paris, L.G.D.J. 2002), xiv + 262 p.

Joshi, M., 'Are Eco-Labels Consistent with World Trade Organization Agreements?', *Journal of World Trade* (2004), pp. 69–92.

MacDonald, J., 'Domestic Regulation, International Standards and Technical Barriers to Trade', *World Trade Review* (2005), pp. 249–274.

MacLaren, D., *Trade Barriers and Food Safety Standards*, (Melbourne, University of Melbourne 2003), 11 p.

Marceau, G. and Trachtman, J., 'The Technical Barriers to Trade Agreement, the Sanitary and Phytosanitary Measures Agreement, and the General Agreement on Tariffs and Trade: a Map of the World Trade Organization Law of Domestic Regulation of Goods', *Journal of World Trade* (2002), pp. 811–881.

Pauwelyn, J., 'Does the WTO Stand for "Defence to" of "Interference with" National Health Authorities When Applying the Agreement on Sanitary and Phytosanitary Measures (SPS Agreement)?', in T. Cottier and P. Mavroidis (eds.), *The Role of the Judge in International Trade Regulation. Experience and Lessons from the WTO*, (Ann Arbor, University of Michigan Press 2003), pp. 175–192.

Peel, J., 'A GMO by Another Name… Might be an SPS Risk! Implications of Expanding the Scope of the WTO Sanitary and Phytosanitary Measures Agreement', *European Journal of International Law* (2006), pp. 1009–1031.

Provost, D. and Van den Bossche, P., 'The Agreement on the Application of Sanitary and Phytosanitary Measures', in Macrory, P., Appleton, A. and Plummer, M. (eds.), *The World Trade Organization. Legal, Economic and Political Analysis*, (New York, Springer 2005), Vol. 1, pp. 231–370.

Stanton, G., *The multilateral trading system and the SPS Agreement*, (Geneva, WTO 2000), p. 19.

Stanton G., 'A Review of the Operation of the Agreement on Sanitary and Phytosanitary Measures', in M. Ingco and A. Winters (eds.), *Agriculture and the New Trade Agenda. Creating a Global Trading Environment for Development*, (Cambridge, Cambridge University Press 2004), pp. 101–110.

Stökl, L., *Die welthandelsrechtliche Gentechnikkonflikt: die europarechtlichen Handelsbeschränkungen für gentechnisch veränderte Lebensmittel und ihre Vereinbarkeit mit Welthandelsrecht*, (Berlin, Dunker & Humblot 2003), 304 p.

Slotboom, M.M., 'The Hormones Case: an Increased Risk of Illegality of Sanitary and Phytosanitary Measures', *Common Market Law Review* (1999), pp. 471–491.

Trachtman, J. and Marceau, G., 'A Map of the World Trade Organization Law on Domestic Regulation of Goods: The Technical Barriers to Trade Agreement, the Sanitary and Phytosanitary Measures Agreement and the General Agreement on Tariffs and Trade', in J. Trachtman (ed.), *The International Economic Law Revolution and the Right to Regulate*, (London, Cameron May 2006), pp. 73–160.

Vergano, P., 'The Sanitary and Phytosanitary Agreement', No. 4 *ERA Forum* (2001), pp. 118–128.

Walkenhorst, P., *The SPS Process and Developing Countries*, (Paris, OECD 2003), 20 p.

Wynter, M., 'The Agreement on Sanitary and Phytosanitary Measures in the Light of the WTO Decisions on EC Measures Concerning Meat and Meat Products (Hormones)', in *International Trade Law on the 50th Anniversary of the Multilateral Trading System* (Milano, A. Guiffrè 1999), pp. 471–526.

6. SAFEGUARDS

Bown, C. and MacCulloch, R., 'Nondiscrimination and the WTO Agreement on Safeguards', *World Trade Review* (2003), pp. 327–348.
Bown, C., 'Why Are Safeguards Under the WTO so Unpopular?', *World Trade Review* (2002), pp. 47–62.
Bronkers, M., 'The Special Safeguards Clause in the WTO Agreements with China: (How) Will It Work?', in M. Matsushita (ed.), *The WTO and East Asia: New Perspectives*, (London, Cameron May 2004), pp. 39–50.
Lee, Y., 'Emergency Safeguard Measures under Article X in GATS: Applicability of the Concepts of the WTO Agreement on Safeguards', *Journal of World Trade* (1999), pp. 47–59.
Lee, Y., 'Reflections on the Agreement on Safeguards in the WTO', *Journal of World Trade* (1999), pp. 27–46.
Mah, J., 'Injury and Causation in the WTO Agreement on Safeguards', *Journal of World Intellectual Property* (2001), pp. 373–382.
Martin Rodriguez, P., 'Safeguard in the World Trade Organization Ten Years After: a Dissociated State of the Law', *Journal of World Trade* (2007), pp. 159–190.
Müller, F., *Schutzmaßnahmen gegen Warenimporte unter der Rechtsordnung der WTO: die materiell-rechtlichen Anwendungsvoraussetzungen der "Safeguard Measures" gem. Art. XIX:1(a) GATT 1994 und Art. 2.1 des Agreement on Safeguards*, (Tübingen, Mohr Siebeck 2006), xviii + 324 p.
Pauwelyn, J., 'The Puzzle of WTO Safeguards and Regional Trade Agreements', *Journal of International Economic Law* (2004), pp. 109–142.
Sykes, A., *The WTO Agreement on Safeguards: A Commentary*, (Oxford, Oxford University Press 2006), xxvi + 357 p.
Sykes, A., 'The Safeguards Mess: A Critique of WTO Jurisprudence', *World Trade Review* (2003), pp. 261–295.
Taylor, J., 'Beggar-thy-Neighbour?: Why the WTO Appellate Body's Enforcement of a Rigorous 'Parallelism Requirement' Limits the Exception of Regional Trade Agreement Partners from the Application of Safeguards Measures', *Manchester Journal of International Economic Law* (2004), pp. 24–53.

7. ANTIDUMPING

Baars, A. and Bischoff-Everding, P., 'Antidumping und Ursprungsregime: das Schiedsverfahren im Mercosur wird zu einer festen Größe', 13 Jahrg. Heft. 11 *Europäische Zeitschrift für Wirtschaftsrecht* (2002), pp. 329–335.
Birnstiel, A., 'Die Abwehr der Umgehung von Antidumpingmaßnahmen im EG-Recht', *Beiträge zum europäischen Wirtschaftsrecht; Bd. 19* (Berlin, Dunkel & Humblot 2002), 274 p.
Boudant, J., 'L'antidumping communautaire', *Travaux de la Commission pour l'étude des Communautés européennes* (Paris, Economica 1991), 344 p.

Buat, A., *L'antidumping: quelles améliorations pour cet instrument de défense nécessaire aux entreprises?: rapport présenté au nom de la Commission du Commerce International et adopté à Assemblée générale du 4 décembre 2003*, (Chambre de commerce et de l'industrie de Paris 2003), 26 p.

Davey, W., 'Antidumping Laws: A Time for Restriction', *Journal of World Trade Law* (2006), pp. 265-297.

Cunningham, R. and Cribb, T., 'Dispute Settlement Through the Lens of Free Flow of Trade: a Review of WTO Dispute Settlement of US Antidumping and Countervailing Duty Measures', *Journal of International Economic Law* (2003), pp. 155-170.

Czako, J., Human, J. and Miranda, J., *A Handbook on Antidumping Investigations*, (Cambridge, Cambridge University Press, 2003), xx + 543 p.

DiSalvo, N., 'Let's Dump the 1916 Antidumping Act: Why the 1994 GATT Provides Better Price Protection for the US Industries', *Vanderbilt Journal of Transnational Law* (2004), pp. 791-826.

Estrella, A. and Horlick, G., 'Mandatory Abolition of Antidumping, Countervailing Duties and Safeguards in Customs Unions and Free Trade Areas Constituted Between WTO Members. Revisiting a Long-Standing Discussion in the Light of the Appellate Body's Turkey-Textiles Ruling', in L. Bartels and F. Ortino (eds.), *Regional Trade Agreements and the WTO Legal System*, (Oxford, Oxford University Press 2006), pp. 109-148.

Finger, M. and Nogués, J., *Safeguards and Antidumping in Latin-American Trade Liberalization: Fighting with Fire*, (Washington D.C., World Bank 2006), xxi + 285 p.

Finger, M. and Zlate, A., 'Antidumping: Prospects for Discipline from the Doha Negotiations', *The Journal of World Investment and Trade* (2005), pp. 531-552.

Grey, R., 'Politiques antidumping et concurrence', in UNDP, *Les initiatives des pays en développement pour les futures négociations commerciales*, (New York, United Nations, 2000), pp. 517-548;

Hallworth, T. and Piracha, M., 'Macroeconomic Fluctuations and Antidumping Filings: Evidence from a New Generation of Protectionist Countries', *Journal of World Trade* (2006), pp. 407-423.

Jackson, J. and Vermulst, E., *Antidumping Law and Practice: a Comparative Study* (New York, Harvester Wheatsheaf, 1990), xi + 520 p.

Kerr, W. and Loppacher, L., 'Antidumping in the Doha Negotiations. Fairy Tales at the World Trade Organization', *Journal of World Trade* (2004), pp. 211-244.

Kostecki, M.M., 'Le système antidumping et l'Uruguay Round', 17 *Droit et Pratique du Commerce International* (1991), pp. 206-225.

Matsushita, M., Ahn, D. and Chen, T. (eds.), *The WTO Trade Remedy System. East Asian Perspective*, (London, Cameron May 2006), 362 p.

Macrory, P., 'The Antidumping Agreement', in Macrory, P., Appleton, A. and Plummer, M. (eds.), *The World Trade Organization. Legal, Economic and Political Analysis*, (New York, Springer 2005), Vol. 1, pp. 485-429.

Petersmann, E.U., 'Settlement of International and National Trade Disputes through the GATT; the Case of Antidumping Law', vol. 7 *Adjudication of International Trade Disputes in International and National Economic Law; Pupil* (1992), pp. 77-138.

Richez, B., 'L'OMC et la pratique antidumping', *Revue de droit des affaires internationales* 2003, p. 79-89.
Van Bael, I., 'Improving GATT Disciplines Relating to Antidumping Measures', in X., *A New GATT for the Nineties and Europe '92* (Baden-Baden, Nomos Verlag 1991), pp. 171-185.
Vermulst, E. and Graafsma, F., *WTO Disputes: Antidumping, Subsidies and Safeguards*, (London, Cameron May 2002), 878 p.
Vermulst, E. and Mihaylova, P., 'EC Commercial Defence Actions Against Textiles from 1995 to 2000: Possible Lessons for Future Negotiations', *Journal of International Economic Law* (2001), pp. 527-555.
Vermulst, E., *The WTO Antidumping Agreement: A Commentary*, (Oxford, Oxford University Press 2005), xxvi + 331 p.

8. SUBSIDIES

Ahuja, R., 'Export Subsidies. Theory, Evidence and the WTO Agreement on Subsidies', in B. Guha-Kashnobis, *The WTO Developing Countries and the Doha Development Agenda: Prospects and Challenges for Trade-led Growth*, (Basingstoke, Palgrave Macmillan 2004), pp. 261-286.
Becker, T., *Das WTO Subventionsübereinkommen: Einfluß auf die Rechtsschutsmöglichkeiten Dritter gegen Beihilfen im Rahmen das EG Rechts*, (Frankfurt am Main, Lang 2001), 292 p.
Bénitah, M., *The Law of Subsidies under the GATT/WTO System* (The Hague, Kluwer Law International 2001), xii + 424 p.
Bourgeois, J., *Subsidies and International Trade: A European Lawyer's Perspective* (Deventer, Kluwer 1991), ix + 214p.
Chambovey, D., 'How the Expiry of the Peace Clause (Article 13 WTO Agreement on Agriculture) May Alter Disciplines on Agricultural Subsidies in the WTO Framework', *Journal of World Trade* (2002), pp. 305-352.
Cross, K., 'King Cotton, Developing Countries and the "Peace Clause". The WTO's Cotton Subsidies Decision', *Journal of International Economic Law* (2006), pp. 149-195.
Delvos, O, 'WTO Disciplines and Fisheries Subsidies. Should the "SCM Agreement" be Modified?', *Victoria University of Wellington Law Review* (2006), pp. 341-364.
Grave, C., *Der Begriff der Subvention im WTO-Übereinkommen über Subventionen und Ausgleichsmaßnahmen*, (Berlin, Dunker & Humblot 2002), 306 p.
Hoda, A. and Ahuja, R., 'Agreement on Subsidies and Countervailing Measures: Need for Clarification and Improvement', *Journal of World Trade* (2005), p. 1009-1069.
Lodefalk, M. and Storey, M., 'Climate Measures and WTO Rules on Subsidies', *Journal of World Trade* (2005), pp. 23-44.
Luja, R., *Assessment and Recovery of Tax Incentives in the EC and the WTO: a View on State Aids, Trade Subsidies and Direct Taxation*, (Antwerp, Intersentia 2003), xii + 311 p.

Meier-Kaienburg, N., 'WTO's Toughest Case: An Examination of the Effectiveness of the WTO Dispute Resolution Procedure in the Airbus-Boeing Dispute over Aircraft Subsidies', *Journal of Air Law and Commerce* (2006), pp. 191-250.
Porterfield, M., 'The US Farm Subsidies and the Expiration of the WTO's Peace Clause', *University of Pennsylvania Journal of International Economic Law* (2005)6), pp. 999-1042.
Reich, A., 'Institutional and Substantive Reform of the Antidumping and Subsidy Agreements: Lessons from the Israeli Experience', *Journal of World Trade* (2003), pp. 1037-1061.
Rice, T., 'Farmgate: the Developmental Impacts of Agricultural Subsidies', in H. Katrak and R. Strange (eds.), *The WTO and developing countries*, (Basingstoke, Palgrave Macmillan 2004), pp. 233-256.
Sánchez Rydelski, M., *EG und WTO Antisubventionsrecht: ein konzeptioneller Vergleich der EG Antisubventions-Verordnung mit den Beihilfevorschriften des EG-Vertrages unter Berücksichtigung des Subventionsübereinkommens der WTO*, (Baden-Baden, Nomos 2001), 355 p.
Schowalter, M., 'A Cruel Trilemma. The Flawed Political Economy of Remedies to WTO Subsidies Disputes', *Vanderbilt Journal of Transnational Law* (2004), pp. 587-630.
Stewart, T.P. and Dwyer, A.S., *WTO antidumping and subsidy agreements: a practitioner's guide to "sunset" reviews in Australia, Canada, the European Union, and the United States* (The Hague, Kluwer, 1998), xv + 268 p.
Steinberg, R. and Josling, T., 'When the Peace Ends. The Vulnerability of the EC and US Agricultural Subsidies to WTO Legal Challenge', *Journal of International Economic Law* (2003), pp. 369-417.
Wouters, J. and Coppens, D., 'An Overview of the SCM Agreement – Including a Discussion of the Agreement on Agriculture', Institute for International Law. *Working Paper No. 104* (November 2007), available on http://law.kuleuven.be/iir/nl/wp/WP/WP104e.pdf.

9. CUSTOMS

Chang, S., 'The Customs-tariff Law of Japan and Its WTO Consistency: A Case-study of the Samsung-Fujitsu PDP Dispute', M. Matsushita, D. Ahn and T. Chen (eds.), *The WTO Trade Remedy System: East Asian Perspectives*, (London, Cameron May 2006), pp. 179-191.
Gürler, O., 'WTO Agreements on Non-Tariff Barriers and Implications for the OIC Member States: Customs Valuation, Pre-Shipment Inspection, Rules of Origin and Import Licensing', *Journal of Economic Cooperation* (2002), pp. 61-88.
Mikurya, K., 'Trade Facilitation: Benefits and Capacity Building for Customs', in United Nations Economic Commission for Europe (ed.), *Sharing the gains of globalization in the new security environment: the challenges of trade facilitation*, (New York, United Nations 2003), pp. 41-48.

Letterman, G.G., *Basics of the International System on Customs and Tariffs*, (Ardsley-on-Hudson, Transnational publishers 2001), xxi + 546 p.

New York County Lawyers Association, *Handbook on Customs and International Trade Law* (New York, New York County Lawyers Association, 1996), ix + 60 p.

Pace, V., 'European Communities: Customs Qualification of Certain Computer Equipment', in B. Stern and H. Luiz-Fabri (eds.), *La Jurisprudence de l'OMC*, (Leiden, Nijhoff 2005), pp. 208-237.

Rege, V., 'Developing Country Participation in Negotiations Leading to the Adoption of the WTO Agreements on Customs Valuation and Preshipment Inspection: A Public Choice Analysis', *World Competition* (1999), pp. 37-117.

Sarsevic, P. and Volken, P., *The International Sale of Goods Revisited* (New York, Kluwer Law International, 2001), xv + 266 p.

Sherman, S. and Glashoff, H., *Customs Valuation, Commentary on the GATT Customs Valuation Code* (Deventer, Kluwer, 1988), xvii + 382 p.

Shin, Y., 'Trade Facilitation and WTO Rules. For a Better Harmonized Customs System', *Journal of World Trade* (1999), pp.131-142.

10. GATS

Adlung, R., 'Public Services and the GATS', *Journal of International Economic Law* (2006), pp. 455-485.

Adlung, R., 'Services Negotiations in the Doha Round: Lost in Flexibility?', *Journal of International Economic Law* (2006), pp. 865-893.

Blouin, C., Drager, N. and Smith, R. (eds.), *International Trade in Health Services and the GATS: Current Issues and Debates*, (Washington D.C., World Bank 2006), xii + 312 p.

Bongini, P., 'The EU Experience in Financial Services Liberalization. A Model for GATS Negotiations?', *SUERF Studies* 2003/2, 80 p.

Clough, M., *Trade and Telecommunications*, (London, Cameron May, 2002), 307 p.

Das, D., 'Trade in Financial Services and the Role of the GATS. Against the Backdrop of the Asian Financial Crises', *Journal of World Trade* (1998), pp. 79-114.

Delimatsis, P., 'Don't Gamble with GATS: The Interaction between Articles VI, XVI, XVII and XVIII GATS in the Light of the "US-Gambling" Case', *Journal of World Trade* (2006), pp. 1059-1080.

Delimatsis, P. 'Due Process and 'Good' Regulation Embedded in the GATS – Disciplining Regulatory Behaviour in Services Through Article VI of the GATS', *Journal of International Economic Law* (2007), pp. 13-20.

Dobson, W. and Jacquet, P., *Financial Services Liberalization in the WTO*, (Washington D.C., Institute for International Economics 1998), xiv + 352 p.

Dutry, J. and Servais, D., 'GATS 2000: Quels enjeux pour les services financières?', *Revue de Droit des Affaires Internationales* (1999), pp. 653-675.

European Communities Commission, *GATS, the General Agreement on Trade in Services: a Guide for Business* (Luxembourg, Office for the official publications of the European Communities, 1995), 68 p.

Gamberale, C. and Mattoo, A., 'Domestic Regulations and Liberalization of Trade in Services', in B. Hoekman, A. Mattoo and P. English (eds.), *Development, Trade and the WTO: a Handbook*, (Washington D.C., World Bank 2002), pp. 290–303.

Grieshaber-Otto, J. and Sinclair, S., *Return to Sender. The Impact of GATS "Pro-competitive" Regulation on Postal and Other Public Services*, (Ottawa, Canadian Centre for Policy Alternatives 2004), 219 p.

Hein, W., *GATS und Globale Politik*, (Hamburg, DÜI 2004), 199 p.

Hopkins, R., 'Liberalizing Trade in Legal Services. The GATS, the Accounting Disciplines and the Language of Core Values', *Indiana International and Comparative Law Review* (2005), pp. 427–471.

Jarreau, J.S, 'Interpreting the General Agreement on Trade in Services and the WTO Instruments Relevant to the International Trade of Financial Services: the Lawyer's Perspective', *North Carolina Journal of International Law and Commercial Regulation* (1999), pp 1–73.

Karmakar, S., 'Disciplining Domestic Regulations Under the GATS and Its Implications for Developing Countries: An Indian Case-study', *Journal of World Trade* (2007), pp. 127–158.

Kelsey, J., 'Legal Fetishism and the Contradictions of the GATS', in D. Lewis (ed.), *Global Governance and the Quest for Justice*, (Oxford, Hart 2006), pp. 133–149.

Key, S., 'Trade Liberalization and Prudential Regulation: The International Framework for Financial Services', *International Affairs* (1999), pp. 61–75.

Key, S., *The Doha Round and Financial Services Negotiations*, (Washington D.C., AEI 2003), xiii + 107 p.

Krajewski, M., *National regulation and trade liberalization in services: the legal impact of the General Agreement on trade in Services (GATS) on national regulatory autonomy*, (The Hague, Kluwer 2003), xxii + 245 p.

Krajewski, M., 'Services Liberalization and Regional Trade Agreements. Lessons for GATS "Unfinished Business"?', in L. Bartels and F. Ortino (eds.), *Regional Trade Agreements and the WTO Legal System*, (Oxford, Oxford University Press 2006), pp. 175–200.

Lang, A., 'The GATS and Regulatory Autonomy: A Case-study of Social Regulation of the Water Industry', *Journal of International Economic Law* (2004), pp. 801–838.

Leroux, E., 'Trade in financial services under the World Trade Organization', *Journal of World Trade* 2002, pp. 413–442.

Lin, T., 'Addressing the Issues of Trade in Services and Public Health in the Case of Tobacco. Are the FCTC Restrictions on Tobacco Advertising inconsistent with the GATS?', *The Journal of World Investment and Trade* (2006), pp. 545–561.

Marchetti, J. and Mavroidis, P., 'What are the Main Challenges for the GATS Framework? Don't Talk about Revolution', *European Business Organization Law Review* (2004), pp. 511–562.

Mattoo, A. and Wunsch-Vincent, S., 'Pre-empting Protectionism in Services: the GATS and Outsourcing', *Journal of International Economic Law* (2004), pp. 765–800.

Mavroidis, P., 'Highway XVI Re-Visited: The Road From Non-Discrimination to Market Access in GATS', *Word Trade Review* (2007), pp. 1-23.
Mengozzi, P., 'Le GATS: un accord sans importance pour la Communauté européenne?', *Revue du Marché Unique Européen* (1997/2), pp. 19-44.
Musselli, I. and Zarilli, S., 'Oil and Gas Services. Market Liberalization and the Ongoing GATS Negotiations', *Journal of International Economic Law* (2005), pp. 551-581.
Ortino, F., 'Treaty Interpretation and the WTO Appellate Body Report in *US-Gambling*: A Critique', *Journal of International Economic Law* (2006), pp. 117-148.
Parameswaran, B., *The Liberalization of Maritime Transport Services: with Special Reference to the WTO/GATS Framework*, (Berlin, Springer 2004), xxiii + 425 p.
Pauwelyn, J., 'Rien ne Va Plus? Distinguishing Domestic Regulation from Market Access in GATT and GATS', *World Trade Review* (2005), pp. 131-170.
Peng, S., 'Multilateral Disciplines on Services Procurement. Architectural Challenges Under the GATS', *The Journal of World Investment and Trade* (2006), pp. 975-996.
Pitschas, C., 'Die Liberalisierung des internationalen Dienstleistungshandels im Rahmen des GATS', *R.I.W.* (2003), pp. 676-689.
Roberts, C., 'Financial Services in the WTO: Are Liberalization and Regulation in Conflict?', *The Financial Regulator* (2002), pp. 54-59.
Sauvant, K.P. and Weber, J., 'The International Legal Framework for Services', in *Law and Practice under the GATT and other trading arrangements* (New York, Oceana 1992-1996), 3 vol.
Sauvé, P. and Stern, R.M. (eds.), *GATS 2000: New Directions in Services Trade Liberalization*, (Washington, Brookings Institution 2000), xi + 544 p.
Sauvé, P. and Steinfatt, K., 'Financial Services and the WTO: What Next?', in R. Litan, P. Masson and M. Pomerleano (eds.), *Open Doors: Foreign Participation in Financial Systems in Developing Countries*, (Washington D.C., Brookings Institution Press 2001), pp. 351-386.
Sauvé, P. (ed.), *Trade Rules Behind Borders: Essays on Services, Investment and the New Trade Agenda*, (London, Cameron May 2003), 541 p.
Trachtman, J., 'Trade in Financial Services under GATS, NAFTA and the EC: A Regulatory Jurisdiction Analysis', *Columbia Journal of Transnational Law* (1996), pp. 37-122.
Trachtman, J. and Nicolaïdis, K., 'From Policed Regulation to Managed Regulation. Mapping the Boundary in GATS', in J. Trachtman (ed.), *The International Economic Law Revolution and the Right to Regulate*, (London, Cameron May 2006), pp. 281-321.
United Nations. Department of International Economic and Social Affairs, *Manual of Statistics on International Trade in Services*, (New York, United Nations 2002), ix + 176 p.
Wang, Y., 'Most-Favoured-Nation Treatment under the General Agreement on Trade in Services – And Its Application in Financial Services', *Journal of World Trade* (1996), pp. 91-124.
Wouters, J. and Coppens, D., 'GATS and Domestic Regulation: the Right to Regulate and Trade Liberalization', in K. Alexander and M. Andenas (eds.), *The World Trade Organization and Trade in Services* (Leiden, Nijhoff 2008), p. 207-262.

WTO, *Guide to the GATS: An Overview of Issues for Further Liberalization of Trade in Services* (The Hague, Kluwer 2001), xxix + 704 p.
WTO, *A Handbook on the GATS Agreement*, (Cambridge, Cambridge University Press 2005), vii + 96 p.
Wunsch-Vincent, S., 'The Internet, Cross-Border Trade in Services and the GATS: Lessons from US-Gambling', *World Trade Review* (2006), pp. 319-355.
Zdouc, W., 'WTO Dispute Settlement Practice Relating to the General Agreement on Trade in Services', in F. Ortino and E.-U. Petersmann (eds.), *The WTO Dispute Settlement System 1995-2003*, (The Hague, Kluwer 2004), pp. 381-420.
Zeiptnig, S., 'Staatliche Wirtschafstregulierung und auf dem Prüfstand des GATS. Das WTO Streitbeilegungsverfahren United States: Gambling and Betting Services', *Österreichische Zeitschrift für Wirtschaftsrecht* (2005), pp. 117-125.

11. TRIPS

Abbott, F., 'TRIPS and Human Rights. Preliminary Reflections', in F. Abbott, C. Breining-Kaufmann and T. Cottier (eds.), *International Trade and Human Rights. Foundations and Conceptual Issues* (Ann Arbor, University of Michigan Press 2006), pp. 145-169.
Bail, C., 'Elaboration of Trade Related Principles, Rules and Disciplines for Intellectual Property', *A New GATT for the Nineties and Europe '92* (Baden-Baden, Nomos Verlag, 1991), pp. 245-259.
Bronckers, M., 'The Impact of TRIPS: Intellectual Property Protection in Developing Countries', *Common Market Law Review* (1994), pp. 1245-1281.
Carvalho, N., *The TRIPS Regime of Trademarks and Designs*, (The Hague, Kluwer 2005), xviii + 537 p.
Carvalho, N., *The TRIPS Regime of Patent Rights*, (The Hague, Kluwer 2005), xxi + 520 p.
Correa, C., 'TRIPS and access to drugs: toward a solution for developing countries without manufacturing capacity?', *Emory International Law Review* (2003), pp. 389-406.
Cottier, T. (ed.), *Trade and Intellectual Property Protection in WTO Law: Collected Essays*, (London, Cameron May 2005), 495 p.
Cottier, T. and Mavroidis, P. (eds.), *Intellectual Property: trade, competition and sustainable development*, (Ann Arbor, University of Michigan Press 2003), xv + 558 p.
Fleet, J., 'U.N. approach to access to essential aids medications, intellectual property law and the WTO TRIPS agreement', *Emory International Law Review* (2003), pp. 451-466
Helfer, L., 'Regime Shifting: the TRIPS Agreement and the New Dynamics of Intellectual Property Lawmaking', *The Yale Journal of International Law* (2004), pp. 1-83.
Hermes, C.-J., *TRIPS im Gemeinschaftsrecht: zu den innergemeinschaftlichen Wirkungen von WTO-Übereinkünften* (Berlin, Duncker & Humblot, 2002), 374 p.
Gad, O., *Representational Fairness in WTO Rule-Making: Negotiating, Implementing and Disputing the TRIPS Pharmaceutical-Related provisions*, (London, British Institute for International and Comparative Law 2006), viii + 333 p.
Gervais, D., *The TRIPS Agreement* (London, Sweet and Maxwell, 2003), xlvi + 580 p.

Greppi, E., *La disciplina giuridica internazionale della circolazione dei servizi: i sistemi di liberalizzazione GATT, OCSE e CE* (Napoli, Jovene, 1994), xi + 387 p.

Kennedy, K., 'The 2005 TRIPS Extension for Least Developed Countries: a Failure of the Single Undertaking Approach?', *International Lawyer* (2006), pp. 683–700.

Kreibich, S., *Das TRIPS-Abkommen in der Gemeinschaftsordnung: Aspekte der Kompetenzverteilung zwischen WTO, Europäischer Gemeinschaft und ihren Mitgliedstaaten* (Frankfurt am Main, Lang, 2003), 322 p.

Matthews, D., 'WTO Decision on the Implementation of Paragraph 6 of the DOHA Declaration on the TRIPS Agreement and Public Health: A Solution to the Access to Essential Medicines Problem?', *Journal of International Economic Law* (2004), pp. 73–107.

Pfeifer, K.-N., 'Brainpower and trade: The impact of TRIPS on intellectual property', vol. 39 *Jahrbuch für internationales Recht* (1996), pp. 100–133.

Pugatsch, M., 'The International Regulation of IPRs in a TRIPS and TRIPS-plus World, *The Journal of World Investment and Trade* (2005), pp. 431–465.

Ribeiro di Almeida, A., 'The TRIPS Agreement, the Bilateral Agreements concerning Geographical Indications and the Philosophy of the WTO', *European Intellectual Property Review* (2005), pp. 150–153.

Rosendahl, G., 'The Convention on Biological Diversity: Tensions with the WTO TRIPS Agreement over Access to Genetic Resources and Sharing of Benefits', in S. Oberthür and T. Gehring (eds.), *Institutional Interaction in Global Environmental Governance: Synergy and Conflict Among International and EU Policies*, (Cambridge, MIT Press 2006), pp. 79–102.

Rott, P., *Patentrecht und Sozialpolitik unter dem TRIPS-Abkommen* (Baden-Baden, Nomos 2002), 385 p.

Rott, P., 'WTO Law and Environmental Standards. Lessons from the TRIPS Agreement?', in D. Lewis, *Global Governance and the Quest for Justice* (Oxford, Hart 2006), pp. 113–131.

Steffens, K., 'Das WTO-Abkommen über handelsbezogene Aspekte der Rechte des geistigen Eigentums (TRIPS) und das chinesische Recht', in R. Heuser and R. Klein (eds.), *Die WTO und das neue Ausländerinvestitions- und Aussenhandelsrecht der VR China: Gesetze und Analysen*, (Hamburg, Institut fur Asienkunde 2004), pp. 319–330.

Sun, H., 'The road to Doha and beyond: Some reflections on the TRIPS Agreement and public health', *European Journal of International Law* (2004), pp. 123–150.

Thomas, C., 'Trade policy, the politics of access to drugs and global governance for health' in K. Basingstoke (ed.), *Health Impacts of Globalization: Towards Global Governance*, (Palgrave, Macmillan 2003), pp. 177–191.

Vawda, Y., 'From Doha to Cancun: the quest to increase access to medicines under WTO rules', *South African Journal on Human Rights* (2003–4), pp. 679–690.

Walker, S., 'A Human Rights Approach to the WTO's TRIPS Agreement', in F. Abbott, C. Breining-Kaufmann and T. Cottier (eds.), *International Trade and Human Rights. Foundations and Conceptual Issues* (Ann Arbor, University of Michigan Press 2006), pp. 171–179.

12. INVESTMENT PROTECTION AND TRIMS

Carmody, C., 'TRIMS and the Concept of Investment under the WTO Agreement', in C. Carmody, Y. Iwasawa and S. Rhjodes (eds.), *Trilateral Perspectives on International Legal Issues: Conflict and Coherence*, (Baltimore, ASIL 2003), pp. 325-339.
Civello, P., 'The TRIMS Agreement: A Failed Attempt at Investment Liberalization', *Minnesota Journal of Global Trade* 1999, pp. 97-126.
Ellis, C.N., 'Trade-related investment measures in the Uruguay Round, The US viewpoint', *Conflict and resolution in US-EU trade relations* (New York, Oceana, 1989), pp. 273-292.
Graham, E.M. and Krugman, P.R., 'Trade related investment measures', *Completing the Uruguay round: a results-oriented approach to the GATT trade negotiations* (Washington D.C., Institute for International Economics, 1990), x + 224 p.
Johnson, J., 'The WTO Decision: MFN, National Treatment, TRIMS and Export Subsidies', in M. Irish (ed.), *The Auto Pact: Investment, Labour and the WTO*, (The Hague, Kluwer 2004), pp. 73-109.
Lester, S., 'Update on TRIMS: the Development of a TRIMS Jurisprudence in the WTO Panel Report on Indonesia: Certain Measures Affecting the Automotive Industry', *World Investment* (1998), pp. 85-97.
Sidhu, K., *Die Regulierung von Direktinvestionen in der WTO: das TRIPS-Abkommen und das GATS*, (Göttingen, V&R Unipress 2004), 357 p.
United Nations, *The impact of trade related investment measures on trade and development: theory, evidence and policy implications*, United Nations Conference on Trade and Development, (New York, United Nations, 1991), vii+ 104 p.

13. PUBLIC PROCUREMENT

Arrowsmith, S., Linarelli, J. and Wallace, D., *Regulating Public Procurement, National and International Perspectives* (The Hague, Kluwer Law International, 2000), xxxii + 856 p.
Arrowsmith, S., *Government Procurement in the WTO, Studies in Transnational Economic Law Vol. 16*, (The Hague, Kluwer 2003), xxiii + 481 p.
Bungenberg, M., 'Die Ausweitung des Geltungsbereichs des Government Procurement Agreement', *Wirtschaft und Wettbewerb* (2000), pp. 872-877.
Dabhi, K., 'A note on the emerging WTO framework for government procurements', *Indian Journal of International Law* (2002), pp. 334-347.
Evenett, S. and Hoekman, B., *Government procurement: market access, transparency, and multilateral trade rules*. World Bank policy research working paper; 3195, (Washington D.C., World Bank, 2004).
Mosoti, V., 'The WTO Agreement on Government Procurement: a necessary evil in the legal strategy for development in the poor world?', *University of Pennsylvania Journal of International Economic Law* (2004), pp. 593-638.

Reich, A., 'The New GATT Agreement on Government Procurement – The pitfalls of plurilateralism and strict reciprocity', *Journal of World Trade* (1997), pp. 125-151.
Suami, T., 'WTO and local government in Japan: examples of the Agreement on Government Procurement', *The Japanese Annual of International Law* (2004), pp. 57-74.
Van Calster, G., 'Green procurement and the WTO: shades of grey', *Review of European Community and international environmental law* (2002), pp. 298-305.
Salvadori, M., *Gli appalti pubblici nell'Organizzazione mondiale del commercio e nella Comunità europea*, (Napoli, Jovene, 2001), viii + 284 p.
Spennemann, C., 'The WTO Agreement on Government Procurement: a means of furtherance of human rights?', *Zeitschrift für europarechtliche Studien* (2001), pp. 43-95.

14. TRADE AND AGRICULTURE

Aggarwal, R., 'Dynamics of Agriculture Negotiations in the World Trade Organization', *Journal of World Trade* (2005), pp. 741-761.
Anderson, K., 'Trade Liberalization, Agriculture and Poverty in Low-income Countries', in B. Guha-Khasnobis (ed.), *The WTO, Developing Countries and the Doha Development Agenda: Prospects and Challenges for Trade-led Growth*, (Basingstoke, Palgrave Macmillan 2004), pp. 37-62.
Anderson, K. and T. Josling (eds.), *The WTO and Agriculture*, (Cheltenham, Elgar 2005), xxiv + 597 p.
Bhala, R., 'World Agricultural Trade in Purgatory: the Uruguay Round Agriculture Agreement and its implications for the Doha Round', *North Dakota Law Review* (2003), pp. 691-830.
Cardwell, M., 'The European Model of Agriculture and World Trade: reconfiguring domestic support', *Cambridge Yearbook of European Legal Studies* (2004), pp. 77-103.
Chambovey, D., 'How the Expiry of the Peace Clause (Article 13 of the Agreement on Agriculture) Might Alter Disciplines on Agricultural Subsidies in the WTO Framework', *Journal of World Trade* (2002), pp. 305-352.
Das, D., 'The Doha Round of International Trade Negotiations and Trade in Agriculture', *Journal of World Trade* (2006), pp. 259-290.
Desta, M., *The Law of International Trade in Agricultural Products: from GATT 1947 to the WTO Agreement on Agriculture*, (Kluwer, Kluwer Law International 2002), xvii + 468 p.
Cardwell, M., Grossman M. and Rodgers, C. (eds.), *Agriculture and International Trade: Law, Policy and the WTO*, (New York, CABI 2003), xiv + 330 p.
Hunter, J., 'Broken Promises: Trade, Agriculture and Development in the WTO', *Melbourne Journal of International Law* (2003), pp. 299-322.

Ipsen, K. and Haltern, U.R., 'Landwirtschaft und internationalen Handel; Beschert die gemeinsame Agrarpolitik der EG dem GATT eine "Missernte"?', *Europaeische Zeitschrift für Wirtschaftsrecht* (1991), pp. 464–469.

Ingco, M. and Winters, A. (eds.), *Agriculture and the New Trade Agenda: Creating a Global Trading Environment for Development*, (Cambridge, Cambridge University Press 2004), xxi + 510 p.

Mah, J., 'Reflections on the Special Safeguard Provision in the Agreement on Agriculture of the WTO', *Journal of World Trade* (1999), pp. 197–204.

McMahon, J.A., *Agricultural Trade, Protectionism and the Problems of Development: a Legal Perspective* (Leicester, Leicester University Press, 1992), ix + 278 p.

McMahon, J.A., 'The WTO Agreement on Agriculture', No. 4 *ERA Forum* (2001), pp. 111–117.

McMahon, J.A., 'The Agreement on Agriculture', in Macrory, P., Appleton, A. and Plummer, M. (eds.), *The World Trade Organization. Legal, Economic and Political Analysis*, (New York, Springer 2005), pp. 187–229.

Mechlem, K., 'Harmonizing Trade in Agriculture and Human Rights: Options for the Integration of a Right to Food in the Agreement on Agriculture', *Max Planck Yearbook of United Nations Law* (2006), pp. 127–190.

Modwel, S. 'The WTO and Agriculture: Why is India so Furious?', *The Journal of World Investment & Trade* (2004), pp. 289–319.

Montañà i Mora, M., *The U.S.-E.C. Agricultural Export Subsidies Dispute: a GATT Perspective* (Bellaterra, Institut Universitari d'Estudis Europeus, 1993), 55 p.

Morgan, D. and Goh, G., 'Peace in our Time? An Analysis of Article 13 of the Agreement on Agriculture', *Journal of World Trade* (2003), pp. 977–992.

Newell, M., 'Cotton, U.S. Domestic Policy and Trade Wars: the Future of WTO Agriculture Negotiations', *Minnesota Journal of Global Trade* (2004–05), pp. 301–344.

O'Connor, B., 'A Note on the Need for More Clarity in the World Trade Organization Agreement on Agriculture', *Journal of World Trade* (2003), pp. 839–846.

Pijnacker Hordijck, E.H., 'La Communauté européenne, la politique agricole communale et le GATT, récents développements dans un perspective juridique', *Revue des droit des affaires internationales* (1993), pp. 27–45.

Sturgess, I., 'The Agenda 2000 CAP reform and the "Millennium Round": negotiations on agriculture', *Negotiating the future of agricultural policies* (The Hague, Kluwer Law International 2000), pp. 97–111.

Stewart, T. and Schenewerk, C., 'The conflict between facilitating international trade and protecting U.S. agriculture from invasive species: APHIS, the U.S. plant protection laws and the Argentine citrus dispute', *Journal of Transnational Law and Policy* (2004), pp. 305–346.

Swinbank, A., 'The Challenge of Agriculture Trade Negotiations in the WTO Doha Round', in N. Perdikis and R. Read (eds.), *The WTO and the regulation of international trade: recent trade disputes between the European Union and the United States*, (Cheltenham, Elgar 2005), pp. 87–108.

Subedi, S., 'Managing the "Second Agricultural Revolution" through International Law: Liberalization of Trade in Agriculture and Sustainable Development', in N. Schrijver and F. Weiss (eds.), *International Law and Sustainable Development: Principles and Practice*, (Leiden, Nijhoff 2004), pp. 191–184.

Valdes, A., 'Special Safeguards for Developing Country Agriculture: A Proposal for WTO Negotiations', *World Trade Review* (2003), pp. 5–31.

von Urff, W., 'Der Agrarhandel in der Uruguay-Runde des GATT; Irritationen zwischen der EG und den USA', *Integration* (1993), pp. 80–94.

Wouters, J. and Coppens, D., 'An Overview of the SCM Agreement – Including a Discussion of the Agreement on Agriculture', Institute for International Law. *Working Paper No. 104* (November 2007), available on http://law.kuleuven.be/iir/nl/wp/WP/WP104e.pdf.

15. TRADE AND THE ENVIRONMENT

Alam, S., 'The United Nations' Approach to Trade, the Environment and Sustainable Development, *ILSA Journal of International and Comparative Law* (2006), pp. 607–639.

Alan, B., 'The World Trade Organization and the marine environment', in M. Nordquist, J. Moore and S. Mahmoudi (eds.), *The Stockholm declaration and the law of the marine environment*, (The Hague, Nijhoff 2003), pp. 109–118.

Aledo, L., 'Instruments nationaux de la politique de l'environnement et tant qu'entraves au commerce international: limitations imposées par le droit international économique', in M. Bothe and P. Sand (eds.), *La politique de l'environnement: de la réglementation aux instruments économiques*, (The Hague, Nijhoff 2003), pp. 115–157.

Bernasconi-Osterwalder, N. et al. (eds.), *Environment and Trade: A Guide to WTO Jurisprudence*, (London, Earthscan 2006), xx + 370 p.

Boisson de Chazournes, L. and Mbengue, M., 'La déclaration de Doha de la Conférence Ministérielle de l'Organisation Mondiale du Commerce et sa portée sur les relations commerce/environnement', *Revue générale de droit international public* (2002), pp. 855–892.

Cameron, J. and Demaret, P., *Trade & Environment: The Search for Balance* (London, Cameron-May, 1994), 2 vol., 475 and 748 p.

Cole, M., 'Examining the Environmental Case against Free Trade', *Journal of World Trade* (1999), pp. 183–196.

Driesen, D., 'What is Free Trade? The Rorschach Test at the Heart of the Trade and Environment Debate', in E. Choi and J. Hartigan (eds.), *Handbook of International Trade*, (Malden, Blackwell 2005), pp. 5–41.

Gaffigan, S., 'Developments in International Trade and Environment', *Colorado Journal of International Environmental Law and Policy* (2003), pp. 87–98.

Gallagher, K., *Free Trade and the Environment: Mexico, NAFTA and Beyond*, (Stanford, Stanford Law and Politics 2004), ix + 125 p.

Macmillan, F., *WTO and the Environment* (London, Sweet and Maxwell 2001), xx + 388 p.

Maljean-Dubois, S., *Droit de l'Organisation Mondiale de Commerce et protection de l'environnement*, (Brussels, Bruylant 2003), 535 p.

Mavroidis, P., 'Trade and Environment after the Shrimps-Turtles Litigation', in S. Henson and J. Wilson (eds.), *The WTO and Technical Barriers to Trade* (Cheltenham, Elgar 2005), pp. 203–218.

Mayer, J., 'Not Totally Naked: Textiles and Clothing Trade in a Quota-Free Environment', *Journal of World Trade* (2005), pp. 393–426.

Montini, M., 'The Interplay Between the Right to Development and the Protection of the Environment: Patterns and Instruments to Achieve Sustainable Development in Practice', *African Yearbook of International Law* (2004), pp. 181–223.

Niño, L., 'Trade and Environment: A Historical Challenge for Sustainable Development', in M. Cordonier-Segger and M. Leichner Reynal (eds.), *Beyond the Barricades: The Americas Trade and Sustainable Development Agenda*, (Aldershot, Ashgate 2005), pp. 281–287.

Ostrovski, A., 'The European Commission's Regulations for Genetically Modified Organisms and the Current WTO Dispute – Human Health or Environmental Measures?: Why the Deliberate Release Directive is More Appropriately Adjudicated in the WTO under the TBT Agreement', *Colorado Journal of International Environmental Law and Policy* (2004), pp. 209–244.

Pacht, L., 'Commerce international du bois tropical et protection de l'environnement: chronique d'une scission annoncée?', *Revue générale de droit international public* (2001), pp. 647–676.

Perrez, F., 'The Mutual Supportiveness of Trade and Environment', *Proceedings of the Annual Meeting of the American Society of International Law* (2006), pp. 27–29.

Petersmann, E.-U., 'Settlement of International Environmental Disputes in GATT and the EC: Comparative Legal Aspects' in *Towards more effective supervision by international organizations: Essays in honour of Henry G. Schermers* (Dordrecht, Nijhoff 1994), Vol. I, pp. 165–203.

Rosenberg, D., 'Trade and the Environment in 2004: Developments in Genetically Altered Food, Air Pollution and Trade in Endangered Species', *Colorado Journal of International Environmental Law and Policy* (2004), pp. 167–181.

Prost, M., *D'abord les moyens, les besoins viendront après: commerce et environnement dans la «jurisprudence» du GATT et de l'OMC*, (Brussels, Bruylant 2005), xix + 232 p.

Sampson, G. P., *Trade, Environment and the WTO: The Post-Seattle Agenda (Policy Essay no. 27)* (Washington D.C., Overseas Development Council 2000), xi + 154 p.

Sampson, G. P. and Whalley, G. (eds.), *The WTO, Trade and the Environment* (Cheltenham, Elgar 2005), xxv + 701 p.

Scott, J., 'International trade and environmental governance: relating rules (and standards) in the EU and the WTO', *European Journal of International Law* (2004), pp. 279–305.

Stillwell, M. and Bohanes, J., 'Trade and the Environment', in Macrory, P., Appleton, A. and Plummer, M. (eds.), *The World Trade Organization. Legal, Economic and Political Analysis*, (New York, Springer 2005), pp. 511–569.

Torres, H., 'The Trade and Environment Interpretation in the WTO: How can a "New Round" Contribute?', *Journal of World Trade* (1999), pp. 153–167.

Van Calster, G., *International and EU Trade Law: the Environmental Challenge* (London, Cameron May 2000), xxvii + 564 p.
Vikhlyaev, A., 'Environmental Goods and Services: Defining Negotiations or Negotiating Definitions', *Journal of World Trade* (2004), pp. 93–122.
Ward, H., 'Trade and Environment in the Round – and After', *Journal of Environmental Law* (1994), pp. 263–295.
Whitehouse, T., 'International Trade and the Environment', *Pace International Law Review* (2006), pp. 243–252.
Wiers, J., *Trade and Environment in the EC and the WTO: a Legal Analysis* (Groningen, European Law Publishing 2002), xii + 502 p.
Wold, C., Gaines, S. and Block, G., *Trade and the Environment: Law and Policy* (Durham, Carolina Academic Press 2005), xlii + 933 p.
WTO, *Trade and Environment at the WTO*, (Geneva, WTO 2004), 46 p.

16. TRADE AND LABOUR STANDARDS

Addo, K., 'The Correlation between Labour Standards and International Trade: Which Way Forward?', *Journal of World Trade* (2002), pp. 285–303.
Barry, C. and Reddy, S., 'International Trade and Labor Standards: A Proposal for Linkage', *Cornell International Law Journal* (2006), pp. 545–639.
Burgoon, B., 'The Rise and Stall of Labor Linkage in Globalization Politics', *International Politics* (2004), pp. 196–220
Compa, L. and Diamond, S. F. (eds.), *Human Rights, Labour Rights, and International Trade*, (Philadelphia, University of Pennsylvania Press 1996), vi + 311 p.
Cottier, T. and Caplazi, A., 'Labour Standards and World Trade Law: Interfacing Legitimate Concerns', in T. Cottier (ed.), *The Challenge of WTO Law: Collected Essays*, (London, Cameron May 2007), pp. 551–585.
de Castro, J., *Trade and Labour Standards: Using the Wrong Instruments for the Right Cause*, (Geneva, UNCTAD 1995), iii + 24 p.
De Feyter, K., 'The Prohibition of Child Labour as a Social Clause in Multilateral Trade Agreements', in E. Verhellen (ed.), *Monitoring Children's Rights*, (The Hague, Nijhoff 1996), pp. 431–444.
Flanagan, R. and Gould, W., *International Labor Standards: Globalization, Trade and Public Policy*, (Stanford, Stanford University Press 2003), 275 p.
Frundt, H.J., *Trade Conditions and Labour Rights: US Initiatives, Dominican and Central American Responses* (Gainesville, University Press of Florida 1998), xxii + 385 p.
Gray, K., 'Labour Rights and International Trade: a Debate Devolved', in M. Irish, *The Auto Pact: Investment, Labour and the WTO*, (The Hague, Kluwer 2004), pp. 277–300.
Grynberg, R. and Qalo, V., 'Labour Standards in US and EU Preferential Trading Arrangements', *Journal of World Trade* (2006), pp. 619–653.

Hansson, G., *Social Clauses and International Trade, an Economic Analysis of Labour Standards in Trade Policy* (London, Canberra, Croom Helm, New York, St.Martin's Press 1983), 198 p.

Hertzenberg, S. and Perez-Lopez, J.F. (eds.), *Labor Standards and Development in the Global Economy: an Edited Collection of Papers Presented at the Symposium on Labor Standards Held in Washington D.C. December 12-13, 1988* (Washington D.C., U.S. Dept. of Labor, 1990), xii + 265 p.

Krebber, S., 'The Search for Core Labor Standards in Liberalized Trade', in E. Benvenisti, G. Nolte et al. (eds.), *The Welfare State, Globalization and International Law*, (Berlin, Springer 2004), pp. 175-230.

Langille, B., 'Eight Ways to Think about International Labour Standards', *Journal of World Trade* (1997), pp. 27-53.

Lenzerini, F., 'International Trade and Child Labour Standards', in F. Francioni (ed.), *Environment, Human Rights and International Trade*, (Oxford, Hart Publishing 2001), pp. 287-312.

Lieberwitz, R., 'Linking Trade and Labor Standards: Prioritizing the Right of Association', *Cornell International Law Journal* (2006), pp. 641-653.

Lopez-Hurtado, C., 'Social Labelling and WTO Law', *Journal of International Economic Law* (2002), pp. 719-746.

Maclaren, R., 'Integrating Environment and Labour into the World Trade Organization', in J. Kirton and M. Trebilcock (eds.), *Hard Choices, Soft law: Voluntary Standards and Global Trade, Environment and Social Governance*, (Aldershot, Ashgate 2004), pp. 266-269.

Meng, W., 'International Labour Standards and International Trade Law', in E. Benvenisti, G. Nolte et al. (eds.), *The Welfare State, Globalization and International Law*, (Berlin, Springer 2004), pp. 371-394.

Pearson, C., 'Labor Standards' in Macrory, P., Appleton, A. and Plummer, M. (eds.), *The World Trade Organization. Legal, Economic and Political Analysis*, (New York, Springer 2005), pp. 171-188.

Shaffer, G., 'WTO Blue-Green Blues: the Impact of U.S. Domestic Policies on Trade-Labor, Trade-Environment Linkages for the WTO's Future', *Fordham International Law Journal* (2000), pp. 608-651.

Thomas, C., 'Should the World Trade Organization Incorporate Trade and Labour Standards?', *Washington and Lee Law Review* (2004), pp. 347-404.

Trebilcock, M. and Howse, R., 'Trade Policy and Labour Standards', *Minnesota Journal of Global Trade* (2004-05), pp. 261-300.

Trebilcock. M., 'Trade Policy and Labour Standards: Objectives, Instruments and Institutions', in J. Kirton and M. Trebilcock (eds.), *Hard Choices, Soft law: Voluntary Standards and Global Trade, Environment and Social Governance*, (Aldershot, Ashgate 2004), pp. 170-185.

Trebilcock, M., 'International Trade and International Labour Standards: Choosing Objectives, Instruments and Institutions', in S. Griller (ed.), *International Economic Governance and Non-Economic Concerns: New Challenges for the International Legal Order*, (Wien, Springer 2003), pp. 289-314.

Vandaele, A., *International Labour Rights and the Social Clause: Friend or Foes?*, (London, Cameron May 2005), pp. 949 p.

Van Liemt, G., 'Trade and Human Rights: The Issue of Minimum Labour Standards', in B. Hocking and S. MacGuire (eds.), *Trade Politics*, (London, Routledge 2004), pp. 238–248.

Von Shöppenthau, 'Trade and Labour Standards: Harnessing Globalization?', in K. Deutsch and B. Speyer (eds.), *The World Trade Organization Millennium Round: Freer Trade in the Twenty-First Century*, (London, Routledge 2001), pp. 224–236.

Wolffgang, H. and Feuerhake, W., 'Core Labour Standards in World Trade Law: The Necessity for Incorporating Labour Standards in the World Trade Organization', *Journal of World Trade* (2002), pp. 883–901.

17. TRADE AND COMPETITION POLICY

Abbot, A., 'Competition Policy as a Welfare-Enhancing Complement to Trade Liberalization: A United States Perspective', T. Hwang and C. Chen (eds.), *The Future Development of Competition Framework*, (The Hague, Kluwer Law International 2004), pp. 77–88.

Alvarez-Jiménez, A., 'Emerging WTO Competition Jurisprudence and its Possibilities for Future Development', *Northwestern Journal of International Law & Business* (2004), pp. 441–511.

Anderson, R. and Jenny, F., 'Competition Policy, Global Development and the Possible Role of a Multilateral Framework on Competition Policy: Insights from the WTO Working Group on Trade and Competition Policy', in E. Medalla (ed.), *Competition Policy in East Asia* (London, Routledge 2005), pp. 61–85.

Balasubramanyam, V.N. and Elliott, C., 'Competition Policy and the WTO', in H. Katrak and R. Strange (eds.), *The WTO and Developing Countries*, WTO, (Basingstoke, Palgrave Macmillan 2004), pp. 301–314.

Bellis, J.-F., 'La politique de la concurrence et l'organisation mondiale du commerce', in X., *Mélanges en hommage à Michel Waelbroeck* (Brussels, Bruylant 1999), pp. 737–767.

Cadot, O., Grether, J. and De Melo, J., 'Competition Policy in the WTO: Where do we stand?', *Journal of World Trade* (2000), pp. 1–20.

Cernat, L., 'Trade and Competition Policy in the Digital Era: Toward a Regulatory Framework for Global E-Business', *The Journal of World Investment* (2003), pp. 987–1010.

Damro, C., 'Linking Competition and Trade', in B. Hocking and S. Macguire (eds.), *Trade Politics*, (London, Routledge 2004), pp. 194–207.

Durand, B., Galarza, A. and Mehta, K., 'The Interface between Competition Policy and International Trade Liberalization: Looking into the future: Applying a new virtual antitrust standard', *World Competition* (2004), pp. 3–12.

Ehlermann, C.-D., "WTO Dispute Settlement and Competition Law: Views from the Perspective of the Appellate Body's Experience", *Fordham International Law Journal* (2003), pp. 1505–1561.

Hoekman, B. and Mavroidis, P., 'Economic Development, Competition Policy and the World Trade Organization', *Journal of World Trade* (2003), pp. 1–27.

Islam, M., 'A WTO Multilateral Framework for Competition Policy and Trade-Induced Development: Debunking Their Complementarity in Developing Countries', *The Journal of World Investment and Trade* (2004), pp. 491–508.

Janow, M., 'Trade and Competition Policy', in Macrory, P., Appleton, A. and Plummer, M. (eds.), *The World Trade Organization. Legal, Economic and Political Analysis*, (New York, Springer 2005), pp. 487–510.

Jenny, F., 'Globalization, Competition and Trade Policy: Convergence, Divergence and Cooperation', Y. Chao *et al.* (eds.), *International and Comparative Competition Laws and Policies*, (The Hague, Kluwer Law International 2001), pp. 31–70.

Marsden, P.B., 'A WTO "rule of reason"?', *European Competition Law Review* (1998), pp. 530–535.

Marsden, P.B., *A Competition Policy for the WTO*, (London, Cameron May 2003), 392 p.

Nicolaides, P., 'Competition Policy and the WTO', in K. Deutsch and B. Speyer, (eds.), *The World Trade Organization Millennium Round: Freer Trade in the Twenty-First Century*, (London, Routledge 2001), pp. 138–147.

Nottage, H., 'Trade and Competition in the WTO: Pondering the Applicability of Special and Differential Treatment', *Journal of International Economic Law* (2003), pp. 23–47.

Sweeney, B., 'Globalization of Competition Law and Policy: Some Aspects of the Interface Between Trade and Competition', *Melbourne Journal of International Law* (2004), pp. 375–433.

Trebilcock, M. and Iacobucci, E., 'National Treatment and Extraterritoriality: Defining the Domains of Trade and Antitrust Policy', in R. Epstein and M. Greve (eds.), *Competition Laws in Conflict: Antitrust Jurisdiction and the Global Economy*, (Washington, AEI Press 2004), pp. 152–176.

Ureana, R., 'The World Trade Organization and its Powers to Adopt World Competition Law', *International Organizations Law Review* (2006), pp. 55–91.

Weinrauch, R., *Competition Law in the WTO: the Rationale for a Framework Agreement*, (Wein, Neuer Wissenschaftlicher Verlag 2004), 206 p.

Wooton, I and Zanardi, M. (eds.), 'Antidumping and Antitrust: Trade and Competition Policy', in E. Choi and J. Hartigan (eds.), *Handbook on International Trade* (Malden, Blackwell 2005), pp. 383–402.

18. WTO AND REGIONAL TRADE ARRANGEMENTS

Bartels, L. and Ortino, F. (eds.), *Regional Trade Agreements and the WTO Legal System*, (Oxford, Oxford University Press 2006), xxxiv + 604 p.

Bernal, R., 'Competition, Competitiveness and Cooperation: Priority Issues for CARICOM in Future EU-ACP Trading Arrangements', in UNCTAD, *Trade Negotiation Issues in the Cotonou Agreement: Agriculture and Economic Partnership Agreements*, (New York, United Nations 2003), pp. 147–159.

Select Bibliography

Cadot, O. (ed.), *The Origin of Goods: Rules of Origin in Regional Trade Agreements*, (Oxford, Oxford University Press 2006), xiii + 332 p.

Choi, W.-M., 'Legal Problems of Making Regional Trade Agreements with Non-WTO Member States', *Journal of International Economic Law* (2005), pp. 825–860.

Choi, W.-M., 'Making a Better Dispute Settlement Mechanism for Regional Trade Agreements: Lessons of Integration Efforts in East Asia' in M. Masushita and D. Ahn (eds.), *WTO and East Asia: New Perspectives*, (London, Cameron May 2004), pp. 423–440.

Choi, W.-M., 'Regional Economic Integration in East Asia: Prospect and Jurisprudence', *Journal of International Economic Law* (2003), pp. 49–77.

Das, D., 'Regional Trading Agreements: the Contemporary Scenario', *The Journal of World Investment* (2001), pp. 333–401.

Davey, W., 'Regional Trade Agreements and the WTO: General Observations and NAFTA Lessons for Asia', W. Davey (ed.), *Enforcing WTO Trade Rules: Essays on WTO Dispute Settlement and GATT Obligations*, (London, Cameron May 2006), pp. 159–183.

Einhorn, T., 'The Impact of the WTO Agreement on TRIPs (Trade-related Aspects of Intellectual Property Rights) on EC Law: a Challenge to Regionalism', *Common Market Law Review* (1998), pp. 1069–1099.

Fabricotti, A., 'The ASEAN Free Trade Area (AFTA) and its Compatibility with GATT/WTO', *Asian Yearbook of International Law* (2003), pp. 37–58.

Gao, H., 'Legal Issues under WTO Rules on the Closer Economic Partnership Arrangement (CEPA) between Mainland China and Hong Kong', *Chinese Journal of International Law* (2003), pp. 629–648.

Hafez, Z., 'Weak Discipline: GATT Article XXIV and the Emerging WTO Jurisprudence on RTAs, *North Dakota Law Review* (2003), pp. 879–917.

Haller, A., *Mercosur: rechtliche Würdiging der außenwirtschaftlichen Beziehungen und Vereinbarkeit mit dem Welthandelssystem* (Münster, Aschendorff, Köln, Schmidt 2001, 3rd ed.), 229 p.

Herzstein, N. and Whitlock, J., 'Regulating Regional Trade Agreements: A Legal Analysis', in Macrory, P., Appleton, A. and Plummer, M. (eds.), *The World Trade Organization. Legal, Economic and Political Analysis*, (New York, Springer 2005), pp. 203–246.

Kwak, K. and Marceau, G., 'Overlaps and Conflicts of Jurisdictions between the World Trade Organization and Regional Trade Agreements', *The Canadian Yearbook of International Law* (2003), pp. 83–152.

Lebullenger, J., 'Les dispositions commerciales de l'accord de partenariat ACP/CE de Cotonou confrontées aux règles de l'OMC', *Revue des affaires européennes* (2001), pp. 75–91.

Limão, N. 'Preferential vs. Multilateral Trade Liberalization: Evidence and Open Questions', *World Trade Review* (2006), pp. 155–176.

Lockhart, N. and Mitchell, A., 'Regional Trade Agreements under GATT 1994: An Exception and its Limits', in A. Mitchell (ed.), *Challenges and Prospects for the WTO*, (London, Cameron May 2006), pp. 217–252.

Marceau, G., 'The Adoption of the "Best Practices" for Regional and Free Trade Agreements in APEC: a Road towards more WTO-consistent Regional Trade Agreements?', in Y.

Tanigushi, A., Yanovich and J. Bohanes (eds.), *The WTO in the Twenty-First Century: Dispute Settlement, Negotiations and Regionalism in Asia*, (Cambridge, Cambridge University Press 2007), pp. 409–422.

Matambalya, F. and Wolf, S., 'The Cotonou Agreement and the challenges of making the new EU-ACP trade regime WTO compatible', *Journal of World Trade* (2001), pp. 123–144.

Mathis, J.H., *Regional Trade Agreements in the GATT/WTO*, (Cambridge, Cambridge University Press 2002), xxii + 328 p.

Mathis, J.H., *Regional Trade Agreements in the GATT/WTO: Article XXIV and the Internal Trade Requirement*, (The Hague, T.M.C. Asser Press 2002), xxii + 328 p.

Montaguti, E. and Lugard, M., 'The GATT 1994 and other Annex 1A Agreements: four different relationships?', *Journal of International Economic Law* (2000), pp. 473–484.

Mota, P.-I., 'Os blocos económicos regionais e o sistema comercial multilateral: o caso da Comunidade Europeia', *Revista da Faculdade de Direito da Universidade de Lisboa* (1999), pp. 71–156.

Mwebeiha, C., 'Re-configuring the Spaghetti Bowl: Reflections on the Issue of Multi-memberships in Regional Trade Agreements in Eastern and Southern Africa', *Legal Issues of Economic Integration* (2004), pp. 243–256.

Pauwelyn, J., 'The Puzzle of WTO Safeguards and Regional Trade Agreements', *Journal of International Economic Law* (2004), pp. 109–142.

Picker, C., 'Regional Trade Agreements v the WTO: A Proposal for Reform of Article XXIV to Counter this Institutional Threat', *University of Pennsylvania Journal of International Business Law* (2005), pp. 267–319.

Sauvé, P., 'Lessons from the Periphery: Comparative Perspectives on Services, the WTO and Regional Trade Agreements', in P. Sauvé (ed.), *Trade Rules Behind Borders: Essays on Services, Investment and the New Trade Agenda* (London, Cameron May 2003), pp. 249–273.

Sen, R., '"New Regionalism" in Asia: A Comparative Analysis of Emerging Regional and Bilateral Trade Agreements involving ASEAN, China and India', *Journal of World Trade* (2006), pp. 553–596.

Smith, F., 'Renegotiating Lomé: the impact of the World Trade Organization on the European Community's development policy after the Bananas conflict', *European Law Review* (2000), pp. 247–263.

Then de Lammerskötter, R., *WTO und Regional Trade Agreements (RTAs): Artikel XXIV und die Enabling Clause im Lichte eines idealen Regulierungssystems'*, (Münster, Lit 2004), 341 p.

Wang, J., 'China's Regional Trade Agreements: The Law, Geopolitics and Impact on the Multilateral Trading System', *Singapore Yearbook of International Law* (2004), pp. 119–147.

Weiler, J.H.H. (ed.), *The EU, the WTO, and the NAFTA: towards a common law of international trade?* (Oxford, Oxford University Press 2001), xx + 238 p.

Williams, G., 'Priority issues for ACP States in respect of negotiating economic partnership agreements with the EU', in UNCTAD, *Trade negotiation issues in the Cotonou*

Agreement: agriculture and economic partnership agreements, (New York, United Nations 2003), pp. 133-146.
Woolcock, S., 'A Framework for Assessing Regional Trade Agreements: WTO-Plus', in G. Sampson and S. Woolcock (eds.), *Regionalism, Multilateralism and Economic Integration: the Recent Experience*, (Tokyo, United Nations University Press 2003), pp. 18-31.
Ziegler, A., 'Lessons for the WTO from recent EFTA bilateral free trade agreements', in R. Buckley (ed.), *The WTO and the Doha Round: the changing face of world trade*, (The Hague, Kluwer 2003), pp. 229-249.

19. LEGITIMACY AND DEMOCRACY DEBATE ON THE WTO

Bacchus, 'A Few Thoughts on Legitimacy, Democracy and the WTO', *Journal of International Economic Law* (2004), pp. 667-673.
Bronckers, M., *Betere regels voor een nieuw millennium: een pleidooi tegen ondemocratische ontwikkelingen in de WTO* (Leiden, Universiteit Leiden 2000), 20 p.
Broude, T., 'The Rule(s) of Trade and the Rhetos of Development: Reflections on the Functional and Aspirational Legitimacy of the WTO', *Columbia Journal of Transnational Law* (2006), pp. 221-261.
Bughdahn, S., *Reforming the World Trade Organization. A Choice between Effectiveness and Equity?*, (Speyer, Forschungsinstitut für öffentliche Verwaltung 2006), v + 49 p.
Cass, D., *The Constitutionalization of the World Trade Organization. Legitimacy, Democracy and Community in the International Trading System*, (Oxford, Oxford University Press 2005), xxvi + 266 p.
Cho, S., 'A Quest for WTO's Legitimacy', *World Trade Review* (2005), pp. 391-399.
Dunoff, J., 'The WTO's Legitimacy Crisis: Reflections on the Law and Politics of WTO Dispute Resolution', *The American Review of International Arbitration* (2002), pp. 197-208.
Greisberger, A., 'Enhancing the Legitimacy of the World Trade Organization: Why the United States and the European Union should support the Advisory Centre on WTO Law', *Vanderbilt Journal of Transnational Law* (2004), pp. 827-860.
Howse, R. and Nikolaidis, K., 'Legitimacy through "higher law"?: Why Constitutionalizing the WTO is a Step Too Far', in T. Cottier and P. Mavroidis (eds.), *The Role of the Judge in International Trade Regulation: Experience and Lessons from the WTO*, (Ann Arbor, University of Michigan Press 2003), pp. 307-348.
Jackson, J.H., *Sovereignty, the WTO and the Changing Fundamentals of International Law*, (Cambridge, Cambridge University Press 2006), xxvi + 361 p.
Krajewski, M., 'Democratic Legitimacy and Constitutional Perspectives of WTO Law', *Journal of World Trade* (2001), pp. 167-186.
Meltzer, J., 'State Sovereignty and the Legitimacy of the WTO', *University of Pennsylvania Journal of International Economic Law* (2005), pp. 692-733.

Moore, M., *WTO Policy Issues for Parliamentarians. A Guide to Current Trade Issues for Legislators*, (Geneva, WTO 2001), 45 p.
Petersmann, E.-U., *Reforming the World Trading System: Legitimacy, Efficiency and Democratic Governance*, (Oxford, Oxford University Press 2005), xx + 569 p.
Petersmann, E.-U., 'Challenges to the Legitimacy and Efficiency of the World Trading System: Democratic Governance and Competition Culture in the WTO', *Journal of International Economic Law* (2004), pp. 585–603.
Steger, D., 'The Challenges to the Legitimacy of the WTO', in S. Charnovitz, D. Steger and P. Van den Bossche (eds.), *Law in the Service of Human Dignity: Essays in Honour of Florentino Feliciano*, (Cambridge, Cambridge University Press 2005), pp. 202–221.
Vedder, A., 'Non-State Actors' Interference in the International Debate on Moral Issues: Legitimacy and Accountability', in A. Vedder (ed.) *The WTO and Concerns Regarding Animals and Nature*, (Nijmegen, Wolf Legal Publishers 2003), pp. 173–182.
v. Bogandy, A., 'Legitimacy of International Economic Governance: Interpretative Approaches to WTO Law and the Prospects of its Proceduralization', in S. Griller (ed.), *International Economic Governance and Non-Economic Concerns: New Challenges for the International Legal Order*, (Wien, Springer 2003), pp. 103–148.
Wallach, L. and Sforza, M., *Whose Trade Organization? Corporate Globalization and the Erosion of Democracy: An Assessment of the World Trade Organization* (Washington D.C., Public Citizen 1999), xii + 229 p.
Weiler, J.H.H., 'The Rule of Lawyers and the Ethos of Diplomats: Reflections on the Internal and External Legitimacy of the WTO Dispute Settlement', in P. Mavroidis and A. Sykes (eds.), *The WTO and International Dispute Settlement*, (Cheltenham, Elgar 2005), pp. 677–693.

20. WTO AND THE EUROPEAN COMMUNITY

Abbott, F., 'GATT and the European Community, A formula for peaceful coexistence, Vol 12 *Michigan Journal of International Law* (1990), pp. 1–58.
Bartels, L., 'The Legitimacy of the EC Mutual Recognition Clause under WTO Law', *Journal of International Economic Law* (2005), pp. 691–720.
Bourgeous, J., 'The EC in the WTO and Advisory Opinion 1/94: An Echternach Procession?', *Common Market Law Review* (1995), pp. 763–787.
Castillo de la Torre, F., 'The status of GATT in EEC law', *Journal of World Trade* (1992), pp. 35–43.
Clough, M., 'WTO and EC Safeguard Measures: Legal Standards and Jurisprudence', *International Trade Law and Regulation* (2003), pp. 70–76.
De Búrca, G. and Scott, J., *The EU and the WTO: legal and constitutional issues* (Oxford, Hart 2001), x + 332 p.
Desta, M., 'EC-ACP Economic Partnership Agreements and WTO Compatibility: An Experiment in North-South Interregional Agreements', *Common Market Law Review* (2006), pp. 1343–1380.

Didier, P., *WTO trade instruments in EU law: commercial policy instruments: dumping, subsidies, safeguards, public procurement*, (London, Cameron-May 1999), 844 p.

Di Gianni, F. and R. Antonini, 'DSB Decisions and Direct Effect of WTO Law: Should EC Courts be More Flexible when the WTO Flexibility Has Come to an End?', *Journal of World Trade* (2006), pp. 777–793.

Dillon, S., *International trade and economic law and the European Union* (Oxford, Hart 2002), xviii + 391 p.

Geeroms, S., 'Cross-border Gambling on the Internet under WTO/GATS and EC Rules Compared: a Justified Restriction on the Freedom to Provide Services?', in A. Aronovitz, *Cross-border Gambling on the Internet: Challenging National and International Law*, (Zürich, Schulthess 2004), pp. 143–180.

Hoogmartens, J., *EC Trade Law Following China's Accession to the WTO*, (The Hague, Kluwer Law International 2004), xxiii + 216 p.

Kerremans, B., 'The European Commission and the EU Member States as Actors in the WTO Negotiation Process: Decision-Making Between Scylla and Charybdis?', in B. Reinalda and B. Verbeek (eds.), *Decision-making Within International Organizations*, (London, Routledge 2004), pp. 45–58.

Krajewski, M., 'External Trade and the Constitution Treaty: Towards a Federal and More Democratic Common Commercial Policy?', *Common Market Law Review* (2005), pp. 91–127.

Messerlin, P., 'The Impact of EC Enlargement on the WTO', in M. Moore (ed.), *Doha and Beyond: the Future of the Multilateral Trading System*, (Cambridge, Cambridge University Press 2004), pp. 146–177.

Murphy, A., *The European Community and the International Trading System, Vol I Completing the Uruguay Round of the GATT, Vol. II The European Community and the Uruguay Round* (Brussels, Centre for European Policy Studies 1990), Vol I, 166 p., Vol II, 140 p.

O'Neill, M., 'On the Boundary Clash between EC Commercial Law and WTO Law', *Legal Issues of Economic Integration* (2005), pp. 65–86.

Ortino, F., *Basic Legal Instruments for the Liberalization of Trade: a Comparative Analysis of EU and WTO Law*, (Oxford, Hart 2004), xxii + 502 p.

Petersmann, E.-U., 'The Uruguay Round of multilateral trade negotiations and the single European market 1992', in Hilf, M., Tomuschat, C. and Bruha, T. (eds.), *EG und Drittstaatsbeziehungen nach 1992* (Baden-Baden, Nomos 1991), pp. 195–212.

Princen, S., 'EC Compliance with WTO Law: the Interplay of Law and Politics', *European Journal of International Law* (2004), pp. 555–574.

Rossi, L.S., *Commercio internazionale sostenibile?: WTO e Unione europea*, (Bologna, Il Mulino 2003), 343 p.

Schaps, J., 'Die EG und das GATT', *Handbuch der Europaeischen Integration* (1991), pp. 552–570.

Senti, R., 'The role of the EU as an economic actor within the WTO', Vol. 7 issue 1 *European Foreign Affairs Review* (2002), pp. 111–117.

Slotboom, M., *A Comparison of WTO and EC Law: Do Different Objects and Purposes Matter for Treaty Interpretation*, (London, Cameron May 2006), 316 p.

Slotboom, M., 'The Exhaustion of Intellectual Property Rights: Different Approaches in WTO and EC Law', *The Journal of World Intellectual Property* (2003), pp. 421-440.

Slotboom, M., 'Subsidies in WTO Law and EC Law: Broad and Narrow Definitions', *Journal of World Trade* (2002), pp. 517-542.

Steinberger, E., 'The WTO Treaty as a Mixed Agreement: Problems with the EC's and the EC Member States' Membership of the WTO', *European Journal of International Law* (2006), pp. 837-862.

Tancredi, A., 'EC Practice within the WTO: How Wide is the "Scope for Manoeuvre?"', *European Journal of International Law* (2004), pp. 933-961.

Van den Broek, N., 'Legal Persuasion, Political Realism and Legitimacy: The European Court's Recent Treatment of the Effect of WTO Agreements in the EC Legal Order', *Journal of International Economic Law* (2001), pp. 411-440.

von Bogandy, A., Mavroidis, P.C., Mény, Y. and Ehlermann, C.-D., *European integration and international co-ordination: studies in transnational economic law in honour of Claus-Dieter Ehlermann*, (The Hague, Kluwer International 2002), xx + 516 p.

Weiler, J.H.H. (ed.), *The EU, the WTO, and the NAFTA: towards a common law of international trade?* (Oxford, Oxford University Press 2001), xx + 238 p.

Wiers, J., 'The Rule of Reason in International Economic Law: Does the EC-WTO Parallel make Sense?', A. Schrauwen (ed.), *Rule of Reason: Rethinking another Classic of European Legal Doctrine*, (Groningen, Europa Law Publishing 2005), pp. 95-108.

Wiers, J., *Trade and Environment in the EC and the WTO: a Legal Analysis*, (Groningen, Europa Law Publishing 2002), xii + 502 p.

Zonnekeyn, G., 'EC Liability for Non-Implementation of WTO Dispute Settlement Decisions: Are the Dice Cast?', *Journal of International Economic Law* (2004), pp. 483-490.

Zonnekeyn, G., 'The Status of WTO Law in the EC Legal Order: The Final Curtain?', *Journal of World Trade* (2000), pp. 111-125.

21. RELATIONSHIP WTO LAW AND GENERAL INTERNATIONAL LAW

Atripaldi, M., Baroncini, E. and Capaldo, G., 'WTO Dispute Panels and Appellate Body: Legal Maxims: Summaries and Extracts from Selected Case-Law', *Yearbook of International Law and Jurisprudence* (2001), pp. 311-489.

Benedek, W., *Die Rechtsordnung des GATT aus völkerrechtlicher Sicht, Beiträge zum ausländischen öffentlichen Recht und Völkerrecht* (Berlin, Springer 1990), xxiii + 557 p.

Cameron, J. and Gray, K., 'Principles of International Law in the WTO Dispute Settlement Body', *The International and Comparative Law Quarterly* (2001), pp. 248-298.

Carmodi, C., 'WTO Obligations as Collective', *European Journal of International Law* (2006), pp. 419-443.

Emmerich-Fritsche, A., 'Recht und Zwang im Völkerrecht, insbesondere im Welthandelsrecht', in Schachtschneider, K. and Emmerich-Fritsche, A. (eds.), *Rechtsfragen der Weltwirtschaft* (Berlin, Dunker & Humblot 2002), pp. 123-209.

Garcia-Rubio, M., *On the Application of Customary Rules of State Responsibility by the WTO Dispute Settlement Organs: A General International Law Perspective*, (Geneva, Graduate Institute of International Studies 2001), 101 p.

Gazzini, T., 'The Legal Nature of WTO Obligations and the Consequences of their Violation', *European Journal of International Law* (2006), pp. 723–742.

Hu, J., 'The Role of International Law in the Development of WTO Law', *Journal of International Economic Law* (2004), pp. 143–167.

Jackson, J., *Sovereignty, the WTO and Changing Fundamentals of International Law*, (Cambridge, Cambridge University Press 2006), xxvi + 361 p.

Jackson, J., 'International Law Status of WTO Dispute Settlement Reports: Obligation to Comply of Obligation to "Buy Out"?', *The American Journal of International Law* (2004), pp. 109–125.

Kuyper, P.J. and Steenbergen, J., 'Het GATT en het Volkenrecht; preadviezen', no. 107 *Mededelingen van de Nederlandse Vereniging voor Internationaal Recht* (1993), pp. 1–75.

Lamy, P., 'The Place of the WTO and its Law in the International Legal Order', *European Journal of International Law* (2006), pp. 969–984.

Mengozzi, P., 'Private International Law and the WTO Law', *Recueil des Cours* (2001), pp. 249–385.

Pauwelyn, J., *Conflict of Norms in Public International Law. How WTO Law Relates to Other Rules of International Law*, (Cambridge, Cambridge University Press 2003), 554 p.

Van Damme, I., 'What Role is There for Regional International Law in the Interpretation of WTO Agreements?', in L. Bartels and F. Ortino (eds.), *Regional Trade Agreements and the WTO Legal System*, (Oxford, Oxford University Press 2006), pp. 553–575.

Van Genugten, W.J.M., *WTO, ILO en EG: handelen in vrijheid: rede in verkorte vorm uitgesproken bij de aanvaarding van het ambt van hoogleraar Volkenrecht aan de Katholieke Universiteit Brabant op vrijdag 6 juni 1997* (Deventer, Tjeenk-Willink 1997), v + 45 p.

Vranes, E., 'Jurisdiction and Applicable Law in WTO Dispute Settlement', *German Yearbook of International Law* (2005), pp. 265–289.

22. WEB PAGES ON INTERNATIONAL TRADE LAW

Global International Organizations

G7/8 (Univ. of Toronto G7/8 Research Centre): http://www.g7.utoronto.ca
Int. Labour Org: http://www.ilo.org
Int. Monetary Fund: http://www.imf.org
Int. Trade Center (< UNCTAD / WTO): http://www.intracen.org
Org. Econ. Coop. & Devel.: http://www.oecd.org
UN Com. Int. Trade Law: http://www.uncitral.org
UN Conf. Trade & Devel.: http://www.unctad.org

UN Devel. Progr.: http://www.undp.org
UN Envir. Progr.: http://www.unep.org
UN Industr. Devel. Org.: http://www.unido.org
World Bank Group (incl. IBRD): http://www.worldbank.org
- Int. Center Settlem. Invest. Disp.: http://www.worldbank.org/icsid
- Int. Devel. Assoc.: http://www.worldbank.org/ida
- Int. Finance Corp.: http://www.ifc.org
- Multilat. Invest. Guarantee Agency: http://www.miga.org
World Customs Organization http://www.wcoomd.org
World Intell. Prop. Organization http://www.wipo.org
World Trade Organization http://www.wto.org
- WTO official documents online: http://docsonline.wto.org
- List of panel, appeal and arbitration rulings:
    http://www.wto.org/english/tratop_e/dispu_e/find_dispu_cases_e.htm
- Edited Dispute Settlement Reports (from IIEL):
    http://www.law.georgetown.edu/iiel/students/materials/reports.html
- Brief Comments on Appellate Body reports (from EJIL):
    http://www.ejil.org/journal/curdevs/AB.html
- Summaries of Dispute Settlement Reports are usually also included in the ASIL's *International Law in Brief*:
    http://www.asil.org/ilib/ilibarch.htm
- WorldTradeLaw.net's Dispute Settlement Commentary (mostly limited to subscribers):
    http://www.worldtradelaw.net

Regional International Organizations

Afr. Car. & Pacif.: http://www.acpsec.org
Asian Devel. Bank: http://www.adb.org
Andean Community: http://www.comunidadandina.org/endex.htm
Asia Pacific Econ. Coop.: http://www.apecsec.org.sg
Benelux Econ. Union: http://www.benelux.be
Car. Community: http://www.caricom.org
North Am. Com. Envir. Coop.: http://www.cec.org
Com. Econ. & Monet. Afr. Centr. (Econ. & Monet. Community of Central Africa):
 http://www.cemac.org
Carib. Devel. Bank: http://www.caribank.org
Com. Labor Coop. (NAFTA related): http://www.naalc.org
Com. Market. East. & South. Afr.: http://www.comesa.int
East Afr. Com.: http://www.eac.int/
Eur. Bank Reconstr. Devel.: http://www.ebrd.com
Eur. Central Bank: http://www.ecb.int
Econ. Com. West. Afr. States: http://www.ecowas.int
Eur. Free Trade Assoc.: http://www.efta.int

Eur. Invest. Bank:		http://eib.eu.int
Eur. Invest. Fund:		http://eif.eu.int
European Commission:		http://europa.eu.int/comm
– DG Trade:		http://europa.eu.int/comm/trade/index_en.htm
– DG Development:		http://europa.eu.int/comm/development/index_en.htm
– DG Competition:		http://europa.eu.int/comm/competition/index_en.html
European Union:		http://europa.eu.int
– Eur-Lex (incl. Treaties & OJ):		http://eur-lex.europa.eu
Free Trade Area Amer.:		http://www.ftaa-alca.org
Gulf Coop. Council:		http://www.gcc-sg.org/index_e.html
Int.-Am. Devel. Bank:		http://www.iadb.org
Islamic Devel. Bank:		http://www.isdb.org
Mercosur:		http://www.mercosur.int
North Am. Free Trade Area:		http://www.nafta-sec-alena.org
South Afr. Devel. Com.:		http://www.sadc.int
South Asian Ass. Reg. Coop.:		http://www.saarc-sec.org
UEMOA (West Afr. Ec. & Monet Union):		http://www.uemoa.int
UN Ec. Com. Afr.:		http://www.uneca.org
UN Ec. Com. Eur.:		http://www.unece.org
UN Ec. Com. Lat. Am. & Car.:		http://www.eclac.cl/default.asp?idioma=IN
UN Ec. & Soc. Com. Asia & Pacific:		http://www.unescap.org
UN Ec. & Soc. Com. W. Asia:		http://www.escwa.org.lb
Union du Maghreb Arabe (Arab Maghreb Union):		http://www.maghrebarabe.org

Government agencies

Canada:	Dept. For. Aff. & Intl. Trade:	http://www.dfait-maeci.gc.ca
	Intl. Trade Tribunal:	http://www.citt.gc.ca
Japan:	Min. Econ. Trade & Ind.:	http://www.meti.go.jp/english/index.html
Jap.	External Trade Org.:	http://www.jetro.go.jp
US:	Trade Representative:	http://www.ustr.gov
	Court of Intl. Trade:	http://www.cit.uscourts.gov
	Customs Service:	http://www.customs.ustreas.gov
	Intl. Trade Commission:	http://www.usitc.gov
	Dept. Com., Int. Trade Adm.:	http://www.ita.doc.gov
NB:	For EU countries, see European Commission, above.	

Others

American Society of International Law Library:
    http://www.asil.org/spgbd.htm
ASIL Intl. Econ. Law Group:
    http://www.fletcher.tufts.edu/inter_econ_law
Center for the Study of Western Hemispheric Trade:
    http://lanic.utexas.edu/cswht
Bridges Trade News Digest (weekly newsletter):
    http://www.ictsd.org/weekly/index.htm

Findlaw:	http://www.findlaw.com/topics/25interntrade/index.html
Intl. Chamber Commerce:	http://www.iccwbo.org
Intl. Inst. for Sust. Devel.:	http://www.iisd.org
Inst. of Intl Econ. Law (Georgetown):	http://www.law.georgetown.edu/iiel/
Lex Mercatoria:	http://www.lexmercatoria.com
LLRX:	http://www.llrx.com/features/wto2.htm
NAFTALAW.ORG:	http://www.naftalaw.org
Natl. Law Cent. Int.-Am. Free Trade:	http://www.natlaw.com
The North American Institute:	http://www.northamericaninstitute.org
North Am. Integr. & Devel. Center:	http://naid.sppsr.ucla.edu

Trade Environment Database:
    http://www.american.edu/projects/mandala/TED/ted.htm

UN Wire (daily newsletter):	http://www.unwire.org
World Chambers Network:	http://www.worldchambers.com
World Trade Institute:	http://www.worldtradeinstitute.ch
WorldTradeLaw.net:	http://www.worldtradelaw.net

INDEX

The numbers refer to paragraphs

A

Absolute advantage 3
Accession process 44, 53, 149, **204-211**, 224, 229, 242, 262, 272, 316
Accession Protocol *See* Protocol of Accession
Accountancy 139–140, 296
Across the board negotiations 17, 54
Administrative Committee on Co-ordination 169, 173
Ad valorem 52, 57, 126
Advisory Centre on WTO Law **195-201**, 366-367
African Group 217, 359
Agriculture 17, 24, 46, **112–119**, 159, 160, 215-216, 218, 221, 257, 280-281
Alliances 212-218
Amendments 19, 152, **247-252**, 254, 259, 283
    Non-substantive amendments 249
    Substantive Amendments 250
Aim and effects test 67
Amicus curiae briefs 359-363
Antidumping 38, **108–111**, 121, 133, 285
Appeal 302, 304, 342, **352-355**
Appellate Body *See* Standing Appellate Body
Arbitration 337, 357
Article IV consultations 177
Asbestos 173, 360, 362
ASEAN-China Free Trade Area 214
ASEAN Free Trade Area 213
Association of Southeast Asian Nations 213-214

B

Balance of Payments 40, 175, 178–180
Basic law 223, 226
Berne Union 184
Bound tariffs 22, 55-56
Brazil 122, 217-218
Bretton Woods 14, 174
Budget 161, 166, **235-236**, 259, 266

C

Cairns Group 215-216
Cancún 24, 217, 218, 221, **257**, 318
Central product classification system 143
Chairman's Text 363, 367
Chief Executives Board of Coordination 173
China *See* People's Republic of China
Chinese Taipei 219, **227-230**
Civil aircraft 44, **154–155**, 270
Closer Economic Partnership Arrangement 225
Codex Alimentarius Commission 26, 94, 221
Coherence in global economic policymaking 20, 165, 167, 176, 181–183, 276
Committees **260-261**, 263
    Committee of Participants on the Expansion of Trade in Information Technology Products 292
    Committee on Agriculture 119, 159, 160, **281**
    Committee on Antidumping Practices 285
    Committee on Balance-of-Payments Restrictions 265
    Committee on Budget, Finance and Administration 166, 177, 182, **235**, **266**
    Committee on Customs Valuation 286
    Committee on Import Licensing 288
    Committee on Market Access 280
    Committee on Regional Trade Agreements 82-83, 268
    Committee on Rules of Origin 134, 287
    Committee on Safeguards 290
    Committee on Sanitary and Phytosanitary Measures 159, 160, 188–189, **282**

Committee on Specific Commitments 295
Committee on Subsidies and Countervailing Measures 284
Committee on Technical Barriers to Trade 267, **283**
Committee on Trade and Development 82-83, 177, 233-234, **264**, 267, 268
Committee on Trade and Environment 177, **267**
Committee on Trade in Financial Services 294
Committee on Trade-Related Investment Measures 289
Comparative advantage 4-7, 33, 193
Competition policy 125, 257, 272, **273**, 274
Concessions 8, 14, 17, **28**, 33-34, 47, 53, 55-56, 96, 205, 280, 356-357
Conformity assessment procedures 100, 221, 283
Consensus 82-83, 102, 217, 231, **239-243**, 302, **312-313**, 336, 342
  Explicit consensus 240
  Reverse consensus 241
  Consensus *in lieu* of voting 242
Consultations 127, 142, 155, 265, 290, **321**, **330-332**, 364-365
Consultative board 313
Context 345, **346-347**
Contracting Parties 204
Cooperation agreements 166, **167**
Cotonou 253
Council for Trade-Related Aspects of Intellectual Property Rights 259, **298-301**
Council for Trade in Goods 82, 125, 247, 253, 259, **278**
Council for Trade in Services 82, 139, 243, 247, 253, 259, **293**
Countervailing measures 40, 103, **104–107**, 108, 110, 117, 121, 133–134, 155, 284
Country assistance strategies 183
Cross-conditionality 176
Cross-retaliation 358
Customs duties 28, 52, 57, 61, 79, 126–128, 129
Customs Union 10, **58**, **78-83**, 219

D
Decision of 1966 365
De minimis 66, 115
Democracy 311-320
De novo review 349-350
Developing countries 6, 24-25, **84-92**, 94, 114–119, 121, 129, 152, 176, 193, 195, **218**, **231-234**, 257, 277, 311-312, 361, **364-367**
Direct effect 222
Director-General 163, 237, 303, **307**, **309-310**, 313, 330, 337, 365-366
Discrimination 25, **29**, 94, 97, 145
Disciplines on Domestic Regulation for the Accountancy Sector 140, 296
Disguised discrimination 36, 42, 66, 76, 94, 141, 147
Dispute settlement 19, 23, 195, 237, 241, 302-304, 311, **321-367**
Dispute Settlement Body 302-304
Dispute settlement reform 363, 367
Dispute Settlement Understanding 252, 363
Doha Declaration **24**, 115, 118, 119, 152, 173, 177, 211, 233, 241, 273, 274, 276-277
Doha Round 24, 115, 125, 140, 149, 158, 216, 218, 221, **257**, 296
Domestic regulation **140**, 145, 296
Drugs 152, 300
Dumping 40, **108–111**, 121, 285
Dunkel Draft 20

E
Economic and Social Council 173
Economic integration agreements *See* Regional trade agreements
Efficiency 269, **311-320**, 341
Enabling clause 82-83, **88-92**, 268
Enforcement 26, 173, 185, 305, **356-358**
European Community 100, **220-222**
European Court of Justice 222
Exhaustible natural resources 42, 74
Expert Review Group 338
Export restrictions 70

F
Factual issues 344, 350, 353
Financial services 44, 294
Fragmentation of international law 347

Free riders 34
Free Trade Area 58, **78-83**

G

GATT Council *See* Council for Trade in Goods
GATS Council *See* Council for Trade in Services
General committees *See* Horizontal committees
General Council 166, 203, 235, 246, 255, **258**, 259, 302, 305
Generalized system of preferences 89
General Working Groups *See* Horizontal Working Groups
General Working Parties *See* Horizontal Working Parties
Goods 46, 56, **136**
Government procurement 44, **156-158**, 257, 271, 275
Grandfathered clauses 55
Groupings 212, 313
Group of 20 218, 257
Group of 20+ 218, 231, 257
Group of 22 218
Group of 33 218
Group of 90 217, 218

H

Harmonized system 56
Headquarters 164
Health 9, 36, 42, 66, **74**, 93, 147, **173**, **300**
Hong Kong 24, 119, 138, 218, **257**, 297
Hong Kong, China 223-225
Horizontal Committees 263
Horizontal Working Groups 262-263, **272**
Horizontal Working Parties 262-263, **272**
Hormones 358, 359

I

Immunities 163
Implementation of reports 356-358
Import licences 132
Import restrictions 71, 132
India 122, 217, 218, 231, 359
Infant industries 11, 40
Information technology products 26, 292
Integrated data base 280
Integrated framework 180, 234

Intellectual property 6, **150-152**, 184-187, 298-301
Intent 67
Interim agreements 79, 81-82
Interim review 340
Internal taxes 6, **64-67**
International Labour Organization **193-194**, 214
International Law Commission 30, 347
International legal personality 161, **162-164**
International Monetary Fund 14, **174-180**
International Office of Epizootics 94, **188-189**
International Plant Protection Convention 94
International standards 94, 97, **141**, **188**, 282
International Telecommunications Union 167, **190-192**
International Trade Organization 14-15, 161, 174
Interpretation 25, 56, **345-349**
Interpretations 246, 256, 259, 309
Inverted consensus *See* Reverse consensus
Investment **122-125**, 257, 274, 289
Issues of fact *See* Factual issues

J

Johannesburg Summit 173
Judicial activism 320, 351
Judicial economy 344, 353
July Decision 24, 118, 119, 158, 218, 273, 274

K

Kennedy Round 17, **53-57**

L

Least developed countries 84, 87, 89, 92, 112, 114, 115, 124-125, 180, 188, 199, 200, **205**, 211, **232**, 234, 264, **267**
Legal standing *See Locus standi*
Legitimacy 311-320
Likeness 29, 63, 66
Locus standi 202, 324

M

Macao 226
Mainland China *See* People's Republic of China

Index

Market access **28**, 48, 114, 118–119, 140, **144**, 145, 211, 218, 269, **280**
Membership 44, **204-211**, 229, 316, 352
MFN *See* Most Favoured Nation
Millennium Round 257
Ministerial Conference 26, **255-257**, 259, 261, 311
Ministerial decision 245
Most Favoured Nation 10, 22, **30-35**, **60-63**, 102, 123, **138**, 151, 157

N

National security 42, 77, 147, 173, 230
National treatment 29, **36-37**, **64-67**, 97, 123, 130, 133, **145**, 151, 157
Negative integration 48, 94
Negotiating new agreements 185, 254
New Quad 217
Non-governmental organizations 141, **202-203**, 243, 308, 319, 323, 363
Non-tariff barriers 6, 19, 28, 46, 55, 90-91, 93, 114, 280
Non-violation complaint 328
Nullification or impairment 326-329

O

Observer status **166**, 177, 182, 192, 194, 205, 228
Office international des épizooties *See* International Office of Epizootics
One country, two systems 226
Ordinary meaning 345, 348
Original members **204**, 206, 219
Origin-neutral 36

P

Package *See* Single undertaking
Panel 173, 178, 302-303, 320, 330-331, **333-351**, 357, 365
Paris Union 184
People's Republic of China 121, 122, 214, 217, 218, 223-225, 226, 227-230, 231
Plurilateral agreement 18, **22**, **44**, 153-158, 210-211, 240, 270-271, 275, 292, **313**
Poverty reduction strategy papers 183
Precautionary principle 94
Preparatory works 349
Protocol of accession 205, 210, 225
Public morals 42, 74, 147

Q

Quad **217**, 231, 312
Quantitative restrictions 6, 28, 51, 60, **68-71**, 96, 114, 120–122, **140**, **144**, 280

R

Reciprocity 17, 28, 35, **53-54**, 85, 88-92
Reasonable period of time 140, **356-357**
Regional trade agreements **39**, 368, 269
    Involving goods **78-83**, 91
    Involving services 148
Regulation **64-67**, 93, **140**, 145, 296
Regulatory autonomy 37, 46, 72, 140
Report on the future of the WTO 313
Retaliation 290, 356-358, 367
Reverse consensus **241**, 243, 342
Rules of origin 58, **133-134**, 287

S

Safeguards 60, **101-103**, 114, 119, 120–121, 225, 290, 297
Sanitary or phytosanitary measures 66, **93-95**, 96, 188, 282
Schedules of concessions **47**, 204
Scientific justification 94, 97
Secretariat 15, 163–164, 196, 203, 237, 304, **307-310**, 330, 365
Services 135–137
Services classification list 143
Shrimp 359, 360
Singapore issues 221, 257, 240, 257
Single package *See* Single undertaking
Single undertaking 14, **21**, **44**, 152, 205, 208, **209**, 312, 317
Situation complaint 329
South Africa 54, 122, 217, 218, 231
Special and differential treatment **84-87**, 118, 157, 211, 216, 218, 233, 264, 282, 367
Specialized Agency of the UN 14, 26, 163, **173**
Specific commitments 22-23, 27, 140, **143-145**, 179, 204, **295**
Standard of review 344
Standing *See* Locus Standi
Standing Appellate Body 302, **352-355**
Steel 230, 360
Sub-Committee 234, 238, 264, 270
Subcommittee on Least-Developed Countries 234

Supplementary means of interpretation 249
Suspension of concessions 102

T
Taiwan *See* Chinese Taipei
Tariffs 6, **51-59**, 79, 280
Tariff bindings 26
Tariff heading 56-57
Tariff quotas 51, 114, 280
Technical Committee on Customs Valuation 286
Technical Committee on Rules of Origin 134, 287
Telecommunications 44, 139, 190–192
Third parties 323, 332, 343, 353, 355
Tokyo Round 18, 54, 88, 127, 154
Trade facilitation 257, 269, 272
Trade Negotiation Rounds 17, 28
Trade Negotiations Committee 20, 177, 269
Trade Policy Review Body 305-306
Trade policy review mechanism 21, 26, **305-306**
Transaction costs 33
Transparency 26, 83, 130, **139**, 267, 273, 274, 282, 291, 298, **305**
  Transparency for regional trade agreements 83, **268**
  Transparency in decision-making 260, 311
  Transparency in dispute settlement 359
  Transparency in government procurement 157–158, 257, **275**
Treaty of Nice 220
TRIPS Council *See* Council for Trade-Related Aspects of Intellectual Property Rights

U
Unanimity **251**, 342
Unfair trade practices 40, 104, 108
United Nations 14, 26, 77, 143, **161**, 163, **168–173**, 232
United Nations Conference on Trade and Development 26, 89, 168, 170, 171, 172, 218, 277
United Nations Development Programme 168

Uruguay Round 20, 46-47, 54, 152, 164, 193, 216

V
Variable geometry 313
Vienna Convention on the Law of Treaties 345
Violation complaint **327**, 328
Voluntary export restraints 70, **102**, 103
Voting **244**, 246, 313

W
Waiver 41, 47, 88-89, 152, 242, 248, **253**, 259
Withdrawal 209–210
Working Groups 262
  Working Group on the Relation between Trade and Competition Policy 273
  Working Group on the Relation between Trade and Investment 274
  Working Group on Trade and Technology Transfer 277
  Working Group on Trade, Debt and Finance 276
  Working Group on Transparency in Government Procurement 275
Working Parties 262, 268
  Working Party on Accession 272
  Working Party on Domestic Regulation 140, **296**
  Working Party on GATS Rules 297
  Working Party on Professional Services 140, **296**
  Working Party on State-Trading Enterprises 291
World Bank 14, 26, 166, 173, 176, **181–183**, 200, 313
World Bank Institute 183
WTO Institute for Training and Technical Cooperation 183